In the Time of Trees and Sorrows

In the Time of Trees and Sorrows

Nature, Power, and Memory in Rajasthan

ANN GRODZINS GOLD AND BHOJU RAM GUJAR

Duke University Press ❧ *Durham & London 2002*

© 2002 Duke University Press
All rights reserved
Printed in the United States of
America on acid-free paper ∞
Designed by Rebecca Giménez
Typeset in Adobe Minion by
Keystone Typesetting, Inc.
Library of Congress Cataloging-
in-Publication Data appear on
the last printed page of this book.
All photos by Ann Grodzins Gold,
except p. 47 by Bhoju Ram Gujar,
p. 261 by Joseph C. Miller Jr.,
and p. 283 by Daniel Gold.

In memory of Sukh Devji Gujar,

Dayal Gujar, Kalyan Mali, Dhapu Mina,

Madhu Nath, Rajendra Joshi,

Milton B. Singer, and Helen Singer

CONTENTS

NOTE ON LANGUAGE

Our fieldwork was conducted in Sawar's Rajasthani vernacular (Magier 1992), in standard Hindi, and quite often in an ad hoc combination of the two. In general, the people we met who knew any Hindi would use it in my company, and most people understood simple Hindi, but the majority of our interviewees spoke only Rajasthani. I have attempted to translate both languages as fully as possible. When Hindi and Rajasthani words appear in the text, I have transliterated them using a standard system and italicized them. Usually, terms used repeatedly are defined on first appearance only and are listed in the glossary. Normally, if a Rajasthani term or phrase has an obvious standard Hindi equivalent, either orthographic or grammatical, I give the Hindi rather than the Rajasthani variant.

Proper nouns are reproduced in roman type without diacritics, and sometimes appear as they are conventionally written, rather than according to exact transliteration. A prime example would be Sawar, which is correctly transliterated as Sāvar. Caste names, which often serve as surnames, are the only proper nouns included in the glossary.

PREFACE

"There Are No Princes Now"

Now his father is dead, the tigers are extinct, and the birds have all gone, except one, which never sings a note and, in the absence of trees, makes its nest in a secret place that has not been revealed. . . . There are no princes now. The government abolished them decades ago. The very idea of princes has become, in our modern country, a fiction, something from the time of feudalism, of fairy tale.—Salman Rushdie, "The Firebird's Nest"

Salman Rushdie's vivid fictional account of a decaying kingdom evokes a landscape and polity that could belong to the region where this book is set: Rajasthan in North India. His tale's magical realism is infused with motifs of meshed ecological and social decay that resonate with the histories offered here. For tourists, whether of Euro-American or Asian origins, Rajasthan is packaged as a feudal fairy tale Elsewhere of the kind sensuously evoked in Rushdie's story, a place where it is possible to enter physically into realms of past royal grandeur. For it is mere decades, not centuries, since princes were abolished (and today many run hotels). Our book is in part about the idea of princes (and kings) as related by their former subjects; an idea that unfolded when we asked these farmers, herders, laborers, and artisans the reasons for the absence of trees. To them, that time is no fiction, but a true story.[1]

Bhoju Ram Gujar and I coproduced this book, but our collaboration is not a simple coauthorship. We cannot write in a collective voice because—although we work as a unit—we do not work as one. Therefore, in much of this book's text, as in this preface, I assume the first-person singular voice and speak of Bhoju as another. Often, though, I write "we" consciously to evoke our double presence. Do not be jarred by these pronominal shifts; they are deliberate. In chapter 2, "Voice," we each describe, with separate tongues, something of our emotional and interpersonal experiences as we brought this book into being. But here, speaking as an American anthropologist, I take stock of a personal trajectory, which chronologically precedes the collaborative endeavor.

In 1979, as the final hurdle for admission to doctoral candidacy at the University of Chicago, I defended a thesis proposal for research to be based in a yet undetermined locality in rural Rajasthan. I planned to live in a village, to go on a pilgrimage with villagers, and to ask them, on and off the road, why they were going where they were going. Through long-term participant observation and unstructured qualitative interviews, I proposed to understand values and meanings in popular Hinduism and in Rajasthani culture. In 1979 this seemed a reasonable and appropriate project for an anthropologist concerned with "indigenous perceptions." Rajasthan as historical entity was incidental to my interests.

At my proposal hearing, as I recall (noting that the theme of memory's selective and creative workings will remain central to this work), someone asked a question about the region's kings, or the princely past, or some such thing. After all the name Rajasthan means "land of kings." Under the British, this region was called Rajputana after the dominant community of Rajputs, a designation meaning literally the "sons of kings." Was it not therefore a place where I would have to reckon with kingship? I know I answered facilely, displaying my awareness of appropriate historical sources in the current literature but asserting that Rajasthan's royalty was of little concern to me. In my naïveté I actually meant that not just royalty but all of history and politics were equally irrelevant. I concluded, definitively (accidentally foreshadowing Rushdie), "Of course, today there are no kings." My advisor, Ralph Nicholas, muttered an audible warning: "I wouldn't be so sure of that if I were you."

For a long while I was able to ignore his prescient rejoinder. It was not a direct assault, and I sailed forward—not just through the hearing but through about a decade of research, writing, and publishing—comfortably ignoring the past's multiple powers as I forged partial understandings of cultural realities in a no longer hypothetical Rajasthan village: Ghatiyali, in Ajmer district. In spite of various indications to the contrary (indications that did occasionally impinge on my projects), I did not much concern myself until 1993 with either history or governance. Thus I had no cause to take account of flesh-and-blood kings, their descendants, or their material and intangible legacies.

That I failed to attend to the realities of a not so remote past of royal dominion may seem especially peculiar given that the village where I did all my ethnographic work was—like so many settlements in rural Rajasthan—dominated in terms of built landscape by its *garh*. The term *garh* translates as "fort" in Indian English, but the structure looks more like a well-fortified castle on a hill. In 1979 Ghatiyali's fort was, as it remains today, a place of residence for members of one branch of the former royal family, along with their show horses. From the roof of Bhoju's house in 1997 I often looked up to the fort's ramparts, and sometimes contemplated these two handsome horses gazing out, imperially it seemed to me, over the village. In the past horses were high-maintenance symbols of power for Rajput rulers. Today, most local royal families still keep one or two in spite of straightened circumstances, and at a time when they have renounced or lost most trappings of their past dominion. These horses are no longer fed through the unremunerated sweat of the low born, yet their presence is not a neutral one. Perhaps the deepest shock Bhoju experienced during our interviews was when we were told that the very poor used to search through royal horse manure to remove the undigested grain, wash it, and grind it for their bread.

During my first period of fieldwork in 1979–81, I rarely took note of the fort's looming structure or thought much about its residents, human or animal. The *thākur*, or village master, residing there, then and now, was Gana Raj Singh. He had a jeep, which did somewhat interest me initially because transportation was often a problem. However, it turned out he rarely gave anyone rides—let alone a no-count foreign woman. In an established tradition of the Sawar Court (as I was to learn years later), he maintained a scornful distance from foreign intruders. At one point in 1979, when I was still fully dis-

Ghatiyali fort viewed from Bhoju's roof.

oriented, Gana Raj Singh did invite me and Joseph Miller, another resident American research scholar, for dinner. I recall little of that occasion, except that I found the strained politeness and the strictly enforced purdah to be uncomfortably stifling. At the time this atmosphere seemed to me thoroughly disconnected from the rest of Ghatiyali's warm sociability, to which I was only beginning to adjust. Let me confess here that except for a brief visit to the courtyard when I was recording a village-wide women's ritual (Gold 1988:126) I never again set foot inside the boundaries of the fort. In the course of researching this book, I have spent considerable time in other such structures, especially in Sawar's fort where Gana Raj Singh's younger brother, Mani Raj Singh, resides.

Because I paid the fort and nobility so little attention, a few early signposts stand out now in my re-collected memories. I recount them here.

Although I developed no ties with the royal family, during most of my time in the village between 1979 and 1981 I lived in a household belonging to somewhat impoverished members of the Rajput caste.[2] Our neighborhood, I came eventually to learn, was called the *rāvaḷo*—meaning "the place where Rajputs dwell." The *rāvaḷo* is usually in fair proximity to the fort, as indeed we were. Many of the household's men were truckdrivers or chauffeurs—and proud of it. From my host family I gathered definite impressions of the high esteem in which the lineages of "sons of princes" held themselves vis-à-vis others. I can distinctly recall my landlady and mentor, Shobhag Kanvar, revealing hierarchy to me with her bluntly tactless didactic style. When she described her relationship with a visiting member of the Charan, or bardic, caste, she enunciated loudly in a simplified language for my benefit: "I am a Rajput, he is a Charan; I sit on a chair, he sits on the floor."[3] The Charan, Indar Dan, whom I had invited from another village to be my research assistant, was a kind of grassroots socialist poet. Understandably, he took an immediate and strong dislike to her.

On the other hand, what I saw around me in the proud homes of the *rāvaḷo* was, from my perspective, not much different in material terms from what I saw in the homes of farming and herding peoples— many of whom lived virtually down the block, as Bhoju did from Shobhag Kanvar. Their basic diet, their topics of conversation, and their religious practices were all pretty similar, although Rajputs sometimes had more elaborate ceremonies. The most distinctive feature I could see about Rajputs in those days was women's adherence to purdah. This was a matter of pride to both genders. In-married women of all other *jāti*s, even Brahmins, might go to the wells and work in the fields, but not the Rajput ladies—the *ṭhukarāṇī*s (literally "queens of the *ṭhākur*s"). I also observed how freely, but discreetly, Shobhag Kanvar rewrote purdah rules to suit her own needs and advantage.

I had been living in the Rajput neighborhood for many months before I learned the word *rāvaḷo* or understood its significance. The term first entered my consciousness only when I was engaged in translating bawdy songs performed for the festival of Sitala Mother's worship, and sung collectively by intercaste groups of women who taunted one another about each *jāti*'s sexual traits. Rajput women worship first on the day of Sitala Mother, and are safely back in their courtyards well before sunrise, whereas the middle-caste groups may be singing their bawdy songs in the streets in the full light of day.

The only mention of Rajputs in these lyrics is indirect: "In the she-buffalo's vagina you can fit the whole *rāvaḷo*."[4] When my helper explained this verse to me I was amused by the song's image with its fanciful size distortions, but nonetheless I failed to grasp its subversive nature. I had zero comprehension then of the anger the farming community harbored toward the rulers. Years later I was told that such lines were taunts to the ruling elite, and were risky to perform, even on carnivalesque occasions such as Sitala's worship.

Until 1993, most of what I knew about the royal house of Sawar, and royalty in general, was gained through conversations and interactions with a woman who had attached herself to me—Lila Damami, an "untouchable" drummer to royalty. Lila regaled me in 1980 with a lively description of one day when the grand ladies from the Sawar fort had decided to visit Puvali ka Devji—Ghatiyali's pilgrimage magnet (Gold 1988). Their visit required sustaining their seclusion from the world's eyes—that is, keeping purdah. On that day, Lila dramatically informed me, the shrine had been closed to all other pilgrims (thereby preventing devotees from viewing or praying to the Lord). I found this startling news, especially since Puvali was a place where I was used to seeing Rajputs and Brahmins rubbing elbows with farmers and herders—Minas, Gujars, and Malis—affliction being everywhere a great leveler of persons. Moreover, in the context of devotion, I was aware that purdah could often be circumvented; some Rajput women, normally subject to purdah, did come as pilgrims to Puvali—including my landlady, Shobhag Kanvar. But evidently, purdah constraints on the ladies from the fort were of a quite different order.[5]

Lila had a primary school education and a lively mind. She was often startlingly quick to evaluate intercultural matters. Perceiving my astonishment, she said to me, with a kind of sigh, "Oh Ainn Bai [my village name] in your country there are no kings-and-great-kings (*rājā-mahārājā log*)." "No there aren't, that's right," I thoughtfully but emphatically agreed.

This bit of conversation echoed in my head. However, it prodded me then to think not about hierarchy in Rajasthan, but rather about my own heritage. It was as if for the first time since learning about the establishment of democracy in the American colonies in second-grade social studies I finally glimpsed what kind of transformation might actually have been implied. In 1980, maybe a little homesick, thinking about the way the great kings could co-opt a whole shrine plunged me into a moment of appreciation for the ideology, if not the actuality, of society in the United States. But also lingering in a corner of my brain was the nagging suspicion that something important remained uninvestigated, at Puvali and elsewhere. Later, when I began to take a serious interest in power plays, and when the great kings' reign had become my research focus, I had reason to recall this neglected epiphany.

The poetics of kingship often caught my attention in minor ways, because it pervades Rajasthani culture and language. I was struck, for example, by the semantic merging of names and terms of address for "god," "ruler," "patron," and sometimes "husband." Most especially, viewing kings as householders par excellence, I found a compelling commentary on worldly religion in the oral epic tales of kings turned yogis (Gold 1989, 1994). Retrospectively, these tales reveal more than I once imagined about the time of kings.

Years after that conversation with Lila, while translating the story of King Bharthari that I recorded in Ghatiyali in 1987, I had particular trouble with a scene where a king confronts his people who have deserted his kingdom en masse, leaving it desolate. He pursues them to the border and demands to know their reasons for leaving. The dialogue of spokesman and ruler goes like this:

> "Grain-giver, we have quit this city, and we ask your forgiveness."
>
> "Why are you asking forgiveness? What is your trouble? Are my land taxes (*hāsil*) too big? . . . Are my guards or my messenger (*syāṇā bāmī*) afflicting you?"
>
> "Grain-giver, you're a very good king. We're troubled neither by taxes, nor by your guards and messenger." (Gold 1992:86)

In 1987, after seven years of research in, and writing on, Rajasthan, I had never taken note of the several terms that made this passage opaque to me: terms for taxes, king's guards, and king's messenger. They were not recorded in my vocabulary cards, nor had they entered my understanding of village life.

Bhoju Ram then explained to me about the practice of placing exorbitant taxes on crop production and helped me to translate the terms for the pair of kings' agents: *syāṇā* as "guards" and *bāmī* as "messenger." This duo of royal agents was used synecdotally by the epic bard to evoke the panoply of the kings' men. I looked up both terms in several dictionaries, found the spelling variants, and wrote appropriate footnotes.[6] When the floodgates of the past opened to us in 1993 and 1997, the overwhelming burden of the old revenue assess-ment and collection system and the obnoxious behavior of the kings' agents echoed and resounded as key themes, as they will in later chapters of this book.

It was an episode concerning Lila's taking refuge in the fort to escape her angry estranged husband's attempt to drag her back to his parents' house that prodded me to write, in the introduction to my first book on Ghatiyali, "After I had been in Ghatiyali for some time I began to perceive that the stone Fort (*garh*) on the central hill where the *thākur* and his family lived was neither so remote nor so powerless as I had at first thought it to be." But, I continue, "It is perhaps a two-minute descent from Ganaraj's stone ramparts to Ghatiyali's dusty lanes" (Gold 1988:28–29). In these lanes my attention remained and remains—among the ruled not the rulers. Even in 1997, I was not nearly as happy seated awkwardly on a chair in the prim parlor of the former chief minister's son, or in the current *tahsīldār*'s office, as I was squatting by farmers' wells or cooking hearths, or rambling over scrubland with goatherds. This book too has its heart in the lower reaches. What has changed is that I am now acutely conscious of the looming stone fort.

Bhoju Ram, born in a small *kachchā* (adobe) house not far from the fort, experienced his own discoveries and realizations as we did research for this book. Whatever due respect he renders to the former rulers, whatever residual disdain he nurses for the former untouch-ables, his identity is firmly planted among the pressed-down people, whose sorrows and pleasures—largely through his ministrations—unfolded in our ears.

It was in 1979 through Bhoju's verbal skills that I first began to understand the meaning of village devotional songs (Gold 1988:xiv). With our focus on the political world we sometimes forgot to think about religion. During my last days in winter 1997, Bhoju and I de-cided to host a *jāgaraṇ,* or all-night hymn singing session of thanks and praise. I was very glad to be going home and my work had gone well, yet I was sad to leave the family whose love had so enveloped me. I sat blissfully listening to hymns to an indescribable lord, hymns I had struggled for months to translate in 1980 when I cared not a whit for history. Now I was newly moved by the fervor of the singers and, during interludes that punctuated the singing, the deep interest they had in conversing about the soul and its possible destinies. How could I have forgotten this? I felt a jolt, a tectonic shift in my brain. My diary entry on the following day, my last in the village that winter, reads: "21 February 1997: Bhoju says I'm like a bird that wants to leave its eggs. . . . Raji wants to know if we have quilts in America. Typing all day with a dogged despair, wondering if any of this was worth it. . . . Flies swarming around my eyes nevertheless I type on. . . . *Jāgaraṇ* was uplifting truly for me. If I could only fuse what I understand of this deep sweet profound and real devotion with the cruelty of history then maybe I could write something whole and true."

ACKNOWLEDGMENTS

From Bhoju

We are indebted to all the elders and youths, women and men, with whom we have talked, who gave us their priceless time and made us emotional partners in their joys and despairs. We have sympathy toward all who, even today when recollecting their past, feel sorrows and frustrations. Today our chief effort ought to be to ensure that every person become happy, free, and fearless, and our country unified and progressive.

I once again offer respectful salutations to all, and I wish that everyone's happiness increase.

From Ann

The fieldwork that enabled this project was supported in 1993 by a senior research Fulbright fellowship and in 1997 by a senior short-term fellowship from the American Institute of Indian Studies, which was funded by the National Endowment for the Humanities, an independent government organization. I am doubly indebted to the endowment because I was fortunate to receive a University Teachers fellowship from the NEH in order to write this book. In 1997–98 Bhoju and I shared a major research grant from the Spencer Foundation for separate but related research that contributed significantly to the understandings put forward here. I thank the College of Arts and Sciences of Syracuse University for supporting a one-semester research leave (and granting two additional semesters of leave from teaching duties). At Syracuse, my department chair James Wiggins and Richard Pilgrim, then associate dean, gave me various kinds of assistance in negotiating my leave, for which I am most grateful. More recently, as chair of the Religion Department, Dick arranged much-needed funding to support production of the maps and photographs in this volume.

My advisors in India in 1993 and 1997, respectively, were Professor T. N. Madan of the Institute for Economic Growth at Delhi University, and Dr. Rajendra Joshi of the Institute of Rajasthan Studies in Jaipur. In both situations I was greatly blessed by the interest and acumen of these senior scholars, whose lively minds and accumulated knowledge enriched my thought and work. Periodic conversations in New Delhi with Bina Agarwal and Ramachandra Guha were also extremely important to this project as it developed, as was friendship and intellectual exchange with Shail Mayaram of the Institute of Development Studies in Jaipur. Thanks to these colleagues, Bhoju and I twice had the opportunity to give joint presentations of our work in progress to seminars—at IEG in Delhi in 1993 and at IDS in Jaipur in 1997—from which we gained invaluable critical feedback. My friendship with Aditi and Ajay Mehta grew along with this project and contributed to it. Aditi was district collector in Ajmer in 1993 and district magistrate in 1997; her hospitality included hot baths, toast served on the lawn, and far-ranging conversations concerning every aspect of our work. We also benefited greatly from Ajay's insightful comments, pragmatic questions, and service perspective.

In Ghatiyali, honor and gratitude beyond words first go to Bhoju Ram's immediate family, for whom I provided huge amounts of trouble. I must mention each of them by name: Sukh Devji and Raji, Bali, Kamalesh, Madhu, Chinu, Ghumar, Monu, and Sandip, who was born during my last visit to Rajasthan in July 1997. I also thank Ugma Nathji Natisar Nath and Shambhu Natisar Nath for invaluable assistance; Shivji Gujar for doing "the work of Eli"; and Lila and both Bhabhasas (Shobhag Kanvar and Motiya Kanvar), as ever.

Many persons have listened to, read, and commented on various parts of this volume, and it has been the substance of numerous lectures. I collectively and inadequately thank these patient and receptive audiences for so much helpful and critical oral commentary.

Graduate students in Susan Wadley's spring 2000 seminar on Anthropology of South Asia read the entire manuscript and their lively responses were helpful and heartening. Discussions with Shubhra Gururani, Smitu Kothari, Michael Lambek, and Pramod Parajuli contributed at various times to my thinking and writing.

To some colleagues who have taken pen in hand to different parts of this work—whether as anthology editors or out of the kindness of their hearts—I owe deep intellectual debts, many of which are not sufficiently acknowledged in the text. These include Bina Agarwal, Amita Baviskar, Daniel Gold, Brian Greenberg, Paul Greenough, Ronald Herring, Anirudh Krishna, Stig Madsen, Shail Mayaram, Archana Prasad, Lance Nelson, Paul Robbins, Gloria Raheja, Anna Tsing, and Susan Wadley. Gloria has been particularly assiduous in correcting errors, pointing me toward perfect sources—even mailing them to me. Since 1992 I have learned much from ongoing conversations with Ron—whose ability to cut straight to the core questions complements his relentless passion for exactitude.

Saurabh Dube and Ishita Banerjee Dube each read in a preliminary draft what are now chapters 2 through 6 and gave me a wealth of advice, some of which I may have squandered but much of which significantly guided the penultimate round of revisions. Wonderfully helpful comments from Saurabh and Gloria, again, as well as Ramachandra Guha, Kirin Narayan, and an astute and demanding anonymous reviewer motivated further revisions, as have consultations with Ken Wissoker. Mark Hauser patiently, carefully, and cheerfully produced the two maps. Jonah Gold helped me to create a database of interviewees.

I thank my colleagues in the Department of Religion at Syracuse for sheltering me as a disciplinary "other" in their midst and giving me a congenial professional home. Phil Arnold's shared concern for religion and environment has particularly helped me to feel I belong. For another form of shelter in Syracuse, plus seven years of comfortable and valuable cross-disciplinary collegiality and limitless pots of coffee, I thank Kristen Schaffer deeply.

Betsy Clarke, Deborah Pratt, and Carol Williams have assisted me in innumerable ways since I arrived at the Hall of Languages in 1993. I owe them profound thanks for seven years, during which my requests were never once greeted with anything but good cheer and efficiency—astonishing but utterly true! During my three semesters on leave, which were supported by multiple funding sources, Betsy managed the accounting complexities—a burden of which I was blissfully unaware until she presented me on my return with the grossly bulging paperwork files.

I must also thank the South Asia Consortium, a national resource center uniting Syracuse and Cornell, for support at both institutions. Center directors (including Susan Wadley at Syracuse and Mary Katzenstein, Shelley Feldman, and Chris Minkowski at Cornell) along with staff (including Jishnu Shankar at Syracuse and Anne Stengle and Durga Bor at Cornell) have assisted me over the years in countless small and large ways. Precious boons granted to me by our consortium include my cool basement space in the Einaudi Center for International Studies as well as Cornell library privileges; these have significantly sustained both my scholarship and sanity in a frazzled commuter's life. Norma Grant's hard work on the home front for over a decade has also meant the world to me.

Once again I praise my mother, Ruth Grodzins, for ongoing assistance of many kinds; now in her eighties she has lost neither her skilled editorial touch nor her legendary generosity of spirit. I am ever grateful to Bert and Sylvia Gold, my husband's parents, who always cheered me in both senses, and gave our family much-needed holiday escapes; Sylvia passed away between this work's two field stages, and we miss her. Kelly and Diana Grodzins, my *kākā* and *kākī*, continue to offer moral and financial succor where it is most desperately needed, and I affectionately thank them. I thank my big sister Mitchell Mariam (Helly) Grodzins, who has shared jokes, empathized with worries, and exemplified attitude at appropriate moments. For over twenty years now, my children Adam Rose, Jonah Gold, and Eli Gold at various ages suffered abandonment when I traveled in India without them, and numerous discomforts when I took them along. I am grateful for their forbearance and forgiveness, and I trust that they may have gained from anthropological parenting something more than a lifelong taste for mangos and *jalebis*.

Periodically in the hot and rainy seasons of 1993 I would hysterically declare my intention to cease this pointless research and return home. Each time, my infuriatingly calm husband, Daniel, was able to dissuade me from making rash moves; I would resign myself and get back to work, promising with more cynicism than faith to thank him in "the book" for thus detaining me. So I do, as well as for much other sound advice and true support throughout our lengthening years.

To the many people of Savar Sattaisa who gave us their time and words I offer my profound gratitude and respect.

None of the institutions and persons named are responsible for the content of this book.

Together, Bhoju and Ann dedicate this volume to departed teachers in India and the United States, with appreciation for their enduring words and lives. First among these is Sukh Devji Gujar, Bhoju Ram's father. Others whose words we were fortunate to record before they became peaceful include Dayal Gujar, Kalyan Mali, Dhapu Mina, and Madhu Nath. In academia we honor the memories of Rajendra Joshi, former head of the Institute of Rajasthan Studies, and of Milton B. Singer and Helen Singer, from whom Ann as a small child caught her first sense of a place called India, and years later received generous and wise mentoring.

1. THE PAST OF NATURE

AND THE NATURE OF THE PAST

These are small voices which are drowned in the noise of statist commands. That is why we don't hear them. That is also why it is up to us to make that extra effort, develop the special skills and above all cultivate the disposition to hear these voices and interact with them. For they have many stories to tell—stories which for their complexity are unequaled by statist discourse and indeed opposed to its abstract and oversimplifying modes.—Ranajit Guha, "The Small Voice of History"

There is good reason to believe vision is better from below the brilliant space platforms of the powerful.—Donna Haraway, *Simians, Cyborgs, and Women*

This book relates some complex stories of a small place: the twenty-seven-village former kingdom of Sawar (Savar Sattaisa) in the modern state of Rajasthan in India. Differing from most accounts of the past in Rajasthan, our book describes conditions and events from the viewpoints of subjects, not rulers. We attempt to portray a critical and pivotal era—the 1930s through the 1950s—in the translated words of largely nonliterate farmers, herders, leatherworkers, and others who recollect the "time of great kings" (*rājā-mahārājā kā jamānā*).[1] Although occasionally we consulted persons who once held power, and also visited archives, the bulk and heart of our book is conversations with those who formerly endured a double oppression under colonial and regional rulers. Through these conversations we present not only appraisals of past autocracy but experiences of the sudden and radical transformation to democracy and modernity as these have been incorporated and interpreted "below" the realms of power.

Early in 2000, Bhoju Ram Gujar proposed seven possible titles for our coalescing manuscript. One possessed rhyme, rhythm, and economy in the original Hindī, but translates rather awkwardly as "The Rulers' Story, the People's Testimony" (*rāj kahānī prajā kī jabānī*). Although we ultimately chose a different phrase, I would like to stress here the importance of Bhoju's deliberate equation in this formulation of "story" (*kahānī*) with "oral testimony" (*jabānī*).[2] We offer these stories, and they were offered to us, as a kind of testimony. By "story" we mean something that has been told, and that is worth retelling, with feeling. By "testimony" we mean something witnessed, stated, and affirmed to be true; another meaning given for *jabānī* is "affidavit."[3]

Urvashi Butalia evokes a similar conjunction of subjective experience with witnessed truth when she argues for the worth of her own work with memories in her book of oral narratives about India's partition. She considers any preconceived contrast between memory and historical fact as a misapprehension: "But to me, the way people choose to remember an event, a history, is at least as important as what one might call the 'facts' of that history, for after all, these latter are not self-evident givens; instead, they too are interpretations, as remembered or recorded by one individual or another" (2000:8). Each person's story has intrinsic value—not just as a crude source to be refined into data, but in the telling. Like Butalia, we do not weigh speakers' interpretations against supposed actuality. Rather, we layer multiple versions to achieve a textured, contoured narrative density.[4]

In the epigraph to this chapter, Ranajit Guha exhorts his fellow historians not just to exert "extra effort" in attending to small voices, but to realize the need to cultivate a "disposition" for such attentiveness. Anthropologists—however maligned they find themselves at present—might be permitted a fleeting satisfaction in this regard. Has not such attention been their bottom-line métier from the beginning?[5]

For me and Bhoju, listening has been a basic mode of operation, although our respective motivations and trajectories are disparate. For Bhoju these voices are after all from his own community; for me, as an ethnographer and a foreign guest, these voices are of people who have not only taken pains to educate me more or less from scratch, but have made me feel at home among them. Certainly, Bhoju and I differ from Guha's presumed audience of Indian historians educated in a predominantly European disciplinary tradition. For better or worse, our capacity to hear small voices has been unimpaired by grand visions.[6] By this I do not mean to imply that either of us came to this work without plenty of preconceptions, but rather that by virtue of stumbling unaware and unprepared into history we had no sense of what the stories we gathered should reveal by way of the larger narratives in which they are, of course, embedded and by which they are to a degree controlled.

Our book is a product not only of our isolated and unique collaboration (a Jewish female cultural anthropologist born in Chicago in 1946, and a Gujar Hindu male schoolteacher, now headmaster, born in Ghatiyali in 1956), but of twenty years of sea changes in anthropology and social science that have filtered into our aims, methods, and styles. Three such changes are perhaps most relevant to this work. First is the shift from univocal to dialogic or polyvocal narration; from monologic claims for ethnographic authority to practices of coproduction, whatever the (considerable) risks entailed.[7] Our collaboratively engendered book gives pride of place to the words of elderly Sawar villagers who, as they sometimes put it, filled our tapes for us. These persons have lived through multiple, radical changes. Their memories include transformations from simultaneous subjection to both a well-known local despot and a remote colonial power, to participation as citizens of a modern, bureaucratic, and postcolonial democracy. Concurrently the Sawar elders have seen their landscape transformed from one rich in biodiversity of trees and wildlife to one where hillsides have been stripped of indigenous growth and are now dominated by a single alien species. Sawar residents experience and evaluate these and many other changes in varied, nuanced, and critical ways.

The second massive trend that influenced our work is the departure from assertions that each culture yields a coherent, systematic, elegantly chartable universe of ordered meanings and values. Some ethnographers now deny any such monolithic constructs, and replace them with sheer revelry in fraught negotiations, contested realities, and displays of cacophonous discourse.[8] We have accordingly attempted to record individual Sawar voices with particular care, to situate persons as social actors speaking from unique life histories, and in general to avoid dissolving disparate identities and positions and to present multiple and sometimes conflicting versions of the same tales.

Finally, and most directly connected with the content of this work, are several strands rebinding anthropology with history and reworking ethnohistory, oral history, and environmental history or landscape memory into the mainstreams of ethnographic knowledge.[9] Originating separately from but eventually converging with and cross-fertilizing these efforts is the influential and vastly important work of the subaltern historians in the subcontinent.[10] From their inspiration, accomplishments, and impact we gather confidence in the worth of our endeavors, while remaining well aware that our project is genealogically different from theirs.

I would argue that all the changes I have evoked here are healthy ones; they keep anthropology worth doing. I sometimes hear colleagues of my generation (trained in the 1970s) express nostalgic yearning for the era of certainties—whether the crisp visions of E. E. Evans-Pritchard or the calm detachment of Louis Dumont. For myself, I am grateful to be a seriously rattled, insecure ethnographer at the millennium rather than a complacent authority of fifty years past. Moreover, it is a pleasure to observe a slightly newer generation flourishing, many of whom themselves belong from birth to more than one world. Their theoretical edges are well-honed and multiple, and they are more at home camping on shifting sands.[11]

Bhoju and I are in the middle. We are differently in the same middle—millennial anthropology; and we are similarly in middles that differ. That is, he in Ghatiyali and I in American academia are both between two generations, our seniors more sure of the terms on which life should be led; our juniors bred to swim in floods of change. Bhoju, too, sometimes sighs after consistency and laments the untamed multiforms of every story we hear. Yet ultimately he lives comfortably enough, as I too try to do, with double doses of multiple realities.

There might be a parallel here with the people of Sawar, who resoundingly prefer their unbalanced, slippery existence under the rule of votes (*voṭ kā rāj*)—despite its dismaying disorders and massive disillusions—to the rule of great kings (*rājā-mahārājā kā rāj*) with its firm hand. They maintain their conviction that the present is happier in spite of the genuinely tragic losses of wooded terrain sheltering biodiversity and of community solidarity (losses far greater than any that social science may have suffered in losing its cherished paradigms). This preference for the present counters nostalgia with something quite other than contentment; it is an important theme in much that follows. In the village, too, a new generation is maturing. This book will not tell you much about them, but the future is theirs.[12]

Our framing question is straightforwardly descriptive: What was it like for poor farmers and herders and laborers during the time of kings (and empire)? All that we learned in this regard emerged from a prior inquiry: What happened to the trees? Our original impetus, then, was to learn the story of deforestation; in the process we found out a great deal about everything else, yet our expanded vision remains ecological in spirit. We seek to substantiate the answers to both questions through accounts of lived experiences located in space and time, often presented dialogically. Some of the qualities of these experiences—rendered as the exploitation and suffering of peasants in early-twentieth-century Rajputana—have been presumed to be generalized conditions for this region in many works of history. But actual recorded recollections are scarce, thin, and too often decontextualized.[13]

Our conviction is that the stories or testimonies gathered here have their most powerful impact as human expressions. To theorize them is not to enhance their worth, but only to locate them in fields of knowledge in order to aid readers in situating and understanding their meaning. Our book's value, then, lies not in making new arguments about human relationships with nature or the course of environmental history; about power witnessed from below; or about the realities of a remembered past. Our claims are considerably more modest: to contribute a few thoughts and a greater measure of grounded substance to three currents of academic discourse—nature, power, and memory. I would characterize these more expansively as scholarship concerned with envisioning nature and tracking environmental transformations, with subaltern consciousness and struggles, and with the relationship between individual recollections and historical truths.

Floating in the confluence of these streams, our work—to pun rather badly but meaningfully—remains an ethnographic craft. It is fieldwork based, at heart an anthropological endeavor with all the baggage those terms have come to hold.[14] In the remainder of this introductory chapter, I will briefly position our voices and labors as we navigate these fluid thought worlds.

Why Say "Nature"?

What is now an oral ethnographic history, made up of fragmented chronicles of dramatic change, began as a timeless study of value. Its impetus reflected my 1970s training at the University of Chicago permeated with romanticized visions of divine conservation (Gold and Gujar 1995), cross-fertilized over five-odd years by Cornell University's more pragmatic agendas in development sociology, natural resources, and environmental engineering.[15] I set out for Rajasthan in December 1992 to research, what I called "cultural constructions of the natural environment." However, my original conception had been to look at "religious constructions of nature." I ran an early version of a research proposal past an advanced graduate student of my acquaintance, and received from him many supportive comments, along with some polite but pointed advice: the project was great, but it would be preferable not to say "religion," and not to say "nature."[16] Fine, I thought; there is always virtue in less-loaded language.

I leave unexamined here the facility with which I was able to substitute "culture" for "religion" and never look back. But I shall have to tangle with the terminological dilemma surrounding "nature" because, having once docilely replaced it with "environment," I eventually returned to it. When in our interviews old people sketched past landscapes before our minds' eyes, we were stunned by the contrast with a denuded present. To understand what happened to the trees in Sawar we had to understand a whole passage in history. For this reason my research proposal for 1997 was titled, as is this chapter, "The Past of Nature and the Nature of the Past." And nature—with all its attendant perplexities—remains central to this book. From semantic issues I shall then turn to the intersections of our work with recent rethinkings of South Asian environmental history; that is, to the past of nature in the subcontinent.

In two often-cited meditations on the meaning of the English word "nature," Raymond Williams has argued both that it is "perhaps the most complex word in the language" (1976:184) and that as an idea it contains "an extraordinary amount of human history" (1980:67). Many other authors have explored the meanings of nature in Euro-American culture in far greater detail than did Williams, but none, to my mind, with greater economy or eloquence.[17] To oversimplify radically the poetics, politics, and evolving historical meanings presented in multiple accounts, we may highlight two constructions that have dominated English speakers' understandings of this noun.

In one construction, nature is and by definition must remain "out there." It is separate from all that humans create and affect; it is, as Williams puts it, "all that was not man: all that was not touched by man, spoilt by man" (1980:77). The second view of nature, elaborated extensively in marxist thought but widely acknowledged, realizes that any pristine nature is only imaginary. Continuing to follow Williams's capsule imagery: "We have mixed our labour with the earth, our forces with its forces too deeply to be able to draw back and separate either out" (1980:83). In other words, any nature that is possible for humans to know they have also produced, even as it has produced them. These two opposing but complementary views have generated many debates in environmentalist thought, and they hold serious consequences for environmental policy and the conflicted politics that often surround it. Both areas are, fortunately, well beyond our present scope.[18]

As Bell's (1994) study of nature in rural England beautifully reveals, both of the views that Williams highlights coexist in commonsense, vernacular understandings—sometimes comfortably, sometimes uneasily. Every other year on the first day of my Syracuse University undergraduate course "Religions and the Natural Environment" I ask students to free-associate on the word "nature." After five or six responses, I invariably have written on the blackboard that nature is other than and beyond humanity, pristine and unspoiled; and that nature is a resource for people, but is endangered by their folly. Now and then the occasional Wiccan, or Buddhist, or, memorably, a Californian "raised by hippies" will help me to turn a corner by suggesting that spiritual life is inherent in nature, rather than garnered from it.

For anthropologists and historians of religions seeking to understand (and teach) cosmologies other than those posed in the three familiar monotheisms, both Euro-American paradigms are problematic. Whether pristine or imbricated in human labor and art, nature as an English term has—at least since the seventeenth century—been largely devoid of consciousness and agency.[19] Both of these concepts are regularly located either in humanity or in a nonimmanent creator. But there flourish many other religious worlds where elements of nature are more often animate—spirited, emotional, and willful.[20]

A second problem for cross-cultural meanings follows closely on any view of nature as devoid of conscious agency. Deeply embedded in the English semantics of nature is a presumed dichotomy with culture, a dichotomy of skewed value, often gendered.[21] Marilyn Strathern, among others, has argued that one of the many assumptions implicit in the nature/culture dichotomy is "the notion that the one domain is open to control or colonization by the other" (1980:181). And it is culture that western humans have traditionally viewed as the proper and inevitable colonizer.[22] That is, nature is to be disciplined, productive, and ornamental. In spite of many critiques lodged against any notion that such dichotomous and hierarchical ideas about nature and culture have universal validity, these ideas inexplicably continue to haunt social science.[23]

The Sanskrit term *prakṛti*, often used as a translation of, and translated as, the English word "nature," suggests some rather different formulations. *Prakṛti* can refer to an active, infinitely multiple, female cosmic principle, and a manifestation of divine female power.[24] Thus, as ecofeminist pioneer Vandana Shiva proclaimed in the first of her many books, third-world women "have challenged the western concept of nature as an object of exploitation and have protected her as Prakriti, the living force that supports life" (1988:xvii). Such a definition might immediately throw into question the dichotomous devaluation of nature, as opposed to culture, and open to colonization by it.

Shiva's rhetoric has been roundly and repeatedly critiqued—perhaps most devastatingly by feminists rightly suspicious of the way ecofeminism essentializes "women" by equating them with nature, even when their intention is to valorize female power.[25] Nonetheless, Shiva calls attention to some very good reasons to beware (as my friend advised me) of loosely employing the term "nature" when talking about Rajasthani interactions with the earth, its atmosphere, creatures, and products. Why then—when it is clearly inappropriate in multiple ways—would Bhoju and I evoke the idea of nature in our accounts of geophysical and social transformations in Rajasthan? I answer this in two explanatory steps dealing with alternatives and translations, followed by a sweeping statement.

Possible alternatives to the term "nature" might include "landscape," "environment," and "ecology." Each word carries a semantic weight that is contextually helpful, and in fact I freely deploy all three throughout this work to convey particular messages. "Landscape" might be the safest word, because it has everything to do with viewpoint and representation, with "traditions of perception and perspective" (Appadurai 1991b:191).[26] Often enough (but not always), I can use "landscape" to talk about transformations in the environment as envisioned and interpreted by Sawar residents, without wishing to imply anything more far-reaching.

In earlier work I used "environment" specifically in order to avoid the cultural baggage of "nature"—it seemed to be a more neutral and prosaic way of saying almost the same thing. Several authors have argued convincingly, however, that "environment" holds specific meanings that "nature" does not. These meanings derive from its etymology as "surroundings." What is surrounded? People. And "environment" is conceived as that which affords them uses (Ingold 1992).[27] In the chapters that follow, those instrumental meanings are often arguably just the sense we require: we are concerned with trees as fuel and fodder, with rain as making crops grow, with wild animals either as edible objects of desire or as agents of economic ruin. This is something flatter and more instrumental than the view of nature as inevitably mixed with human labor. Missing from "environment" and its implications is any larger understanding beyond the anthrocentric and the functionalist/materialist.

The term "ecology," in direct contrast to "environment," effectively decenters our understandings from human needs. More important, ecology suggests whole systems, fragile and multiply interdependent. For me the term implies a highly sensitized causal web. Sawar villagers gave me this weblike vision, although they had no single word for it. They also taught me its moral dimensions, and I have roughly translated my derivative understanding with the abstraction "moral ecology."[28]

In Sawar residents' interpretations, biophysical well-being or ill-being depends on soil, livestock, grain, and weather, but it is also in mutual formation with human temperaments and behaviors—whether generous or selfish. Interviews portray the tree-covered hills of the past as completely intermeshed with the bygone rule of kings. To evoke only a few of the factors at play: the past was a time of less dense population, less intensive land use, more cattle and milk, organic fertilizer, coarser but more nourishing and tasty grains, stronger digestions, greater compassion, more leisure to tell stories, and many fewer consumer goods to crave and to arouse envy.

Among other things, such a complex vision helps us to understand why ecological recovery may seem a remote prospect in Sawar villagers' views. The visible ruin of nature is tied not only to the equally visible and highly appreciated freedom from despotic government, but also to the invisible and highly deplored corrosion of ordinary human goodness. Some Indian scholars and activists argue persuasively that South Asian environmentalism differs from American movements in making social justice an absolute requirement in any plan for conservation or regeneration. Their positions take a stance that reveals in urban political terms some of the same moral discourse I heard in Sawar—insisting that the fate of the earth and the character of human society are inextricably interlocked.[29]

Turning to issues of translation, we immediately acknowledge that in the interview texts that are this book's chief substance, readers will find scant talk of nature, landscape, environment, or ecology. Not one of these terms has a precise equivalent in the everyday local language of Sawar. Rather, they are all part of the academic prose with which we elaborate meanings.

While Shiva's vision of *prakriti* as a divine force manifest in nature may well convey something akin to Rajasthani understandings, in Sawar villages we encountered the word *prakriti* only in the Sanskritized language of the learned. Most others spoke of trees, or animals, or grass, or weather, but rarely required a concept embracing them all. If they wished to refer to all of "creation" or "nature writ large," Hindus as well as Muslims were more likely to use the Urdu/Perso-Arabic word *kudarat*.[30] Like *prakriti*, *kudarat* implies creative power. In Islam that power would be associated with male divinity understood as singular, while *prakṛiti*, by contrast, would imply activity, proliferation, and plenitude—all expressions of the goddess who is herself multiform. In common, however, *kudarat* and *prakṛiti* imbue the natural world with value and meaning beyond human purpose or calculation—the main import with which they were charged. All told, with the exception of schoolteachers, neither term was spontaneously produced in more than half a dozen interviews.

Another word derived from Sanskrit, *paryāvaraṇ*, has begun to move into common speech largely due to government efforts to introduce "environment" as a subject in primary school curriculums. *Paryāvaraṇ*, like the English word "environment," literally means "surroundings" and conveniently lacks the religious or philosophical implications of *prakṛiti* or *kudarat*. I found that by 1997 this word—traveling via teachers and schoolchildren—had gained some currency, but not among the elderly, who were our chief sources.

I retain the term "nature" in my interpretive writing not for accuracy but for ambiguity, complexity, and uncertainty. I use it willfully, at the metalevel, to evoke something more richly meaningful and potentially confusing than landscape or environment or ecology in the minds of academic readers. With "nature" I call on that culturally posed, nonexistent abstraction of something out there that is beautiful, fearsome, and untouched by humans yet intrinsic to their beings and of great worth to them. I want to remind us of ongoing, accelerated histories of use, exploitation, degradation, and extinction that are transnational and transcultural. Above all I use "nature" as a word that will allow readers to connect the barren hills of Sawar with all other places on the earth where trees once grew.

If one significant aspect of Euro-America "nature" is its utterly separate existence, the work of environmental history, according to one of its better-known American practitioners, deals exclusively with the other vision—that is, "the role and place of nature in human life." According to Donald Worster, the main task of environmental historians is to analyze "the various ways people have tried to make nature over into a system that produces resources for their consumption" (1990:1090). Most significantly for us, Worster goes on to observe that in the process of transforming the earth, "people have also restructured themselves and their social relations" (1090). Large and sometimes heated debates have swirled around how to interpret such environmental transformations and social restructurings in the South Asian subcontinent, focused on the impact of colonialism.

Indeed, Ramachandra Guha in his cogent update on these debates speaks of "The Great 'Ecology and Colonialism' Debate" (2000:215–20).[31] At issue is whether or not colonial environmental interventions were a "watershed," unleashing destruction unprecedented in India's environmental saga, as Guha believes to be the case. Others, notably Richard Grove, have doubted this narrative's total vision, without seeking to whitewash imperial impacts. Guha calls attention to a recent spate of monographs on India's environmental history that have massively documented not only colonial policy but also how attempts to implement it met with varied local responses.[32] These works provide strong evidence for what Ajay Skaria has called "the violence of colonial environmentalism" (1999:192).[33]

Our own intentions and capacities are not to judge whether or not colonial legacies were purely exploitative and uniquely devastating. Chapter 3, which in part draws on archival investigations, discusses some of the policies established by the colonial power in Ajmer that would have had significant impact on Sawar in the late nineteenth and early twentieth century. And we shall sometimes point to some of the ways that some British ideas about environment, especially about forests, affected this single, small locality with its idiosyncratic history. However, in our interviews within Sawar's villages, we heard little about the forestry agenda of the British Raj. This was in part doubtless a result of the Sawar Court's largely successful strategy of keeping the English well beyond arm's length. The marks of colonialism on Sawar's environmental circumstances and policies will be readily apparent, but we treat them largely as context rather than subject.

We have learned much from some of those meticulously documented histories of environmental change that, as Guha points out, are the fruits of at least a decade of extraordinary interest in these issues. Political energies have infused scholarly labors in this field, under the merged pressures of increased awareness of environmental deterioration and dramatic conflicts over environmental management.[34] Although comparative analysis is not our aim, we draw occasionally from these works to contextualize Sawar's stories more broadly. One important observation to emerge is that the ways that elements of nature have been viewed and treated in different eras and regions are highly variable according to local political and ecological specificities.

Taken together, for example, monographs by Skaria and by Sumit Guha complicate previous understandings of South Asian environmental history. Drawing on oral narrative traditions of Dangis in western India, Skaria is able to track transformations in configured relationships among power, identity, gender, and what he calls "wildness" in the Dangis' own historical understandings. Juxtaposing these to outsiders' views, he achieves a multifaceted portrait of politicized environmental history. Skaria shows how Dangis identified wildness with power, although that power was ambivalently construed. He observes that their relationship with wildness as power changed with changing circumstances in surrounding political and social structures that in turn impacted the internal political dynamics of the Dangis. Thus Skaria offers us the "complexities of wildness, and the many sites at which it was produced" (1999:43).

Sumit Guha's historical study of environment and ethnicity is based in western India as is Skaria's, but it ranges more widely, both geographically and historically. Like Skaria, Guha is interested in, among other things, the relationship between kingship and ideas about forests and their inhabitants. In legendary accounts of regional history, he finds a clear message: "Pushing back the jungle and subduing jangli [indigenous forest peoples] were central elements in the kingly role" (1999:154). Forest-dwelling Dangis in Skaria's study once thought their power continuous with untamed wildness; Guha shows us kings who located their royal identity in part in their capacity to tame a dangerously wild landscape and its inhabitants (which would include Dangis). Guha also notes an affinity between "dominant forest communities" and warrior/rulers that intersects with and corroborates those ideas of power and wildness that Skaria portrays.

From these two important studies we may gather that configurations of power, forest, and wildlife, and relations between forest and farming peoples, may vary widely within a single region according to internal situations and external pressures. Still greater are variations ensuing from varying climates and polities. Elsewhere on the subcontinent, royal identity has evidently involved fostering and protecting endangered wildness, rather than overcoming the double threat of wild spaces and their human and animal inhabitants. In semiarid Rajasthan, this has often been the case. In several kingdoms, not all as small as Sawar, rulers may have hunted dangerous beasts, but they also guarded woods and wildlife with vigilance, as did Sawar's own fabled Vansh Pradip Singh, who reigned from 1914 to 1947.[35]

When I began to write this book, I felt at first uneasy that a tension or confusion lay between our initial focus on deforestation and the broader historical processes we eventually took as our task to comprehend. But increasingly I have come to see the tale of Sawar's dwindling jungle as a tale of conjoined natural and social transformations.[36] Moreover, I am convinced this merging is less an accident of Bhoju's and my stumbling research path than a global actuality we inevitably came to realize (Gold 2001a). In Sawar, the time of nature's abundance was also the time of abundant sorrows endured under the rule of kings who protected the trees.

We hope to portray the ways that nature—as trees and grasses, as berries, wild pigs or rain—was experienced, produced, and internalized in the twenty-seven villages, not only as sustenance but as meaning, not only as goods but as identities and tales. Elements of the environment become emblems of satisfaction and deprivation, submission and confrontation. One person recalls blistering his feet in the dry riverbed on a frivolous errand for the king; another remembers the exquisite thrill and dire risk of poaching and consuming savory wild boar. Experiences of power impinged upon experiences of nature; the king's passion for trees made it harder to get firewood, but never impossible.

Voices from Under a Stone

As a schoolteacher and research assistant, Bhoju was fully aware that books on the Rajasthani past are filled with the deeds, words, and affairs of kings and armies. In 1993, as our history work first unfolded, he began to formulate a concept of largely uninscribed pasts, of submerged voices and lives such as those of his neighbors, his relatives, and his own mother and father. He called these "voices from under a stone" (Gold with Gujar 1997). Although Bhoju had not encountered the writings of the subaltern school of historiography, his understanding expressed in this phrase is something close to subalternity. It was not only that the words and views we taped were rarely heard beyond village courtyards or caste meeting spots, but that during the past era not just these elders' voices but their very beings had been suppressed. At the same time their capacity to speak was indisputable, and their lively tongues articulated not only what they had endured but how their spirits had not been crushed by it.[37] It was with an increasing sense of urgency that Bhoju worked with me to elicit and record these memories. Both of us were gripped not only by accounts of past suffering, but by lucid appraisals of power's insidious workings.

The subaltern studies editorial collective began publishing anthologies of historical essays in the early 1980s. Rapidly overflowing the outdated boundaries of area studies in unprecedented fashion, their contributions have had a profound impact on the disciplines of history and anthropology, and have cross-fertilized the burgeoning field of postcolonial studies, striking chords with recent foci of theoretical interest including resistance and creative cultural hybridity. Subaltern scholarship set out to locate and listen to the nonelite voices of history—voices that countered hegemonies both of colonialism and of the indigenous elite. However, as Dipesh Chakrabarty put it in one much-cited essay, in that "ruling class documents" have constituted the major sources for the historian's craft, often it was not speech but "silences" that had to be interpreted (1988:179). Much of the subaltern collective's work has been to highlight and interpret elusive traces of recalcitrant subaltern consciousness, in vivid descriptive and incisive analytic strokes. Expanding their scope well beyond rulers' records to other textual sources such as regional literatures, they have called attention to multiple resources for new understandings of historical processes.[38]

When scholars associated with the subaltern studies project have included oral testimonies in seeking to understand the more recent past that is also the remembered past, tropes of silence give way to vibrant voices and contesting narratives. Authors such as Shahid Amin (1995); Saurabh Dube (1998); Shail Mayaram (1997); Gyan Prakash (1990); and Ajay Skaria (1999) brilliantly interweave oral historical material with archival work to portray nuanced complexities of consciousness in full-bodied ways that could not easily be imagined if their research had been confined to written sources. In these works, multiple versions and visions are portrayed, and the quest for a single plot or a truer truth is relinquished. Amin, for example, writes: "Incongruence with known facts has not been construed as a lapse of memory, but rather as a necessary element in the stitching together of the story" (1995:197).

Our work, as we have already shown, has its separate hybrid genealogy. We only stumbled inadvertently into history; thus our project was not originally framed either in historical perspectives or methods. However, over the past seven years, subaltern histories have increasingly influenced us so that we might, after the fact, claim some affinity to them while acknowledging our deficiency in their two highest achievements: broad theoretical visions and meticulous archival craft.[39] The strongest evidence of this affinity emerges when we encounter the experiences of radically disempowered persons. In Dube's study of religious transformations within an untouchable community in Chhattisgarh, for example, critical voices from the bottom of the social hierarchy speak of landlords in a fashion very similar to the way Sawar people speak of the king's men. That is, we hear appraisals from below of power's workings, framed sometimes in terms of helplessness but incorporating astute understandings of the structural conditions under which that helplessness is perpetuated.[40]

In the era before Independence, most of what is now Rajasthan was composed of princely states and existed under that particular configuration of royal and colonial power that the British called paramountcy. However, the administrative district of Ajmer-Merwara, where Sawar is located, was under direct rule, with consequences we shall briefly address in chapter 3. European historians' fascination with India's princes has resulted in much scholarly attention to the pinnacles of power in Rajasthan. This may be one reason that, until recently, there has for this region been less writing focused on subaltern perspectives.[41]

Mayaram's richly textured study of community memory in Rajasthan, however, provides a source of particularly insightful interpretation. She shows the ways that different forms of power—colonial, princely, and nationalist—have impinged on Meos, her central research focus, and have been interpreted by them. Mayaram writes that she examines "the construction of sovereignty in terms of the perceptual understanding of the reflexive subject" (1997:13). In recording and presenting memories from the kingdom of Sawar we do not focus on sovereignty, but our interests have been in just such perceptual understandings. Power relations at local, state, national, and transnational levels all condition what has most captivated our attentions: the ways that everyday lives, including pressures from above, are experienced and interpreted. It is this experiential level that we feel equipped to portray and convey: textures of a life-world in which power's subtleties are rendered vivid in memories.

In chapter 9, for example, Kalyan Mali as an old man recalls the slight provocation that pushed him from complaint to action and mobilized a brave and successful act of protest. This was no more than the king's chief minister familiarly clapping him on the shoulder while he was expressing his outrage over the wild pigs that were damaging his crops. Relived fifty years later that patronizing gesture provokes him to rage, and one of his listeners responds by commenting on the brutality of the man who made that insolent gesture: "He had no pity."

Just as our portrait of environmental history has not centered on colonial policy, our general portrait of Sawar subjects, unlike much writing within the field of subaltern studies, has not highlighted colonial circumstances. Subalternity in Sawar was always multiply mediated. Sawar residents were fully aware of the machinations of the English in Ajmer, but the majority did not foreground imperial pressures when describing the "time of kings." I had to comb through scores of recorded interviews to locate a few mentions of the "double administration" and its impact on farmers and herders. Interestingly, when the English were discussed the assessments were not consistent; some saw them as potentially more benign than the kings, while others portrayed the kings as squeezed from above and squeezing below in turn.

Rup Lal Khati, a carpenter with an astute understanding of history, put it this way: "It was their time, the great kings' time, and that's why we were afraid. We were not afraid of the English. At that time there was a double administration [*doharā śāsan*]. If the Rajputs did something bad you could complain to the English and they would do something about it, but no one would [complain], because of fear of the Rajputs—because we had to live here, and complaining outside would only get them more angry."

A Brahmin man, by contrast, directly blamed the English for the kings' exploitative behavior—a valid position, but one we rarely heard so blatantly expressed: "Before the English came, the kings would help the people, but at this time the British collected a fixed tax, and the great kings collected the grain tax, and no one took responsibility (*zimmedārī*)." In both of these statements, the English power is realistically placed at a remove from local impact. It was in the end the king and the kings' men with whom people had to live on a day-to-day basis; the benign colonial power was impotent; the malign colonial power was mediated through local force.

In his call to attend to small voices, Guha also stresses the power these voices may have to disrupt the master narratives of history: "If the small voice of history gets a hearing at all . . . it will do so only by interrupting the telling in the dominant version, breaking up its storyline and making a mess of its plot. . . . Insofar as the univocity of statist discourse relies on . . . order, a certain disorderliness . . . will be an essential requirement for our revision" (Guha 1996:12). Guha sees the advent of disorder and polyphony as an inevitable consequence of admitting small voices to historical understandings.[42] Thus history, not unlike anthropology (if perhaps somewhat later), comes to question clean models and admit discord if not incoherence.[43]

Along with the effort to attend to small voices, whatever confusion that may entail, some participants in the subaltern collective project have also urged a shift from concern with "flashes of rebellion" to "quotidian consciousness." Thus Partha Chatterjee proposes: "In the long intervals between open, armed rebellions by peasants or the spread of the great heterodox religious movements, one is likely to notice, if one looks for it, a continuing and pervasive struggle between peasants and the dominant classes in everyday life" (1993:170). He goes on, however, to argue that because "the domain of the quotidian" is also "the domain of the seeming perpetuity of subordination," historians still need the "flashes of open rebellion" to convince themselves of an "undominated region in peasant consciousness" (171). This is the magic appeal of Kalyan Mali's tale of three days of pig slaughter—the denouement of his story presented in chapter 9. From the moment I first heard it I was thrilled by the "flash of rebellion" it revealed.

I recorded dozens of accounts showing that for long years prior to this gleeful moment, most farmers had resentfully adjusted their work routines to deal with the increased population of wild boars. Camping in their fields was the only way to maintain damage control. The king punished anyone who hurt a pig, and at the same time he made every effort to increase the wild boar population within his domain. I would like to think that these accounts of quotidian accommodations, no less than of that one rebellious flash, also display undominated consciousness—if what we mean by that is the capacity to think critically and to have a sense of self unblighted by unfortunate circumstances.

I am therefore less willing than Chatterjee to name the everyday the "domain of the seeming perpetuity of subordination" unless "seeming" were to be italicized. Jean Comaroff and John Comaroff suggest that all kinds of creative possibilities may lurk in the everyday. Although they characterize the everyday negatively as "not the extraordinary or the mythic; . . . not the macrocosmic or the transcendent, the philosophical or the heroic" and as "frequently situated beneath the level of philosophical reflection or historical self-consciousness," they declare it nonetheless rich in potential with a significance that "lies in its paradoxes, in its absent presence" (1997:31). It is a space where subtle but genuine transformations may insinuate themselves. These transformations would not be flashes of rebellion, but neither are they dull and perpetual resignation.

I might borrow again from Ranajit Guha, a master of language, and describe conditions under the great kings as "dominance without hegemony." Guha defines hegemony as "a condition of Dominance" where "Persuasion outweighs Coercion" (1997:23). However, in Sawar (and elsewhere, as Guha of course discerns and elucidates) the distinction between coercion and persuasion turns out to be surprisingly elusive. Is it a distinction between externally and internally imposed controls, between physical and psychological forces?[44] In the first half of the twentieth century in Sawar the rulers had no institutionalized military or police force. Thus, as chapter 5 explores in detail, Sawar's rule might appear to be a perfect example of hegemonic dominance.[45] It seems that Sawar people by and large obeyed a cruel regime that rarely if ever carried out threatened coercive measures, and that even its threats were more about damage to honor than anything corporal.

But we would argue that those whose lives were regulated by threatened sanctions from the Court simultaneously saw through the ruses of those who threatened them, and despised and often successfully manipulated them in return. Many of them also revered the ruler and exonerated him from blame for their sufferings. Was their consciousness dominated or undominated? Or might any attempt to create such categorical distinctions result in misunderstandings of the complex sources motivating human beings as they struggle to have good lives. The Comaroffs's views are germane when they write: "Not only is hegemony never total . . . it is always threatened by the vitality that remains in the forms of life it thwarts. It follows, then, that the hegemonic is constantly being made—and, by the same token, may be unmade" (1991:25).

That remainder of vitality is at the heart of Sawar narratives. The unmaking of hegemony in everyday forms of resistance, of which James Scott's work (1985, 1990) especially has made us so aware, is evident in multiple tales of the kings' time. Beyond these small defiances perhaps, are the still larger undominated regions of dignity and struggle.[46] In picturing Sawar people's description of their lives in the time of kings, as "voices from under a stone" we reiterate that it is the voices, not the stone, that captivate us.

We hope it is not too large a claim to make if we say we have attended to small voices, and that we have heard in them an "undominated region in peasant consciousness" rooted in the quotidian. By no means is this a unique accomplishment; the kinds of critiques we recorded in Sawar have been recorded wherever the views of disempowered subjects are elicited (for example, Dube 1998; H. Singh 1998; Pande 1988; and Sundar 1997). But we have given rather more space to "the people's testimony" than have many other accounts. By thus expanding the play of voices we have necessarily and quite consciously made short shrift of other sources. We make no claims for thorough coverage here of economic and bureaucratic structures, of ecological conditions, or of political transformations. By providing textured, layered, and multiple recollections we hope modestly to supplement larger projects of historical understanding.

Pivotal Memories

When I returned to Rajasthan at the end of December 1996, four years almost to the day after initiating my research on cultural constructions of the environment, my topic at last had a name that translated perfectly: history (*itihās*). Bhoju and I told people that our work this time was to learn and record nothing less than "the history of Sawar." But, we would always add, *this* history would not be the tale of the ruling Shaktavat clan's battles, marriages, and edifices; rather, it would be the experience of the great kings' rule viewed from below; or, to use a term that has become part of Rajasthani even among those whose vocabularies contain almost no other borrowed English, the views of the *publik*.

I was stunned and awed by the instant rush of memory our questions evoked. Perhaps it should not have been a surprise. When my son at age fourteen interviewed my mother at age seventy-nine for his eighth-grade social studies oral history project, she spoke almost as readily (unaccustomed as she was to being taped) of victory gardens and rationing during World War II as did the Sawar elders about their past. In general she was not prone to reminisce in this way, and neither were the old people in Sawar. For elders in our shared millennial present, it may be that just to be asked to recollect is a powerful release.

I take it that recollections of the past are common to all human beings and all societies, and that we can therefore talk about memory, loosely to be sure, across many human contexts. Certainly the Hindi *yād* or *smaraṇ*, the Rajasthani *har,* and the English "memory" do not cover identical semantic fields. Nonetheless, when we asked someone, "Do you have memory (*yād*) of the kings' time?" they understood our question and responded to it in a fashion very similar to the way my mother understood and responded to a question about what she remembered of World War II.[47]

Ghatiyalians of Bhoju's age—familiar with the barren landscape and pompous, ineffective government servants—may only vaguely conceive of the lush woods and abusive royal agents their elders knew so intimately. Even so, in the overstocked and overfed surroundings of America today, I am not easily able to envision people waiting in line for hours for poor-quality meat, as my mother recalls from the war years.

Most of the content of this book is transmitted through memories and composed of memories.[48] In working with this material, we join other postcolonial fieldworkers for whom memory allures as a curative potion (Gold with Gujar 1997). Speaking memories, the voices from whose testimonies ethnographers have ever woven synthetic fabrics of meaning and knowledge, cannot sound frozen in time.[49] An anthropological turn to memory allowed ethnographers to accommodate history while retaining the essence of their disciplinary identity. One facet of ethnographic identity lies in the fragile, vulnerable heart of anthropological practice: fieldwork experience generating intimacies, dependent on human interactions.[50] Another facet of our discipline remains bound to a quest for patterns. From divergent, even clashing, memories within a single community there may emerge not only vividly positioned views of reality, but some of those designs with which anthropologists remain concerned, in spite of dissolution, fragmentation, and globalization.[51]

Well beyond anthropological predilections, memory emerged in the 1990s as thematically "hot" and politically fraught throughout the humanities and social sciences. It became a focal lens for recovering lost histories—usually painful and suppressed—including those of African American enslavement and of the social universe of Jewish society in Eastern Europe and the horrific truths of its annihilation.[52] Displaced persons and transformed landscapes are another main current flowing into the rapids of memory.[53] As we have seen, environmental histories, finding ample documentable substance in colonial forestry records, have begun to tap living memories as well, particularly in South Asia and also in Africa. In most of these studies loss predominates, as it does in the ecological history of Sawar's jungle.[54]

It is understandable that memories of struggle, crisis, violence, and displacement are those most invested with academic and emotional attention. In the South Asian context, Amin (1995) takes a pathbreaking approach to memory in his study of the complicated causalities and repercussions of a single pivotal and violent event: an antipolice riot in 1922 in which twenty-three policemen were burned to death. One immediate result was Gandhi's decision to suspend civil disobedience. Amin shows how this violent disruption of nationalism's narrative has been subject to a kind of erasure, losing its "distinctiveness and specificity and multiple peculiarities" in the process (9). All of these he is able to restore through careful memory work. Other recent oral history and memory studies have centered on partition, and the communal violence that accompanied it (Butalia 2000; Menon and

Bhasin 1998; and Pandey 1999).[55] These are limited foci for articulated memories and sometimes poignant silences—standing here not for imperfect recall but for an anguish that disrupted language itself (as Das and Nandy [1986] have argued).[56] In Sawar no event was so sudden, radical, or terrifying. Sawar memories are poignant in their ordinariness, making vivid what Sherry Ortner has described as "the intricate webs of articulations and disarticulations that always exist between dominant and dominated" (1995:190).

I have asked myself why memory was suddenly so important, not just to me but to so many people. My intuitive answer began with two broad commonsense notions. The first has to do with our times: a generation of people (including my own parents) who have been witness to extraordinary geopolitical and sociocultural, technological, and ecological changes is gradually passing. All over the globe from Tibet to South Africa, from Germany to Bali, from Chicago to Rajasthan, unimaginable changes have taken place between the 1930s and the 1990s. Social and cultural landscapes, as well as geophysical ones, are transformed sometimes beyond recognition. Margaret Mead observed that "everyone born and bred before World War II is . . . an immigrant in time" (1970:56). Mead's specific concern was that the new generation's knowledge exceeded their elders'. She asserts persuasively: "Today, nowhere in the world are there elders who know what the children know, no matter how remote and simple the societies are in which the children live. In the past there were always some elders who knew more than any children in terms of their experience of having grown up within a cultural system. Today there are none" (60–61).

Our work, and that of many others who gather memories, deals with the other side of this coin. If the young know "more" than their elders, their knowledge is of a different "place" in time.[57] To them knowledge of the past could seem both irrelevant and incomprehensible. But with this knowledge something is lost. So-called salvage anthropology has a bad name, but we would be dissembling if we did not admit that recording what could otherwise be lost was part of what drove us to create this book.

My second notion is squarely within academia, where various suspicions have converged in recent years. These include the postmodern suspicion of any entity labeled factual or real as well as the postcolonial

Generations: Mangi Lal Kumhar and granddaughters (Mehru, 1997).

and feminist suspicions of master narratives. I have already noted that Bhoju's and my work is part of the disciplinary turn to privilege polyvocality and highlight contested or negotiated realities: in short, following Guha's admonition with which we began, to admit discord to disrupt monolithic, reductionist accounts. It follows naturally that this turn should favor memory over document; subaltern over rulers; and multiple, fractious voices over omniscient observer. It distrusts records and listens to stories, as we have done—stories of abundant trees and multiple sorrows.

Chapter 2 in this volume, "Voice," addresses Bhoju's and my joint authority, ethnographic methods, and collaboration in order to foreground them as integral to any knowledge we have to offer and to treat them as issues rather than givens. We attempt to disclose our collaborative practices, and to expose the ways this book emerged as a product of two minds and lives that, while originating in very different places, have come to be closely intertwined. In chapter 2 I detail some of the ways physical, emotional, and interpersonal conditions of fieldwork have shaped and informed our project, and Bhoju summarizes what this work means to him, in practice and in principle. He speaks both as a member of the community being researched, and as an experienced observer of its collective and individual behaviors.

Chapter 2, then, is about the collaborative process of gathering voices and learning from them, motivated by our aspiration to create responsible representations of their vivid, gripping cadences. My perilous choice of loaded words—"representation" and "create"—is deliberate. Much as I would prefer to be nothing but a channel, I am extremely conscious of acting as a mixer and synthesizer. Writing from a very different context, Nancy Scheper-Hughes affirms the worth of such imperfect efforts as ours: "And though I can hear the dissonant voices in the background protesting *just this* choice of words, I believe there is still a role for the ethnographer-writer in giving voice, as best she can, to those who have been silenced" (1992:28). To counter the inherent possibilities of claiming authority we do not have, without surrendering to postmodern paralysis and postcolonial angst, she recommends "an ethnography that is open-ended and that allows for multiple readings and alternative conclusions" (30), as I hope ours does.

In "Place," chapter 3, I sketch some geographical, ecological, and historical contexts for the locality in the Banas River Basin, colloquially called Sawar Twenty-Seven. These sketches provide backdrops or frames in which the recounted experiences that follow are set. Chapter 4 treats memory as subject and practice. This book is nothing but memories, but when in 1993 I began the project that would bring it into being, I never set out to collect them. When I found myself collecting them, I was sure Bhoju and I had stumbled on this mode of fieldwork by sheer happenstance. When I returned to the United States in autumn 1993 with tapes, disks, and notebooks loaded with old people's memories I was astonished to find a proliferation of seminars, conferences, and volumes on memory and history. Moreover, within this scholarly efflorescence, ecological memory—with which I was most particularly concerned—was an important subfield and genre.[58] However baffled I was by this coincidence, in chapter 4 I humbly acknowledge zeitgeist—and locate myself within it. The chapter closes with an extensive interview with Jamuni Regar, an old leatherworker woman who releases a stream of linked memories that presage all that follows.

In chapters 5 through 9 lie the substantial heart of these oral histories. Each chapter attempts, largely through the medium of transcribed interviews, to convey a selected set of recurrent themes in memories of "that time" under the great kings' rule. Taken together, these themes form a fragmented and partial political, economic, environmental, and social history of Sawar. Although only a few of these recollections are specifically dated, most speakers vividly recall three decades—the 1930s through the 1950s. Vansh Pradip Singh's death in 1947 is the watermark, the end of an era, but not quite the end of our focal period.

These chapters are preponderantly concerned with the old days—when Sawar's Court, in the person of Vansh Pradip Singh, was alive and radiated power.[59] Nonetheless, ruminations on things past, expressions of vanished circumstances, are sometimes made most vivid through contrasts with the experienced present.[60] In this memory collage we find persons—king, kings' men, farmers, herders, artisans, laborers, males and females, elders and juniors—interacting with one another. Thus we hear of situated persons in various settings transacting power through different, varying strategies and media. We often heard of love and generosity, playfulness and cooperation, as past modes of sociability. But the nature of our inquiry, our initial curiosity about the vanished jungle and our subsequent exploration of royal authority that protected it, conspired to focus our findings on power relations.

The portrait of "that time" that emerges is by no means a complete social history. For example, we attend only slightly to patron-client relationships (the famous "Hindu *jajmānī* system"), in spite of their pervasive influence on village economy and ritual during the time period under scrutiny. We also speak little of the village counsel (*panchayat*) and its operations. We have truthfully followed those recurrent themes reverberating through our recorded interviews. We are aware and remind readers of a selection at work that came synergistically from interlocutors and respondents.

It will be evident that each chapter's thematic focus—shoes, Court, homes, fields, and jungle—is a strand thoroughly intertangled with the other four, despite my authorial efforts at grooming them. But so indeed are the themes of ecology and polity; herding and farming; woods and fields; rulers and ruled; center and hinterlands; men and women; parents and children; domesticity and political economy. An ecological history by definition recognizes the mutual impingement of causalities. For example, wild pigs may belong in the jungle, but pig stories figure often in character sketches of the Court, as well as in talk about crops and grain taxes.

Spatial configurations are the chief ordering principle for chapters 6 through 9. Each has a particular kind of setting as its focus: Court (Sawar itself, the center place, embodied in both ruler and administrative apparatus), homes, fields, and jungle. Preceding these contextualized examinations, chapter 5 attempts to portray power itself. Although power was from time to time expressed in sanctions or laws, these by no means confined its play. Power seeps through interstices, pervading all localities, as something akin to climate or atmosphere; the inquiry is not localized. Chapter 5, then, introduces subtle and gross persuasions of rank, honor, and force; it confronts as prior a gross and subtle violence of the everyday. Direct analogies and reflected behaviors link the Court's power over farmers, herders, and laborers with those of men over wives, sisters, and daughters-in-law. In short, chapter 5 is about shoes. It dwells on this singular image with multiple ramifications. Issues of rank attach themselves to shoes in Sawar, like iron filings to a magnet.

Chapter 6, "Court," details the former ruler's legendary persona, his conspicuous consumption, his self-respect and occasionally soft heart, and his hunting prowess and excessive love for animals and trees. It examines the bureaucratic apparatus and the system of *begār*, or conscripted, unpaid, enforced labor on which much of the ruler's government and lifestyle depended. Chapter 5 closes by detailing the death of the Court and its multiply conflicted aftermath. These are the pivotal moments when everything changed for the people of Sawar.

Chapter 7, "Homes," turns from governance to domesticity. It looks at individual lives, families, work, and gender roles. These contexts and subjects might appear to display the most evident continuities between past and present in that health, wealth, and progeny, along with weddings, births, and funerals equally are concerns of both eras. However, the Court's agents once stomped into kitchens and conscripted more than labor, as we shall see. The change of rule from kings to votes entailed many transformations beyond the political.

In "Fields," chapter 8, we talk about agriculture and herding, then and now the sources of village livelihood. Recollections of the time of kings stress the multiple harassments of farmers by relentless taxations of crops and subtler degradations. We trace the oral history of a dispute over a farmer's right to the tree growing in his own field. Herders were less afflicted than farmers, but they too had to cope with royal taxations and controls on their flocks; they too have tales to tell of resistance.

The predations of tax collection often merge in farmers' talk with those of wild animals, to which we turn in chapter 9. This chapter, "Jungle," treats the Court's conservation practices, which were evidently more in the service of the king's pleasure, reputation, and corporal identity than any dream of wild nature or posture of benevolent governance. No wood was available, we were told, without requesting the Court's permission and rendering a share to the fort. The only exception, an ironic generosity, was fuel for the cremation fire—always "free of charge." From the Court's vigilance over trees we turn to pig tales, which are legion. Chapter 9 concludes by chronicling how deforestation accelerated madly after the ruler's death, presaging chapter 10, which concerns altered landscapes and lives.

"Imports," the final chapter, turns from a focus on the past to appraisals and apprehensions of present and future. The same old people who described to us the time of great kings epitomize transformations they have witnessed and their experience in the present, expressing both strong appreciation and strong dislike for different elements of their current circumstances. In concluding we evoke the future, embodied in children as they happily participate in replanting indigenous species of trees.

2. VOICE

A fundamental questioning of the privilege and politics of knowledge has made any representation problematic. There is now no escaping the questions "who is speaking here, and who is being silenced?—Amitava Kumar, *Passport Photos*

Here at the beginning we—two authors—must speak of voice. This book is not about us, nonetheless we describe our teamwork and identify ourselves. These descriptions may neither be fixed easily in a brief note (then conveniently assumed or forgotten); nor be blanketed smoothly with collective pronouns. There are many other persons residing in and near the kingdom of Sawar who speak in this text, in distinctive, named voices. We acknowledge each of them as coproducers, but they are not equally authors in the sense that Bhoju Ram Gujar and I are.

We hope in this chapter to explain the nature and circumstances of our collaboration. Given the ongoing postcolonial circumstances haunting most ethnographic research, including ours, Bhoju might have remained a shadowy figure, the invisible research assistant recognized only in the front matter. We have taken a different path in naming Bhoju coauthor. But as Kumar warns in the epigraph above (and as several colleagues and students have similarly warned), other perils lie on our chosen route. If my own voice dominates the text, if authorial power is in my hands, have I not falsely appropriated Bhoju's name? This is one risk I cannot avoid; we have imagined this book of history and brought it into being as a shared endeavor over the course of about eight years. Moreover, we are convinced that to submerge our practices of coproduction would be disastrously to diminish our work's value. Put another way, any history we have to offer emerged from the methods we hope to disclose.

Bhoju Ram Gujar belongs to the Gujar *jāti* or birth group; that is, a "caste" in the sense of birth-given professional identity, and a community in that Gujars—as do most caste groups in present rural Rajasthani society—have a collective social life, a vital oral tradition, and a caste organization dedicated to reform and improvement. Bhoju's Gujar identity is not incidental to our work together, but figures largely in the creation of this book. His being Gujar is considerably more important than my being a "sixties" person, a Jew from Chicago, and a cultural anthropologist who teaches religion—although all of these factors are probably also relevant.[1]

There are castes called Gujar throughout North India. Their roles and statuses in different regions range from nomadic herders to powerful landlords, their religious identity from Muslim to Vaishnavite.[2] Many Gujar groups are associated strongly with pastoralism. In Sawar and generally in eastern and central Rajasthan, Gujar identity—both in folklore and in practice—is bound up with livestock and often most specifically with dairy production. Although in western Rajasthan herding is associated with transhumance, the Gujars of Sawar and its vicinity are a settled people and have been for generations.[3] Today most Gujar families in this region have at least small landholdings; some, like Bhoju's household, have entirely given up herding for farming, and keep animals only to satisfy domestic dairy consumption needs. But this change took place in Bhoju's lifetime.

Before 1947, in the time of kings, Gujars were privileged in several ways. They had a reputation as fierce fighters, and consequently they were sometimes employed as soldiers and as guards to protect small states from endemic banditry.[4] By tradition, Gujar women suckled the children of Rajput rulers, and their milk was understood to transmit courage as well as physical strength (because an ancestral figure was said to be nursed by a lioness). Therefore, within Gujar communities there were always favored lineages called *dhābhāī*—literally "wet-nurse brother." *Dhābhāī* were accorded special privileges and sometimes were even educated along with their Rajput milk siblings. For these reasons, most Gujars paid less grain tax than did other farmers and herders.

Bhoju, holding recorder, interviews Ladu Loda; Ugma Nathji
Nath (in turban) participates (Ghatiyali, 1993).

Today, Gujars are a numerically powerful caste in Ghatiyali. In
recent years they have entered electoral politics at the local level with
intermittent success. A Gujar village council leader, or *sarpanch,* was
elected in 1995. He was a neighbor of Bhoju's, and Bhoju's support was
instrumental in his election.[5]

When I first employed Bhoju in 1980 he was still a youth, and
although his family was justifiably proud of his education, he did not
have particular status in the community.[6] In the 1990s, when we did
research for this book, I was made extremely aware of a major transformation in his position. He had become a respected leader among
the local Gujars because of his status as a teacher, his family's much
improved economic condition, and not least his strength of character
and personal integrity. The births in succession of two sons, in 1995
and 1998, have capped in local visions Bhoju's visible fulfillment of the
good life.

Bhoju emerges in this work most apparently as primary interlocutor in the majority of interviews that are simultaneously substance
and substantiation of our historical account. The dialogic form in
which we present much of our material thus reads on the explicit
surface as a document of his efforts. Perhaps less evident, but equally
crucial, are his roles as source and channel, as mediator and inter-

preter in the broadest sense. What we learned had everything to do with Bhoju's own evolving vision of local history.

I proceed here to describe and differentiate our two research periods, in 1993 and in 1997, briefly treating intellectual agenda and research circumstances and highlighting the ways in which the two factors were mutually constructive. I then attempt to characterize just how Bhoju and I constitute a collaborative whole. Bhoju's account of his experience of gathering oral history in his own community follows. His prose, less rambling and more power-packed than mine, concludes this chapter.

From Culture and Environment to Memory and History: 1993 and 1997

Complicating the composition of these histories and the operational strategies of their harvest, our book is based about equally on two very different research efforts. The first segment of work was gropingly and sporadically accomplished during my twice-fractured eight-month stay in Rajasthan in 1993; the second was undertaken with sustained, concentrated effort during nine winter weeks in 1997, with a distracted summer coda. In 1993 my husband and two children, then ages ten and five, were with me, and we set up our own household five kilometers from Ghatiyali proper, but only two kilometers from Sawar. In winter 1997 I came to India alone and lived for two months at Bhoju's house in the heart of the village. That same year I returned with my husband and my sons (then fifteen and ten) in the rainy season, but not for long.

While the results of these two periods are thoroughly interspersed and integrated in the chapters that follow, and while both projects produced interview texts of similar structure and genre, many important differences characterize the emergence of these conversations.[7] Acknowledging the frank extractive metaphor, I might characterize these as the difference between prospecting for gold and mining ore. The terms of my collaboration with Bhoju during these two periods were also very different.

1993: (ALIENATED) IN THE PRINCE'S GARDEN
"The fieldwork of my discontent" describes 1993. This unease was doubly manifest in intellectual flounderings with the abstractions of

"nature" and multiple stresses of everyday life. My family's housing situation in 1993 was a major source of frustration. We were living in the Sawar nobility's "garden house"—used before our arrival mainly as storage for bootleg liquor and as a scenic picnic spot. It was a lovely setting, with shade trees, a good well, a beautiful view of Sawar's hillside fortifications, and above all a private bathhouse. Although rats and insect life were overwhelmingly populous, my real problem was the five kilometers that separated me from Ghatiyali, no matter how I traversed them. Traveling by bicycle was best, until full summer heat fell upon us around the end of April. Even so, my tires were always getting flats from the omnipresent thorns, and my "ladies" bicycle (the first in the village) had other flaws. I sometimes rode on the back of my husband's motor scooter, but my pathetic inability to overcome a fear of driving it myself was a source of animosity between us, and he had his own work to do. As for the bus, I perpetually miscalculated its timing; it always seemed that everyone else knew what was going on with the bus while I alone was wholly in the dark, either sitting stupidly by the road until a passerby informed me it wasn't running that day, or being still in the house as it rattled past in a swirl of dust.

Living in the prince's garden did, of course, bring me much closer both physically and cognitively to Sawar, the seat of rule, and its royal family. Our house was set back from the road, two kilometers from Sawar proper. The resident watchman—a Bhil whose relationship with the Court was somewhere between bonded laborer and "old family retainer"—was aged and decrepit. His dog was not much more alert than he. Many friends and well-wishers gave us stern warnings about danger from bandits. To live alone in the jungle was folly, and we were especially admonished that I should never spend the night there when my husband was gone. But, because his own research schedule frequently took him away, for me to spend the night elsewhere became increasingly inconvenient. One night I said, "I'll stay there, I'm not worried," to a small group of acquaintances. To my surprise, instead of arguing with me, they suddenly agreed, but not on the basis of my being able to take care of myself. Rather, they nodded and said "Who will come in the prince's garden? Nobody!"[8] Thus they affirmed the continuing power of the Sawar Court, a power that ap-

peared to extend—forty years after democratization and land reform—quite a bit further than the law.

In what did this lingering power consist? It seemed above all a
power over minds and spaces. Perhaps, as this book will propose, it
always was that. What protected the prince's garden was neither so
tangible as an army nor so subtle as prestige. He did have strong arms
in his service, or so it was rumored, but they were certainly not visible
in our vicinity. Rather, just as fear of shoe-beatings underpinned the
king's rule in the early 1940s (chapter 5), so the reputation of the
modern Court for acting swiftly and violently when provoked protected our garden home in the 1990s.

Almost daily, the scion of the royal family rode his handsome
horse, to no apparent purpose, around the grounds. It was not for our
benefit; he barely deigned to nod at us, and the rent had been collected in advance. Perhaps he was checking on his well and on his
fields that lay behind the house, but mostly I believe he was exhibiting
himself—with horse and mustache as a figure of traditional Rajput
power and receiving due respect from subordinates. This was still his
land. No comparable figure appears today in the fields that villagers
now are able to claim as their own. Yet the beautiful mango trees by
the water reservoir in the heart of Ghatiyali still belong to the Court,
and few but the boldest children would dare to sample their tempting
fruits.

In 1993 Bhoju was working full-time as a government middle
school teacher in another district, where he kept a room. Whenever
he was free from teaching duties—Sundays, occasional evenings, and
several longer school vacation sessions—we worked intensively together, as we had in 1980–81 and more briefly in 1987. When Bhoju
was not free, four other persons occasionally helped me to conduct
interviews—Ugma Nathji, Shambhu Nath, Lila Devi Chauhan, and
Bali Gujar, Bhoju's wife. Although each of these companions enriched
my understandings and expanded my networks, I am certain that my
bad moods and existential despair in 1993 were in part a result of
Bhoju's long absences. Another problem, of course, was my very hazy
sense of what I meant to do.

When as usual, people in Ghatiyali asked me to tell them just what I
was doing, I found that research on cultural constructions of the

environment was even harder to explain than my earlier research on concepts of liberation and life after death. As elaborated in chapter 1, there was no key word to cover my project. I would literally sputter and improvise, inconsistently telling one person I was working on farming techniques, while telling another I was interested in herbal medicine, and another that I was working on festivals celebrated by farmers. In fact, I had hoped to approach the cultural construction of the environment through observing the intertwining of rural North Indian Hindu practices with agriculture and herding. As it turned out, agricultural rituals were dramatically on the wane—nonetheless, I doggedly attempted to record them.

When there were no rituals to observe, which was most of the time, I followed what seemed a pragmatic path—wandering the fields trying to amass indigenous agricultural knowledge. I asked: How deep do you set the plough for different kinds of seeds? How far apart should the furrows be? What kinds of fertilizers are applied when? All villagers were veritable founts of knowledge on these topics. Having grown up on Chicago's south side, I was a blank slate when it came to agricultural knowledge, and I was seriously daunted by this information (and not a little bored). Moreover, my heart just was not into learning how to plant barley as opposed to wheat, or the details of how much urea needs to be spread for which crops.

As farmers held forth to me, I found myself yawning and changing the subject: Why do you have a shrine to your ancestors here by the well? Almost everyone does, and the simple answer is that a spirit lingers where attachments are formed: a farmer's heart, of course, is in his fields, just as a merchant's is in his shop. "Yours," one man added portentiously, "will linger around your books."

I recalled being told in 1980 about a dense (*gaharā*), dark, and frightening (*bhayānak*) forest inhabited by dangerous wild animals, where now we saw scrubby, barren, largely open land. I had found such a forest hard to imagine and paid it little special attention then. I was also aware from the general literature on deforestation and the decline of common property resources in Rajasthan, that the landscape had undergone radical transformations within the last half century, and thus within living memory.[9] In 1993, desperate for a way of getting ideas about nature, and more than a little baffled by where to find them, on a weekend in January Bhoju and I asked an old man,

Kalyan Mali, about the vanished trees. He told us a tale of wild pigs that would be our first thread leading to ecological history in its fullest ramifications—and later to this book. But it was not until months later that we knew where we were going.

During Bhoju's hot-season holidays, the interlocked patterns of social history and ecological change dawned on us full force. With the dangerous seasonal scalding wind (*lū*) blowing, which prostrated us for hours a day, Bhoju and I nonetheless found ourselves increasingly gripped and energized by narratives of the past and of historical changes. We began to see disruptions in the ritual cycles (those I originally intended to study) as part of an accelerated transitional flux—a flux intrinsic to and conditioned by broader historical developments.[10] Having departed from a one-dimensional concern with cultural constructions of the environment, I soon learned that these never existed except as shaped by political forces.

Between arriving home in August 1993 and returning once more to Rajasthan in late December 1996, I wrote and rewrote, presented, discussed, and in some cases published fragments of research thematically organized around topics that would continue to pervade the 1997 interviews: pigs and kings, sin and rain, foreign trees, and abandoned rituals.[11] Each of these topics is a thread, a strand in a braid. I was only able to start composing these histories by moving back and forth between the strands and having each progress along with the others. As the initial fragments of this book began to take shape, I saw that I needed to go back. I wanted to understand Sawar's history from locations other than Ghatiyali among the twenty-seven villages in its dominion, as well as visit neighboring kingdoms and the state archives.

1997: (EMBRACED) IN THE HEART OF THE FAMILY

Grant proposals envisioning the present work bore fruit in the form of airplane tickets and research stipends that allowed my return to Rajasthan at the end of December 1996, four years after initiating the environmental research. My topic at last had a name that everyone understood perfectly: history (*itihās*). Moreover, in the pleasurable winter season I was living as I had always wished to live, in a household that surrounded me with kindnesses and love. This was Bhoju's home, where I stayed from 30 December 1996 through 23 February 1997.

Bhoju was released from his teaching duties most of the time during this period, and no other person participated in the research; I worked exclusively with him, often for twelve-hour days.[12] When Bhoju was absent on other business I tended just to revel in the company of women and children, or to roam the hills and fields with old friends and no particular agenda. I want to describe in detail the comforts of Bhoju's home because there is a seamlessness to the qualities of my life there, the nature of our partnership, and the nature of this book. My wretchedness isolated in the royal garden and my happiness within the warm sociability of a Gujar household are not accidental circumstances in which "objective" fieldwork took place. Rather they are continuous with our book's realization and meanings.

Since I first arrived in Ghatiyali, uninvited, in 1979, I had boarded in several other households, always as a rent-paying outsider. Never in my past sojourns had I known the kind of substantial incorporation that other foreign anthropologists have described for India.[13] Envious of such descriptions, and a little incredulous too, I could not have anticipated it would happen to me after so many years. Bhoju's wife, mother, daughters, and niece enveloped me with attentions, explanations and services; patience, indulgence, and beyond all of that or perhaps generating and sustaining it, some kind of sweeping, kinship-generated love that took me by surprise. This was a household dominated numerically by females. Bhoju's father—a very old man with trembling hands but a tenacious grip on life, work, and daily habits—never dealt much with me at all. "Have you eaten?" he would inquire almost every day, to which I would reply "Yes," to which he would reply "Wāh!" (meaning "that's great!"). The day I left in February, to my embarrassment, he made his longest-ever declaration, telling me with a kind of insistent fervor that—if he did not live to see me again—I must surely come and eat his funeral feast. Thankfully, he was just as vigorous when I returned in August, and I at last recorded his memories of what he called his "days of sorrow" (chapter 7). Sukh Devji passed away peacefully in 1998, around the time I was translating that interview.

My altered status in 1997 was appropriately marked by a change in what I was called; no longer Ainn Bai ("Lady Ann"; Gold 1988), I become Ainn Buaji ("Auntie Ann"). Every chilly winter morning, as we all huddled with unabashed eagerness around the cooking hearth waiting for the first, blessed, scalding dose of sweet tea, my wistful foreign greed must have seeped across my face; not only did I receive my tea in the largest cup ("Ainn Buaji *ko mago,*" they called it) but I was the only person over age six who got seconds. At first I tried to refuse, I said, "It's not necessary," or I said "*bas bas*" and weakly attempted to cover my cup with my hand. But they read my desire and, disconcertingly to my own conscience, I came gradually to expect this as my due (and even to feel disgruntled if for some reason "my" mug was not located). Every day of the two months I was there, one of the girls or women would summon me when the precious pot of hot water was ready for my bath, to be used immediately before it cooled. This too was a gift—of fuel, comfort, and care.

It was pleasant, even luxurious, to live in Bhoju's home in spite of what would strike many urban folks as myriad physical "hardships": no running water, no indoor plumbing, no refrigeration, irregular electricity (including eleven days with none at all when the village transformer burned out), and two fairly monotonous daily meals of flat bread and spicy vegetables or lentils, supplemented with rich yogurt and sometimes a large lump of brown sugar. But I can only describe my life, enmeshed in this family's expansive care for my well-being, as pampered. At times, though, I prowled like a caged animal wishing for a chore of any sort. They cried out in sorrow when I picked up my dirty dishes just to deposit them in the washing place. And, on top of all this, they came into my room regularly to sigh with apparent deep sincerity: "Oh Ainn Buaji when you are gone we will miss you."

I had an experience the day I left that is difficult to describe. I was perceptibly happy to be on my way home to my husband and children. However, Bhoju's mother, Raji, disapproved of this, as did Bhoju, because a daughter going to her husband's house is supposed to look glum, not radiant. When I went to part from Raji—who was squatting by the cooking fire as usual in the early morning—I felt a sudden, forceful blow of grief right in my heart, and tears began to seep from my eyes, tears a daughter leaving ought to shed. Later I pondered her personal power—the parting gift of tears meant more than any other, as it physically validated our kinship. By living in this household I learned from personal experience that documentable hierarchical structures—whether of caste, gender, or literacy—are only part of far more complicated stories of relationships and interactions.

In 1993 Bhoju and I began our oral history work by attempting to speak with members of many different communities in Ghatiyali. These people were old, smart, articulate, and male.[14] I had interviewed some women independently of Bhoju, but high on my research agenda for 1997 was the need to redress a gender imbalance in our material. Bhoju would occasionally agree, but then again resist. In part, of course, this was because of the strong constraints on inter-gender conversation imposed by his society. It was much easier to surrender to these constraints than attempt to transgress them. But also, I believe, Bhoju felt in most cases that it was men who would best know and best be able to tell us what we wanted to learn. Throughout our work together in 1997, I stubbornly pressed the gender issue.

Sometimes, without making it a big production, I would be able casually to include women in a conversation initiated with men. It often happened during an interview that an elderly female appeared from nowhere and approached to listening distance. I might unobtrusively tilt the microphone in her direction and interpolate questions directed to her; a subtle subterfuge, sometimes fruitful. Nonetheless, I failed more than once in my attempts to gather female voices. My sourest memory is of a Brahmin house in the small village of Vajta. Devi Lal, the head of the household, had been the Vajta *sarpanch* for decades; he was a man of substance and presence. With him was his educated son, who had trained in pharmacology. An old woman approached us, and happened to squat on a low wall next to a large potted *tulsi* plant. *Tulsi* (sacred basil) is a form of the goddess (a consort of Lord Vishnu) that all Brahmins have in their courtyard. Because the woman was clearly seeking to join us, I asked, "Who is this?" gesturing to her. But Devi Lal's son answered, "It is Tulsi Mother" as if there were no human female there.

In this exchange, I had clearly pronounced the word *kaun*, "who"; not *kyā*, "what," as one might say about a plant (granted, if the *tulsi* plant were taken as a goddess, "who" would work). Evidently, the young, educated son had assumed that my anthropological attention had been properly captivated by the goddess plant, but that the old lady poised beside it, with her expressive face and bright eyes, would

Brahmin woman and *tulsi* plant (Vajta, 1997).

and should remain invisible. My diary records our subsequent interactions, as I brooded over them: "I try to include her but they drown
her out. Her natal home, I learn, is Sawar, the capital. I ask her if she
liked being married out of Sawar into Vajta and the men interrupt,
'she's not like you, she doesn't think, our Rajasthani women don't
have choices like you do in your country'—as if women did not spend
a deal of time evaluating their marital homes as good or bad places,
and comparing them to the villages of their birth. This is patriarchy,
like a miasma in the air, thick, a weight, tangible, I never felt it before
in all my years of research." I had failed abysmally to control the
situation. Men had never tried to stop me from talking to women
about women's things—rituals, stories, songs, and so forth (Raheja
and Gold 1994)—but the topic of history was different.

In Ghatiyali we started with women of the leatherworker caste
who, as young brides, were forced to grind grain all day for the kings'
horses, while their men carried messages, or opium, or condiments,
from village to village at the royal family's whim. Bhoju found it
reasonable to visit these women because their work was different from
their menfolks' and because they were at the core, if also the bottom,
of the workings of the kingdom. Their testimonies were totally gripping and sometimes emotionally exhausting. Jamuni Regar, the first
voice we will hear at length in this book, was of course one of these.

Inside Sawar Fort.

In addition to women we were missing the voices of former rulers. Having self-consciously avoided Rajputs in 1993, we now sought out a few, along with persons from some other formerly powerful families, going straight to the center, to Sawar proper. On 2 January 1997, our first trip to interview in Sawar, it happened that we met Gana Raj Singh, Ghatiyali's *ṭhākur*, on the road and learned that his brother, Mani Raj, was currently in residence in the Sawar fort, on vacation from his city home in Ajmer.[15] We immediately paid a courtesy call to Mani Raj. He gave us the obligatory tea and put me in the capable hands of his youngest daughter, Rashmi. At that time she attended an English-medium high school in Ajmer, and she told me she was the only one among her siblings with a taste for studies. Rashmi struck me as an independent-minded and high-spirited young woman; she appeared to have recognized the limits to her freedom as a female Rajput but was making the most of the spaces to which she was confined. Appropriately imperious in her bearing, she was nonetheless friendly. Moving like quicksilver, Rashmi changed rapidly from Indian dress into jeans (more easily to climb around the ramparts), and led me on an efficient, rapid tour of the fort, inside and out.[16] I shot almost two reels of film.

The tour culminated, appropriately enough, with a visit to a baby wild pig that the family were keeping in confinement—however oxymoronic this may sound. They were raising it to slaughter for the symbolic savor of its meat. I could not readily have distinguished this small captive from the ordinary domestic piglets I regularly observed with their noses in the muddy open gutters of Sawar town. Having just sent our "Wild Pigs" article to press before leaving the United States, I was astounded and charmed (though I don't believe Bhoju was) to encounter this emblem of past power in the flesh (Gold with Gujar 1997). The former Court once fostered a multitude of free pigs in his jungle; now, with no jungle left, the royal family nursed this tiny remnant within the walls of the fort.

On Collaboration

My collaboration with Bhoju dates back to 1979, but my discussion here is focused on the periods of research for this volume. The years before 1993 gave us a comfortable groundwork for this more recent and intense collaborative coproduction (Gujar and Gold 1992). Starting from very different places the two of us, during seventeen years of intermittent fieldwork, have developed habits of practice for our shared time and have settled into comfortable grooves of interdependence. These ways sometimes felt wonderfully secure, while at other moments they would rankle, lead to edginess, and occasionally impel one or the other of us, temporarily at least, to strain to break free. Bhoju and I have persistently suspected one another's assumptions of authority, even while acknowledging our own deficiencies. This results in a balance that is intellectually precarious and emotionally tumultuous, but ultimately curiously secure. Above all we talk and talk, absorbing one another's thoughts like two sponges until neither of us knows what originated with whom.

In winter 1997, while I was living at Bhoju's home, I drafted the following (now slightly edited) text in an attempt to portray, while I was experiencing it, the interplay of our personalities and powers, our talents and weaknesses.

Bhoju consistently takes the lead and plays the major part in identifying speakers and eliciting the memories and interpretations of the past which compose the important part of our work. I quite literally ride behind him [on his black Suzuki motorcycle], legs to one side as a woman should sit according to Rajasthani proprieties, but wearing a protective helmet as no village woman would, though mine, from Ajmer city, is gendered powder blue.[17]

Bhoju controls the cultural geographies and contingencies of our research. Without him I would literally be lost; he guides us over the land and among the houses. He knows the roads, paths, and neighborhoods; the kinship networks; the lunar calendar with its opportunities and constraints; the shrines where we often stop for *darshan*, rest, and sometimes knowledge. Bhoju readily recognizes allusions—however elliptical and cryptic—to proverbs, songs, and local knowledge (gossip, legend, history). He appears, in short, to mastermind the daily progress of our research, while I tag along. He can almost read my mind, after a dozen years of fruitful collaboration and deep friendship. Yet he repeatedly asks me, "What do we have to do today?"

So, I make lists in advance of where to go, of topics to be explored, of whom we must contact, of what we must ask. Yet, no matter how well plotted I believe our day's journey to be, as often as not the Suzuki halts at a place I had no idea we were going. This is usually a Gujar house; if not, a home with daughters married into Ghatiyali; or, possibly, a home of schoolteachers who form a kind of occupational *jāti* of their own; or of devotees of Dev Narayan; always a place where tea and information are available. Sometimes, these stops yield actual interviews; sometimes, they are simply Bhoju's way of reconnoitering a largely unknown place. After exchanging cordialities he probes: "Who is left alive around here who remembers the old days? Who among them will talk? Where do they live?" We drink in this knowledge with our tea and move along.

Without Bhoju, I have very limited access to these voices. How would I ever have found my way to the hamlet of Mori where lives the younger brother of Hazari Mina, the famed boar hunter now deceased? How would I have the nerve to barge into an open-air, roadside tailor shop in Devli asking if anyone there knows the story of a tailor called Hanuman who was said to have once received a shoe-beating. We never learned more of this Hanuman, but the leatherworkers-turned-tailors with whom we spoke that afternoon revealed new facets of the old days that were key links in our understanding of the nature of forced labor as abjection and its raw-nerve residues today.

Our Hindi interviews, which I can conduct and translate pretty well, are often downright boring; almost never as interesting as those in the local language where my production fluency drops to superficialities and my comprehension remains, even now after seventeen years, partially murky until we replay the dialogues—on the roof, in the benign winter sun. Then Bhoju unlocks their nuances while I feverishly type on my lamentably sticky keyboard (ashes, dust, and bugs embedded in its depths).

Most of the time when we are out working together I feel passive, almost a spectator, my presence alone and my equipment testifying to the foreign impetus of our seemingly quixotic project. When I hear people describe me as a photographer I'm offended, but this is merely their best guess, based on limited opportunities to observe what I do.

Without me, Bhoju has no impetus, no tapes, no time. He is enmeshed in the complex life of a successful householder in his prime: full-time job with enforced, unpaid overtime; four children under age ten and another in the womb; aging parents for whom he must care; multiple households of problematic uncles, cousins, nieces; agricultural land to supervise; no brothers to share the burden. Since I first knew him, he has become an important figure in his community, and he is pressured to attend numerous time-consuming social affairs, which—to my disgruntlement—I see that he enjoys. He would not do research at all did I not come flying in with my agenda and my funding.

Yet, I hasten to add, this does not make him my tool or even my employee, just as my own lack of initiative in many situations does not actually reduce my part in the research to nothing but pho-tographer and typist. Bhoju becomes deeply and autonomously involved in each project. Such was the case from his first research assistant experience. This—his penchant for intellectual involve-ment—must be why we continue to collaborate after so many years; why I so value his assistance; why he, unlike others who worked for me in the past, still continues to be engaged in field-work.[18] I doubt, truth to tell, that I would have continued to revisit Ghatiyali and learn these histories were it not for Bhoju Ram and the boundless possibilities our collaboration brings to me.

What I wrote in Ghatiyali captures pretty well our different contri-butions to this collaboration. Beyond holding (figuratively) the pen (the keyboard, the megabytes), I control the overarching aims, the successful grant proposals, and the banking, as well as the English prose, translation, theory, secondary literature, computers, and thus, inevitably, the final text—these words you now are reading.

Therefore it would appear that, beyond language, in the pages that follow I have evidently controlled the selection and ordering of mate-rial. But do not be so sure; in a sense we return here, in circular fash-ion, to Bhoju, whose improvised interview strategies create threads braided through our conversations from which the patterned tapestry I produce in words is consequently woven.

While working together we each surrender part of our selves, per-

Ann interviews Ram Narayan Daroga (Jasvantpura, 1997).

haps part of our self-respect too. Certainly ego-downgrades take place; each of us at times has to admit to helplessness or cluelessness. The academic world in which I move at ease is partially opaque to him; the village world in which he moves at ease is partially opaque to me. Inevitably, in the process of leading and being led by one another we risk damage, chinks in our public and private identities. I sometimes have to wonder how can I, a fifty-year-old professor of religion, be so utterly dependent on this proud schoolteacher who loves to instruct under all conditions. I must on our day-long travels by motorcycle rely on him not only to tell me where our next interview will be, but where to relieve myself (and then I scramble awkwardly into the brush beside the road, catching and frequently ripping my baggy clothing on the thorn scrub).

Bhoju must sustain his Gujar honor before his community, even though everyone can see that he devotes his time to the unpredictable whims of a graying foreign female. He must explain to others why my work takes priority: my time is short; our grant funds have produced imperatives; and—as I have heard him argue authoritatively—our efforts will save something worth saving in the alien libraries of the West. "Your children will have to go *there* to learn about your culture," he harangues, and I find this inexplicably shames me.

I must in turn accept that, in reality, my work often does not truly take priority. If Bhoju's mother's brother's unbalanced son's unhappy wife bolts one morning, it is Bhoju who is honor-bound to track her; if wheat must be bought for a feast, it is Bhoju who must chase around the villages after a good price; if a castefellow needs a literate man-of-the-world visible at his funeral feast, it is Bhoju (there are truly no alternatives among the local Gujars) who must spend two days there, looking appropriately urbane. Yet his autonomy is compromised in certain ways by me, even as my sense of identity is taxed by him. We both go on faith that these mutual sacrifices produce something of value, culminating if not fully captured in our book.

I hope our strategies in all that follows are relatively transparent. Nonetheless, I want to highlight a few conditions under which we steer our perilous course of authorial choices. As our own knowledge grew, as our ability to spin the narrative frames and elicit elaborations improved, we inevitably refined our questions. Our mode of research was intuitive, not systematic (and the two may well be mutually exclusive). Often we became excited about a particular theme—whether pig poaching, or shoe-beating, or grain taxes—and trailed it single-mindedly until it grew stale or led to another theme that gradually replaced it in our priorities. Only in a few instances did we return to reinterview persons with whom we had already spoken to ask about themes that had emerged later. For this reason some persons were explicitly pumped on some subjects and not on others.

Sometimes a particular topic would evoke the same responses so repetitively that we would drop it. Now and then, however, when we were anticipating no surprises, someone would offer a radically different perspective. For example, many people otherwise bitter about the kings' rule—its enforced penury and other blatant humiliations—would praise dispute settlement in the time of the *darbār*. In those days, many told us, justice was "hand to hand" (immediate). Nowdays the "disease" of litigation drags cases on literally for generations, draining energies and resources. But Mumtaz Ali, interviewed in February 1997, spoke scathingly of the kings' so-called justice, which he saw as nothing but another facet of arbitrary autocracy.

Earlier in the fieldwork, Bhoju was troubled whenever accounts seemed to lack consistency. Sometimes I nervously heard him trying to persuade people out of divergent opinions, in the interests of gleaning a single truth.[19] My attempts to interrupt this were usually futile. Eventually, Bhoju came to appreciate the ways that differently positioned persons necessarily had different perspectives—something he stresses in his portion of this chapter. For example, herders understandably have more regrets for the lost grazing land and tree cover than do farmers.

The order Bhoju and I have imposed on these materials—both in collection and in presentation—is partially arbitrary and thoroughly constructed. At the same time it will strike some as a rather imperfect order. I could say that the interview texts, both in process and as processed, refused to submit to our ordering wishes. I have cut interviews into pieces so that I may illuminate topics, loosely grouping voiced memories around some major recurrent themes and segregating these themes within chapters as best I can. Had I refrained altogether from sorting and selecting—and merely transcribed and translated—readers could have floundered and dozed in reaction to content both jumbled and repetitious.

Balanced against the authorial urge to order, however, was another urge: to retain chunks of voiced expressions as they emerged dialogically and to translate these as closely as possible, as befits oral performances. Consequently, some speakers' trains of thought transgress my artificial chapter boundaries. I hope this in turn allows readers to experience something of the flow of associations through which both questions and answers emerge; and to hear things I may well have missed.

Had I wished to distill dialogues to monologue, and to forego lengthy citations of actual interviews, it would have been much easier to pack topical chapters under tamperproof seals and have each deliver a discrete punch. I have taken a risky middle way thus to offer chunks of dialogue selectively arranged, and I anticipate that critics will see either too much artifice and imposition or too much unanalytic free form. Eventually a layered, mottled narrative emerges, and whatever truth force it has derives from substantial reiterations and cohesive convergences. This does not mean that stories do not directly discorroborate and clash; often they do. Some are so vicious, dark, and potentially scandalous they cannot be entered here; sometimes our heads spin.

Bhoju spent most of September through December 1997 in my home in Ithaca, New York, where our relationship subtly altered. In Ithaca his expertise no longer prevailed in every area of daily life. Here, typing in *devanāgarī* font on a Macintosh computer and writing in fine literary Hindi prose, he composed the following account, which I have translated.

The Story of the Sawar Twenty-Seven Community, from Their Own Testimonies: "From the Squirrel's Sins the Pipal Tree Withered"

I had heard this saying many times but had never taken any interest in its depth, its hidden meaning. Behind every saying is the long experience of a people's thought, offering assistance and instruction to coming generations.[20]

We asked people about the conditions of those times: under the rule of great kings. How were their lives? What were their chief occupations? Were they happy? What were their experiences? When we asked, they searched their memories, and lines of joy and despair appeared on their faces.

When we asked people, "What were your sorrows in those times?" each ordinary person said that the king was the king, and from his direction came no sorrow. But, there was a lot of trouble from the king's bosses (*hākim*).[21]

When they told us about their troubles, it seemed to us that in those times the low workers were barbarically exploited, but their troubles were not known. They were sorrowful, but there was no one to listen to their sorrow. Inside the fort, the grain bins were full and the king's horses and oxen ate their fills every day. But farmers might be starving for grain. In times of famine, in exchange for labor, some grain was distributed, but this was not sufficient for the farmers' families. Many old men and women, when speaking about the times of famine, were very troubled to recall them.

People still tell of the year [*samvat*] 1856 [1908] when conditions were heartrending. At that time, grain was like medicine. You may imagine how difficult it was for ordinary people to survive, from the following couplet:

chhapanyā thārā rāj meṁ augad hogyā ann
nārayāṁ nakharā chhoṛ diyā marad khānchgyā man

O year Fifty-six, in your kingdom, a grain is precious medicine
Women no longer adorn themselves; men are indifferent

In that era all the classes did separate work; every *jāti* had a role to play. If anyone objected, then they were physically punished or fined. In the twenty-seven villages, the Court was the master and had rights over the whole jungle, all the grazing land, all the settled places, and all the fields on the earth. Whatever agricultural work was done, it was by the *darbār*'s order only. In exchange for granting the right to farm, he took a fixed portion of the produce in the form of grain. Grain tax was different for different castes.

Even if they are happy today, many people, when they remember those times, which they don't even want to do, feel as if their souls are yoked to pain. Just think what kind of a time it was when, after laboring in the fields for an entire season, farmers could not harvest their crops without the ruler's order, or rather, the boss's (*hākim*'s) order.

Some castes were happier than others then: Rajputs, Gujars, and Minas sometimes praise those times. The Gujars' chief occupation was keeping animals; and in the *darbār*'s time there was a lot of jungle, so there was no trouble. Under today's government the jungle has been destroyed, and this is a major sorrow. Gujars had to pay only a one-quarter share of their agricultural production. This is because some Gujars were wet-nurse brothers to the king. Mina did the guard work, and they also gave only one-quarter. These people sometimes think of that past as a good time.

But for many farming people, and for others, it seems that those times were sorrowful, and that they were forced to do much that they did not want to do. Some people were prohibited from wearing shoes, or sitting down, or riding in certain streets and neighborhoods. Some always lived dependent on others' compassion. Many are happy today because the rule of kings is over. Many remember Indira Gandhi's rule, and say that she raised us up and that during her rule we realized that we are free.[22] Today we are not so oppressed, we lead respected lives.

When we heard the Sawar people's whole story of misery, it seemed as if they had no knowledge of enslavement by the British. Except for the Court, no one knew of it. For them the greatest happiness of freedom is to have escaped the oppressions of the kings' men and of forced labor.

To obtain this knowledge by searching each village was not so easy. If we have been successful in this—in recording and transmitting their moments of joy and despair—it is because our sympathy and sadness would equal theirs. This was natural, too, because when they remembered that time they would be lost in the depths of their own past, and no perception of the present remained.

I always questioned the villagers with sympathy and showed them the connection between our souls. When I met some old man, or woman, and talked with them at their home, they sometimes struck me as a little agitated; I could not comfort them sufficiently. But I tried to comfort them, even more than I do in my own house. This is true: when I interview someone I always forget who I am. What is most important for me is where I am and with whom I am talking. I give them my deep attention. And with my demeanor I show them great respect and, always, personal sympathy. This is one method of doing my work.

When I talk with Rajputs or Brahmins, I remain very careful. I go along in the conversation following their leads and observing the proper respectful etiquette, giving attention to their status. For how long have we been free? Nonetheless, even today the old generation keeps social status as its first concern. So whenever I interview them, I am very attentive. If I were even a little lazy about this, then it would be harmful to our work.

This is my feeling: even now our elders must struggle to make today's youthful generation hold their own past in esteem and appreciate its dignity. My personal efforts are to bridge this ideological gulf so that there will be a meeting of minds among all who are alive to witness the present. I think that whoever would help our country's development should have the mental disposition to understand the elder generation's mentality and spirit. Let us envision the road to development on the basis of their experiences.

3. PLACE

If place-making is a way of constructing the past, a venerable means of *doing human history*, it is also a way of constructing social traditions and, in the process, personal and social identities. We *are*, in a sense, the place-worlds we imagine.—Keith Basso, *Wisdom Sits in Places*

A village is not just a collection of different lineages, it is a place marked by memories and particular spirits inhabiting particular spots. Specific stones and bends in the river, specific trees and paths—all have their stories.—Nandini Sundar, *Subalterns and Sovereigns*

The storied place that fills our minds and those of our teachers—the senior citizens of Sawar—is multiply situated. In this chapter, laying no claims to comprehensiveness or singular truth, we attempt to sketch some contexts—geophysical and historical—for what follows.

The Banas Basin: Physical and Geographical Groundings

The kingdom of Sawar is located in the southeast portion of present-day Ajmer district, and is surrounded on three sides by other districts: Bhilwara to the south and west, Tonk to the northeast, and Bundi to the southeast. Sawar is part of the Banas Basin, which is named after its major river, the Banas. The Banas River is a tributary of the Chambal River, which ultimately flows into the Yamuna in Uttar Pradesh (Misra 1967:36).[1] One of the lesser rivers draining into the Banas is the Khari, and most, but not quite all, of the villages belonging to Sawar's

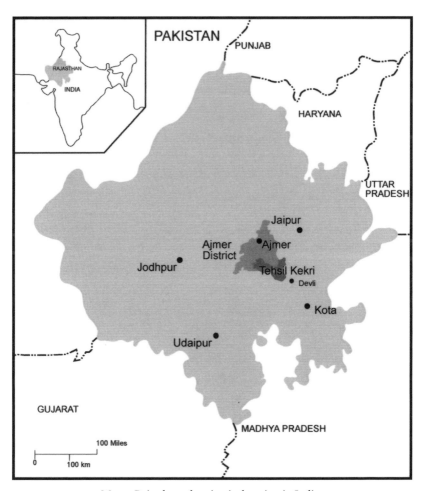

Map 1. Rajasthan, showing its location in India.

old territory lie between the Banas and the Khari. People in Sawar, who do not often look at maps, think of their particular piece of the earth as positioned between these rivers, which in the rainy season present strategic barriers to all travelers.

The Banas Basin is relatively homogeneous in geophysical and climatic features, and it has a distinctive ecological identity. Nonetheless, each village has its characteristic microecology, and the erratic, seemingly willful rains of Rajasthan may sometimes bless one locality's crops while leaving its neighbors dry.[2]

Colonial documents regularly comment critically on the dearth of "good" year-round rivers in Rajputana; the *Imperial Gazetteer of India* declares disparagingly of Ajmer-Merwara that "the Province does not possess any rivers of importance" (1989 [1908]:149). But for Sawar folks, the Banas, with its seasonally changing character, is central to regional identity, geographical and cultural, and it is a source of livelihood as well as hazard and hassle. When its waters cease to flow in the hot season, the Banas supplies luscious melons and cucumbers, which are cultivated by gardeners in its fertile bed and are gratefully consumed at a time of year when fresh green vegetables are almost unavailable.

Crossing the Banas to reach Ghatiyali, or to depart from it, has given me diverse adventurous experiences over the past twenty years. I have waded it when there was a knee-deep current, and I have trudged heavy-footed through its sandy bottom when it was hot and dry. My most exciting (if abortive) crossing was one rainy September twilight in 1980 in a bullock cart bound home from Devli, laden with a colleague's cumbersome video equipment. The water was rather high and swift and the oxen balked at mid-stream. We were treated to their driver's marvelous vocabulary of curses, but all to no avail. By the time the oxen's will had definitively prevailed we felt lucky to return to the bank, and we spent a rather hungry, damp, and disconsolate night in a pilgrims' rest house belonging to the Ganeshji temple that overlooks the river. The next day, towed by calmer animals, we successfully crossed less turbulent waters. In 1997, sometime after I departed at the end of February, a fine new bridge opened at the place where the road from Ghatiyali (via Jasvantapura) meets the river. Now the shortest route between Ghatiyali and Devli City—the nearest junction with direct links to India-wide transportation—no longer involves the riverbed. I happily crossed this bridge in July with my whole family in a taxi, and I shall determinedly resist nostalgia for past fordings.

Quarrying for rocks and minerals has long been a supplementary economic activity in this region, one expanding very rapidly at present, doubtless with profound ecological and sociological consequences that we will not address here. Nonetheless, the basis of life in the Banas Basin, and hence in the Sawar Twenty-Seven, has been in past centuries and remains today a mixture of agriculture and herding. The soil is fertile in this region (Misra 1967)[3]: wheat and corn are the staple grains, although minor trends in cropping patterns may vary greatly from locality to locality in Rajasthan and even within Ajmer district.

In 1993, Shambhu Nath—a literate young farmer who was working for me as research assistant—created three scrapbooks, including one on local trees, another on other wild plants, and another on agricultural crops. In the latter, he described Ghatiyali's two major agricultural seasons and their principal crops, which he designates "modern" (*adhūnik*) crops, because patterns have changed in recent years.[4] The *rabī* crop, cultivated between October and March, is called *unyālū* in Rajasthan—meaning the crop harvested in the hot season. The chief *rabī* crops are wheat, barley, mustard, cumin, fenugreek, coriander, chickpeas, sugarcane, *tārāmīrā* (a kind of brassica, *Eruca sativa*), fennel, alfalfa, and other kinds of fodder crops. For wheat, new and non-indigenous varieties have become dominant—notably *kalyāṇ sonī*.[5] Most *rabī* crops depend on irrigation and therefore are planted only in fields where there are sources of water.

The *kharīph* crop, cultivated from July to October, is called *siyālū* in Rajasthan—meaning the crop harvested in the cold season. The chief *kharīph* crops are small millet (*jvār*), large millet (*bājrā*), corn, peanuts, sesame, cotton, and many varieties of legumes (*dāl*), including *mūng, moth, uṛad,* and *arahar.* The *kharīph* crop is of greater importance, Shambhu writes, because "this crop can grow on every kind of land, and in all places, whether fertile or only slightly fertile, sandy or stony. This crop is called the poor people's crop. For this crop there is no need of irrigation. It grows with rain water only. For this reason, in Rajasthan, people call it *dharmasākh*" (Nath 1993). Bhoju explains that "the *kharīph* crop is called *dharmasākh* or *dharmaphasal* because the farmer does not have to do any special hard labor; there is no irrigation, just faith in God. Production depends on His desire alone, and if the rain is good then the crop is good; and if not, then there is nothing."

In the past the most significant cash crop was cotton. Around Sawar and Ghatiyali cotton has become perceptibly scarce, even within the last two decades.[6] It takes longer to grow and is labor intensive (although not water intensive). Its abandonment in part reflects new irrigation technologies. In *rabī*, increasingly, the oil seed cash crop of mustard holds sway. Bhoju was uneasy in January 1997 when there seemed no end to the vistas of brilliant yellow flowering fields in every direction we gazed. He too had planted mustard and was worried not only that the market would glut and the price plummet, but that wheat could become expensive and scarce. In that year, mustard continued to do well. But it is increasingly the case that people who once grew all the grain they consumed now purchase food grains for their families with profits made from oil seeds. This is part of a recent statewide trend.[7]

Livestock varieties in the area include cows, buffalo, and goats all raised largely for dairy products, although goat meat is eaten—most often in the context of sacrifice to the goddess. Sheep are raised for wool and meat, and their milk is also sometimes consumed domestically. In the regional ecology that today appears degeneratively unbalanced for reasons that will gradually unfold, a semisymbiotic mix of herders' and farmers' productive activities has always been crucial (Tambs-Lyche 1997:144).

In the past, agriculture totally depended on cattle; bullocks enabled both plowing and irrigation, and dung was the source of fertility.[8] Farmers would pay herders to have their livestock pasture overnight in their fallow fields—leaving their droppings to enrich the soil.[9] Milk is a pure, cooling, "truthful" (*sattvik*) food, considered to nourish both body and soul.[10] Everyone desired and valued milk products for food and health. Ghi, churned from yogurt made from whole milk is a condensed, powerful, and strengthening substance—and is also offered to the deities. One claim we heard often in villagers' narratives of change is that far more dairy products were consumed in the village in the past, which led to larger physiques, better human health, better tempers, and, hence, to community harmony and morality (see chapter 10). In the very arid districts of Rajasthan west of the Aravali Mountains—which people in Sawar colloquially call the "hungry land" (*bhūkhā deś*)—herding communities were often seasonally migrant peoples.[11] But in the Banas Basin most herders are permanently settled in villages, where they own houses and some farmland.[12]

The population density in Rajasthan is significantly lower than in less arid parts of North India. Nonetheless, growth in population, mentioned by many interviewees, is statistically confirmed for Sawar's large and small villages.[13] Today, as pressures on the land increase owing to increased population and increased desires for consumer goods, herders may speak with resentment of rich and powerful farmers' illegal but successful encroachments on what was once grazing commons (charāgāh). Moreover, as we will discuss below, conflicts between herders' needs and forestry conservation efforts are a recurrent theme in local and statewide forestry narratives, both past and present.

When in 1993 I began to elicit oral histories of environmental change, I knew nothing about indigenous tree species in Rajasthan, and I was only aware of trees with particular significance in ritual and myth. Predictably, these were the pan-Indian, religiously emphasized species of nīm, pīpal, and banyan (bāṛ; or in Sanskrit vata),[14] none of which were numerous enough to be a major economic resource or play a major part in local ecology. However, all three species were generally praised for shade and beauty, and were multiply employed religiously and medicinally. These culturally valorized trees do not grow in the jungle, but are cultivated with care by humans and are located near houses, temples, meeting places, water tanks, and wells in the fields. Nīm, pīpal, and banyan were named as the three species of trees that the last ruler of Sawar planted along the roadside and protected militantly. In the aftermath of his death, they were cut and sold—amoral acts that chartered or coincided with the free-for-all attack on forest commons that resulted in today's barren hills (chapter 9).

What were the trees that once covered Sawar's hills? When we began interviews in Ghatiyali on the remembered jungle, we found that many people would readily name trees that had once been numerous and valued but were now scarce or gone. A single species was the first on everybody's tongue. This was dhokaṛā, which was colloquially, or affectionately it seemed to me from intonation, called dhok. Numerous sources confirm that this tree (Anogeissus pendula) was indeed the dominant indigenous species for the Banas Basin area.[15] Just as do nostalgic citizens of Sawar, geographic and botanical studies praise A. pendula's wood for its strength and multiple uses. The value and versatility of dhokaṛā wood was doubtless a key to its near disappearance.[16] After dhokaṛā, lists given to us by individuals are bewilderingly varied, suggesting ample biodiversity in the area.[17] In chapters 9 and 10, we follow in detail the oral history of Sawar's deforestation—from its disastrous acceleration after 1947 through its ecological consequences in the present.[18]

The fruits of all productive interactions of Sawar's people with the land, as far back as any can recall, have always been subjected in varying degrees to rulers' substantial extractions. We turn now to embedded political histories, but our eyes will not be off the trees for long.[19]

Embedded Histories

Through books and documents we can trace for several centuries the rather undramatic political fortunes of the Sawar Twenty-Seven.[20] These written records are histories of the highborn, recounting their ambitions and accomplishments, and are wiped clean of all but the flimsiest traces of the "public," or *riyāyā*. Even the agglomeration of twenty-seven villages under one king is a structure imposed from without and above, although, as we have seen, it has some geographical logic.[21] Rulers play with villages as if they were uninhabited, inert, alienable property. "You can have these villages," they say to their favored soldiers, or bards, or wives—as if there were no people in them. What they mean by this, of course, is "You can have the income from these villages." When we superimpose our collection of orally transmitted histories upon the last half-century of princely chronicles, we see that rulers and farmers did inhabit, almost, the same spaces. What we learn from rulers' histories is the magnificent number of horses, and even more admirably, elephants, in the kings' stables. From the old Regar women who—their energies diverted from their own families' needs—were required to grind grain all day without pay to keep those beasts well fed, we gain a rather different perspective.

An alternative history of indeterminate depth exists in some elders' memories. Without implying a false partition of oral and written traditions, and aware of the crisscrossing mutual influences blurring the boundaries between them, I attempt here first to trace some fragmented narratives of non-Rajput local history, before turning to Rajput and colonial versions of Sawar's past.

OF THIEVES AND PRINCES: MINA ORIGINS

For Ghatiyali, within Sawar, we learn from landscape and memory of a pre-Rajput past, a time conceived as an era of thieves, shifting sand dunes, and divine retribution. The ruins of an ancient settlement that predated Ghatiyali are located on a desolate sandy rise known as Ghugh Thala, the "Owl Dune,"—a place where a few eccentrics and magicians still seek buried treasure (and some claim to have found it). My field notes of 7 February 1993 record a walk with Bhoju to the Owl Dune "where the buried city is said to be; where Gopi, maybe using the power of his magic armband, obtained silver coins, but Sukh Devji and Narayan Gujar went mad; where on festival nights the mysterious lights flicker." The place had an eerie ambiance, a ghost-ridden, sub-rosa reality around which rumors of wealth and danger flourished.

This settlement was wiped out, we are told, by some kind of natural or magical disaster. From oral accounts we gathered tantalizing fragments of alternative narratives. They do not concern ruling families who live in castles and fight great wars. Rather, they center on Minas—former "tribals" now well settled in the area as farmers—and suggest that an original village of "thieves" occupied a site near today's settled area.[22]

Bhoju and I hoped to elicit the Minas' versions of local history, because it was generally agreed that they were the first to settle this area. Like Gujars, Minas are known as a fierce community: sometimes they are cast as desperadoes from whom farmers and kings equally required protection; sometimes they are appointed guards, ensuring safe passage to others.[23] Doubtless they operated at times in both modes, and perhaps more usually in neither.[24]

In Mori, a village dominated by Minas, Bhairu Mauja Mina gave us one fragment about the Owl Dune. He said that the ruined houses still visible there had belonged to bandits (*ḍākū*) living in hamlets in the jungle. He did not specify Mina bandits. According to Bhairu, the bandits had underground hideouts in the area, including one at the Owl Dune. He added that Sawar itself once was a group of hamlets called Savad ka Khera.[25]

Bhairu told us a story of the bandits' bad end, in which he introduced a figure well known from Ghatiyali's religious history, the Gufawala Baba, or "Holy Man of the Cave," shortened here (as in earlier publications) to "the Cave Baba." The Cave Baba was an ascetic whose shrine, on one hillside, is an important site in the local sacred landscape and is associated with protection from natural disasters

Bhairu Mauja Mina (Mori, 1997).

(Gold 1988:50–53). Bhairu said: "The Cave Baba finished them [the bandits] off. Once he was sitting doing ascetic practice (*tapasyā*); and his [female] disciples went on begging rounds but they didn't receive any food in the whole settlement [*kherā*]: Kapuri washerwoman, Gangali oil Presser, no one gave them any alms." These names of a powerful guru's female disciples, a washerwoman and an oil presser woman, are standard legendary figures in North India and are associated with Nath yogis (Gold 1992:226–59). Bhairu continued:

> Then the guru came out of his meditation trance. His women disciples were bathing, and he noticed they had marks on their heads [from carrying heavy burdens of firewood].
> They told him, "In this settlement [*kherā*], no one ever gives us alms and so we have been collecting wood and selling it in order to feed you."
> The guru told them to announce to all the people, "Leave this area before tomorrow morning. Cross the Banas River."
> So the disciples told the people, "The guruji is angry," and some left. Those who didn't leave were swallowed up, destroyed: the earth turned over (*prithvī palaṭ gayī*, like an earthquake), and everything was finished.
> Then the guru left Kantola [the dense, wooded hillside] and the cave.[26] As he was leaving, his clothes stuck in the *dhokaṛā* trees and he cursed the jungle, "Your wood will never be straight!" So from that day, if you wander through all of Kantola, you cannot find any straight wood.
> Sometimes [in the Owl Dune] you find old things, wealth, remnants of houses, but it was all finished off at that time. And Sawar [as we know it today] was settled later.

This story is evocative. It suggests that a natural disaster (with religious causality) destroyed the area's former inhabitants. Its geographic and environmental motifs include the former abundance of *dhokaṛā* trees, and an explanation of their awkward, not aesthetically pleasing forms. The Banas River—a kind of imprecise boundary for the kingdom of Sawar, which in the era of this story had not yet been established—is set as a boundary for the edge of the place that is cursed. This suggests that the whole kingdom of Sawar developed over cursed ruins. The story does not reveal much about pre-Rajput polity, however.

Sitting in front of Ghatiyali's Mataji temple with Ganga Ram Mina and Shri Kishan Regar, we gathered another bit of Mina history glorifying the heroic bandits who dwelt in the Owl Dune. Bhoju asked who had "ruled" in Ghatiyali before the Rajputs, and Ganga Ram told us that a certain lineage had lived in the "place where the sand is." He explicitly identified the bandits as Mina, and told us something we had not heard from others: they were "the ones who installed Balaji."

Balaji is a name of Hanuman, and Ganga Ram refers to a shrine called Kantola ka Balaji (Balaji of the Thorny Hill) or, more commonly, Jhamntha ka Balaji (Balaji of the Pubic Hairs). The latter is another linguistic recollection of the environmental past—the trees in this area, crooked though they may have been, were once as thick as pubic hairs. Ganga Ram then described the forefather of these Mina worshippers of Hanuman as "a man, or a thief, a criminal. And nobody knew what his caste was; he came here and said, 'I am a Mina.' He married a Mina in Mori village and he is the person who settled this area; from his generation came the Minas of Ghatiyali." He then contradicted his assertion of the founder's unknown caste, and identified him as "a Rajput of the Panvar lineage of Rajputs."[27] This says something about the arbitrary and fluid nature of caste identity in ancient, "lawless" times. To claim identity, at least for a desperado, was to possess it.[28]

The only other information Ganga Ram divulged was that this founder bandit had once stolen "the entire Gangaur with all its ornaments" from Jaipur, and brought them back here, to Ghatiyali. In the major princely state of Jaipur the festival of Gangaur occasions a magnificent procession honoring the goddess Parvati. This performative display of power and grandeur was integral to Jaipur's identity. Elsewhere in Rajasthan the Gavri drama, still performed by Minas and Bhils in Udaipur district, includes an episode in which the Jaipur Gangaur procession is attacked; it seems likely that the source of Ganga Ram Mina's tale lies in these still vital traditions.[29]

We were not able to find anyone who could give a fuller account of the non-Rajput past. The skimpy stories of the Owl Dune and the antisocial elements it formerly harbored have in common a notion that the area's earliest citizenry were given to illegitimate, amoral feistiness, but received their comeuppance in the end—giving way to a tamer society. On the other hand, the bandits' legacy to Ghatiyali turns out to be not only the spooky buried city of the Owl Dune, with its elusive and dangerous treasures, but the still active and beneficent shrine of Balaji. To characterize them as amoral bandits who failed properly to respect holy persons and were duly destroyed does not quite jibe with their having established the shrine of Hanuman, an important place of protection and assistance.

Among other things, the stories suggest that the line between rulers and bandits is a very fine one, and that the goods of life must be shared for society and nature to prosper safely. Both stories encode multiple references to the formerly lush woods on Kantola.

OF THIEVES AND PRINCES: SHAKTAVAT ORIGINS

Sawar's documented history offers specifics of dates and details but less substance for ecological visions. From its exclusive focus on rulers we nonetheless gain some crucial context and background for the experiences recounted in the remainder of this book. Much that is in the brief written narratives of Sawar's ruling house is equally part of the corpus of collective memory. But in the oral histories we hear also the prices of rulers' accomplishments voiced by their bonded laborers and dissatisfied sharecroppers.

In 1997, while Ghatiyali was experiencing an eleven-day blackout due to slow government action in replacing a burned-out electricity transformer, I happened to be looking at a collection of papers pre-served by the sons of Jivan Lal Mathur.[30] Mathur was the last chief minister (*divān*) of Sawar state. I found there a letter, in English, dated 1937 and addressed to the ruler, Vansh Pradip Singh, concerning the installation of electricity in the fort. In the thirty-six-page pamphlet published by the Sawar royal family in 1977, authored by Jivan Lal Mathur himself, Sawar's history is presented as a genealogical chro-nology of rulers, listing each great king's accomplishments (Mathur 1976). This slim volume praises Vansh Pradip Singh for fostering development (*vikās*), including installing electricity in the fort. It does not, of course, mention that this "progress" took an additional forty years to reach villages only a few kilometers distant, and then

Jivan Lal Mathur's history of Sawar, original manuscript, title page.

only selectively. Even today night schools for working children are often illuminated only by kerosene lamps (or are canceled because of darkness).

Following Jivan Lal Mathur's history, we learn that the rulers of Sawar belong to the Shaktavat lineage (*vansh*), tracing their ancestry to Maharana Uday Singh of Udaipur's younger son, Shakti Singhji.[31] Sawar's Shaktavat heritage commences at a particular moment, one that links it to great doings in the subcontinental past. One of Shakti Singhji's many sons was Bhan Singhji, whose younger son was a soldier prince named Gokal Das. Gokal Das, the first Shaktavat ruler of Sawar, received his dominion as a land grant reward for heroic service in battle from the Mughal emperor Shah Jahan. According to Mathur's pamphlet, Gokal Das fought on behalf of Shah Jahan when, in 1623 C.E., the future emperor attempted to lead a revolt against his father, Jahangir.[32] In a great battle near Banaras, Gokal Das received eighty-four wounds—an auspicious number.

A few years later (in *samvat* 1684; 1628 C.E.), after the death of Jahangir, Shah Jahan ascended the Mughal throne. On the ninth day after becoming emperor, Shah Jahan called Gokal Das into his presence to reward him for his heroic and loyal service. He assigned him dominion over large areas, of which the Sawar Twenty-Seven, what remains known of the kingdom today, were but a small part.³³ Thus the written history of Sawar's Shaktavat rulers—which has its own legendary quality—commences in the late seventeenth century.³⁴

Each generation succeeding Gokal Das to the Sawar seat had its own accomplishments. Sawar never captured the attention of historiographers as did the greater Rajput states.³⁵ However, its existence is noted by art historians, who sound a somewhat patronizing note in characterizing a miniature painting style of the Sawar Court.³⁶

In spite of kinship ties with Mewar, Sawar geographically and politically fell under the dominion of Ajmer, which is far closer than Udaipur. From the seventeenth century through the early nineteenth century, Ajmer was a prize that frequently shifted hands and was ruled in turn, until the British took over, by Mughal, Rajput, and Sindhia of Gwalior (also referred to as Maratha) (Sarda 1911:160–175).³⁷ These administrations all left their marks—mostly on bureaucratic systems of administration and taxation.³⁸

Within Ajmer were sixty-six estates held under the *istimrāri* system. These estates were "permanent" land grants, dating back to a time when chiefs ruled land under obligation of military service, an obligation that had been converted under the Maratha rulers to one of "fixed tribute." Among these estates were fifteen classified as *tāzīmi*, or "aristocratic," and among these fifteen Sawar was second in order of precedence (*Imperial Gazetteer* 1989 [1908]:474),³⁹ only Bhinai ranked higher. Even in today's greatly reduced circumstances the Sawar royal family retains a strong sense of their own importance and status.

We conducted some interviews in two kingdoms adjacent to, and smaller than, Sawar: Mehru, with twelve villages the ninth-ranking *tāzīmi* state; and Gurgaon, a single-village non-*tāzīmi* state.⁴⁰ The rulers of both Mehru and Gurgaon were Rathor Rajputs (out of Marwar). We found that little in these two places differed strikingly from Sawar except, predictably, by scale. We heard of forced labor in both places, and of a sanctioning shoe (see chapter 5) in Mehru. In both places the jungle was protected by the Court's will and by guards. However, in neither place was there a ban on hunting wild animals that was anywhere near as strict and unpopular as the one Vansh Pradip Singh rigorously upheld in Sawar (chapter 9).

Ajmer district, and with it Sawar, was ceded to the British in 1818 during the reign of Jasvant Singh, who had begun to rule Sawar in

1812. Ajmer then became part of the combined administrative districts called Ajmer-Merwara, a territory of 2,711 square miles thought of as "isolated" because it was the only part of Rajputana under direct British rule.[41] As the *Imperial Gazetteer* states: "The long tale of battles and sieges is now closed; the history of Ajmer becomes one of its administration" (1989 [1908]:454). By "administration" the British meant above all tax assessment and revenue collection. The *Gazetteer* further states: "When Mr. Wilder took over charge of Ajmer in 1818 [he found the people] 'sadly thinned by oppression' " (475). He nonetheless proposed to take *half* the estimated value of the crops as revenue, a policy that, the *Gazetteer* reluctantly acknowledges, further thinned the people and reduced the district "to a state of abject poverty" (1989 [1908]:475).

Colonel Dixon's Settlement, made between 1849 and 1851, lowered the government's share from one-half to two-fifths of the produce in Ajmer, and to one-third in Merwara. Perhaps in response to the public distress, Colonel Dixon relinquished all government control over forest lands—a step that had significant repercussions for environmental history, as we will explore more fully. A resettlement conducted by Sir James La Touche between 1872 and 1874 developed a more nuanced approach to collection, taking into account soil quality and making more lenient provisions for bad seasons. At last, the *Gazetteer* reports, "the Province made substantial progress" (1989 [1908]:476).

Local ruling Rajputs in Ajmer's tributary kingdoms were subject to pressures from above and elsewhere (whether Ajmer, Delhi, Gwalior, or, in living persons' experience, London). But, as we have already observed, the persons whose memories compose this book only infrequently note this. To most villagers it was the great kings and their agents who controlled conditions of daily life, and whose rule was, both literally and figuratively, taxing. The ruler whose presence dominates Ghatiyali's remembered past, Vansh Pradip Singh, was a strong personality. He reigned over Sawar for more than thirty years, from his youthful ascension to the throne in 1914 until his death in 1947. In our interviews, Vansh Pradip Singh is usually referred to as the *darbār* (literally, "the Court") a term of reference commonly applied to rulers of large and small kingdoms in Rajasthan, and a practice that we follow here.

In the following section of this chapter I do not look in detail at Sawar's Court, but rather I follow some trails through documented colonial policy. Chiefly, I emphasize the British government's concern about depleting forest cover in Ajmer, a concern initially expressed almost three-quarters of a century before Vansh Pradip Singh's reign. This reign coincided with the years of India's struggle for Independence, during which the British cared less for forestry. Vansh Pradip Singh, however, as chapter 8 reveals, sought with great deliberation to shape Sawar's environmental conditions.

Colonial Tales of Deforestation and Reboisement

From published sources and archival documents on British rule in Ajmer-Merwara we may gather something of the area's recent ecological history as it was distinctively manipulated by colonial authorities and practices, often mediated by Rajput landowners and rulers. A caveat is in order here regarding my archival research—it is a beginner's effort. In the Rajasthan state archives in Bikaner, armed with a catalog of Ajmer records that I had pored over in advance, I was able rapidly to sift through preidentified materials and to have copied a significant number of files that were relevant to my specific interest in environmental history (Rajasthan State Archives 1980).[42] In the Ajmer branch of the state archives, I had no list before arriving and there were no photocopy facilities available. However, I found a wealth of interesting material there and gathered what I could under severe time constraints. I doubt I unearthed anything of great import in either place that has not been scrutinized and synthesized by more meticulous and dedicated archival researchers before me. My own obsessive capacities lie elsewhere.[43]

E. P. Stebbing's comprehensive and synthesizing four-volume work, *The Forests of India* (1923–26), has provided me with one usefully condensed account of affairs in Ajmer-Merwara, and I have frequent recourse to it, although I am aware that it is a positioned work.[44]

Impressions I gained from the archives and hope to transmit here are twofold. Most important, I gathered a sense of colonial attempts to prioritize their agendas in spite of conflicting rationales, and to keep forestry in mind—especially because of its purported links with climate change. At the same time, pragmatics of the imperial purse appear never far from any officer's consciousness. Forestry in Ajmer (unlike in Bengal, for example) never seemed likely to yield much profit.

Also, the archival material revealed daily administrative business in the colonial capital, especially the ways in which local people's claims on access to livelihood continually bumped into government policy. Strikingly, this situation is perpetuated today under a different regime. Almost from the time forest reserves were first established, there is an increase in documents concerning "complaints" and "disputes" over grazing rights in protected areas—an ongoing issue for Sawar herders of the late twentieth century.[45]

Ajmer was a drought- and famine-prone area. There was deep concern among colonial administrators about avoiding famine, with its high costs in human suffering and production, as well as to be prepared to deal with it in the event of the inevitable, given the climate.[46] Long before the post-Independence period of accelerated deforestation—to which our oral histories amply testify—British officials assessed tree cover in the dual province as threatened if not devastated.[47]

When did deforestation first become a perceptible problem in Ajmer? Nineteenth-century interpretations suggested that it was a recent and direct result of Colonel Dixon's Settlement of 1850. In the settlement Dixon had included a component that was to have enduring consequences for the district, and that was later decried by many concerned with forest conservation. In the assistant conservator's report on forest reserves we read that, according to the settlement, "all the waste lands were made over to the zamindars of the different villages to do with as they pleased. This proceeding altogether contrary to the ancient rules and regulations of the native states of Rajpootana has been attended with the most fatal results from a Forest point of view, but was no doubt decided upon at the time with the best and most liberal motives, these districts, especially that of Mhairwarrah, being in an unsettled state."[48] Speaking from a somewhat later point in time, Stebbing, closely following an account by Brandis, also attributes accelerating deforestation in the region to Dixon's ill-conceived decree—except that, rather curiously, he has replaced culprit "zamindars" with "people."

Colonel Dixon, Stebbing writes, in 1850 had handed over to the people "the whole of the waste and forest lands in these British districts" (1926, 3:104). According to Stebbing, the "inevitable" result that followed was that "the forest disappeared, the areas became barren and unproductive, and the water supplies diminished and became uncertain" (104). The "people" is an ill-defined term, perhaps Stebbing just means "Indians." But he goes on immediately to suggest that in neighboring areas where a zamindar's strong hand still prevailed, so did the trees.

Seventeen years after Dixon's Settlement, in the years 1867 to 1869, "Rajputana was subjected to a terrible famine." Stebbing tells us that in 1869, Brandis visited Ajmer and "painted with a vivid pen the contrast presented by the British area and the adjacent territory of the Thakur of Bednor. . . . In the latter the forest had been carefully preserved as a game sanctuary for pig (wild boar). These forests provided a plentiful supply of fodder for the cattle of the Thakur's people, whilst on the British side, to quote Brandis, 'the cattle had perished, the people had fled, large villages were deserted and the country was almost depopulated by these years of drought and famine'" (1926, 3:104–5). Brandis, cited by Stebbing, observes forgivingly that Dixon had "possessed no knowledge of forestry or of the enormous value of the forest as a preserver of water in a dry climate" (105). Brandis goes on, however, to point out the ironic results of Dixon's supposed "magnanimity." In his settlement, he had "presented all these lands to the people, not foreseeing that the gift would ruin and kill off numbers of their descendants within a score of years" (1926, 3:105).[49]

Something does not add up here. According to the archive report, landowners (zamindars), not the "people," were the beneficiaries of Dixon's settlement, and the ones charged with rapid deforestation. But Brandis and Stebbing both saw zamindars as preservers of trees. Just what were the "ancient rules and regulations" that, according to Ajmer's first assistant conservator, Colonel Dixon had violated in his action? A best guess would be that he was speaking of traditional commons rules, perhaps enforced by village panchāyats (with the agreement of rulers). He would seem then to suggest that Dixon's settlement had given the zamindars authority over commons land formerly regulated by communities, and that wanton, exploitative deforestation resulted. The conservator's report mentions traditions of reserved forest areas called "Beers" (bīr), as well as sacred groves:[50]

"Notwithstanding this dry climate some extensive wood lands exist throughout the territories of Rajpootana, it being the custom in most of the native States to conserve certain tracts of jungle and grass generally called Beers to furnish cover for game, and in order to give a supply of grass, firewood and small timber, also in other cases certain tracts have been reserved for religious purposes."[51] Sawar's oral accounts, presented in chapter 9, also speak of the Court's *bīr*.[52]

Stebbing's view, following Brandis, gives a nearly opposite interpretation of the problem of deforestation in Ajmer. As Stebbing formulates it, the "people" have been empowered and allowed to destroy forests that *thākurs,* or their overlords in Ajmer, would have protected—albeit for selfish reasons. Interestingly for us, the Bednor *thākur* is praised for preserving his woodlands for the sake of hunting wild pigs, much as Vansh Pradip Singh would do so effectively in Sawar three-quarters of a century later. As far as any of our oral sources reveal, Sawar forests were decidedly under the control of the Court, not the "people," in living memories. But Vansh Pradip Singh had founded Sawar's Forest Department (*jangalāt*) and established forest guards. We do not know if before his rule the lands over which he so effectively exercised control were village commons.[53] None of the reserves established by the British were within Sawar's boundaries.

In the wake of the 1869 famine, associated as it was with environmental deterioration, the British administration in Ajmer had systematically turned its mind toward reestablishing central control over the province's forest resources, scrubby and lamentably unlucrative as they were. Initial assessments of reserve operations told of rapid successes. The assistant conservator states for one area that "the result of three years conservancy however has been such that the natural growth is now so thick that pathways have to be cut in order to facilitate inspection."[54] However, the venture never became lucrative, and the British raj did not see its interests greatly served by forestry operations in Ajmer-Merwara, where costs were often weighed against product and were found to be imprudent.

A theme that recurs persistently in colonial discourse is the questionable association between forest cover and rainfall. The British strongly suspected that there might be a direct causal connection linking deforestation with drought and famine. Richard Grove (1995), and after him Ajay Skaria, have discussed this perceived nexus as a theory

of "desiccationism" defined as "the loose and often internally contra-
dictory set of ideas about the relationship between people and environment that emerged in the eighteenth century . . . characterized by
its assertion that there was a connection between the depletion of tree
cover and phenomena like droughts or soil erosion" (Skaria 1998:
597).[55] In Sawar minds, a thoroughly reworked "desiccationism" inte-
grates ideas about sin and selfishness, God's attitude toward humans,
and humans' appropriate and inappropriate behaviors toward trees
and toward one another (chapter 10 of this volume). Skaria points out
that for colonial powers as well, desiccationist discourse had "tran-
scendental implications and [an] apocalyptic nature" (1998:597).

Tracing colonial desiccationist notions in the archives on Ajmer
tree cover, we see that the theory was never unanimously held and was
never fully stabilized into uncontested policy. J. Nisbet noted in a
memo dated 1906 that the famine commission had "not paid enough
attention to the connection between forest and water," even though
an inquiry had been ordered as far back as 1847. However, in 1911
Captain Pritchard observed that the experimental stations set up in
various parts of the province to test this connection had been "found
valueless."[56] A direct "less trees, less rain" causality nexus was not
satisfactorily proved, and is still debated today.

Nonetheless, the colonial government knew beyond debate that in
drought years areas where forests were protected fared better than
deforested areas. Forest reserves meant fodder resources, which sustained both livestock and their owners through meager times. At least
as far back as the mid-nineteenth century, district administrators in
Ajmer had addressed the problem of forest-cover loss in general,
linking it to the impact of unchecked grazing on trees and grasses.
They sought as methodically as possible to establish more rigorous
control over these processes—although collected documents reveal
how tortuous the paths of paperwork had to be to attempt this aim.

Among the British forestry records, a great bulk concern contested
grazing rights. Wherever forest reserves are established, the "villagers"
are likely either to "complain" or to "take the law into their own
hands." They are generally viewed as foolishly motivated, and at
counterpurposes to the government. A hand-written document dated
1891 declares of people in Merwar that "the villagers are so utterly
improvident that they will sell their grass without taking the least

thought of the difficulty they will afterwards have in feeding their own Cattle."[57]

In 1892 Hira Singh, then assistant conservator of forests, reported on villagers who wanted to prevent establishment of a reserved area. He wrote that the area was "destined to ruin if immediate steps are not taken to check the ceaseless cutting of wood." A year later, the *bīr* had been established. The same document file contains an Urdu letter naming violators of the reserve: "The persons named below by sheer force and determination let their goats into the bir, do much damage and do not mind the guard who warns them—nay it appears that they are determined to take the law into their own hands." I note that among those named, all are Singh and one is titled *kāmdār* or "manager"—a generic term for high-ranking agents of the Court. Hence they are Rajputs and one is a designated official. This supports my earlier supposition that it was zamindars, not people, who may have exploited forest reserves.[58]

One memo from the Ajmer archives strikes a rather comical note, complaining that "large numbers of useless cattle wander in the forest, consuming grass which is meant for more valuable beasts and trampling down more grass than they consume." This is followed by strong statements on the need for rules, and some kind of "admissions standards" for cattle to be allowed in the reserves. While one administrator objected that "the selection of cattle for admission to forests is beset with many difficulties and is generally impossible," another actually offered the bright idea that tickets be issued—which I find rather hard to picture.[59]

From the point of view of a self-consciously conservation-minded government, "villagers" are collectively defined as improvident, unable to think beyond present circumstances or to appreciate what their foreign masters are trying to do for their own good. A quarter of a century later, the colonizers' scornful attitude had not changed. Stebbing cites a memo that conveys one administrator's typically irate feelings: "In 1924 the Divisional Forest Officer reported that 'the attitude of the villagers towards the Department has always been most unfriendly despite their depending on the Department for keeping body and soul together in famine years—the fact is that in those years (and all the time between) they wanted the free run of the forests to help themselves as they pleased with no thought to the future'"

(Champion and Osmaston 1983:360). Thus the colonial government's rhetoric persistently maligns the local folk in regard to forest conservation consciousness.[60]

One thing we learn with certainty from archival sources is that deforestation—a central trope of our oral histories—has been a concern in the Banas Basin region since at least the mid-nineteenth century. This is in itself an interesting backdrop to the ecological histories narrated to me and Bhoju by the people of Sawar, who date the period of ecologically disastrous transformation of their landscapes from the late 1940s through mid-1960s. Rather than assuming this is evidence of memory's green-tinted glasses, we must keep in mind that (at least for the thirty years that Vansh Pradip Singh kept his jungle in the palm of his ever-so-sensitive hand) Sawar diverged from the regional norm, as Bednor did in Brandis's memo, because of the Court's keen interest in keeping his woods dense and populous with wildlife.

Double Jeopardy: Rajput Rule under Colonial Rule

Nandini Sundar writes: "What we should be focusing on here is not the distinction between kingship and colonial rule, between custom and its opposite, but the nexus between them, especially in terms of how the British cashed in on traditional legitimacy and at the same time attempted to upstage it through their own version of paternalism" (Sundar 1997:89). In concluding this chapter of meshed backgrounds, I want to stress the double jeopardy under which citizens of the Sawar Twenty-Seven toiled and celebrated, the powerful nexus to which Sundar refers. Sawar's environment, though far from lush, would usually yield sufficient and valued goods of life. It was extractions from above that imposed scarcity. The British were in the collection business. The Rajput rulers (whether we call them "chiefs," "princes," or "great kings") had to pay the colonizers as well as sustain themselves in the style to which they were accustomed.

Whether "feudalism" as an economic and political system comparable to something that once existed in Europe appropriately describes the system of peasants, small estate-holders, and overlords in pre-Independence Rajasthan (and elsewhere in India) continues to be intensely debated. Thankfully, we need not engage these debates here, Eurocentric as they are both in origin and ultimately in implication.[61]

I have been unable totally to eschew the word "feudal," however, because many of my sources employ it as a useful descriptive handle for pre-Independence conditions in Rajputana (for example, Darda 1971; Pande 1974; Sagar and Ahuja 1987; and K. L. Sharma 1998). But I shall attempt to use it sparingly and always with actual or implied quotation marks; to me it evokes not so much an economic structure as the ambiance of rank and tribute that characterized at least the final half-century of kings' rule in Sawar. A signal caveat to bear in mind is that indigenous arrangements in the period with which we are concerned were ever severely stressed by colonial pressures.

Three specific elements constitute the essence of the bad old days under the great kings' rule in Sawar, as it was narrated to us by multiple voices. These are the named afflictions of the regime of the great kings about which we heard repeatedly: forced labor (*begār*), grain collection (*lāṭo-kūṭo*), and prohibitions (*pratibandh*). All of these are described and elaborated throughout the rest of our book.

Forced labor, or *begār*, was fairly widespread in North and Central India. It refers to labor conscripted by rulers for no pay (Gold 1992:187; 1994:88) and is contrasted with wage labor, however poor the wages. Jaideep Negi writes of *begār* in a Himalayan region: "The obligation of begar was part and parcel of the revenue system . . . man's physical strength was considered to belong as much to the raja as to their owner" (Negi 1995:16). Dube (1998:90–92) describes *begār* in Chhattisgarh, and Sundar (1997:55–57) reports it in Bastar. Both K. L. Sharma (1998) and H. Singh (1998) tell of its impact in other areas of Rajasthan. Sharma, speaking of Shekhawat, describes *begār* as "the most cruel method of exploitation," and notes that "except Brahmins and Rajputs, no other caste was exempted from begar in one or other form" (1998:25). As we will hear, even Brahmins and Rajputs were constrained to serve the Court, like it or not.

A peasant doing a day's *begār* in Sawar received at best a minimal meal for him or herself, but never a scrap for dependents. Moreover, the crux of the system was that a person had no choice whether to go when called or not, no matter if a child was sick or a crop needed irrigation. The only way safely to avoid going was to send a substitute. Otherwise, as one of our interviewees so succinctly put it, "the shoe fell."[62] In chapters 6 through 8 we hear often of *begār* as chief among the sorrows of those times.

The linked terms *lāṭo-kūṭo* refer to the Court's system of assessing and collecting its share of farmers' agricultural labors. A large portion of the assessed amount then had to be rendered to the British, who were overlords of the Rajputs. The system left farmers with myriad vulnerabilities, as they were subject to various skimmings off the top by predatory agents of the Court. These additional payments are often referred to in the literature as *lāg*.[63] When the government's share was set at one-third of the crop, the farmer frequently had to give at least another third to pay various fees. The knowledge that the fruits of one's labor would be ravaged by the Court's men, and that they would take far more than the official "share," all the while treating their victims rudely, was a weight on cultivators' minds.[64] *Lāg* was not a term used by our respondents in Sawar, but interviews presented in chapter 8 treat these skimmings in detail, as farmers recollect experiencing them.

Oppression during the great kings' regime operated on a different register with prohibitions (*pratibandh*), which were as much psychological as physical. People were forbidden certain comforts, luxuries, or signs of rank that the kings and those they favored possessed. These included jewelry and shoes, white sugar and stone houses, and the privilege of riding on horseback.[65] Chapter 5 explores the shoe ban among these in detail. The most common way that people we interviewed explained these bans to us strongly emphasized their symbolic potency. The standard explanation is as follows: "The great kings thought, 'If you eat sugar what will we eat?' 'If you live in stone houses where will we live?' and so forth." This formulation is telling, for while acknowledging the capacity of rulers to dominate, it denies genuine difference and subversively undermines the foundations of hierarchy as birth-given or based on inherent worth. Rather, it makes clear that the whole artifice rests on nothing more than possession and consumption.

Forced labor and grain taxes, but not prohibitions, were identified as rulers' abuses by popular political activists in the early twentieth century. One of these was Mukat Beharilal Bhargava, one of the few public figures other than Gandhi and Nehru whose name appeared in some of our interviews. Mukat Beharilal Bhargava joined the Indian National Congress in 1930, and was twice president of the Ajmer Pradesh Congress Committee in the late 1940s and early 1950s—the crucial years in which the conditions of rural life changed in the former Rajputana. His papers, collected by Ram Pande, focus on "various problems about the British province of Ajmer Merwara including law and order and abolition of Istamrari tenure" (1998:xiii). Bhargava was responsible, according to Pande, for having enacted soon after Indian Independence an ordinance making both *begār* and the various *lāg* illegal.

In an address to the Ajmer-Merwara Provincial Political Conference in 1938, Bhargava declaimed:

> The condition of the peasantry in the province in general and in the Istamrari area in particular is indeed miserable. In the latter the system of Begar is in vogue and the tenants have to pay a number of "lags" (cesses) besides the usual share of the produce, and are liable to be ejected at the whim and caprice of the Istamradar though they may have been cultivating the same plots of land for generations. . . . The rural indebtedness is already too high and on increase day by day and almost whole of the produce of the tenants soon falls into the clutches of the creditors even before it is removed from the field.
>
> The lot of the five and half lacs of people of this important but unfortunate province is no better than the hewers of wood and drawers of water and they drag on their miserable existence as mere dumb driven cattle, devoid of all voice in shaping their destiny. (cited in Pande 1988:5–6)[66]

All this came to an end, fast. A single decade encompassed the events of the death of Sawar's Vansh Pradip Singh, India's Independence, land reform, and the creation of the state of Rajasthan. Much of this larger story is well documented and has been well told elsewhere; we need not dwell on it here.[67]

In the chapters to follow, however, we hope to show clearly that the residents of the province—subjected as they were to colonial and ruling Rajput pressures—were far from being "dumb driven cattle" submitting to destiny without reflection or resistance. First, however, we examine more carefully the use of memories as sources, and our practices of eliciting them.

4. MEMORY

From the anthropological perspective recollections are equally valid material for the reconstruction of the past not "in spite of" but precisely "because of" the significant cultural selection inherent in them. . . . In some sense the sprouting "oral history" is based in a corresponding acknowledgment of the validity of popular recollection.—Kirsten Hastrup, introduction to *Other Histories*

Can it be surprising to us that we find ourselves longing to get *back into place,* whether by memory or in some other way? Getting out of place, being displaced, is profoundly disorienting. . . . No wonder, then, that we so much prize memory of place and often seek out "old haunts." Places and their memory sustain us in our everyday lives, subject as these lives are to fragmentation and rupture of so many sorts.—Edward Casey, *Remembering*

Repressed and rendered invisible, they form the Other of history, the constitutive outside which defines history and yet cannot be acknowledged. This Other is often conceived of as memory, a category thought to hold everything—including epic, chronicle and myth—which is premodern or non-western. It is to this Other, memory, that we need to turn.—Ajay Skaria, *Hybrid Histories*

As we have already related in fair detail, in 1993 circumstance transformed Bhoju and me into gatherers of memories. From there it was only another half-step to becoming self-styled oral historians. No one ever said to us in 1993 or in 1997, "why bother with the past?"[1] I am pretty certain it was not very common to chat about the bad old days, and that most people under thirty-five were not greatly interested. Now and then, however, we encountered exceptions. Some persons too young to have their own memories spoke to us about old times authoritatively, as if they had shared them. They did not say "my grandfather told me," but rather "it was like this." Their contributions testify to a collective or social memory not limited by personal experience.[2] It was also evident that a few stories had entered particular persons' performative repertoires and were well known to the broader community of all ages. For example, Kalyan Mali's story about wild pigs, which we transcribe in chapter 9, had evidently been told and retold; it was a recognizable and bounded oral performance with punchlines his audience knew in advance.

Ghatiyalians' memories include discourses of the good old days as well as of the bad old days, and the same persons speak them. There is a cherished past of community harmony; of winter storytelling by fires that these days there is no spare wood to fuel; of organically grown, tasty, and strengthening food, stone-ground by stronger and more modest women (and older female voices concur in this apparently male slant); and of a government that assumed responsibility for protecting valued trees. There is a hated past of conscripted labor and brutal suppression of personal freedoms. With the former goes a dense woods where herbs, berries, and wildlife flourish; with the latter goes a dense woods that shelters rampaging pigs.

Almost everyone, no matter how dark or how cheerful their recollections, agrees that life in the past was slower, more loving, more interpersonally harmonious, and in a landscape that was more lush. These pasts are the same past, these woods are the same woods. Love was greater then, but so were taxes. The landscape was more lush, but life was far harder. Thus, complexly nuanced ecological nostalgia is one poignant theme playing through the texts we elicited; bitterly recollected stark and even brutal oppression is another.

As the literature on memory proliferated before my eyes, I could not help but wonder what serendipity or fate had meshed our gropings toward an understanding of Ghatiyali's barren hillsides with what appeared to be a burgeoning academic trend whose momentum was far from spent. Combing these studies for inspiration, I found my attempts to argue for the power of the voices we had recorded illuminated and strengthened by many parallel, intersecting, or partially congruent exercises. I began to gather a more textured foundation for thinking about witnessed history in the kingdom of Sawar.[3]

Thinking Memory

I wish to highlight here as relevant to our project some strands or repeating themes in literature on memory, oral history, and environmental history. Heuristically, I have grouped ideas into four sets.[4] (I borrow freely from others' words and thoughts in the following condensed summary; all are fully acknowledged and annotated in the discussions that immediately follow.)

1) Oral history is a natal event, an emergent process having much in common with performance.

2) Oral histories or narrated memories offer multiple and conflicting versions of the same event; rather than obscuring the nature of the past these present a more robust, multidimensional reality—giving access to polysemy, multiple meanings that may challenge dominant discourses.

3) Memory has a "thick autonomy"; its thickness reveals modes of embodiment, sensuousness, places, materiality, the everyday, and vanished landscapes.

4) Memory is a "social fact," belonging to collective mentalities, but (paradoxically) it is individually experienced.

1) *Oral history is a natal event, an emergent process having much in common with performance.* When memories are gathered through ethnographic or oral historical strategies, the interaction of researcher with rememberers in the production of historical narratives is not simply a side effect of the research or a condition to be taken into account, but rather is a central feature—giving an emergent (performative) nature to the results.

Anthropologist C. Nadia Seremetakis, from whom I take the birth metaphor, writes: "Here sensory memory, as the meditation on the historical substance of experience is not mere repetition but transformation which brings the past into the present as a natal event" (1996:7). Other, perhaps less poetic, practitioners of the historian's craft also identify this interactive, creative character of oral history as critical to its practice. Social historian Paul Thompson produced a book in praise of oral history that is simultaneously a handbook on how to practice it. He reflects: "The living humanity of oral sources gives them a third strength which is unique. For the reflective insights of retrospection are by no means always a disadvantage. . . . We are dealing, in short, with living sources who, just because they are alive have, unlike inscribed stones or sheaves of paper, the ability to work with us in a two-way process" (1988:148–49). With a similar insight, drawing on a different kind of context (more formal oral-historical performance traditions in nonliterate societies) Elizabeth Tonkin, in *Narrating Our Pasts: The Social Construction of Oral History,* insists that "one cannot detach the oral representation of pastness from the relationship of teller and audience in which it was occasioned" (1992:2). All three of these authors treat different aspects of memory as history. But whether elicited or observed, in each case the emergent, interactive qualities are stressed.

Consoling to me are the lavish praises anthropologist Barbara Myerhoff gives to the work of memory. She asserts that for aging persons to remember and retell is not only a creative but a healing process. Bhoju often worried about the way our interviews stirred up old pain, or prodded buried but still raw wounds. Yet both of us at times sensed an electric charge in our interview situations, its voltage infinitely larger than the two double-A cells that spun our cassettes. At these times it seemed that being asked about the past, and tape recorded by us—a teacher and a foreigner—allowed speakers to wield their words with new potency. They had no agenda and no expectations, and yet their verbal performances were almost always compelling and, sometimes, truly electrifying.

Myerhoff's observations help me to express such charged moments: "Time is abolished not only by myth and dream but occasionally also by memory, for remembering the past fully and well retains it. Life experiences are not swept away as if they had never been. They are rewoven into the present. . . . Such moments are gifts, numinous pinpoints of great intensity. Then one's self and one's memories are experienced as eternally valid" (1992:238–39). In the case of our Sawar interviews, I would perhaps say "externally" valid rather then "eternally" valid. For voices from under a stone to speak freely of those times, to be heard and recorded, was a kind of validation.

Sociologist Karen Fields has worked on oral history both in Africa and in the United States, using African American family memories. With an emotional fervor similar to Myerhoff's, she also testifies to the different kind of truth that elicited memories may reveal:

> Memory fails, leaving blanks, and memory collaborates with forces separate from actual past events, forces such as an individual's wishes, a group's suggestions, a moment's connotations, an environment's clues, an emotion's demands, a self's evolution, a mind's manufacture of order, and yes, even a researcher's objectives. . . . As researchers we bind ourselves to skepticism about memory and to a definite methodological mistrust of rememberers who are our informants. We are fully attentive to the fact that memory fails. . . . But memory also succeeds. It succeeds enormously and profoundly; for it is fundamental to human life, not to say synonymous with it. (1994:89)

Fields too conveys the natal event quality of oral history research—a collaboration in the success of memory.

2) *Oral histories or narrated memories offer multiple and conflicting versions of the same event; rather than obscuring the nature of the past these present a more robust, multidimensional reality—giving access to polysemy, multiple meanings that may challenge dominant discourses.* Memories reveal alternative versions of the past, allowing polyphony and discord to break through previous silences (whether coercive or self-imposed); and to oppose monolithic, dominant accounts. W. Roseberry describes this in terms of challenge. In his *Anthropologies and Histories,* he writes: "No order of domination is total. There are always relationships and meanings that are excluded. Therefore, alternative meanings, alternative values, alternative versions of a people's history are available as a potential challenge to the dominant" (1989:27). He does not find closure but stresses rather the increase and opening up of a discourse world. Tonkin has a similar perspective, locating "truth . . . in the intersection of narrator and discourse," and stressing the significance of "polysemy" (1992:8). If there are multiple, emergent authorities, truth may lie in process rather than in conclusion, in moving pictures rather than static compositions.

Jacques Le Goff portrays a coursing collective memory as "overflowing history." He does not confine alternative versions to dissonant voices, but finds them in documents and monuments as well: "Over-flowing history as both a form of knowledge and a public rite, flowing uphill as the moving reservoir of history, full of archives and documents/monuments, and downhill as the sonorous (and living) echo of historical work, collective memory is one of the great stakes of developed and developing societies, of dominated and dominating classes, all of them struggling for power or for life, for survival and for advancement" (1992:97–98). Struggle is perpetual and by implication inconclusive.

Some memory theorists and oral history practitioners seem ready to accept multiple truths possessing equal validities as the very nature of historical reality. They would discount any final resolution from multiple to singular narratives. Others insist that ultimately an enriched but more unitary truth might emerge from multiple tales. Shahid Amin, for example, states in the introductory chapter to his *Event, Metaphor, Memory:* "But for me it was not a question of counterposing local remembrance against authorized accounts: the process by which historians gain access to pasts is richly problematic, as is the relationship between memory and record, and the possibilities of arriving at a more nuanced narrative, a thicker description, seem enhanced by putting the problems on display" (1995:4). Amin's book has the sharp focus of a single famous event: a "crowd of peasants" that killed twenty-three policemen in 1922, causing Gandhi temporarily to suspend his noncooperation movement. Around such a known moment, plural memories may be arrayed and examined.

Nandini Sundar puts it differently but with equal clarity, speaking of her fine anthropological history of Bastar in Madhya Pradesh: "The fact that they can disagree about particulars indicates that there is a shared discourse, a framework within which the past can be recreated and contrasted to the present" (1997:25). Much the same is true of our Sawar narratives; from divergent versions expressing divergent situations we gather a surprisingly robust singular vision. Amin also argues that "meanings get glued to events" and "memory plays upon the certitude of facts" (1995:11). That is, he calls attention to the ways that popular collective memory may also be conditioned and constrained by dominant narratives. Heeding Amin, it is well to keep in mind that any apparently shared discourse may be a product not only of inner convergence but of exterior molding.

Material traces may embody impenetrable ambiguities, but serve also to limit the imaginary.[5] Michel-Rolph Trouillot, in his personal and historical account of events in Haiti, insists that the materiality of history imposes certain priorities on the truth value of narratives:

> What happened leaves traces, some of which are quite concrete—buildings, dead bodies, censuses, monuments, diaries, political boundaries—that limit the range and significance of any historical narrative. This is one of many reasons why not any fiction can pass for history. . . . A castle, a fort, a battlefield, a church, all these things bigger than we that we infuse with the reality of past lives, seem to speak of an immensity of which we know little except that we are part of it. Too solid to be unmarked, too conspicuous to be candid, they embody the ambiguities of history. . . . We suspect that their concreteness hides secrets so deep that no revelation may fully dissipate their silences. (1995:29–30)

The multiple forts and hunting towers of Sawar never spoke clearly to me of conscripted labor or economic exploitation until I listened to people who worked in and beneath them. Trouillot points to material traces as adding a kind of molecular weight that counters multiple narratives, but is by no means transparent. This brings me, somewhat indirectly, to the third motif.

3) *Memory has a "thick autonomy"; its thickness reveals modes of embodiment, sensuousness, places, materiality, the everyday, and vanished landscapes.* This set of insights has to do with the embodied qualities both of individuals and of collective memory processes, as well as with selective operations that may work in tandem with these, lodging memories in things, or acts, or locations.

"Thick autonomy" is Edward Casey's expression. Casey, a philosopher, uses this term in his tome on remembering, especially to characterize the association between memory and place. It has not to do with political autonomy, or the ability of consciousness to escape structures of dominance. Rather it has to do with a relationship between individual memory, body, sensuality, and exterior locations. I find Casey's ideas helpful for understanding memories "inscribed" in place names, or nostalgia for scenes and sensualities no longer available to the senses, for example, in vistas or fruits. Thus in chapter 9 we hear persons recall the formerly dense jungle using visual and tactile imageries.

Casey tells us that "places are *congealed scenes* for remembered contents; and as such they serve to situate what we remember." He questions how "such an intimate relationship between memory and place is realized," and his answer is *"through the lived body"* (1987:189). Not just pleasurable recollections are thus embodied; such an instance would be when women reexperience the pain of an entire day spent grinding grain in the fort for the king's horses. Casey then argues that memory's "thickness" gathers its potency from human sensuality. He continues: "Rather than a mere repository of experience, remembering becomes thereby a continually growing fund for experience: a source itself, indeed a resource" (1987:284). He thus returns us from memories as thickly embodied to the natal event as portrayed by Seremetakis and by Myerhoff.

Keith Basso is an anthropologist influenced by Casey whose work with the Apache community has given him a profound understanding of one culture's poetics of place history. In Basso's view, memory's thick autonomy regarding place is a source of both separate and collective identity: "For what people make of their places is closely connected to what they make of themselves as members of society and inhabitants of the earth. . . . If place-making is a way of constructing the past, a venerable means of *doing* human history, it is also a way of constructing social traditions and, in the process, personal and social identities. We *are*, in a sense, the place-worlds we imagine" (1996:7). People who inhabit present altered landscapes retain knowledge—linguistic, legendary, visceral—of their past forms and meanings.

Seremetakis also brings the senses to bear on place, and she tells us that "the sensory landscape and its meaning-endowed objects bear within them emotional and historical sedimentation that can provoke and ignite gestures, discourses and acts—acts which open up these objects' stratigraphy" (1996:7). Thus, she suggests a "sensory archaeology," where the excavation tool would be memory. Paul Stoller's apprehension of the way "sensuous modalities provoke memories—and histories . . . of the dispossessed" (1997:47) adds a political dimension to our understanding that is more clearly developed by Jean and John Comaroff. Describing an "ethnography of the historical imagination," the Comaroffs are concerned with the poetics of landscape and its coded, loaded, nonverbal signs. In a passage that seems brilliantly to condense everything about Bhoju and my project, they suggest that: "A historical ethnography must always go beyond literary traces, beyond explicit narrative, exegesis, even argument. For the poetics of history lie also in mute meanings transacted through goods and practices, through icons and images dispersed in the landscape of the everyday" (1992:35). In a more recent publication, the Comaroffs return still more vehemently to the often neglected salience of the quotidian, and insist that it is not by any means to be equated with the apolitical (1997:31). Power inhabits ordinary landscapes and routines, more subtly but no less effectively than it inhabits the trappings of power—a theme to which we return in the meditation on shoes in chapter 5.

Similar conjunctions of place and power are evident in studies of environmental history that evoke both mundane and dramatic aspects of human interactions with nature. Authors such as William Cronon (1983), Simon Schama (1995), and Donald Worster (1993) tap many types of sources, including orally elicited recollections, to exemplify in varied ways how people interact with landscapes over time. These environmental historians explore both the poetics and the ecologies of such interactions in particular localities.

Such joining of performative poetics with thickly sensuous place memory is evident in one term of reference for an area of farmland in Ghatiyali: the berry wilderness (*bor kā mangarā*).[6] Casually used in today's conversations, this name reflects transformations in nature. I learned about it when my work still focused on stories. In the oral epic of Gopi Chand, recorded in 1981, there is a moment when desperado lady magicians turn fourteen-hundred yogis into donkeys and drive them into the jungle (Gold 1992:246). Later, freed by their compassionate guru, the yogis turn the tables and transform an entire kingdom's women into donkeys. Although this episode is set in Bengal, the Rajasthani bard—as so often happens in oral performances—locates the action in the immediate environment, so as to engage his listeners and draw them into the tale. Thus, the gardener reports to the king, "The yogis made your women into donkeys, and they are braying in the berry wilderness" (Gold 1992:252).

In 1990, helping me to translate this story, Bhoju explained that berry wilderness refers to an area just outside of Ghatiyali, where berries once were plentiful. It is now under the plow, and is no longer common property but private agricultural land. Just as people still refer to the predawn hours as the "time of grinding flour," even though flour is now ground whenever there is power to run the electric mill, so people still call this area "berry wilderness," even though today there are no berries on it.

The loss of the berry wilderness as a common property resource did not in fact leave Ghatiyalians without berries. For the time being, berries still grow in other spots not too far from home, and still in the 1990s these small fruits of the village commons are picked, shared, and relished. I may speak from my own sensual memories to evoke *bor,* the berries in question. They are the size of blueberries, but are 80 percent pit; they taste of sunshine and dust. For me their flavor epitomized the Rajasthani environment. But if I think of *bor* season, I recall more than flavor. These tiny, chewy fruits with wrinkled, red skins are gathered from prickly bushes by young and old, male and female, and by castes big and small, and they are eaten and given in a spirit of sharing. Berries were equalizers—a medium for generosity that did not depend on land ownership or wages.

During *bor* season, small, scruffy, boys—happy to have something to give—would come to my room at twilight with their grubby hands and pockets full of berries, and present them to me with serious pleasure. They wanted to hang around and watch me eat and enjoy their gifts. For them, these fruits of village common property were a brief source of economic independence. It would be difficult indeed to fill one's stomach even on buckets of *bor* (which may be why defeated magicians are consigned to bray in the berry wilderness, dying of hunger), yet with the loss of berry land go other subtler losses.[7] Here story and memory merge, as do the everyday and larger patterns of environmental history.

4) *Memory is a "social fact," belonging to collective mentalities, but (paradoxically) it is individually experienced.*[8] This fourth motif is both straightforward and hard to grasp. We contend here with an ill-defined and unchartable slippage when we try to characterize interactions between personal and collective memories. Different thinkers observe this playing out in different modes.

Maurice Halbwachs, one of the first theorists of social memory, influenced strongly by Durkheimian French sociology, insisted that there was no individual memory separate from social memory, and that "the mind reconstructs its memories under the pressure of society" (1992:51). This is an extreme position. Tonkin states that memory is "a key mediating term between individual and society" (1992: 98), but she does not unpack the mechanics of this mediation or the cross-cultural validity of its terms.

James Fentress (1992:201) locates memory within the individual, but insists that it acts socially as a source of collective representations and by extension of identity. Social historian Peter Burke finds the individual/collective relationship in memory perplexing even as it is compelling. He writes of the term "social memory," that it "sums up the complex process of selection and interpretation in a simple formula and stresses the homology between the ways in which the past is recorded and remembered" (1997:45–46). Burke finds the analogies between individual thought and group thought to be "elusive" and "fascinating." He concludes that access to both past and present is through cultural categories—a basic anthropological premise that brings us back to the different constructions of memory itself within varying contexts.

Jonathan Boyarin offers one of the most accurate descriptions of what memory is and isn't—so accurate I fear it approaches obfuscation. That is, he lays out genuine complexities in full array, and, like Burke, he stresses the interpenetration of group and person when we speak of memory, or for that matter of identity: "Memory is neither something preexistent and dormant in the past nor a projection from the present, but a potential for creative collaboration between present consciousness and the experience or expression of the past" (1994:22). He adds further:

> Memory cannot be strictly individual, inasmuch as it is symbolic and hence intersubjective. Nor can it be literally collective, since it is not superorganic but embodied. The conundrum disappears as soon as we remember that what we are trying to understand is not really a relation between body and group via culture. What we are faced with—what we are living—is the constitution of both group "membership" and individual "identity" out of a dynamically

chosen selection of memories, and the constant reshaping, reinvention, and reinforcement of those memories as members contest
and create the boundaries and links among themselves. (26)

Boyarin almost says it all.

If Boyarin has made the nature of collective memory slightly mysterious or obscure, we could turn to David Lowenthal, whose more
straightforward prose reaches nearly the same conclusions: "In the
process of knitting our own discontinuous recollections into narratives, we revise personal components to fit the collectively remembered past, and gradually cease to distinguish between them"
(1985:196). Lowenthal uses the phrase (borrowed from a novel by L. P.
Harley) "the past is a foreign country." This brings our oral historical
and ethnographic work into close conjunction.[9]

Saurabh Dube, in his work on "untouchable pasts," reflects both
on the interplay between individual and social memory and on the
possibility (pointed to by Shahid Amin) that not only do memories
reveal history but history creates memories. Thus he writes of the
memories he has tapped as sources for his work, that they are "more
than a collection of disconnected individual voices." Rather, he argues, "the individual accounts were bound together by a broad area
of agreement and a shared sense of community experience." Dube
goes on to acknowledge "a danger" that the persons he interviewed
"were not actually recalling their own experience" but instead "retelling what had become a standardized list of untouchable disabilities."
He discounts this, however, on the grounds that these persons "made
a clear distinction between what they had seen and lived through,
on the one hand, and what they had merely heard about, on the
other" (1998:88–89). Bhoju and I, like Dube, wish to respect each
individuals' knowledge and version as genuine even as we recognize
their stories as part of a common culturally and historically shaped
narrative.

Taking together the four themes discussed above—the *emergent*
quality of oral histories through memories; their *multiplicity* and
polysemy; memory's autonomous, sensuous, and thick *everydayness;*
and its *elusive* position between individually embodied and collectively known—I draw one very simple conclusion about memory in
relation to historical knowledge. All the writers I have discussed here

in a sense celebrate just those qualities that make memory suspect as a source of history; the very qualities that make it suspect are those that make it vital and valuable.

In the chapters that follow all four themes are at play. I like to think, following Seremetakis, that our research—as it took place in courtyards and fields, on curbsides and in Rajasthan's commodious doorways, and only occasionally in rooms—was a natal event. We retain the natal event quality in transparent fashion by retaining the interview texts. Questions create memories, memories create questions. Our texts feature multiplicity, polysemy, and challenges to the dominant both oblique and blatant. Kalyan Mali's and Himmat Singh's conflicting pig stories in chapter 9 are both truths that overlap the same fields and woods. Thus we show how multiple histories of a single time and place may diverge and converge in differently situated memories.[10] Memory's sensuous thickness, as evocative poesis, will equally pervade these chapters. We interview many individuals, and attempt to tell the stories of a people.

Veena Das writes with special urgency of the memories of victims and the importance of releasing victims' voices from oblivion, thereby recovering them. But simultaneously she insists that this recovery not involve disembodiment: "If it is the recovery of 'voice,' it cannot be a disembodied voice. . . . To recover such embodied narrations seems to me the only way in which one can resist the totalizing discourses" (1995:22).

The people whose voiced memories create our book are not victims in the sense that persons imprisoned, tortured, or assaulted by violent crowds (as Das has studied) are victims. But, in the old days— the sorrowful times of the great kings—many of them suffered a severe measure of pain and humiliation. Certainly their experiences were less disorienting, but the quotidian quality of multiple adjustments to abjection does not necessarily diminish its impact on souls.

Thematically clustered, differing sets of memories are like transparencies showing different features on the map of a single place that may be held up separately to highlight elevation, or population, or crop production. When overlaid they produce a denser image, harder to read though closer to reality. The chapters of this book are such transparencies, conceptual contour maps of a thin slice of time and a very small part of the earth.

Doing Memory

Because this book is based on the memories of living persons it is easily circumscribed in scope: at most we might claim that it covers approximately sixty or seventy years in the kingdom of Sawar, the late 1920s through the late 1990s. This spans roughly two decades of kings and half a century of democracy. It includes the doubly liminal period between 1947 and 1951 that was critical to environmental history—the interregnum known in Sawar as the Court of Wards (Kort aph Vards) time.[11]

Dealing with age was always difficult. Hierarchy, literacy, and dependence on astrology determine who has knowledge of their own age. Most Brahmins knew the year of their births, as did many members of the other two "twice-born" castes, Rajputs and Baniyas. By distinct contrast, few members of the farming or service communities, and almost no women among these, knew their birth years. Approximations ("the time of the red fever," or "the time of the road being built") serve instead. The dates remain fuzzy for most of these events. Moreover, they seem more often to date not birth but first memories.

What we know about ages of speakers here, then, is almost always approximate. I give one example of the trouble with age questions from an interview with Gori Regar. I asked, "About how old are you?" And she replied, "Friend, I don't know anything about my age and such (*ūmar-phūmar*)." I tried again, "You don't know? Well, about when were you born?" She then said she guessed her age was, "maybe eighty, maybe ninety." A man present, perhaps her grandson, chimed in, "I am thirty-five years old, how could you not be at least eighty?" To this, Gori responded, "Who says I'm eighty years old? No I'm not." The young man concluded, "O.k., it doesn't matter, it doesn't make any difference to you if you are eighty or one hundred!" Experiences like this led me to drop the age question, but Bhoju persisted most of the time to attempt it.

Given this general uncertainty, we can say that the oldest people with whom we spoke were in their mid-eighties in 1997, which would mean they were born around 1910, were adolescents in the late 1920s, and were in their primes in the late 1940s and early 1950s when everything changed. However, by far the majority of our interviewees were in their sixties, born in the 1930s. Thus, the major sweep of vivid shared recollections that not only fill but structure this book flow most copiously from the late 1930s, and encompass the *darbār*'s last decade (1934–45), the upheavals that immediately followed his demise, and the end of British rule in India and eventually, with less fanfare, in Ajmer. In Vansh Pradip Singh's waning years he was acutely aware that his rule, and the rule of kings, was doomed. We have more than one account of his responding to some complaint by saying, "Just wait a little while and all this will be over," or "I'll be dead and all this will be over." He seemed to know, or perhaps he willed, that trees and wild animals would pass with him.

The methods whereby we recorded memories were remarkably straightforward, given all that lay beneath them as recounted in the preceding chapter. Here is how it usually worked: we would ride up out of the blue—unannounced and unanticipated, and undoubtedly startling in our appearance because of my foreign face. Together we would explain who we were and what we wanted, very briefly, to whomever we approached. Bhoju talked briefly about me and my past connections in the area, emphasizing that I was someone who had been there many times before, that I was the author of books, and that my new project was the history of Sawar. Usually he elaborated in greater detail on his own identity, familial and professional.

In any case, these explanations were rarely lengthy and often pro forma. We would conclude by stating our desire to learn about the past. At some point we would discreetly but deliberately and visibly slide the small tape recorder out of its fuchsia-colored drawstring bag, push the red record button, aim the internal mike, and set it down, unobtrusive but present. Then we began to ask questions. Not a single person ever declined to recollect the past on tape. Even those initially hesitant (whether shy, self disparaging, suspicious, or just reserved) would grow involved. Almost without exception every person interviewed spoke with passion; articulate, coherent streams of memories poured forth.

Whenever I expressed my astonishment at this readiness and immediacy, Bhoju had a simple explanation: people remember acute sorrow and acute happiness acutely; this is why these recollections, too many of which are histories of sorrow, seem so fresh. A few persons, mostly women, directly identified memory as pain. They were the ones to say, "Don't ask about those times." Some had tears in their voices, some brushed them unshed from their eyes. Men too had suffered acutely in those days. In some interviews with both men and women anger was more palpable than grief.

Jamuni Regar's Memories Unfold

An interview we conducted fairly early during the 1997 field period touches on almost every motif of Sawar's past that follows in the remainder of our book. It also exemplifies the four themes in memory and history described above. To reproduce much of it here will serve as a disorderly, but I hope evocative, introduction to the contents of the chapters that follow, as well as previewing something of their flavor.

Regars were Ghatiyali's largest population of former "untouch-ables," their traditional occupational identity was as leatherworkers, but it will be apparent that many other tasks were assigned them under the old regime. Today the entire community has ceased all work having to do with dead animals and their hides. Regar women who would remember the days of forced unpaid labor (*begār*) were the first women we approached in 1997. There were four *begārī* women alive in reasonably good health in Ghatiyali that winter. Three lived in the old Regar neighborhood, very close to the Gujar houses where I was staying with Bhoju's family. Jamuni Regar, with whose words we at last commerce these oral histories, had moved along with her family to the new Regar colony, on the edge of the village on the road to Sawar.[12] We interviewed her there in her courtyard on 8 January 1997. My diary for that day records: "One beautiful interview in the Regar colony with Jamuni who used to go in begari who spoke clearly to the past and present, blind, thin, crouching, wrapped in a red orhni, her weathered face alive strong. . . . *These are the voices I want.*"

In the interaction between Bhoju as interlocutor and Jamuni as interviewee, the emergent, natal-event nature of our work is perfectly obvious. That the past and its regime is open to multiple interpretations is also evident here. Strikingly, even within a single speaker's testimony we see closely juxtaposed some opposing views of the rule of kings. On the one hand, there is a whiff of nostalgia for the benevolent grandeur in the image of the Court camped by the water reservoir as his queen summons the village women to sing and dance for her. On

Jamuni Regar, Regar colony (Ghatiyali, 1997).

the other, the torment of those times, laborious and hungry, is re-called in voice and gesture as well as words. Neither is hypocritical. Both are truths.

Perhaps the multiple views of the Court emerge most vividly in the quick shift in Jamuni Regar's recollections—between the wild pigs ravaging farmers' fields (which condemns the Court's selfish wildlife policies) and an episode where Vansh Pradip Singh's hunting skill saves the life of a Regar man. This memory leads Jamuni to recall her community rewarded with feasts when the king's hunt is successful; it starkly contrasts with her earlier plaintive testimony—that for her routine, conscripted grinding work she was fed nothing.

The sensual quality of memory, its thick autonomy, is readily evi-dent in Jamuni's recollections both of pleasure and of hard labor, as when she speaks of the pain in her chest from grinding all day so horses could eat. Also, her memories of places that formerly existed as part of her landscape of servitude are poignant.

Finally, we note her frequent shifts of perspective in the course of one interview. She sometimes recounts her individual life experiences as a woman, sometimes expresses collective memories of her *jāti* (male and female Regars), sometimes speaks for all of her generation, dissolving gender and caste differences. Memory in action reveals how individual and social memories are distinguished and intermingled.

I have rearranged some sections of the interview in order to retain a topical grouping, but I retained the original order in which either Bhoju or Jamuni introduced them. In other words, if a topic once introduced is resumed later, I have moved the second and third con-siderations of that topic next to the original mention; but each initia-tion of a subject comes in the order in which it actually occurred.

INTERVIEW WITH JAMUNI REGAR, JANUARY 1997

As in all subsequent interview translations, four dots indicates my omission of intervening words or passages; three dots a pause in speaking, a trailing off without closure. I use parentheses either to show the original term being translated from Hindi or Rajasthani; or, occasionally, to give an English gloss of a Hindi or Rajasthani word I have retained in the text. In brackets are small syntactical insertions made for the sake of fluidity and/or comprehension, and our length-ier interpretive commentaries.

BHOJU: How old are you?

JAMUNI: Oh *Nātājī* [respectful term of address; literally, "grain giver"]. I don't know; I was born when the road [from Sawar to Kekari] was begun; my natal home is Napa ka Khera.

BHOJU: When you came to Ghatiyali, was it under the rule (*rāj*) of the English or of the great kings?[13]

JAMUNI: The great kings—Vansh Pradip Singh ji [each syllable is enunciated fully and carefully, including the honorific "ji" which may be attached to a name or used independently].

BHOJU: Did you see him?

JAMUNI: Yes I saw him. They used to give us bread, feasts, and I have seen both the queen and the king.

[Vansh Pradip Singh had two wives but probably did not travel in state with both at once.]

BHOJU: In Sawar or here?

JAMUNI: They used to come here, riding in a motor car; and they used to sit on the bank of the water reservoir (*talāb*); we came from this side and from that side and in the middle was the king; and the queen would call the unpaid female laborers [*begārī-wālī*, among whom Jamuni would be numbered], and we used to sing songs to her and dance for her.[14]

BHOJU: Did the Court call you, or did the queen?

JAMUNI: The Court, they both called.

BHOJU: When did he come here?

JAMUNI: When he felt like it . . . about once every eight days. The king and queen used to stay together.

BHOJU: When the Court came here, what kind of conscripted labor (*begār*) did you do?

JAMUNI: Cots: we used to carry their beds from the fort to the banks of the water reservoir; or if they went to Vajta, we carried them to Vajta.[15]

[Vajta is a nearby village, perhaps a thirty-minute walk through the fields—a hike I have enjoyed, at my leisure, in pleasant weather. However, I can well imagine the discomforts of this distance, bearing a heavy wooden cot, in heat or rain.]

BHOJU: Who were the king's men?

JAMUNI: The bosses (*hākim*) were Akka Singhji, Bhopal Singhji,

Chattur Singhji, they were all bosses.[16] And the *kiledār* (commandant of the fort) was Bhairu Dhabhai.[17] They all were with the
Court: and Ram Chandra Babaji [whose role is unidentified]. All
these people could tell us what to do; what they said, we did.

And besides this, we ground grain for the horses. [Now she
begins to speak on women's special work.]

On the road to Dev Narayan [a shrine to the side of one main
road leading out from Ghatiyali's center] there used to be a step-
well.[18] From there we took the barley and alfalfa crops to the fort
[as fodder for the horses].

And the place where Shobhag Mal Jain now lives—that was the
rulers' livestock pen (*nohrā*). There we used to do the work of
collecting cow dung—for twenty to twenty-five cows.[19]
[Note how embedded in the now transformed landscape are her
memories; how she locates these memories precisely in the present-
day landscape, but in the context of vanished or altered landmarks.]
. . . .

BHOJU: What did he give you?

JAMUNI: He gave us nothing at all, it was *begār*, we worked for
free [her voice becomes high-pitched, plaintive, expressive, almost
comical or teasing].

BHOJU: Did you take bread?

JAMUNI: No, no bread, no day wages (*mazdūrī*), nothing [emphatic]!
It was only the farmers who gave us grain for repairing their shoes,
but from the rulers we got nothing.

BHOJU: Sometimes when there was a famine, at that time did they give
any help to the farmers?

JAMUNI: They gave nothing.
. . . .

BHOJU: Suppose you didn't go in *begār*, what would happen?

JAMUNI: They would give insults.[20]

BHOJU: Did they beat?

JAMUNI: No they didn't ever beat; well, sometimes they did. Once
Sukka Regar didn't go and the boss Akka Singh beat him.

BHOJU: Did the Court find out?

JAMUNI: No, who would tell him? But the Court himself didn't do
these things, he did not give this trouble.

. . . .

BHOJU: I heard that when you went to grind for the horses, he gave two or three maunds of grain to one single woman to grind.[21]

JAMUNI: We would get a pain in our chest from grinding but still we had to grind. One woman, ten bundles; and we tossed two carts of cow dung daily. We had to collect it and throw it into the dung pile.

BHOJU: What did you get for that?

JAMUNI: Nothing, nothing! [Jamuni is by now thoroughly exasperated with Bhoju's seeming denseness.] He would give one *seer*, two *seers* of grain and that's all.[22]

BHOJU: What *jātis* went?

JAMUNI: Only Regar and Chamar went.[23]

. . . .

BHOJU: If there were things to send from one village to another, was it done with *begārī*?

JAMUNI: Yes.

BHOJU: What were the other villages?

JAMUNI: Nadi, Vajta, Khera; and as far as Sawar, we were going every day, so often.

BHOJU: What kind of things did you take to Sawar?

JAMUNI: Onions, opium . . . suppose they don't have any onions, [they say] "Go get them from Ghatiyali," or whatever; or suppose someone runs out of opium, "Go get it from Sawar" . . . or "from Ghatiyali."

. . . .

BHOJU: For how many years did you go in *begārī*?

JAMUNI: From my birth, from when I came to Ghatiyali,[24] until the Court died, after his death.

BHOJU: Did you do *begārī* for the Chausala-*vāla*?[25]

JAMUNI: No, never.

. . . .

BHOJU: Did the Napa ka Khera people have to do *begārī*?

JAMUNI: Only if there was work there [in Napa ka Khera], but they didn't come here; here there was more work.

Sometimes the Court came to spend the night. So in the day the Malis and Gujars took the beds, and made you sleep on the floor. And even if a woman was in childbirth labor, they would put her on the ground. [This outrage was given as an example in numerous interviews, with farmers as well as leatherworkers. Whether it happened once or never, it has become a condensed sign of past oppressions.]

BHOJU: Did they take beds and bedding too?

JAMUNI: They just took beds . . . maybe they [the nobility] had their own bedding [she muses].

BHOJU: How long did they keep them?

JAMUNI: After they [the Court and his party] left, the bosses told the farmers to take them back.

BHOJU: Where did you get your firewood in those days?

JAMUNI: At that time we used to get dry wood from the jungle, and one bundle we would send to the fort—a smaller one—and one we could take home.

. . . .

But when someone died, he [*the Court*] gave the fuel to construct the cremation pyre. They used to gather fuel from the jungle—the Bhils[26] and the *begārī* workers. They piled it up where they made limestone, and anyone could take wood from there for cremation.

[It seemed that the single stringless and unfailing generosity of the Court was to give fuel for the cremation pyre; person after person mentioned this. Some mentioned it uncritically, as a genuine boon, while others spoke of it with palpable cynicism. Soon this often-repeated information became a somewhat macabre joke between me and Bhoju.]

. . . .

BHOJU: And if you have a mango tree in your field, do you eat the fruit or bring it to the Court?

JAMUNI: He would eat all of them, take all of them; but we would steal and eat.[27] The children could take the unripe fruits (*keri*),[28] but the adults couldn't take anything.

. . . .

BHOJU: What did the Court take from the farmers?

JAMUNI: Whatever their field was, he used to send a rope, and measure it, and then say, "In this much space, so much grain will be produced."

And then, the royal crier (*rāj balāī*) and the land-record officer (*kānūngo*) [would show up]—and for the two of them, *begārī* workers went cutting and filling two sacks—one for the royal crier and one for the land-record officer—off the top.

. . . .

And if the farmer had nothing he still had to send grain, and if he ended up with no grain he had to take loans from the *baniyā* (merchant and moneylender).[29]

. . . .

BHOJU: So at that time were you ever troubled by wild animals?

JAMUNI: We were very much troubled by pigs. Before we planted the seeds we took our bedding there [to the fields]. And our women took the grindstones to the fields too [so they could make bread!]. If we returned to the village long enough to grind flour, the pigs would eat the grain in the fields.

BHOJU: He didn't let you kill them?

JAMUNI: No, only the Court could kill them, nobody else could. We used to beat the bushes for him.

[Note the subtle quick transition here between the oppression caused by the Court's protection of pigs and memories of heroism and largesse.]

Once Bardu Regar's father was beating the bushes, and a tiger (*śer*) grabbed him. His hand was in the tiger's mouth, and the Court shot the tiger and saved him.

When his hunt was successful he [Vansh Pradip Singh] would give a feast to those who had been beating the bushes.

He was so big that five or six people had to help him into the hunting tower (*mālo*) and sit him down there.

. . . .

BHOJU: Was that time happy, or now?

JAMUNI: Recently, we have had a lot of trouble, for the past year [because production has not been good]—but in the time of Indira Gandhi there were no difficulties, it never happened.

But in *that* time [*ū ṭaim*, the deeper past, the time of the great kings] we were really unhappy. He wouldn't let us sleep on beds and women couldn't wear silver; at that time we had to wear thick cloth; we couldn't wear fine cotton. But now there are no such difficulties: you sit on a bed, I sit on a bed. . . .

[As Jamuni's photograph reveals, she is not at this time sitting on the bed; Bhoju and I have been politely seated on a cot, and Jamuni herself is squatting on the ground.]30

He didn't let us wear shoes in the village; and in the fields if some *hākim* came, then we had to take off our shoes.

BHOJU: In cold, heat, and rain [the names of the three seasons, hence, all kinds of weather] . . . always?

JAMUNI: Yes, we used to wear shoes in the field, but when we came close to the village we took off our shoes.

. . . .

And at that time, they made us wear black cloth, no beautiful clothes, and we couldn't wear an open shirt with buttons; we could only wear hand-woven cotton cloth, thick. And the turban could not have a tassel.

Now these laws, they are all gone.

. . . .

BHOJU: If the rule of the great kings came back, would we live happily?

JAMUNI: Who knows? I am going to the cremation ground, and I don't know what the new generation is thinking. If those who come after me think it's good, or not good, it is their business, not mine, because I am going to the cremation ground.

But [reconsidering], it would be sorrowful to have to go back to *begār*. Now it is well.

. . . .

BHOJU: At that time, what *jāti*s were rich?

JAMUNI: Many, but we Regar were very badly off.31 At that time those who had sheep and goats were happy, and those who had cows and buffaloes were happy, and those who had fields with good grain production were happy.

BHOJU: Were Mali (gardeners) and Loda (farmers) happy?

JAMUNI: Yes, because then there was a lot of rain.

BHOJU: So now you said there used to be a lot of rain . . . why is there less rain today?

JAMUNI: I don't know why. . . . Well, there used to be more dharm; people's behavior was good. There was love, conviviality (*baiṭh uṭh*).32 But now there is conceit (*abhimān*).33 Today you do your work, and I do my work. [That is, people don't help one another as in the past.]

In the cold season we used to make a fire and sit around it all night.[34] The way that humans have changed, the Lord also has changed. [She implies that for this reason there is less rain.]

BHOJU: There used to be a lot of trees? Where did they go?

JAMUNI: The kings and the trees both went, they were all consumed. There used to be *dhok* trees, but when the rule of the kings was over the *dhok* went too.

And a wind came and *vilāyatī bambūl* seeds came in the wind and now they will never be finished, who knows where they came from![35]

. . . .

Nowadays, in our colony, all things are finished. Nowadays, Brahmins and Baniyas eat meat, all our chickens are finished because of that. [I did not understand this, but Bhoju explained to me later that high-caste people buy and eat the Regars' chickens. Now the poor folks who raise chickens can no longer afford to eat them. This is a sign of degenerate times, as Brahmins and Baniyas ought to be pure vegetarians.]

Today neither sin nor virtue remains; [*people*] have become corrupted (*bhriṣṭ ho gayā*); [*people*] have become conceited (*abhimān ho gayā*).

BHOJU: Were you happy in that time, or today?

JAMUNI: Today there is happiness . . . well, even now there is sorrow in the house, but what can we do?

But in *begāri* we *always* remained sorrowful.

ANN: How can you say virtue is finished when all the temples have been improved?

JAMUNI: There are people who give donations, and of their own accord do this kind of work. For some people have a moral feeling, and others work with them.

[I think what she means here is that although no general community spirit remains, individual persons may practice moral virtue; there is a way this is merely a more positive outcome of conceit, rather than proof of morality enduring within the community.]

. . . .

BHOJU: Your grandchildren, do you send them to school to learn to read?

JAMUNI [pointing to a child present, perhaps eight or ten years old]:

He is my grandson and he goes to school, and we will have him
study as long as he will study (*jab tak tab tak*).

BHOJU: Could you Regars go to school, then, in the time of the Court?

JAMUNI: They [*children*] could go but they didn't; we would send
them and they would go somewhere else on the way, hide—but it
was not a problem with "Regars." [That is, she insists, untouch-
ables were not legally forbidden education.]

In Ghatiyali, the middle school has been here since the time of
the Court, and we sent them, but—who knows? They would slip
away. They went to the fields or into the jungle, but they didn't go
to school. But the Court never *forbade begārī* children to go to
school.

. . . .

[Because of the close association between schooling and jobs, Jamuni
launched into a lengthy narrative about her son, who after minimal
education tried to get into the army but was rejected because of his
undersize chest measurement. Jamuni had prayed to the goddess that
the army would reject him, while her husband prayed that he would
be accepted.]

His father said to Mataji [the goddess], "If he enters the army I
will offer you a splendid feast (*savāmaṇī*)" and his mother said, "If
he *doesn't* enter the army I will offer you a splendid feast."[36] I said,
"Let my son return! let my son return!" I didn't eat bread for all the
time he was gone, I only ate when he came back.

BHOJU: Think, if he had gone in the army how good it would have
been.

JAMUNI [emphatically disagreeing]: I would have no one with me.
Who would stay with me? Now he has had children. . . . [Jamuni's
voice again sounds as if she is close to tears, reliving the long past
anguish of contemplating losing her son to the army.]

BHOJU: Now this new generation, if someone wants to go will you let
them go?

JAMUNI: Yes, I will let them go and that's why we are sending them to
school, and you people should help them.

Recurrent motifs emerge and repeat in this and many of our interviews. This is partly because we deliberately elicited them once we
identified them. But it is also because there exists—as collective mem-

ory—a set of common tropes for the narrative of "that time" (ū ṭaim), the time of great kings. These tropes both evocatively epitomize and help to organize memories. Most of these appear in the interview with Jamuni Regar, and for this reason I placed it first. From her words much that follows might be extrapolated.

Jamuni begins, at our request, with the persona of the Court. She describes the ways he maintained his regal power, through insults more than punishments. The abjection of forced labor was a major part of the wretchedness of those days, as were the prohibitions on desired goods. At the same time, we gather from her embedded account a sense of family and community as strongholds even under conditions of cruel deprivation and incursion. Jamuni elaborates on the lāṭo-kūṭo, or grain tax, even though her largely landless community did not suffer so much from this tax. The jungle with its forest products and wild animals is a recurrent space and resource throughout her fluid narrative. As do many others, Jamuni links today's decreases in trees and rain with increased selfish egotism. She describes the transformed landscape colonized by alien vegetation and the children educated to alien futures.

5. SHOES

Rajasthan is perceived by an outsider as a land of chivalry, heroism and self-sacrifice. It is also known by the "styles of life" and cultural uniqueness of its princes. . . . Not many sociological studies are available on how feudal lords exploited peasants, artisans and workers.—K. L. Sharma, *Caste, Feudalism, and Peasantry*

The shoe was ready for everyone, whether they did something wrong or not. . . . Whatever the village crier [*gāṅv balāī*][1] or the king's man says, it is always the Truth. "Why did you piss in front of the sun? Let's beat him!". . . . Whoever was happy was happy, and whoever got the shoe, got the shoe, and kept on getting it.[2]—Mumtaz Ali, interview, 1997

In the last days of the kingdom of Sawar, shoes were what American cultural and symbolic anthropologists in the 1970s might have named a key or regnant symbol ordering coherent galaxies of meanings as well as shaping praxis.[3] In the 1980s, we might have traced shoes, playfully or dolefully, as a narrative trope—noting the intertextualities loosely knitting individual testimonies into a discourse of power where shoes are fluid signs of hegemonic rule, abjection, and at times, muted resistance.[4] As we think about shoes from the vantage or despair of the thoroughly post-all present, they may serve as evocative if elusive media of contested power in its multiple refractions. Shoes—depending on which hands wield them, or which feet they grace—generate fear or pride, surrender or defiance, and on occasion, black comedy. There are quite a few Rajasthani jokes about shoes, but much that they represent is not really funny.[5]

Rule of the Shoe and Rules of the Shoe Games

In this chapter we consider several distinctive modalities of shoe power. First, we conjure the violent essence of local hegemony lodged in an oversized shoe, a crushing sanction against resistance to despotism. This shoe may have hung in the royal forts of Sawar and in neighboring kingdoms. Second, we show how ordinary shoes—taken for granted on nonchalant privileged feet—become outrageous. We hear of occasions when well-shod kings' men stomped insolently into farmers' kitchens or gardens without slipping off their shoes. The latter act is a given of common courtesy and mutual respect automatically performed even today. The *darbār*, we heard tell from one probably unreliable source, even wore his shoes into the temple; but he was the *darbār* and hence, by virtue of birth and nature, incorrigible. The troubling obverse of this second dimension of shoe power is the way that low-born persons (including all females) were subject to punishment if caught wearing shoes in the presence of superiors. To my imagination, stirred by these histories from below, the most poignant aspect of shoes is lack: their absence from the naked and suffering feet of the poor and of women. In closing this chapter we apprehend the hated abjection of forced labor, or *begār*, with a painful story of bare feet.

Speaking the language of shoes, our aim is to pace off gross and subtle parameters of hierarchy and its underpinnings in the last half-century of Sawar's history. Shoes are partially about display. They are leather, and may be embroidered; they have attributes of color, shape, and smell, as well as function. But the discourse of shoes/power is interlocked with several other discourses that are less tangible: shapeless and odorless, if not purposeless. Prominent and heavy among those discourses meshed with the language of shoes is that of honor—*ijjat*.[6] To simplify: a shoe-beating, if administered, would destroy honor. But to resist a shoe-beating is to sustain honor, and hence to rise in others' estimation. Wearing shoes in front of superiors affronts their honor, and is accordingly insufferable. If persons offended do not act against the challenge, they themselves lose face.

The rules of the shoe game were based on complex emotions having more to do with honor and shame than with violence and pain. No one ever spoke of pain in connection with shoe-beatings, only dishonor. Bare feet, at times, were an acknowledged source of physical suffering. Of course, the personal pain experienced on violated honor may be as or more acute than the pain experienced on a beating. Haidar Ali, a Muslim shopkeeper in Ghatiyali, bluntly states that shoe-beatings dishonored their victims. He was not one to mince words in his critique of the time of kings. Bhoju asked him about justice in the old days, which many persons praised in contrast to the prolonged, costly, corrupt legal system of modernity. Haidar Ali had this to say about "justice" under the kings: "It was nothing, it was just that whatever the boss (*hākim*) said people did, and nobody wondered, "is it true or just?" Whatever he said, that's correct. . . . Today we can go court, but it used to be that the great kings had a shoe for beating, and they would dishonor people with it [make people *beijjat*]."

Beyond honor, more implicit than explicit in our Sawar narratives, another domain of shoe talk would have to be located within the anthropologically famous Hindu concern for purity [*pavitratā; śuddhatā*]. Shoes are, of course, doubly impure: first because they go on feet, which are lowly in myth and function; second because they come in contact with the literal filth on the ground: feces, saliva, and other bodily effluvia, all prime sources of pollution.[7] Note, however, that not one of our interviewees ever spoke directly of impurity in connection with shoe-beatings. The result of a shoe-beating was always interpreted not as pollution but as dishonor. I think pollution is salient in helping us to understand why it would be such an outrage for the king's men to wear shoes into a potter's kitchen (where he is likely to have his family deities enshrined) or into a gardener's plot (which he himself thinks of as a Shiva temple, and where economic damage is likely to compound the purity violation).[8] Purity is evidently linked with honor; to have one's purity defiled, without resisting, is to lose face.

The language of shoes expresses some blunt, obvious assumptions of rank: ruler over subjects, master over servant, male over female. Shoe-beatings were threatened sanctions, stylized violence. In terms of its efficacy in upholding a king's regime, the shoe in Sawar may be reminiscent of the concept of *daṇḍa:* the stick, defined by Kautilya in his *Arthashastra*—the classical Hindu guidebook for rulers, which was composed during the first centuries of the common era.[9] *Daṇḍa*, as "the coercive power of the state" consists in fines and punishments (L. N. Rangarajan 1992:94). Fines were part of the ruling apparatus in Sawar also. In fact, sentences of beating were often commuted to fines through rulers' acts of clemency. But I think it would be an error simplistically to equate Sawar's shoe with Kautilya's stick. The shoe in Sawar seems to be more subtle and more polyvocal, its calculated violence psychological rather than corporal.[10]

DISHONOR DOUBLED

In 1993 persons we interviewed often alluded to the sanction of shoe-beating in the context of our questions, which we frequently focused on the protection of forests and wildlife under the *rājā-mahārājās*. Assembling the basic details from numerous accounts, I can offer a composite, speculative description of the situation. I stress that neither Bhoju nor I were ever able to corroborate all the details to our perfect satisfaction.

An untouchable "sweeper" employed in the fort was "ready" to administer a "shoe-beating" to anyone who defied the Court's orders. These infractions included game poaching and wood cutting. But they might be any violations of a requirement stipulated by power, however petty or arbitrary, as Mumtaz Ali so eloquently expresses it in the epigraph to this chapter. While some of our recorded accounts specify "two shoe-blows" others refer to "five hundred." Significantly, far more persons tell of threatened than of administered shoe-beatings.

The sweeper, whose blows personified dishonor, was almost universally referred to in our interviews by the degrading caste name Bhangi. I was struck by this because, at least in my company in the 1980s and 90s, it was far more common for people to use the polite "Harijan" in ordinary conversations. I believe that, in the context of explaining the genuine potent efficacy of the shoe-beating sanction, the degrading caste name Bhangi was required as a linguistic marker. To speak of a beating by the hand of a Harijan would simply not evoke the powerful repugnance immediately conveyed by Bhangi.[11] Evidently, what inspired public fear of the shoe was not physical pain but intense humiliation.

The shoe itself was often described as special, oversized ("one and one-quarter hands long" *savā hāth lambā*), and dedicated to the purpose of punishment.[12] It was not an everyday shoe, and was kept ready—hanging on the wall in the fort (in each fort, that is, for Sawar was not the only place where the shoe ruled). Some persons located it specifically in the stables. As a symbolic, unworn shoe it is more dignified, courtly, and less polluting in the common "dirty" sense. Yet a beating with it, held in the hands of the untouchable sweeper, would be no less dishonoring. A few embellished accounts included the notion that the especially long shoe had little bells on it. Perhaps the little bells would jingle insolently when beatings were administered. Perhaps the entire village could hear them ring and thereby know that something degrading was happening to whomever had been so rash as to disobey the authorities. This fanciful detail does not appear in any recorded interview, and I am not sure who planted it in our minds. I am, however, pretty sure that the jingling of little bells from inside the fort would not easily reach the ears of villagers below. Nonetheless, the aural image is compelling.

The effective power of the combination of polluted Bhangi and polluted shoe seemed limitless, if not mythic. As we conversed about it while these histories unfolded, Bhoju coined the term *jūte kā rāj* ("rule of the shoe") to describe the time of kings. For royal authority to be vested in shoe and sweeper was emblematic of ugliness and abjection, as if all that upheld the court's grandeur in that time were degraded. But there were, of course, other sides to the story of rule.

The other recurrent, narrative motif involving shoes—who may and who may not wear them in front of whom—also has to do, less dramatically but more immanently, with dominion and abasement, with symbolic enactments of rank that are equally an everyday violence. Real shoes either adorning and protecting or absent from real feet are indicators, both abstract and material, of caste and gender hierarchies in that time.[13] Very simply, the rules are that persons of rank wear shoes anywhere, but persons of no account must go barefoot—at least when near superiors. Who wears shoes in whose presence indexes rank. No human being should wear shoes in the presence of God. In every household the kitchen is a pure place where no person wears shoes. Gardeners hold their garden plots to be like Shiva's temples, and therefore their caste customs forbid shoes to be worn into gardens.

The ban on wearing shoes in the company of rulers, or any social superiors, was one among many bans (*pratibandh*, introduced thematically in chapter 3 and elaborated by Jamuni Regar in chapter 4). These *pratibandh* included bans on wearing gold and silver adornment, on wearing finely woven cloth, on eating or serving guests foods cooked with white sugar or white flour, and on bridegrooms riding a horse through the village streets on their wedding day.[14] For the sake of argument, we might bracket the emotional investment such display items definitely hold, and their consequent weight as sources of prestige, clout, and honor. Given this, all these restrictions might well strike outsiders as deprivations of what were, in any case, rare luxuries. For the poor, as many of our interviewees bluntly stated, these prohibitions truly were symbolic. Most persons forbidden them could not in any case afford them. The extreme example of this was a ban on building *pakkā* (brick or stone) houses, which many frankly laughed off when we asked about it. In those days people could barely fill their stomachs, we were told, so where would they find the resources to build houses?

The ban on shoes differs from the other bans. Shoes are not as costly as gold, horses, or fine cloth. Although they do represent an investment of scarce resources, their practical value, enhancing physical capacity for productive work, makes them "worth" it in a way different from adornment. Bare feet cause obvious discomfort and represent health hazards in mud, hot sand, or winter chill, all of which are met in the Rajasthani seasonal cycle. Unshod persons are vulnerable to thorns, snakes, worms, cuts, and blisters.

In the sections that follow we speak first of shoe-beatings avoided and received; and second of shoe bans where the subservient behavior demanded of subjects before rulers is immediately parallel to the behavior required of women before men.

SHOE-BEATINGS MANQUÉ

Many of the shoe-beating tales we were able to elicit with any amount of realistic detail were of shoe-beatings avoided—threatened but never ultimately inflicted.

In a 1993 interview, Ugma Loda told a comical story about an abortive shoe-beating. Ugma was a farmer, almost sixty-six years old.

He told us he had first grazed cows; then studied for two years; then left school to join his father in farming, which has been his métier ever since. He related his story in the context of describing sanctions for wildlife protection. In this particular case, however, the infraction was sheer disobedience.

UGMA: And the wild animals destroyed our fields and we could do nothing.

BHOJU: If you killed an animal, then what?

UGMA: Well, if they found out then they would call us and punish us, but if no one knows, then, no matter! And they had a Bhangi who would beat people with a shoe: this was the worst punishment, to be beaten by a Bhangi!

Once they called Gopal Chamar to the fort, and he couldn't come.

[Chamars, like Regars, are leatherworkers and also stigmatized as untouchable, but they would hold themselves superior to sweepers. Presumably the Chamar was called to perform *begār* or unpaid work by the king's men.]

So they called him the next day, and they asked him why he had not come before, and he said, "Because my children were hungry and their mother wasn't there."

They said, "You must be punished; we will have you beaten with the shoe."

So they sat him down, and several hours went by and they didn't beat him or let him go; so he begged them, "Please beat me with the shoe if you're going to beat me, I'm late!" So they started to laugh, and they let him go. At that time he was the only earning person in the family.

What might this anecdote reveal about the "rule of the shoe"? That good humor and a patronizing compassion mitigates its severity, or that the arrogant bosses have amassed sufficient symbolic capital to enable them to be generous, arbitrarily, on whim? Which of these morals, we might wonder, did Ugma Loda want to convey to us with this tale? We were too new at the game then to probe further, but I suspect it would be both. There is also a whiff of trickster resistance here, which emerges more sharply when we contrast this episode with another.

Amba Lal Loda, also in 1993, narrated another episode of an averted shoe-beating, this one involving a direct appeal to the *darbār,* and perhaps a veiled heroic challenge to the *darbār*'s sense of honor. This is evidently a risky game, but in this case the proud peasant succeeds in winning. Whereas in the preceding episode a Loda tells with mingled humorous compassion and slight scorn a story about a Chamar; in this case we hear a Loda speak with pride of another Loda who stands up fiercely for his honor. His triumph is shared by his community, and there is clear relish in narrating it. The subject of the story, Dhula (now deceased), belonged to a highly respected and prosperous family in the Loda community, and he was the father of Ladu Loda, who appears elsewhere in these pages.

Although in the first anecdote the king's men are the deflected punishers, seen as vulnerable to self-deprecating trickster tactics, here the *darbār* himself is an actor. He is portrayed as responsive—displaying appropriate compassion and magnanimity. He dramatizes his own humanity and compassion; he recognizes and appreciates his subject's gutsiness. He maintains authority through a charmed combination of all these gambits.[15]

Amba Lal is describing the "sorrows" of those times and the particular duties of Lodas vis-à-vis the Court.

AMBA LAL: If he [the Court] had a guest, then he would say, "Hey, I have a guest, so bring me mattresses and cots!" And suppose we [Lodas, farmers] didn't do this work, what would happen? He would have the Bhangi apply the shoe to us!

BHOJU: When he had the shoe applied to us [Bhoju uses an inclusive "us" speaking as a fellow-sufferer from the broader peasant community], could we take our opposition (*khilāph*) to a court of law or some such thing?

AMBA LAL: No no no! Nobody went to the courts. Once something happened: Dhula Loda, he refused to do something, to give a cot or something, and the *darbār* called him to the fort, and gave an order to the Bhangi: "He didn't do my work, so give him two blows with the shoe."

So at this time Dhula Loda said [to Vansh Pradip Singh directly], "Only you can beat me. If the Bhangi beats me, I'll kill the Bhangi, or I'll kill myself, but I won't let him beat me."

So the *darbār* let him go, and he didn't beat him. The *darbār* said, "You have made mistakes one hundred times, and I forgive you, but never come here again as an offender!"

This is a no-fault conclusion; everyone maintains their honor. Of course, the *darbār* has an imperial edge, but at the same time he is portrayed as appreciative of Dhula's stance. There is a hint that Dhula's self-respect has gotten him in trouble more than once, but also a hint that the *darbār* respects this strength of character.

Note the striking difference between these two narratives. Dhula the clean-caste farmer escapes the shoe-beating by standing on his honor, even though his threats of suicide and murder are likely to have been understood as bluffs by all the players, including himself. By contrast, Gopal the untouchable leatherworker evades the shoe through apparent simple-mindedness. Moreover, his single-minded concern for his children, his absent wife, and hence his consequently emasculated house-husband role, all contrive to make him a figure of amusement for the nobility. He does not avoid this identity, but rather exploits it to his advantage.[16]

WAS THERE A SHOE?

In 1997 we sought to flesh out our understanding of the foundations of authority in pre-Independence Sawar. If it truly rested on a shoe one and one-quarter hands long, we wanted to document this. But we found that it was extremely difficult to obtain specifics. Most everyone was vague. Some, especially Rajputs, denied with fair regularity the very existence of a shoe, asserting its chimerical nature. Many others said that there was indeed a shoe but it was never used, or at least they had never witnessed its use. One man claimed that beatings had taken place in Ghatiyali's fort by a man belonging to a known Harijan family, and he named names. But we were unable to confirm his account because the named persons were deceased.

Early in 1997 we spoke with Bankat Singh Kamdar Shaktavat, a member of the Court's own lineage who lived near the Dark Garden ("Andhera Bagh," a lovely tree-filled park belonging to the Sawar royal family) in the Sawar Ravalo just below the fort. He gave his age as about sixty-nine years old. In his youth, as a Kamdar, he had been an active participant in the administrative apparatus of the *darbār*.

BHOJU: I heard about a shoe, one and one-quarter hands long, with little bells on it.

BANKAT: No one has seen it and no one was ever beaten! [His swift denial strikes me as rather abrupt.] It's just that the *darbār* would say, "Have the Bhangi give him one hundred blows!" But he never carried it out. I never saw it.

Bhoju's interpretation of this denial, proffered as we transcribed the tape, epitomized to me one important aspect of the "rule of the shoe." He suggested that "people understand that there was no such shoe, and no Bhangi would apply it, but still they were afraid." In a way, whether there was or was not a shoe is of no import. In collective memory the regime's credibility was fueled by the idea of a shoe. Nonetheless, we have enough accounts of actual events to convince both of us that shoe-beatings probably did occasionally, if rarely, take place in Sawar in the twentieth century.

The following short tale, told by Kishan Lal Gujar of Sawar in 1997, reveals that pride and bravery and bluffing did not always succeed in fending off the shoe.

BHOJU: Did the Bhangi really beat people? Was that real or just a fear?

KISHAN: No, it's true, the Court did have people beaten by the Bhangi. Once . . . the manager was Samān Singh, and our Kalyan Gujar said to him, "Please distribute the grain quickly, because we are troubled at the threshing ground."

And they had a fight—Kalyan Gujar and Saman Singh. So, Saman Singh had him called in, before the Court, and the Court had him beaten by the Bhangi. And Kalyan Gujar said, "The Court is here with us now, but if I ever meet you alone I will kill you." [It is not clear whether he is speaking to Saman Singh or to the Bhangi; and we were unable to trace more details or learn the aftermath of this tale.]

From a Sawar Brahmin that same month we heard another tale of a shoe-beating averted for the sake of honor. Sampat Lal, the narrator here, came from a Brahmin family affiliated with the fort as royal priest. He told us he had reached an age of understanding (eleven or twelve) when Vansh Pradip Singh was ruling. His father, Ganpat Lal, had been *Tehsīldār* (subcollector of revenue). At this point in the interview we were discussing a judgment the *darbār* passed on a sexual offender. This was one of the few crimes the *darbār* himself abhorred sufficiently to punish with more than threats. Sampat Lal states:

> There was also a Jain mahajan [member of the merchant community] who was misbehaving [doing *badmaś;* may mean any kind of naughtiness in children, when applied to adults it implies sexual misconduct].[17] The Court did not send him to jail, but he fined him. This was Bhavar Lal's father. The *darbār* condemned him to five hundred shoe blows.
>
> The other Mahajans requested, "Don't let the Bhangi do it, it will hurt our honor [*ijjat*]." So he gave a five-hundred-rupee fine instead. The Court threatened, and because of this people were afraid.

In this case the offender was a member of the merchant class, for whom the dishonor of shoe-beating, particularly as administered by a Bhangi, would have been an unthinkable fate worse than death. Moreover, the shame was not confined to the individual; his entire community would have been implicated, as the *darbār* well knew.[18] Thus, in spite of his rage at sexual misconduct, the Court responded with clemency, commuting the sentence to a steep fine.

Chalak Dan, a Charan in Rajpura, just outside Sawar, told us he was still a child when the *darbār* died. He testified to actual shoe-beatings, but without providing details of case or name.

CHALAK DAN: During the time of Vansh Pradip Singh the peasants were very sorrowful (*dukhi*). Chotu Bhil used to come to our village, and people used to bring him cups full of milk, ghi, yogurt because he was the king's man, the Court's Bhil! [enunciated with scorn]. That's how afraid people were![19]
[Bhoju comments: "They paid him as much attention as today they pay the chief of police!"]
At that time there were many wild pigs, and the *darbār* still didn't kill them, and if someone else did then he called them into the fort and had them beaten terribly. . . . If the farmers slept then the pigs would destroy their crops.
BHOJU: Didn't they complain?

CHALAK DAN: If they did, he beat them with his shoe: "The pigs are eating your crops, you eat this!"

As noted above, the verb "to eat," coupled with blows, combines incorporation with humiliation and degradation. The parallel structure here confirms the salience of eating in this locution: to eat shoe blows is to internalize the degradation of a shoe-beating.

Chalak Dan, whose entire interview revealed hostility to the Court, does not bother to pose a Bhangi as intermediary, or even to employ the causative "to have beaten with a shoe" rather than the transitive "beat." He makes it sound as if the shoe would be in the Court's own hand, which is quite unimaginable.

Ganga Ram Mina was very close to Bhoju's family, and since 1980 we had interviewed him many times on a variety of subjects. He possessed an enormous store of knowledge about festivals and myths, agriculture, and local history. In 1997, having farmed for fifty years, he had "retired" from physical labor and was regularly to be found sitting on the raised platform surrounding the Mataji temple, just a few yards from Bhoju's house. Often he was knitting (not a common occupation for men, but after a lifetime of labor it troubled him to sit idle).

We probed him about the source of the *rājā-mahārājā*'s authority: why would people agree to work without pay?

BHOJU: Suppose someone said, "I won't do *begār*." What then?

GANGA RAM: No, he had to do it, and if he refused, the shoe fell.

BHOJU: Yes, I've heard there was a shoe and he had people beaten by the Bhangi—is it true?

GANGA RAM: Yes, it is true. The Bhangi used to beat. He always stayed in the fort, and whenever any boss wanted to have somebody beaten, the Bhangi would do it in the place where horses were tied. They would tie him [the offender] up and have him beaten.

From this we gather that a lowly location, the stable, was used as the setting for the degrading punishment. It is also realistic, as members of the sweeper community performed their conscripted labor in the royal stables.

Speaking with another long-time friend, Gokul Mali, in his field in 1997, we covered the by now familiar nexus of the *darbār*'s conservation policies, his protection of trees and wildlife, and the threat of shoe-beatings. Gokul told us he was in his teens at the time of Vansh Pradip Singh's death in [*samvat*] 2005; he is still a vigorous and active farmer in his sixties.

BHOJU: Were there a lot of animals?

GOKUL: Yes a lot. And no one else [besides the *darbār* himself] could kill them. If someone did, they [the king's men] would have that person beaten. If someone killed some animal, then he was beaten.

BHOJU: Did the Court know about this?

GOKUL [sidestepping the question]: They called us into the fort and had the Bhangi beat us.

BHOJU: I have heard there was a shoe that was one and one-quarter hands long (*savā hāth lambā jūtā thā*).

GOKUL: Bhajjalal Bhangi [his son Gopi Lal still lives in the fort and takes care of the *darbār*'s horses]—this was the Bhangi who did the shoe-beating.

Once, a boy, Bhura Mali, Bhagirath Mali's son, he killed a boar. He was the leader, and the knowledge came to the fort. Everyone ran away, but they caught Bhura. Someone from the fort caught him. And they took Bhura along with the pot of meat he was cooking [boar meat]. They took him to the fort and beat him badly (*khūb pītā*). And they also fined him.

Because the *darbār* scattered grain for them [the pigs], and set up water tanks for them, by the fort and on the hill.

Gokul's account includes a youth of his own community who was punished with a terrible beating for pig poaching. There is no rescue, no sentence commuted, no honor upheld in this story. Perhaps because it is a "boy," the blemish is less acute to recall. Note the deliberate contrast set up here between the Court's kindness to pigs and his cruelty to the Mali boy.[20]

From a respected Muslim shopkeeper, Mumtaz Ali (with whose words I prefaced this chapter), we gleaned some powerful critiques of the kings' rule. Bhoju asked him about the bans (*pratibandh*):

BHOJU: I heard that . . . they didn't let you wear nice clothes, was it like that?

Gokal Mali poses with papaya tree, outside Ghatiyali, 1997.

MUMTAZ: Yes, even if we did not greet the guards and chiefs and bosses [*syāṇā sardār hākam*] then they beat us with shoes.
. . . .

BHOJU: Did they beat people in Ghatiyali fort?

MUMTAZ ALI: People say that they beat.

BHOJU: I know that the Malis had to do forced labor.

MUMTAZ ALI: It wasn't about Malis or whatever . . . the shoe was ready for everyone, whether they did something wrong or not. . . . Whatever the village crier [*gāṅv balāī*] or the king's man says, it is always the Truth. "Why did you piss in front of the sun? Let's beat him!". . . . Whoever was happy was happy, and whoever got the shoe got the shoe, and kept on getting it. In those times, the poor were dying, and today too, they are dying; and those rich people who were blissful then, today too they are blissful.

Although Mumtaz is one of the most acerbic in his critiques of the former rulers, he waffles slightly nonetheless on the actuality of beatings in Ghatiyali: "People say they beat." He has no personal testimony, no witnessed moments, to offer. He is also more cynical about the genuine "trickle down" impact of democratic reforms than many other speakers are.

The oversize shoe—myth or reality—was not unique to the kingdom of Sawar. In Mehru we spoke with Ram Dev Regar from Choti Mehru, who was then about fifty-one years old. His *thākur* [*darbār*], a Charan (or royal bard), was Pratap Dan (Singh) Charan.[21] We asked Ram Dev about forced labor (*begārī*) in Mehru:

BHOJU: Did you have to go there [for *begār*]?

RAM DEV: I had to go, and if I didn't go, then he sent a worker to call: "This person, why didn't he come?" And, he had a one-and-one-quarter-hand-long shoe and he would bring us there and give five *jūte* [five shoe-blows]. The shoe was kept hanging in a special place.

Power's Insolence as Shod Feet

Our conversation with Polu Ram Kumhar in 1993 serves as an introduction to the second form of shoe violence. A potter by birth, Polu had, through a riverbed gardening venture, attained an economic status beyond most of his caste fellows. A reflective, articulate, and successful man, Polu spoke thoughtfully. His train of thought makes a rapid transition from offensive shoes in the kitchen to the shoe for beating—revealing how close the two shoe complexes are in thought; they are very nearly the same shoes.

BHOJU: What kind of work did you do in *begār*?
POLU: My son! We gave water to forty horses in this fort! We took water from the reservoir, we took water for forty horses up to the fort. And for their baths and water we also brought, on top of that.

Twenty-four hours a day, two of us sat here with our ears turned toward the fort; at anytime they can call us, "O Potters, come for *begār*!" And we would go, and if we didn't go they would *beat us with the shoe*, and that's why we kept our ears turned toward there.

Sometimes we are boiling milk on the cooking hearth, and if someone in the fort needs the milk they will *come with their shoes on*, and walk in the kitchen, and take the milk and go, and we can't stop them.

If we stop them, they have a shoe one and one-quarter hands long, and they beat with that shoe.

And suppose our child is sleeping on a cot and some guest comes, they won't even wake up the child, they will just take it off the cot and take the cot. That's the kind of work they did. In this way all castes were sad, believe me.

Kalyan Mali in 1993 also told a story of offending shoes on the feet of the powerful—or at least of a person imbued with power by association with the Court. The story also highlights his own resistance, as did all of his well-spun tales. Instead of using the standard interview format here, I have reworded his story and tell it in the third person. This is because my notes were made after the fact, rather than directly transcribed from a recorded interview, and I do not want to attribute words to Kalyanji who, as we will see in chapter 9, has a unique storytelling style.

One day Kalyan Mali was busy running the *charas*—the laborious and tedious irrigation system in which the farmer drives his oxen backward and forward, yoked to a pulley system that lowers leather buckets into a step well, hauls them out full, and spills the water into irrigation channels. The king's servant, whose title was village crier, came past the well and walked into Kalyanji's garden with his shoes on. In the process he broke plants and picked vegetables without asking permission. Kalyan said to him, "Take off your shoes when you enter the garden-temple."

The village crier answered, "I'm measuring and I need my shoes." Kalyan repeated, "Take off your shoes."

"Who are you to tell me?"

Kalyan Mali became angry and responded, "Your mother this-and-that" [*terī māṅ aisī kī taisī*] and, "You are like a Regar!" [both offensive insults].[22] And he picked up a stone to throw, and the crier ran away. He ran and told another of the king's men, "Kalyan Mali beat me!"

So two men came and dragged him to the fort. Akka Singhji [a well-known *kāmdār* in Ghatiyali] asked him, "Why are you beating my Balai?" and added that he was going to beat him in return.

Kalyan Mali replied, "If you want to beat me, fine, but first listen!"

"O.k., speak."

So Kalyan Mali said to Akka, "Do you let us go in your royal neighborhood [rāvalo] wearing shoes or not?"

"No we think it's very bad."

"Well," Kalyan Mali said, "My garden is like your rāvalo."

Then Akka Singh told the Balai, "It was your mistake."

Once again a bold farmer is justified, vindicated, and goes unpunished. His boldness, moreover, extends to comparing himself with the Rajputs, making an analogy between his garden and their neighborhood. It works. But note that Balais are very low in the social hierarchy. Had Kalyanji's dispute been with a Rajput manager and not the lower crier, things might have developed quite differently in this encounter and given it a different outcome.

Abjection as Bare Feet

In all of our interviews, only one account directly links the shoe-beating theme with the shoe-wearing ban, and it is a second-hand narrative that was probably pure fabrication. However, it is worth examining for its several idiosyncrasies, and as an interface of the two shoe-power matrices. It was among the few testimonies we heard that declared that a specific shoe-beating to a named individual was actually administered.

This episode emerged during a conversation with a group of Regars in Devli Gaon, one of Sawar's tehsil headquarters. We had been speaking with Ram Lal Regar, who was quite elderly and extremely articulate. There were several others present, including another senior Regar and a youth of the same community, probably in his late twenties. He was therefore too young to have witnessed those times or even to have appreciated the conditions that prevailed during the rule of kings. Although the older men present had already narrated acutely painful personal histories of abasement and suffering, they hotly denied this youth's second-hand story of a beating.

BHOJU: Did they ever call you into the fort to have you beaten with a shoe?

RAM LAL: No, I never heard of that, and I never saw it either.

REGAR YOUTH: There was a man in Devli named Hanuman, who does sewing. One time, Hanuman was telling me, "I walked in front of the fort wearing my shoes and the big shots [ṭhākur sāheb] were sitting there, and I said "Jai Śrī Jī kī" to them, and I went along my way. [This is a polite greeting, "Victory to Shri Kalyan ji," referring to the deity Shri Kalyan ji, of whom the royal family were devotees. It would be the polite and proper thing to say.][23] Then they called me back, and a Bhangi was working there, and they called him over, and he took off his shoe and struck me twice."

RAM LAL [and another older listener, speaking almost simultaneously]: This is a lie! It didn't happen; such things did not happen.

This story is so unlike the usual references to shoe-beatings, in several ways, that I am inclined to share the elder men's skepticism. First, the shoe is not a special shoe kept in the fort as a reminder of potential sanctions, but a real shoe on a real Bhangi's foot. No symbolic filth this—it is beyond the pale. Second, the episode does not take place in the seclusion of fort or stables but on the street. Finally—although punishment is meted out for the offense of a low-caste person disrespectfully "wearing shoes" in the presence of nobility, the anonymous Bhangi himself, who happens to be on the scene, happens to be wearing shoes—handy to take off and beat with but contradicting the narrated event's total logic. This contradiction seems to discredit the entire story: "Such things did not happen." Yet I found this anomaly provocative. Bhoju and I searched for a Hanuman among the Regar tailors in Devli City, but we never found one. During the same session in Devli Gao, from the elderly Ram Lal Regar, we heard what struck me as the cruelest account of the abusive nature of the forced labor system involving bare feet. It is not at all likely that in this case bare feet signify anything more than poverty. Ram Lal makes his painful trek all alone, and he might have worn shoes if he had owned them. Yet the pain of Ram Lal's memories suggests not only physical suffering but an abjection of the spirit that is difficult to bear recalling, even fifty years later:

> I was my father's only son, and once they sent me from Devli to Napa ka Khera with a case of Coca-Cola (*kokā koyalā kī peṭī*). The manager wrote a note with the name of someone from Napa ka Khera [to whom it should be delivered]. So, it was my duty to take it to Napa ka Khera, and it was the hot season, June. It was my turn, and I didn't have shoes; they put the case on my head and gave me the note, and I had to take it to Napa ka Khera.
>
> I had a very miserable time (*bahut pareśān huā*). My feet hurt, but I couldn't put it down because if I put it down who would put it back up? And I was very thirsty, but I couldn't drink.
>
> I was the son of a poor man, I didn't have shoes, and when I walked into the river [that is, the dry river bed], I got blisters on my feet [from the hot sand], and I was crying. But what could I do? I had to bring it there. There was a Mina in Napa ka Khera. There I wrapped cloth bandages around my feet, and returned home with great difficulty.
>
> Such was our condition in the time of the *rāj*!

Ram Lal's pointed concluding words indicate that he has deliberately given us this story for our history. As if he were saying to us, "You asked me what things were like, I'll tell you." This episode also may not recall an event exactly. Coca-Cola, I am told, could not have been available before 1947. But it does not really matter what was in the case; what is salient is that the disempowered, barefoot Regar goes thirsty and anguished while carrying as a head burden a bottled luxury drink destined for kings. He is unable to lower this burden.

Ram Lal Regar in Devli Gaon, 1997.

Women, when asked to describe the strictures on their behavior in the old days, often spoke of not wearing shoes in front of men. Although the term *pratibandh* is not used here, this struck me as a direct domestication of the courtly ban on anyone of low rank wearing shoes in front of nobility, or those associated with nobility. Gender hierarchy evidently mirrors other power configurations. For women, too, this ban was inconvenient and health-threatening. Shoes protect feet, and women were always walking—often, like Regars, carrying heavy head loads.

In the barber's spacious courtyard we talked with a group of neighbor women in 1997. Ratni Nain told us, with some humor but little nostalgia, about the ways women had to behave in the old days in front of elders and males. To signify respect was necessary even if the men were not actually present. Women had to show respect for the men's meeting place by passing it barefoot and veiled when no men were there. Ratni Nain states: "We kept our faces veiled. At the men's meeting place (*hathai*), whether men are there or whether no men are present, even so we cannot pass it with our shoes on; even if no one was there, we veiled our faces. And if there *were* men there, we would pass it with our backs turned [a sign of respect as well as modesty, and a way of keeping purdah even in the street]."

When Bhoju asked Dhapu, a very old Mina woman in Napa ka Khera about the kind of modesty she used to practice in her in-laws' home in the old days, it was shoes that she first thought of in responding: "In those days it was different, not like today. In that time, if my father-in-law saw me wearing shoes, and if I was just this far from him, he would let out insults. He would '*yū yū yū* . . . she seems like she is climbing on my head' [that is, quite literally, getting uppity]. . . . And when we went to the field, and if there were four or five men, we had to take off our shoes before those men; that's how much etiquette [*kāydā*] there was in those days."

The old woman's memory of her father-in-law's taunt, "*yū yū yū* . . . she seems like she is climbing on my head," is expressive of this chapter's main themes. Shoes have to do with one person putting himself or herself above another, and with the Court and his men holding themselves above all, but never without a modicum of give and take, and never without a toll of rebellious resentment.

6. COURT

The raja himself was not blamed for maladministration, only his corrupt officials.—Nandini Sunder, *Subalterns and Sovereigns*

The *mai-bap* [parental] image of the feudal lords despite extortions and oppression, and the devotion of the people to their rulers despite despotic rule, . . .
created some basic contradictions in the system.—K. L. Sharma, *Caste, Feudalism,
and Peasantry*

We begin this chapter with the Court himself—Vansh Pradip Singh,
who reigns in living memories. We then turn to more mundane matters of state: the administrative apparatus of the twenty-seven-village
kingdom that annually had to deliver a fixed amount of revenue to the
British collector in Ajmer and still maintain pomp according to its
own standards. This is an overview of fiscal affairs, some aspects of
which are treated elsewhere in greater detail. We focus on taxation in
chapter 8, on the agents and mission of the forest department in
chapter 9. Conscripted labor could not be confined to any chapter; it
pervades this entire book. Here all these matters are touched on
briefly, as we try to grasp the Court's operations from the center in
Sawar. In describing the bureaucratic workings of pre-Independence
Sawar, as in all other matters, we follow the lead of our interviewees.
Accordingly, we do not cover every aspect of the kingdom's political
economy with equal care. For example, in collective memories the
role of merchants has generally been underplayed, although they are
frequently casually or bitterly mentioned among the "eaters" of the

farmers' production. Perhaps a sifting of memory makes them less highlighted as oppressors here than elsewhere. In Sawar so much anger is centered on the king's agents, the merchants get a smaller share. It is also true that merchants still play important roles in village economy today, and people may deliberately refrain from speaking ill of persons upon whom they still depend for critical economic resources.[1]

Much of the information in this chapter and the next ought to be straightforward and factual, but as it emerged in interviews the details resisted consistency and precision. This may be as much the nature of the system as it is the nature of memory. Several historian colleagues have gently advised me that it might be well to check against the Ajmer district settlement records the inconsistent and fuzzy oral historical versions of, for example, what percentage of the harvest was taken from whom by the Court. I have not done so, preferring to devote my time to living voices. I also suspect that if those records make the facts sound simple and straightforward, it is more likely that their authors have glossed over fuzziness and fluidity than that our interviewees have confused things in their memory. I have been myself tempted more than once in composing this chapter to gloss over rampant inconsistencies.

In a final section of chapter 6 we look briefly at the ways people talked about the Court's death and its aftermath—the Court of Wards period.[2] During the time that the Court of Wards—a lame-duck regime if ever there were one—controlled Sawar, the princely states of Rajputana were gradually, with difficulty, welded into a new state called Rajasthan.[3] Here the preceding segments on Vansh Pradip Singh and his bureaucracy merge, for the death of Vansh Pradip Singh in 1947 was the end not only of one man's personal history and one ruler's moderately excessive lifestyle, but of a relatively effective administration and the injustices endemic to its nature.

In Sawar, Vansh Pradip Singh's widowed queen engaged in an ultimately successful lawsuit to install her choice of successor, Vrij Raj Singh, whom villagers always call the Chausala-*Wala* ("the Fellow from Chausala"), thus emphasizing his external and not so glorious origins. He ascended the throne in the month of Asoj (June-July), *samvat* 2008 (1951 C.E.).

Much is swept away almost simultaneously with the *darbār*'s death:

his dogs die; his elephants and horses also perish or are rapidly dispersed; *begār* is terminated. One year the land taxes are paid as usual, but by the very next harvest the whole game is finished (*khel khatam*), including, as chapter 9 traces carefully, the abundant trees and wild animals. Thus we begin in this chapter to sense and delineate an unimaginable transformation from despotism to democracy as Sawar people retrospectively recreate its unfolding.

Vansh Pradip Singh on the Record

Two brief, locally published Hindi sources on Vansh Pradip Singh's life and accomplishments supply few details absent from oral accounts. Both are composed in a hagiographic mode (Goyal 1987; Mathur 1977:20–23). These written histories are also based on oral accounts, and many of the same themes to appear in our interviews also appear on paper concerning the court's personality and accomplishments. But the written versions, published in Sawar, tend to omit critiques of the oppressive nature of Vansh Pradip Singh's administration. The oral and the written converge in seeing Vansh Pradip Singh as larger than life—a man of many passions and one tragic lack: an heir.

Both of the written sources provided me with an important fact missing from every oral account we collected: Vansh Pradip Singh attended Mayo College in Ajmer. I must assume this was a setting beyond the horizons of most of our interviewees. Established by the British in 1872, Mayo College was one of four public schools "set up by the Government of India specifically in order to 'fit the young Chiefs and Nobles of India physically, morally and intellectually for the responsibilities that lay before them'" (Allen and Dwivedi 1984:120).[4] There, according to Goyal's hagiographic sketch, our Sawar *darbār*-to-be mixed with the sons of Rajputana's great ruling families (Goyal 1987:7). Mathur's brief history of Sawar also mentions the *darbār*'s education at Mayo College, adding that "he knew Hindi and English very well" (1977:20).[5] If this is true, Vansh Pradip Singh's linguistic competence exceeded that of the family currently in residence in Sawar's fort. In my limited experience socializing with them, only one household member, the youngest daughter, Rashmi (my tour guide through the fort, as described in chapter 2), is fluent in English.

Painting of Vansh Pradip Singh, Sawar Fort.

Neither her older brothers nor her father and uncles spoke any English in my presence, and most often they preferred the local Rajasthani dialect to Hindi.[6]

I reproduce here, in my slightly condensed translation, those three pages of Jivan Lal Mathur's history of Sawar that concern Vansh Pradip Singh. The former chief minister's style is not scintillating; but it conveys well the way local history is narrated on paper, from the ruling point of view. Mathur's account can stand as confirmation and foil to the oral accounts that follow. Mathur did not organize his information in a particularly coherent or fully chronological fashion, and I have not, in my flat translation, tampered with his arrangement of the facts.[7]

This great king [Vansh Pradip Singh] was the only son of Ummed Singhji, and was born on the dark moon of Māgh [January-February], in *samvat* 1949 [c. 1893 C.E.]. His education took place at Mayo College in Ajmer. He knew Hindi and English well. He had two queens, the elder queen Khangarotji was from Padalai estate [in Jaipur], and the second queen, Bagheliji, was from Sohaval State (in Madhya Pradesh). The Great King came to the throne on the dark ninth of Posh [December-January] in *samvat* 1971 [c. 1915 C.E., at the youthful age of twenty-two]. He had no progeny from either queen.

His greatest interests were in houses, buildings, hunting, planting gardens, and constructing small and larger water reservoirs; building roads and planting trees; having silver and gold ornaments, and silver vessels and such, crafted. He bought quite a lot of rifles and swords.

From his childhood he was interested in physical exercise and musical knowledge. He had hunting posts constructed in the hills, and hunted several tawny lions.[8] His greatest interest was in construction. In his time, in Sawar, Devli, and Ghatiyali, throughout the state, there was quite a lot of construction work. . . . [I omit an inventory of numerous building projects Vansh Pradip Singh undertook in the Sawar fort.] He also had a garage built, and stables. In the fort, he knocked down Four-Armed Vishnu's old temple, and built a beautiful new temple.

He installed electric light and a flour mill in the fort, and he bought two buildings in Ajmer. On Shrinagar Road, the name of "Sawar House" is famous. He had quite a lot of interest in reading books and newspapers, and he had quite a lot of collections in his library. During his time, all kinds of progress took place in the *ṭhikānā*. But a huge lack remained: he had no progeny.

In his youth, he did a lot of touring, making journeys around the country. Later, in the time of Maharana Bhopal Singh, he went to Udaipur frequently, and the Maharana treated him with great respect. He had good connections with the states of Kota and Alvar, and there was much coming and going between them. His senior queen, Khangarotji, died in his presence. The great king was a devotee of Four-Armed Vishnu, and held to merit and faith. His was a meritorious soul, and in all the tehsils[9] [of Sawar] he spent quite a lot of money to make fire oblations. He made many kinds of charitable gifts and did all kinds of charitable works.

Once, while hunting, he was shot in the foot, and he had several operations to remove the bullets; he was very courageous and endured the pain in silence. He always had a great interest in horses, and had as many as one hundred, as well as keeping three elephants, several cars, carts, trucks, and quite a few camels.

Since the time of Ummed Singhji [father of Vansh Pradip Singh], Sawar had a connection with the great court of Kashmir, and Vansh Pradip Singh maintained this with dignity, and attended two or three weddings in Shrinagar and Jammu.

The Maharaja left the *thikāna* free of debt; he left it in good condition. In his time there were about 250 workers.[10] There were five tehsil.

The first chief minister (*dīvān*) under Vansh Pradip Singh was Pancholi Kaliyanrayji, who served for about fifteen years. After his death, Pancholi Mangilalji served for approximately one and one-half to two years. After his death, the position of chief minister was entrusted to the author of this book, Pancholi Jivan Lal. He had previously served for twelve years as the tehsildar of four tehsils. After this he remained in the position of chief minister until the time when the *darbār* went to his reward.

The great king's health was very good. He had a well-built, muscular body, a fair color, and an attractive character; he was a gentleman of great majesty. At the age of fifty-five he fell ill and was sick for some time, attacked by disease. In Ajmer, at Sawar House, in the night, on the bright 12th of Bhadva [August-September] in *samvat* 2004 [1947 C.E.], he became a dweller in heaven. His funeral took place in Sawar.

Queen Bagheliji had come to Ajmer, and she traveled with his body to Sawar. After the great king died, the state came under the charge of the government Court of Wards. Personages from Chosala, Madara, and Rud were fighting over the right to the throne.

Queen Bagheliji made the *ṭhākur* of Chosala, Vrij Raj Singhji, her adopted son, and when the government of India's president accepted this, the Court of Wards' control was lifted, and Sawar's charge was entrusted to Vrij Raj Singhji.

In memory of Vansh Pradip Singh, Queen Bagheliji had the temple of Ban Mataji [a Goddess temple] constructed; also, after the death of the great king Vansh Pradip Singhji, by her efforts, there was a memorial dome [*chhatarī*] built for him in the Great Satis Garden [a garden near the Sawar fort where stand ancient monuments to *satis* who predated by many centuries the Shaktavat regime in Sawar]. The honored Queen Mother Bagheliji's death took place in her natal home, Sohaval.

King Vansh Pradip Singhji planted new gardens, called Jovan Vilas and Parvati Vilas, and he built the reservoir of Ganesh Sagar.[11] He gave stipends to many students for their education, and this was a symbol of his generosity. He also set up watering troughs for livestock, and drinking places for travelers; he helped widows and orphans; he always showed compassion. (Mathur 1977:20–21).

Although Mathur mentions gardens, planting trees, and a love of hunting, he gives no attention to the Court's orally famed protection of pigs and other wild animals and his avid conservationist policy. Yet oral accounts all agree these had not merely sustained but substantially improved the jungle. These passions of the *darbār* were strong and universally acknowledged. They were more a part of his public persona than his love for planting shade trees in gardens and beside roads. Possibly, this omission is deliberate. The chief minister writes only good of the Court, and perhaps therefore he desires to suppress any conflict between the Court and the people. Yet the jungle and especially the pigs were contested areas of dominion. By contrast, Vansh Pradip Singh's fostering of garden greenery was fully appropriate to kingly behavior and never a source of popular complaint. Goyal notes, in his account of the life of Vansh Pradip Singh: "he was so concerned about the protection of the gardens that if he saw a tree branch cut he would become extremely angry" (1987:7; my translation). Thus, shifting the focus from jungle to gardens, he portrays the Court's emotional identification with trees (chapter 9).

As the last ruler of Sawar in the time of the great kings, Vansh Pradip Singh emerges vividly in oral accounts. From these accounts we paint with broad strokes a color poster portrait, larger than life. When descriptions diverge or conflict, we record alternative views, but we have by and large refrained from attempts to assess facticity, or to compare a "legendary" Vansh Pradip Singh with a historical figure. This was not our quest. Eschewing biography (which no one provided) we focus on his habits and passions, his idiosyncrasies, and their implications for the tellers.

When people reminisced about the *darbār* as a person, two poles of his character were usually evoked: his daily regimen (*niyam*) and his passionate interests (*śauk*).[12] This conjunction is not insignificant: on the one hand is self-discipline; on the other are strong and intense predilections, firmness and excess, sternness as taskmaster and impulsive generosity as gracious lord. Vansh Pradip Singh fed wild pigs on popcorn and pet dogs on halva, but gave little or no famine relief to poor farmers in lean years. Yet he might suddenly grant two oxen to an impoverished Brahmin petitioner, or show clemency to a convicted wrong-doer. Vansh Pradip Singh indulged in all strong intoxicants but never displayed a hint of being drunk or stoned. He spent huge amounts of money on religious work but wore his shoes in the temple and refused to fast on holy days.[13] In the latter case, his passion for meat and his repetitive daily schedule converge.

In Sawar, our first major interviews, carefully plotted out and tracked down by Bhoju, were with persons who were closely associated with the former Court's administrative operations. Govind Singh Rathor was the former *tehsīldār*—a high-ranking position in the Court's administrative hierarchy.[14] We found Govind Singh at home, crouching outdoors in the winter sun, poking among the pebbles with his walking stick for purposes I could not discern. We persuaded him to sit down with us indoors and, walking slowly but erect, he led us into a beautiful round room painted blue, with pictures of Sawar nobility on the walls. Although the old man himself did not immediately strike me as a former figure of power, this room was impressive. I had not been in another like it, except in forts.

Govind Singh recalled the *darbār*'s daily regimen. Like many others from Sawar proper, he described this as so constant that it served as a kind of clock for Sawarites, as well as a stable topic more predictable than the weather, around which people could pass the time of day:[15] "The *darbār* had a fixed time for eating and for taking a shit. All the people knew when they could find the *darbār* and what he would be doing at what time. [They would say], "Now the Court is taking a shit, now the Court is doing his exercises."

We asked Govind Singh about the *darbār*'s *śauk*, his passionate interests, and he continued to reminisce, his general recollections corresponding closely with the biographic excerpt translated above, but contributing additional, intimate details: "The *darbār* had a great deal of *śauk* in many things: constructing tanks [water reservoirs], planting gardens, buying weapons. Any new thing that appeared, he wanted to buy. He told the farmers to bear it for a few more years." That is, Vansh Pradip Singh knew the time of kings was ending, and he chose not to change his ways. Unspoken but assumed here is a direct causal relation between the people's suffering—tacitly acknowledged by the Court himself in Govind Singh's account—and the Court's acquisition of goods to feed his fancies and finance his construction work. These were bought with his subjects' labors. Although some of them benefited the people, most merely enhanced the status and comfort of the royal family.

Govind Singh continued: "All the cots [in the fort] had springs so that if you sat down on one without paying attention you would bounce." The *darbār,* as we will see, kept his distance from the British. Nonetheless he was, it seems, selectively intrigued by some European goods such as bedsprings.

Sampat Lal, a Sawar Brahmin whose father had also once been a tehsildar under Vansh Pradip Singh, reported a similar list of the *darbār*'s interests:

Collecting weapons, debates, hunting, gardens—he had many interests. He also had interests in cultural fields (*sanskritik kṣetra*). He was a great flute player.

And he was interested in physical exercises! He had two wrestlers. . . . And he called the children to do exercises on Sundays; the *darbār* would have them come, and sit there himself [to observe]. He gave a *pāv* [one-quarter kilogram] of sweets to the winner and half a *pāv* to the loser.

. . . .

At that time the *darbār* partook of every kind of intoxication: hashish, marijuana, opium, wine, they were all his passionate interests! But no one could tell that he was intoxicated.

When we put the same question about the Court's passionate interests to still another of his admirers, Ram Narayan Daroga, another helpful detail emerged: Vansh Pradip Singh's kindness to domestic animals.[16] (In chapter 9 we discuss in detail the Court's passion for wildlife.)

BHOJU: What were the *darbār's* special interests?

RAM NARAYAN: Planting gardens, planting trees, and keeping fine pairs of oxen. If his oxen were ever dispirited (*udās*), he would always call, "What's the matter, are they out of food, are they out of water?" and the servant would attend to them. The *darbār* kept the brown sugar and oil for the oxen right in his sight. Why? If there were three kilograms of oil, the servant might take two home and only give the oxen one, so the *darbār* kept his eye on all of it.

A conversation followed this, a kind of speculative footnote, about how the lineage of the *darbār's* servants in charge of oxen had been wiped out, left without descendants; might this be a divine punishment for their having stolen food from oxen?[17]

The *darbār* treated not just his oxen but all of his domestic animals very well, even royally. One person told a story of Vansh Pradip Singh's dog turning up its nose at a meal that had been served to the *darbār* himself when he was on a rare visit to Bhinai. This was a fine put-down for the rival neighboring court, but it also testifies to how well the dog was fed at home. Many told us that the Court's dogs did not survive their master's death by more than a few days; they were not only grief-stricken but unable to eat the food given to them by others.

From Ram Narayan we also learned of some of the *darbār's* personal eccentricities which extended to eating meat on days considered appropriate for "fasting." In this anecdote, the people are troubled by their king's behavior but he completely refuses to bend an ear to them.

RAM NARAYAN: They [the Court and his retinue] used to eat goats on the eleventh, dark moon and full moon [as well as all other days]. Once all the people of Sawar decided to ask him not to eat goats on those days, and all the villagers went there to request.

All the public* went into the fort, and the *darbār* saw them, and came down, [and asked them] "What happened? What bad work did I do?"[18]

So, someone said, "In our Sawar, please don't eat goats."

The *darbār* joined his hands to the public*, and said, "Starting today I will eat nothing at all."

After that nobody said another word, and they all left. The *darbār* gave up nothing. Everything was permitted.

BHOJU [not quite following]: So, did the *darbār* give it up?

RAM NARAYAN: No, neither food nor goats! He performed a lot of religious acts [*dharm*]—gifts of cows [to Brahmins]; feeding grass and grain to cows—lots of religious acts, but this work [*kām;* that is, meat eating] he would not give up.[19]

In his relations with the gods, it appeared, the Court sustained his imperial personality. He was studiously careless of conventional respect; simultaneously, Vansh Pradip Singh made sure to retain divine favor, and popular approval, with appropriate largesse to priests, temples, and cows.

Ram Narayan told us another story demonstrating this high-handed religiosity:

RAM NARAYAN: Once a lion (*nār*)[20] was killing cows and buffaloes, so the people of Jaswantapura went to the *darbār,* and he had a hunting platform built on top of a tree, and sat there, in Ram Bagh [a garden off the road]. The *darbār* was sitting, waiting for the lion. He heard some sounds of animals moving, and fired his gun in the direction of the sound, and killed a cow. The *darbār* was very sorry, and he made a golden cow and offered it at Char Bhuja temple in Sawar.

BHOJU: After that did he make a vow not to hunt again?

RAM NARAYAN: No, and he still ate meat on the dark moon and full moon!

Repentance and atonement were not for Vansh Pradip Singh.

Gokul Mali gave the most extreme report on the *darbār*'s uncon-

Sawar's "Lake Palace."

ventional disrespect for religious formalities—indeed, it verged on the unbelievable. According to Gokul, "People said that when Vansh Pradip Singh went to the temple he did not remove his shoes, and he took his dog with him, and he did *namaskār* but he did not prostrate himself." When pressed as to whether he had personally witnessed any of this, Gokul denied it, and we have no witnessed confirmation. It seems too outrageous to be true, but even as a memory trope the Court's self-exemption from every expression of human humility is certainly striking. It differs, moreover, from strategies of piety and identification with divinity associated with other Indian kings.

The Court's relations with the British, as popularly acclaimed, displayed a similar mixture of arrogant attitude and dutiful rendering of obligations, both fiscal and social. Oral accounts show Vansh Pradip Singh treating British administrators with exactly the minimum required deference, and not one iota more. His main wish was to avoid their company altogether. Reputedly, he was haughty toward most other Rajputs as well—even those whose kingdoms were greater than his own.

Vansh Pradip Singh had especially prickly relations with neighboring Bhinai, where it is said his dog turned up its nose at cuisine meant for royal humans, and from where he reputedly sought to lure wild animals to Sawar's woods. The Court received respect, and the gift of an elephant, from great Mewar, where his status would only have been that of a poor and distant cousin. A Brahmin astrologer, Mul Chand Joshi of Kalera—who except for his deafness was remarkably astute and alert for his many years—told us a detailed story of how Vansh Pradip Singh acquired this elephant. The tale portrays the Court as the opposite of humble. Indeed, he played the honor game among his betters with a great deal of pizzazz.

Mul Chand had been describing, as others already had, the avoidance strategies Vansh Pradip Singh practiced with the British: as soon as he heard they were coming, he would take off for another place. Bhoju asked what the reason was for this. Mul Chand explained that it had to do with the proud Mewari lineage of the Shaktavats, which made Vansh Pradip Singh despise the "barbarian" English: "Because he belonged to the family of the Udaipur Rana, who also would never meet with the English, for this reason he wouldn't shake hands or meet with any English. There was no other reason; he was imitating the one in Udaipur!"[21]

Mul Chand then launched into the following narrative about an occasion when Vansh Pradip Singh went hunting with the Rana of Udaipur, as a result of which Sawar acquired its third and last elephant in the years preceding 1947:

> Once the Udaipur *darbār* invited Vansh Pradip Singh to Udaipur; so the *darbār* went there and he was standing before him. Vansh Pradip Singh said, "Why did you call me here? Why did you remember me today?"
>
> And the Rana said, "I have heard that you have a great aim in hunting. That's the reason I called you."
>
> So the *darbār* went hunting with the king of Udaipur, Vansh Pradip Singh went. The king of Udaipur was Bhopal Singh.[22]
>
> . . . .
>
> They [Vansh Pradip Singh and Bhopal Singh] were both on elephants and they [Bhopal Singh's retinue] were beating the bushes. Some small lions came before them, and Bhopal Singh said, "Shoot them," but Vansh Pradip Singh said, "No they are too insignificant (*chhoṭī moṭī*). Let a big lion come!"
>
> And then a nine-hand lion came, and Vansh Pradip Singh said, "This is a good animal to hunt. You aim and shoot."

But Bhopal Singh said, "You aim and shoot!" So Vansh Pradip Singh fired one shot and hit the lion in the forehead and the lion fell right there. It died with a single shot.

Then, the Udaipur Rana patted him on the head and back, and said, "*Śābāś!* (Splendid!) I'm so happy there is someone in my lineage who is such a good shot." [Note the praise plus acknowledgment of kinship.]

And at that time the Mewar Maharana gave Vansh Pradip Singh seven hundred silver coins and a double-barreled gun as a reward (*inām*).

But right on the spot the *darbār* distributed the entire seven hundred coins to the beaters, and he only kept the gun as a souvenir.

The Udaipur *darbār* asked, "What are you doing?"

Vansh Pradip Singh said, "I have plenty of money in my treasury, so what do I need this money for? But I accept the gun." Then, he added, "I have a male elephant and if you want to give me something, give me a female elephant so when they take their pleasure (*anand karte*), I can watch them."[23]

So the Maharana gave an order to his chief minister to give Vansh Pradip Singh a female elephant, from Kumbhal Garh.

But Vansh Pradip Singh said, "No, I want an elephant from Udaipur, I want the elephant on which I was riding when I went hunting!"

So now he had three [elephants]. He had one, and he got one from his in-laws [in dowry], and now he got the third. But they were all three finished during the Court of Wards.

Although many testified to Vansh Pradip Singh having an elephant from Udaipur as a reward for his marksmanship, I heard no other versions of this detailed story.[24] Whatever the truth of this account, Mul Chand's narrative tells us a lot about Vansh Pradip Singh's character in the minds of his admiring subjects. The Court's stubborn and prideful behavior did not desert him in the presence of Rajasthan's highest nobility.[25]

We gathered numerous other sketchy, anecdotal accounts of Vansh Pradip Singh's self-elevated demeanor. He practiced some rather blatant strategies of one-upmanship in matters of rank. For example, by keeping only one chair in the room when meeting with other dignitaries, he ensured that no one would sit down. If all stood, then no one could be acknowledged superior, or even equal, in rank on the basis of where they sat, who sat first, or the mere fact of being allowed to sit.

Popular stories related with particular relish the ways Vansh Pradip Singh kept the impure British at arm's length. According to Govind Singh, Vansh Pradip Singh allowed the British commissioner to come into the garden but not to enter the fort, and he refused to meet with him personally. Govind Singh described the Court's attitude toward visits from the British in this way: "He said, 'I am not consuming liquor, I am not giving trouble to the public, my relation with my people is very good, so why do I have to meet with the commissioner? I have no work with them!' "

According to several persons, his wish to minimize contact with the barbaric English caused him deliberately to prevent the construction of proper roads within his boundaries in order to deter, or at least minimize, visits from British "sahabs." He never allowed the English to hunt in his own favored hunting grounds, carefully keeping them secret. He sometimes deliberately directed visiting sahabs to bad hunting. We heard one story in which the *darbār* recommended a certain hunting area to some British sportsmen, and then surreptitiously sent runners ahead to frighten off the game with gunshots. The disappointed intruders never returned.

Vansh Pradip Singh's attitude contrasts with some notably Anglophilic behavior on the part of some other members of the Rajput nobility, from kingdoms far greater than Sawar. I do not suspect these Sawar narratives to be nationalist revisionist accounts. Scorn for the British as impure, clumsy, and barbaric was real enough at every level of society, as I learned in my earliest field experience there (Gold 1988:269–70).

Most of Vansh Pradip Singh's haughty strategies are displayed in an account given to us in 1997 by Mangal Singh Rathor, the principal of Sawar's higher secondary school. Mangal Singh gave his age in 1997 as around fifty to fifty-two, but he spoke of the *darbār* and his times as if he had witnessed them. He gave us these details of Vansh Pradip Singh's behavior both toward fellow nobility and colonial officers:

He only sat when he was alone; because if he himself sat with company, then he would have to give someone else a chair.

He would sit with the Shahpura *darbār* and the Udaipur *darbār;* but he wouldn't even meet with *ṭhākurs* from other districts—not even from Kota. Shahpura and Udaipur were both Shaktavat (his own lineage; see chapter 2).

He trusted nobody. If some commissioner came, and he had to shake hands, then he folded his hands behind his back and a Daroga [his personal servant] would wash them with water.[26]

. . . .

He had a great interest in hunting, but he wouldn't let . . . British people hunt . . . and he wouldn't let them build a road from Ajmer to Sawar, or from Kekari to Sawar, he wouldn't let them build that road. He thought, "If there is a road, the British people will come," and he didn't like it.

Vijay Prakash Mathur, the son of Jivanlal Mathur, the last chief minister under Vansh Pradip Singh, supplied some of the most detailed accounts of the *darbār's* relationships with the English. These revealed his behavior to be studiously cagey.

VIJAY PRAKASH MATHUR: When the English came—they were called sahab—whenever they came from Ajmer, people would say, "Today the sahabs have "nobly arrived." [He uses the verb *padhārno,* part of Rajasthan's special vocabulary implying exaggerated respect for Rajputs or other superiors].

When they were coming, then a telegram would come [in advance], but the *darbār* took no interest in this. He wanted to avoid them. He would say to my father [Jivanlal Mathur, the *dīvān*], "You take care of them." He did not like to walk around with them. When he knew they were coming he would go to Shahpura, or to Jaipur.

BHOJU: Why didn't he like the English?

VIJAY PRAKASH MATHUR: Because he had an independent nature; he didn't like to shake hands with them or wander around in their company.

[He avoids the explicit attribution of impurity, perhaps out of courtesy.]

BHOJU: He didn't let them in the fort?

VIJAY PRAKASH MATHUR: Well he might, but only into a decided place, they couldn't go everywhere. Even so, he had all comforts for them, no lack, he had a guesthouse and took good care of them. It's just that the *darbār* didn't like to meet them, that's all.

In Rajpura, just outside of Sawar, we met with Chalak Dan Charan, who belonged to the family of bards that once sang the praises of the Court on public occasions, and were much involved in manipulating affairs of state.[27] He was clearly less well disposed to the memory of Vansh Pradip Singh, and argued that his passive resistance to the British had a deleterious impact on Sawar's development: "He [Vansh Pradip Singh] didn't like any British officer. Whenever one came, he wandered off; or he wouldn't let him sit down. And, if they wanted to put some factory here, he would refuse to cooperate; so he let nothing new come [to Sawar]—because he didn't want the English to come here; [thinking] 'It will be a bother to me.' He thought, 'They will come here and I'll have to sit with them.' So for this reason Sawar remained backward." We do not have a clue as to what "factory" this might be; no one else mentioned such a proposition.

The *darbār's* unbending nature was mitigated by generosity, as displayed in the following anecdote, also related by Mul Chand Joshi of Kalera, this one from his own family history. It demonstrates the *darbār's* compassion and largesse to a poor but respected Brahmin. The same tale served as a lesson on the culpritude of the king's men, even the king's Brahmins—a familiar theme and one Bhoju Ram has also stressed when summing up what he heard of the Court (chapter 2).

In this way the troubles were from the king's managers (*kām-dār*) and not from the Court; there was a big difference between them. Once, after my grandfather died, there was only one boy in our family [who later became a schoolteacher]; at the time he was studying.

He had sold all his oxen and equipment after his father died because he wasn't a farmer and there was no sharecropper (*sīrī*), because of the way the government took half the crop.[28] And so our field was sitting there [fallow] and the managers were bothering us about the tax, because we had land.

My brother was courageous. The *darbār* was riding in a cart on his way to Devli, so he [the brother] stood in front of the cart with his hands joined.

The *darbār* asked him, "Who are you and where did you come from?"

"I am a Brahmin from Kalera, and I am Kalaji Mishra's son."

"What is your problem?"

"My father died and I have land but I am not farming it because I don't have any oxen and your bosses (*hākim*) are bothering me about the tax."

So at that time, there was a manager with the Court, Ganpath Lal Purohit [the father of Sampat Lal]. And Vansh Pradip Singh said to him, "Ganpath Lal, give two good oxen to this Brahmin from our herd in Tankavas."

But instead, Ganpath Lal gave small weak oxen that were near death.

So you can see the difference between what the Court said and what the bosses did.

Mul Chand went on to reflect bitterly on the fact that this particular *hākim* was a Brahmin who nonetheless ill-treated a fellow Brahmin. It is also true that if the family had not been Brahmins—to whom generosity was meritorious—their unproductive land would likely have been peremptorily transferred to an active agriculturist.

Administrative Matters in the Last Days of the Kingdom of Sawar

From a number of interviews with individuals who had been personally involved in the Sawar Court in the time of Vansh Pradip Singh we gathered some basic understanding of governmental workings in the state of Sawar.[29] In this section, I diverge from my practice of delivering information through interview texts, mainly because there was little expressive emotion or poetics in these interviews. I merge them in an attempt to give a coherent and substantial picture, although it is still rather imperfect.

Our primary source of information was Govind Singh, who, for sixteen years, held the post of chief tehsildar for all of Sawar. We visited him initially in 1997 looking to gain a sense of the administrative apparatus in Sawar from the top—to complement all we had learned in 1993 from Ghatiyali herders and farmers about its impact on the people. Govind Singh knew a lot, although he did not always present it in the most convenient order. What we learned from him we used as the basis for questioning others. Among these were three other chief sources.

The first source was Bankat Singh Kamdar, who lived near the Sawar fort, just next to the Dark Garden where monuments to Sawar's ancient Sati Mothers stand. He was himself a Shaktavat, about sixty-nine years old at the time of our interview.[30] Two Brahmins—Bhairu Lal, who served in the temple of Four-Armed Vishnu inside the fort, and Sampat Lal, who was the *rāj purohit* (royal priest)—also contributed much to our portrait of Sawar in its last decades. In addition, a view from the "provinces" was contributed by Kana Nai—a barber from Gorada.

The state (*ṭhikānā*) of Sawar, according to Govind Singh and others, contained five *tehsīl* headquarters: Devli Gaon, Ghatiyali, Sawar, Gorada, and Tankavas.[31] When we asked him how many villages there were all told, he replied "We call it twenty-seven, but really it was forty. Twenty-seven of them were important."

Govind Singh rattled off a list with fair facility, but it turned out to be only one version among many of the exact twenty-seven. Given the leeway of twenty-seven special villages but forty all told, I finally with relief relinquished the goal of determining the precise twenty-seven; no two lists ever matched. Map 2 shows the extent of Sawar, without a precise boundary. Most of Sawar's territory appears embraced by the Banas and Khari rivers, as by two long arms. The map locates eighteen villages that were on all the lists we collected—including, of course, Sawar, the capital; and Ghatiyali, the largest village and Bhoju's home. The locations of three other administrative centers—Devli Gaon, Gorada, and Tankavas—are included in the eighteen.

Govind Singh told us that in his time there were between 225 and 300 people working for the court. First below the Court was the *divān* or chief minister. Then there was the treasurer (*khajāncī*). Those two positions each were responsible for keeping complete written records. Beneath the *divān* was the chief *tehsildar*, and below this personage would be five sub-*tehsildar*—theoretically, one for each of the five *tehsils*. But it appears that one person might serve in more than one

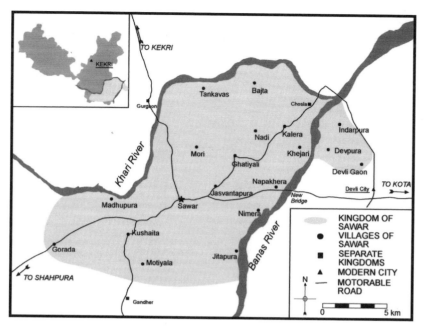

Map 2. Sawar, showing its location in Rajasthan.

tehsil. Sampat Lal's father, for example, had been tehsildar in Gorada, Ghatiyali, and Devli. According to his son, his duties included supervising the biannual collection of the Court's share of agricultural production, in cash or grain. For the *rabī* harvest he went to the threshing ground and oversaw the distribution of the Court's grain.

In each tehsil, beneath the tehsildar would be two managers (*kāmdār*), so there were ten managers all told.[32] One of these, according to Bankat Singh, would always be a Shaktavat—belonging to the same lineage (*vaṃś*) as the Court; the other was a "local"—a village headman (or *lambardār*)—whether a Gujar *dhābāī*, or someone belonging to one of the high castes (Brahmin, Rajput, or Baniya). The chief minister, sub-collectors, and managers received salaries from the Court in money, or grain, as they preferred. In addition, each village would have a revenue accountant (*paṭvārī*), and a village crier (*gāṅv balāī*). Bhairu Purohit used the term *nāyab kāmdār* for the lower-status manager.[33] He told us that the *lambardār* were below these.[34]

Administrative departments (*bhāg, vibhāg*) numbered six or seven: the Agricultural Department (*kriśī vibhāg*); the Jungle Department (*jangalāt*); the Stables (*rasālā*);[35] the Kitchen (*rasovaṛā*); the Grain

Storage (*ambār*); and the Treasury (*khajānā*). Another department was later added to the list by Govind Singh—the Liquor Department (*śarāb khānā vibhāg*).

The Agricultural Department was also the Revenue Department. It had its headquarters in Sawar. Everyone agreed that taxes were collected twice yearly at harvest time. According to Govind Singh, from the *rabī* crops—comprising wheat, barley, and other grains—approximately twenty thousand maunds of grain were collected as tax. But in the *kharīph* the Court collected a cash amount of twenty thousand silver rupees—because the chief crops were not food grains but fodder. The former administrator was evidently still thinking of the cash amount required by the British rulers in Ajmer. Farmers, of course, could not pay cash because they had none. Many farmers did deliver fodder from their fields to the Court. They usually spoke about this when describing conscripted labor, but it was also of course a form of taxation. More prosperous farmers may have obtained cash demanded by the king's men by taking loans from the merchants on the basis of the coming grain crop; merchants also would advance needed cash to the Court on the basis of the rulers' claims on farmers' future crops.[36]

The Court collected either one-half or one-quarter of a farmer's production. According to Govind Singh, speaking from the top, the decision of how much to assess a farmer was not based on caste but rather on the land's productivity. However, no one else in administration said this, and we will hear many accounts in chapter 8 that testify otherwise. Out of all the Court collected, twice yearly a fixed amount was due to the British in Ajmer. Govind Singh recited the figure to us stiffly but without hesitation, a number obviously burned in his memory: "Eight thousand, ten annas, four paise." This was for six months. So in one year, he continued, "sixteen thousand, one rupee, four annas, eight paise."

Bhoju asked Govind Singh what the basis was for this assessment, and he replied without hesitation: "In one rupee there are sixteen annas, so they took six anna out of sixteen [very roughly 35 percent]. The court had to pay this much to the Ajmer commissioner."

In the Ajmer archives, I learned that Sawar's revenue, with Colonel Dixon's sanction, was enhanced from 2,012 to 8,000 rupees some time after the death of Jaswant Singh (great-grandfather of Vansh Pradip

Singh) in 1856.[37] Clearly, it was still hovering around 8,000 in the era with which we were concerned. Govind Singh told us that Sawar continued to pay this tax to the British Court of Wards until 1955. However, all the farmers testified that the grain collection at harvest ceased altogether just one year following Vansh Pradip Singh's death in 1947.

Of the persons we interviewed, Gajanand Sharma Buvalia was one of the few to stress the direct link between British taxation of the kings and the kings' exploitation of the farmers: "Before the English came, the kings would help the people, but at this time the British collected a fixed tax, and the great kings took the grain tax, and no one took responsibility." He was the only person I heard within the Sawar Twenty-Seven who looked back to precolonial times under the kings as having been better for the people, and significantly, perhaps, the only one who said that responsibility was lacking under the Court's rule.

Bhoju attempted to elicit something about the purpose and work-ings of each administrative department. Sampat Lal summed up suc-cinctly the purview and purpose of the Jungle Department: "*Jangal* (wooded areas), *bīr* (protected grasslands), and *pahar* (literally hill, but here common grazing land)—they all came under the *jangalāt*; they all existed previously, but Vansh Pradip Singh developed them. There was a prohibition on hunting. No one could hunt. No one could cut trees."[38] The Jungle Department was based in Ghatiyali. There were maybe ten men in it referred to as the "jungle bosses" (*janglāt kā hākim*). Under each boss were five to seven forest guards (*syāṇā*) whose duties were to protect the jungle—above all from those who attempted to cut green wood or to kill wild animals. They had horses, so they could wander around easily, patrolling the jungle. The Court also saw to the watering of newly planted roadside trees, but it was unclear what department took care of this. Several persons men-tioned that the water was only for the plants the king had planted.

Those areas of uncultivated land designated *bīr* were set aside solely for the Court's use. Farmers were not allowed to graze their animals or cut grass in these areas, we were told, as the Court wanted this grass for his horses.[39] Part of the conscripted labor required from the Mali and Loda communities was to cut these grasses and bring them to the fort in carts. A few persons agreed that in times of scarcity the Court would permit people to take grass from his *bīr* for their livestock. This is the only "famine relief" we heard about in Sawar.

The common grazing land (*charāgāh*) also came under the Forest Department. At that time this land also belonged to the Court, and was used on the Court's sufferance or grace. Some told us that the people could graze their animals and pay no tax. Others said a grazing tax was levied on all animals except cows, so that buffaloes, sheep, and goats were taxed. In chapter 8 we will hear the legendary charter for cows grazing tax-free.

The *jangalāt* also strictly limited tree cutting. Certainly concessions were made when wood was needed—to make agricultural tools, for example—but the general rules prohibited cutting green trees without permission from the Court. This applied even to trees growing in farmers' fields, a source of bitterness and disputes. Some said people were allowed to take dry wood freely; others said that for every bundle taken, one had to be delivered to the fort. As previously mentioned, dozens of interviewees pointed out to us that the *darbār* always donated wood for cremation, no strings attached.

The Stables Department was much smaller than the *jangalāt*. The duties of the stables manager (*kāmdār*) was to look after the horses, with much of the work being done by conscripted labor from the Regar community. The Balai also served in the stables, and sweepers dealt with the horse manure. Sampat Lal told us that there were eighty men serving in the stable, and that they were mostly from leather-worker and weaver communities. Their main work was feeding the horses and keeping them clean. Sampat Lal also told us that there were eighty horses all told in Sawar (eighty is clearly a convenient figure), adding that there also were three elephants and seven or eight camels. The main function of all these burdensome animals was sheer display: if there was a procession, the king would send them to march in it. For weddings among the privileged communities—Brahmin, Rajput, Mina, Gujar—the Court contributed a horse upon which the groom could ride, and from which he would perform the symbolic act of *toraṇ mārnā,* or "striking the wedding emblem."[40] Only a token coconut was expected in return—to be given to the king's man who held the rope of the horse. This was evidently one service the Court offered favored subjects.

Vansh Pradip Singh's three elephants were an important part of his legend. Everyone knew their respective origins: one came to him in dowry; one he bought from some traveling holy men; and one—as related above—was a gift from the Udaipur Rana in appreciation of Vansh Pradip Singh's marksmanship (and boldness).

It is equally important to the Court's legend that his animals did not long survive his death. Many told us that one elephant was sold by the Court of Wards and the other two died, probably of neglect. Ram Narayan Daroga put it more poetically, telling us, "All the animals died crying in three days."

The Treasury Department included a granary (*ambār*), and although Govind Singh had named them separately, we learned nothing to distinguish the Treasury from the Grain Storage Departments.[41] The treasurer, or bookkeeper, maintained all accounts, writing down "who was paid what for wage labor, how much grain went to the servants, how much to the horses, and so forth." Figures given to us for Sawar's annual income varied from forty thousand to one hundred thousand rupees. Even at the lower estimate this would give a fair disposable surplus over and above the sixteen thousand due to the colonial government in Ajmer.

No one said much about the Kitchen Department. We know that the labor of Brahmins and Barbers was conscripted for its operations, and that the Court ate very well. Only Govind Singh described the Liquor Department. He said that although the Court himself drank English liquor, he kept a fire pit always burning for making high-quality local brew. He used two hundred kilos of brown sugar at a time, and *mahuā* (a flower widely used in India for making liquor). It took ten days to ferment.[42] He gave one bottle a day to each manager. Bhoju believes this local liquor was of a high quality, and today would be worth 200 to 250 rupees per bottle. Govind Singh added that the queen gave out bottles as gifts to people who came to respectfully view the Court on festival days such as Holi or Dipavali. He added, however, that no one gave liquor to the peasants.

One thing we learned from traveling to the more remote margins of Sawar was that in many ways life was easier there. No king's men lived permanently in the outlying villages; they arrived only at collection time. Conscripted labor was a less constant pressure. In Ghati-

Gate to the former royal quarters, Gorada.

yali, Polu Kumhar had told us that potters had always to "keep their ears turned toward the fort," listening, under peril of the shoe, in case they should be summoned to labor. No such alertness was required in the outskirt villages. Even in Gorada, named as a tehsil headquarters, the presence of the Court was not felt as strongly or frequently as it was in Ghatiyali or Sawar.

A barber named Kana Nai described the Gorada administration:

BHOJU: How many villages were there in Gorada tehsil?

KANA NAI: There were five villages: Huna ka Khera (Gujars); Kirva ka Jupara (Minas); Loda ka Jhupara; Tikhalya (Mina), and Goroda. [Note that the four hamlets are inhabited by single *jātis*, and that they are too small to be named among the twenty-seven.][43]

BHOJU: Who were the bosses in this tehsil?

KANA NAI: Govind Singh, Chattur Singh, and one Nayab Saheb [assistant to the tehsildar, see above] and one Ram Singh.

BHOJU: Did they always stay here?

KANA NAI: No, they only stayed at the time of the *lāṭo-kūṭo*.

BHOJU: Where did they stay?

KANA NAI: In the *rāj ka noharā* (the ruler's enclosure)

. . . .

BHOJU: How many horses would come here?

KANA NAI: Two or three horses would come, at harvest time.
BHOJU: Did the *darbār* himself come?
KANA NAI: No, only his bosses.

Thus even as tehsil headquarters, remote Gorada was under the eyes of the king's men for only a few days of the year. Places like Mori and Vajta received even less attention.

Two Handfuls

As related at the close of chapter 3, there were three chief sources of painful memories of the Court's rule: forced labor (*begār*), grain taxes (*lāṭo-kūṭo*), and bans (*pratibandh*). In the preceding chapter we discussed bans, especially in relationship to the multiple hierarchical meanings of shoes. The grain taxation system is explored in greater detail in chapter 8. Forced labor pervaded every interview and every setting, and references to it appear in every chapter. It affected family life as much as it affected the Court's operations. Here we will touch on the management of *begār* from the center, and also exemplify its most poignant impacts on lives—which in turn strongly affected people's attitudes toward the Court.

The nature of *begār* is easy to define. Yet from the perspective of different communities it is described differently. The paradigmatic *begārī-log* (people who do *begār*) were the untouchable Regar community. Yet *begār* in one form or another was demanded from persons at every level of society. Brahmins told us that they had to do a kind of *begār* in the form of food preparation for the Court. Persons from Rajput and Charan (bard) communities told us that they were required to perform *baiṭ-begār*—literally "the conscripted labor of sitting." In other words, they had to ornament the Court with their presence on many occasions when they might well prefer to be elsewhere. As one Charan elaborated, it involved "traveling with the king, sleeping with the king's party, having to sit there even if there wasn't any work to do at all. And if someone from that family died we had to sit there, and shave our heads: this was called *baiṭ-baigār*." Of course this is a far cry from grinding grain all day or carrying head loads, but it reveals the lack of personal freedom experienced at every level of society.

The following fragments from our interviews epitomize the nature of *begār* among the lower castes. I begin again with a view from above:

BHOJU: Tell about conscripted labor (*begārī kā kām*).

GOVIND SINGH: The special castes (*khās jāti*) for conscripted labor were Regar and Chamar [both leatherworkers]. In all the villages; they had to grind grain for the horses, and to clean it; and to clean the stables: Regar and Chamar. And the Lodas and Malis [farmers and gardeners]—they carried the grain in their carts. Those who did *begārī* got two handfuls of grain.

The line between conscripted labor (*begārī*) and wage labor (*mazdūrī*) was evidently a thin one. Govind Singh told us that construction work went on all year, ceaselessly, and was done with wage labor. We asked what the wages were and he responded, "One day's wages was probably less than four annas [one quarter of a rupee]—so little it might as well have been *begārī*."

A sympathetic Brahmin, Gajanand Sharma, described the Regars' *begār*, speaking specifically of Regars in Ghatiyali:

GAJANAND: Twelve Regar men [every day] had to go [to the fort] in *begār*, and they didn't give them any food.

BHOJU: Did they go to Sawar?

GAJANAND: No, to this fort, in Ghatiyali.

BHOJU: What kind of work were they doing?

GAJANAND: They had to unload grass from carts and take it to the storeroom; or do construction work in the fort, like preparing plaster; or carry some guest's or some functionary's stuff to other villages where carts could not reach.

Poor things, in the evenings they ate at home when they returned [that is, they had received no meal all day]. No one even asked them, "Do you want bread or water."

Kana Nai described a similar system in Gorada, but he also made the Regars' hunger excruciatingly vivid by telling us about the practice of picking food grain from dung.

BHOJU: Who did *begārī*?

KANA NAI: Barbers, potters, leatherworkers [he uses *boḷā*, a derogatory term].

BHOJU: What work did barbers do?

KANA NAI: They washed all the dishes and lit the lamps—that's the work the barbers did, and the potters did the water-carrying work. And the Balai's work was to gather the villagers to make announcements—that was the Balai's work.

BHOJU: And the Regars?

KANA NAI: The Regar women did the grinding of grain for the horses. There were twenty to twenty-two horses here [in Gorada].

And also they could take some grain for themselves, from the horse's grain. . . . [Sometimes] they ate dung, so people called them "Gobarya." At the threshing ground when the oxen ate grain, then they would take this dung and dry it on top of a *charpoy* (cot), [then remove the grains], clean them, wash them, and eat them.

As we heard from Gajanand Sharma, two handfuls (*do mati*) was standard payment for an entire day's *begār*. Gendi Regar, interviewed in 1993, told me this about her life:

GENDI: In this way I passed my days with a great deal of sorrow. From the day that I came out of my mother's stomach and gained understanding [became *samajhdār*], from that day I never had any happiness. Now I will get happiness in the cremation ground.

[Her younger male relative says to me: "Fill your tape with the old lady, send the poverty of Hindustan to the outside world!"]

ANN: In the time of the great kings?

GENDI: It was not good, the penis-eaters! (*phodo-khābo*).⁴⁴

. . . .

[A number of people are talking simultaneously, confusedly.]

GENDI: The great kings: we went over there to deliver firewood; to bring the horses' grass inside; to grind the grain for horses.

ANN: What did they give you?

GENDI: In the evening the village crier gave us two handfuls [of grain; as much as his two hands together could hold in one scoop].

We interviewed Gulabi Regar in January 1997. She looked very old and small. She told us that her *begārī* work was only grinding grain, and she emphasized that the sweeper dealt with the horse manure and watering the horses and cleaning the stables. Bhoju then asked her, "What did you get for grinding the grain?" What followed was for me

Gulabi Regar's two handfuls (Ghatiyali, 1997).

one of the most poignant moments in 1997, when the nature of the Court's rule was impressed on me by someone who had experienced it from near the bottom.

Gulabi filled her two hands with sand and dust, let it sift through her fingers and fall back to the ground, enunciating in an excruciating quaver, "Two handfuls, only this much."

BHOJU: Did they give you enough grain for your family?

GULABI [repeating in exasperation with our stupidity]: It took all day to grind the grain and all I got was those two handfuls.

She added that she only did *begār* for a few months of her life, until, as she said, "The Court died and it was over." I whispered to Bhoju that I wished I had taken Gulabi's photo at the moment she had demonstrated the two handfuls. She was happy to repeat the gesture, but the look on her face had totally changed.

The Death of the Court and the End of the Game

Because Vansh Pradip Singh died in 1947, his death is thoroughly intertwined with the end of an era. In many accounts he is said to have been fully aware of the coming deluge. Ram Narayan Daroga gave a poignant, bittersweet summary of the Court's death as initiating a period of mourning by nonhumans and sympathetic deaths:

BHOJU: Where did it all go?

RAM NARAYAN DAROGA: It all went along with him, all of it went with him. After the *darbār* died, the elephants died, the horses died; so many died at once they couldn't bury them, and thirty to forty dogs all died at once. By the third day after his death, they all died. When the corpse came in, all the animals started to cry, and they died, crying, within three days. When his corpse came the animals were crying and by the time they came back from the cremation ground they became ill and started to die.[45]

Most persons who talked of the end, described the *darbār* as steadily uncompromising. However, Ugma Loda in 1993 recalled a moment of weakening, when public protest had an impact on policy in the final days of Vansh Pradip Singh's life.

After 1947, we gathered and planted barley for the animals; and the fort people took a whole square of it to feed their horses without permission.

At this time this Suraj Karan Chasta came from Hyderabad and we told him what happened and he wrote a letter and sent it to the (district collector): and then an order came [to the Sawar court]: "You should pay them for the grass you took." This was the first time that the people's opposition, their voice, had effect.

So at this time a party came [of the kings men] and summoned all the farmers to the *darbār* in Sawar; the four men above were named leaders; and the *darbār* asked, "Did you yourselves complain of me?"

"Yes we did."

So the *darbār* asked them, "Did you know what you were doing?"

"Yes sir we knew, we were opposed to you, we were complaining."

So then he compromised. And at that time he gave his minister an order to do something to compromise, because [he said], "I'll die in a couple of years and I don't want any blemish [on my name]." Six months later he died.

In many other accounts of public petition, the Court is said to have always refused to compromise. People depict his position as an insistence that his good name depended on his not yielding to public demands (see chapter 9). But here, near the time of his death, he is said to have acquiesced, under duress, for the same reasons.

Another rather confused account told of the *darbār* responding foolishly to revolutionary words played on a *ṭep* (a tape player, but probably it was a radio). This we heard from Kisan Lal Gujar, an educated farmer belonging to Sawar proper:

And at that time, a cassette came [and was broadcast in Sawar, announcing]: "News has come on paper, India will be free; Gandhiji will come; and every man will be king of his own house (*har ādmī ghar kā rājā*)! This is the kind of times that will arrive in the villages. There will be schools, and everyone will be bosses [*hākim*] in their own homes.

When the Court heard this voice, he went out and said "Who is speaking? Shoot him!"

But they couldn't see anyone because a tape was speaking. And at that time, no one had a tape, so everyone wanted to see [what was happening].

. . . .

The *darbār* died in 1947. When people were troubled he had told them, "There is only a little time left, don't be troubled."

Bhura Mali, a Ghatiyali farmer, also described the Court's last days and summed up the changes at Independence with reference to Gandhi's influence:

BHOJU: So how did all the wild animals and the great kings come to an end?

BHURA MALI: It was the influence of Mahatma Gandhi; at that time Mahatma Gandhi came and we fought for freedom from the British, and at that time the great kings and the British both knew "our time is almost finished" (*hamārā samāī khatm hone wālā hai*), so they stayed quiet.

We started to kill the boars and they did nothing. And at the threshing we threshed without waiting for the *lāṭo-kūṭo*, and we took all the grain to our own homes. And if someone was coming over there [to the threshing ground] from the great kings, we gave them abuse words and chased them right away (*phara bhagā diyā*).

This would, of course, have been unthinkable during Vansh Pradip Singh's lifetime. In people's minds the British and the kings went together, but it was freedom from kings that meant the most to them in their daily lives. The shoe no longer reigned.

Two other Brahmins, Bhairu Lal and Suva Lal, also placed similar events in the context of the Independence movement. The details they give permit us to see more clearly how the transformations sweeping through India also took place in Sawar, under local leadership. Bhairu Lal speaks here about the suffering under the kings, and its end.

BHAIRU LAL: No farmer could eat even a piece of grain while harvesting. And at the time no one could make any protest (*virodh*); even after 1947 they didn't know about the changes . . . people were illiterate; and there was no one to give advice. . . .

BHOJU: Were there any organizations or unions in Ghatiyali who could make objections or motivate the public?

SUVA LAL: In *samvat* 1992 there was Suraj Karan [a Chasta Brahmin and a relative of Suva Lal] who went to Hyderabad and came back, and he was a leader of the Arya Samaj. . . . And at that time he read to people, he read . . . about the leaders of the Independence movement: Mahatma Ghandi, Sardar Patel, Subash Chandra Bose, Jawaharlal Nehru, these kind of men, and people thought about their ideas, and their attitudes (*bhāvanā*) changed, they got excited, and Suraj Karan told the people of Ghatiyali, this has happened in the country and you should be clever and should change yourselves, and I will help you.

And so, whenever the great kings did something wrong, we objected, and little by little change came. They also called meetings around the area, like in Ganeshpura and other places, and told people, "You are your own master, you are free!" He wandered in Kekari and Ajmer, through this whole area, and in this way he [Suraj Karan] had the *lāṭo-kūṭo* finished.[46]

We collected a number of accounts of the succession dispute that followed the Court's death and—after years of legal strife—brought the current Sawar *ṭhākur*'s father, Vrij Raj Singh, the Chausala-wala, to the throne. Some of these were fairly detailed, but I have pruned and condensed here, as they are less relevant to our aims, being the affairs of rulers.[47] According to Gajanand Sharma and others, Vansh Pradip Singh's younger widow, whose sister was married into Chausala, had with the help of a lawyer in Ajmer ritually and legally adopted Vrij Raj Singh in the pilgrimage center of Pushkar in *samvat* 1904. The final court decision that brought him to the throne was pronounced in *samvat* 1908. Relevant to our interests are the accounts of a groundswell of popular opposition in Sawar to the decision to install Vrij Raj Singh as legal heir. Apparently in the early 1950s a large crowd of Sawar citizens gathered to protest this and had to be dispersed by soldiers.

Some told us that the "entire twenty-seven" wanted a different candidate, the Mandara *ṭhākur*, who was also reputed to have been the choice of Vansh Pradip Singh. In any case, there was a collective protest. Chalak Charan described these events for us:

At that time, I was eight or nine years old, and at that time, 4,000 to 5,000 men collected against the Chausala-wala, to stop him from coming.

In the fields and the streets all told there were probably 10,000 to 20,000 with sticks and weapons in their hands.

They, they sent a wireless to Ajmer. And 200,000 or 250,000 policemen came from Ajmer [this is likely an exaggeration].

Mostly they were ordinary police, but some had sticks and some had rifles and some had small sticks. First the rifle men covered the whole *kīlā* [the ruined fort on the hill top above Sawar], and the lower fort [the royal residence], and the others spread around them; and they made an announcement: "In five minutes the whole public should leave. We are putting Sawar under curfew."

First they gave them five, and then four, and then three more minutes. The children had come from the school to see.

They gave them one minute; and then they began to beat the public, the policemen beat them, and many ran away and some were so badly beaten that they died.

Later, after this, the game was finished and Sawar went into the hands of the Chausala-wala.

This is one dramatic moment when the people of the Sawar Twenty-Seven did gather in collective protest, although they were easily dispersed by force. Gauri Nath, an elderly widow with a sharp and cynical tongue, vividly described the scene:

GAURI: For four days all the people from all twenty-seven villages gathered in Sawar.

. . . .

At that time he [Vrij Raj Singh] was in the fort and he didn't come out, he stayed hidden within. Who knows how he made a phone call! But the police came and fired a cannon, and there was smoke everywhere [Bhoju believes it was not a cannon but a gas bomb, a riot control device].

People ran away, and some left their shoes, and some left their *dhotis*, and some left their turbans—they were in such a hurry!

ANN: Did you see it yourself?

GAURI: Nobody from our house went on that day. We were harvesting our *moṭh* [a kind of dal]. It is a good thing we didn't go, because people fell and skinned their knees.

Gauri's recollection, "Nobody from our house went . . . we were harvesting our *moṭh*," points us toward the next two chapters, on homes and fields, where the concerns of daily life may have little to do with courtly passions but everything to do with courtly powers. It seemed to me increasingly that Vansh Pradip Singh, flesh and blood though he was, became a story the people of Sawar told themselves. He was part of their identity as much as they were part of his. Vansh Pradip Singh as portrayed by his "subjects" reads in some ways as a composite stereotype—merging elements of "degenerate princes" and elements of legendary kings from Rajasthani oral epics.[48] Nonetheless, the composite adds up to a unique character that surely reflects in part a real human personality.

Now and then we glimpse behind the proud, aloof, insatiable, immovable figure a man well aware of his own vulnerability. Vansh Pradip Singh is especially vulnerable at a personal level because he was childless—a situation all Rajasthanis view as the ultimate tragedy. But, the *darbār* was also historically vulnerable because his life coincided with the last days of a doomed regime. Serendipitously, the two vulnerabilities—biological and historical—merged to make Vansh Pradip Singh fully cognizant that his death would mark the end of an era.

From the many reported encounters and dialogues we recorded, it seems fair to surmise that Vansh Pradip Singh participated self-consciously in creating his own story. He was well aware of his legendary self and was on good terms with it. He may indeed have cultivated it under the influence of notions circulating in the Rajasthani imagination of how a prince should behave. Often in reported speech the Court above all is concerned with protecting or projecting his reputation (*nām*) or preventing the spreading of ill repute (*badnām*).

Princes in the last days of parmountcy had various reactions to the common foreknowledge of their own doom. Some were hedonists; some were Anglophiles; a few became involved in the struggle for Independence.[49] Some, like Vansh Pradip Singh, simply determined heart and soul to ignore, for as long as possible and with maximum dignity, the changes they knew would overwhelm their worlds. As far as we have been able to discover, our *darbār*'s attitude was not strategic, not designed to promote an outcome. His lack of progeny perhaps gave him a more reckless spirit. His was in every way a holding operation. Indeed, his attitude of *après moi le déluge* seemed a point of honor, and was often very bluntly articulated in his reported speeches.

As we have heard both peasants and nobility describe, Vansh Pradip Singh would turn to his people, his "public," when they complained to him, and ask or command them to indulge his excesses and exploitations just a little longer: "Wait till I die!" "Bear it a little while more." "Soon you won't have me." And they accepted this.

There was no significant movement or uprising (*andolan*) against Rajput abuses in Sawar, although such movements did take place against similar abuses in nearby Bijoliya in Bhilwara district, and elsewhere in Rajputana.[50] My sense, which Bhoju expressed at the opening of his statement in chapter 2, is that because people focused their resentment on the Court's managers and bosses rather than on the Court or on the British, any potential for collective revolutionary action was at least partially undercut.[51] Admiration for Vansh Pradip Singh did not in any way efface his subjects' dislike for the terms of life under his regime, but it may have worked to quell any impulse toward action against the Court as an institution embodied in his person.

Only a few of the old people with whom we spoke—who were educated and had traveled—had been aware in advance of the magnitude of change about to engulf their worlds. For most villagers the changes that came with the end of the great kings' rule were not only radical but unanticipated and disorienting. But they almost immediately brought many improvements, at least in material conditions. These transformations were incorporated into lives centered, then and now, on family, social networks, and food production; and infused with a sense of deities present and capable of intervening in human affairs, both before and after death.

7. HOMES

Not only is hegemony never total . . . it is always threatened by the vitality that remains in the forms of life it thwarts.—Jean Comaroff and John Comaroff, *Of Revelation and Revolution*

Here we turn our backs on the Sawar fort with its oversized ruler and oversized shoe, its fabled elephants and well-fed horses, its rich cuisine and regimented schedules, its treasury and the staff of relentless managers and bosses who saw to keeping the kings' coffers and grain bins full. We shift our focus to domestic spaces, to families and their struggles to survive and prosper under the rule of the great kings as that rule emanated from the visible seats of power. In this chapter we hear fragments of lives, including accounts of extraordinary events and of the daily grind. We hear evocative recollections of sorrow and trouble, of difficult accomplishments and occasionally of pleasures and contentment. We also learn of violent ruptures in domesticity perpetrated by powerful men, and how their victims may sometimes respond in unexpected ways. Throughout chapter 7, our primary concerns are families, work, land, and the multiple bonds of kinship within and across generations. For all of these, the word "home" (*ghar*) stands meaningfully.[1]

My fieldwork design, such as it was, had no life history or domesticity component. Most of our early interviews were pitched at a level of common conditions, and were consciously topical. We most often asked men to talk about "the way things were" in past times, rather than about their own lives. When speaking with women, however, a turn to personal narratives was often the most expedient way to elicit their memories. The question "Tell me about the time of kings" addressed to women could be shrugged off with a "What do I know?" But a different question, "Tell me what it was like for you as a young bride in your in-laws' place," almost always received a voluble response from elderly females. That we have many more descriptions of domestic life in interviews with women than we do with men is in part a result of this interview strategy, as the transcripts that follow make obvious. But such interview strategies result from the way gender roles in rural South Asia locate women's expertise in homes. Gendered positions, therefore, not only affect interview style but condition the tropes of memory.

Some aspects of the Court's rule affected women differently from men; others affected both sexes similarly. Throughout this book we place women's voices alongside those of men, whether describing the lost trees, grain taxes, or conscripted labor. All of the repeatedly stressed key features of "that time" are reported by both sexes in a broadly similar fashion. But in this chapter on homes, there are only two male voices: Bhoju's father and Modu Lal Regar. We simply did not elicit much men's talk about domesticity, housework, or familial trials. And because we found that men, unlike women, were always ready to speak about society rather than selves, it was easier to allow them to do so.

Nonetheless, homes are inhabited by both sexes, and it is clear that men's domestic concerns can be just as strong as women's, as shown below in the narrative of Sukh Devji Gujar. It is also evident from Modu Lal's discussion of Rajput sexual abuse of Regar women that a community's males are deeply involved, and in multiple ways, with the sufferings inflicted on their women. Prosperity and reputation, and the capacity to negotiate successfully in social transactions, depend and reflect on both sexes in the household. It is true that the fruits of economic successes pass largely from fathers to sons, but women participate not only in obtaining but also in enjoying these fruits, and they have their ways of diverting household resources as well.

When activist Mukat Behari Lal Bhargava gave passionate speeches on the sorry condition of Ajmer's rural folk before Independence, he charged the feudal system with reducing them to psychological passivity as well as economic bondage, as we saw in chapter 3. Similarly, many studies of South Asian women have found patriarchy's cages to be at least partially internalized.[2] It seems too easily forgotten that within oppressive systems individuals live full, complex, and sometimes satisfying lives. In this chapter on homes we see many ways in which the rule of kings intruded violently on its subjects—including commonplace conscriptions of milk, furniture, and precious labor time, as well as sexual assaults, altering lineages and characters. But we also see that home life in those days had its meaningful patterns, goals, and fulfillments that were certainly not independent of royal power but rather outside its immediate grasp. This is not to deny that domestic hierarchies were constructed in the shadow, and too often in the image, of political hierarchies. We have seen this to be the case with shoes. I only observe that the well-being of families was multifaceted, and not every facet reflected only the center.

Many of those interviewed who have allowed us to glimpse moments of their lives seem to have challenged those lives' limits in different ways. Some challenged economic limits, as Sukh Devji did when he joined the army or as Gauri Nath did in embroidering blouses at night to double the amount she might earn in twenty-four hours. Others challenged gender structures, as does Raji Gujar when she plots to transfer wealth to her daughter, or Jhamku Bhuvalia when she tells of her girlish resistance to drudgery in her marital home. Regarding the impositions of the Sawar Court, almost everyone who mentioned limits on wood collection, or on eating one's own crops in the fields, talked also about ways of subverting these rules. And we shall hear defiant stories addressing even the most painful aspects of leatherworkers' subjection to royal power. If there is a single motif, it is struggle (Wadley 1994). Such accounts of personal struggle are important to keep in mind as we contemplate Sawar's past under the rule of the shoe with its subtle and gross manifestations of oppression.

The following section, "Intertwined Lives," gives the lengthy narrated experiences of Bhoju's father and mother, recorded on separate occasions. The second section, "Domestic Economies and Ecologies," deals especially with women's work, with the ruptures of marriage, the education of young brides in their marital homes, and interactions with the Court's power as part of daily routines such as fuel gathering. The final section, "From Grinding, Grinding, Grinding the Stone Wore Thin," uncovers the most violent aspect of the regime's penetration of homes and families—rape and procreation.

Intertwined Lives

Neither Sukh Devji Gujar nor his wife Raji had what any of their contemporaries might portray as ordinary, or ideal, life courses. Sukh Devji was orphaned as an infant, and he labored for many years as a landless servant in other men's houses. He then took the extreme risk of joining the British army, and with the salary he earned he was able to begin to transform his own destiny. It made him (in some respects) an attractive match in spite of his lack of paternal kin—he was able to purchase sheep and land. Later, he changed his only son's destiny by allowing him the education that virtually none of his fellow Gujars, at least locally, were encouraging their children to have in the 1970s.

Raji was married off at an early age to this soldier of fortune. In telling her story she dramatizes the pathos for a young girl of such a marriage: "My husband was a pebble in a barren field. This is where my father arranged my marriage." Yet she finds herself with much fulfillment now, and acknowledges the contentment of her mature years. Unlike the vast majority of village women, Raji has spent her entire life in the village of her birth, with her three younger brothers and growing families surrounding her. Because women always complain of the sorrows of going to their in-laws, I had presumed Raji's situation would be considered enviable among women. I was surprised to learn that it was not. Out-married daughters long to visit their natal homes, but this does not mean they want to live in them. As one woman put it, "There is nowhere to visit if your natal home (*pihar*) is your marital home (*sasurāl*)." Women's double identities offer double opportunities.[3] But Raji has made the best of her situation; she is known throughout Ghatiyali as Buaji, or "Father's Sister."

I recorded Raji's story in 1993 and Sukh Devji's in 1997, but Raji is at least ten years younger than her husband. In deciding where to position their stories, I was torn between fieldwork chronology, which would begin with Raji and stay logical in terms of my own knowledge; or "real" chronology. Choosing the latter, I begin with Sukh Devji's interview, followed by Raji's. With the information given in Sukh Devji's story, readers will know more as they read Raji's account than I did when I first heard it.

Bhoju's father's narrative is the very last that I recorded, and the only one I deliberately elicited with a blanket request: "Tell me your life." Bhoju had often suggested that I interview his father, but somehow the time never seemed right, and I also felt awkward about it. When I finally sat down quite formally with Sukh Devji and Ugma Nathji (who was not only an old friend of Bhoju's family but my former research assistant) in summer 1997, Sukh Dev was primed to deliver his unique story. He had listened in on many other interviews over the years, as had his wife.

It is certain that Bhoju's parents' unusual backgrounds have shaped his unusual character, accomplishments, and aspirations. Bhoju's parents' stories, which Bhoju helped me to translate (although not to record) and which held a few surprises even for him, add to an understanding of the deeper origins of this book.

SUKH DEVJI GUJAR (RECORDED ON 3 AUGUST 1997)
Although this chapter is titled "Homes," Sukh Devji's story begins with the loss of his home and a kind of homelessness. He then gains, after great effort and against all odds, a new home, yet never forgets his orphaned beginnings and his lack of male ancestors in Ghatiyali, where he now lives. His birth village Gokulpura—empty though it is for him—remains an important place. For Bhoju, that absence of a strong paternal line in one's own place of residence is often at play in his sense of self. Raji, too, has not forgotten how it felt to be married into nowhere. And yet the intersection of her life with Sukh Devji's produced a remarkable home—a place of comfort not only for the couple as they aged, but for their only son Bhoju, for his growing, flourishing family, and for me.

UGMA NATH: How did you start?
SUKH DEV: When I was six months old my mother and father died. It was the "year of the knots" (gāṇṭhyā kā sāl). It was plague*— within fifteen days they both died, husband and wife. I remained. We were three—older than me were a brother and a sister. My sister's wedding had already taken place; they had given her in

marriage. Both brothers were saved, me and another. Then my paternal aunt and uncle took care of me and raised me.

[Ugma Nathji explained to me that the sister, who also survived the plague, went to her in-laws' place.]

And when I got a little bigger, I worked at different houses and ate. In this way, little by little, I started to grow up. Together with my brother, who also grew bigger, I started to herd some buffalo calves. And they gave me one paisa, for my labor fee.

ANN: One paisa, only one paisa!

SUKH DEV: So, working like that, in this fashion I spent those sorrowful days. And when I was ten years old, I came here to Ghatiyali.

ANN: You came here when you were ten? Did you have relatives here?

SUKH DEV: My uncle's mother-in-law was from here, from Ghatiyali; and her husband died, here in Ghatiyali. So she brought my uncle here, and that would have left me alone in Gokulpura, so I too came to Ghatiyali.

Chhitar Gujar was here, and he said, "Please send this boy to me. I need a servant to herd sheep, and I will feed him." So I started herding sheep.

So in this way I came from there to here. At that time I had nothing—just this [he gestures to the clothes he is wearing, a loincloth (*dhoti*) and a shirt]; a loincloth like this.

ANN: Nothing else?

SUKH DEV: I had nothing at all. I spent seventeen years herding this man's sheep; and he didn't even give me one paisa for a labor fee; I did not receive any labor fee; only food and drink and clothes. . . . Then I left it all and went to stay with a *ṭhākur*. [This is Bhavar Singh Chauhan, a key figure in Sukh Devji's life.] I got one rupee a month! All day I ran the irrigation buckets (*charas*) and the cultivator (*kuḷī*). I did agricultural work all day long.

UGMA NATH: Did you get clothing too?

SUKH DEV: Yes, clothing and bread and one rupee a month. So I spent two years with him and he gave me twenty-four rupees. But after that, came the year of [*samuat*] '96, the famine![4]

. . . .

[Sukh Devji's benefactor has no male progeny, and his daughter's husband also dies; in the hard times of the famine, he sells his oxen, which means there is no longer agricultural work.]

I had no job, it was noon, and that *ṭhākur* and I, we were resting in the Niranjani temple [presumably a pleasant place for a cool nap; it is in the *rāvalo*]. And that *ṭhākur* said to me, "Lālū [an affectionate term of address, meaning "boy" or "son"], we have one famine now, one '96 famine. But if there should be ten '96 famines on this earth, I won't let you die. All you have to do is to bring me one pot full of water in the morning and one pot full of water in the evening."

UGMA NATH [explaining]: "You do this work of getting water and stay with me."

ANN [thinking that fetching water is not men's work]: Were there no women to bring water in the *rāvalo*?

SUKH DEV: No, there was no one else. So [he told me], "Eat well, and live happily!" But I thought to myself, "How long can I spend my life like that!"

. . . .

[Unlike herding or farming, strenuous but respected labor, to be a water carrier doubtless strikes the Gujar youth as demeaning. Soon follows the decisive moment in a tale which Ugma Nath has obviously heard before.]

SUKH DEV: I left at eleven o'clock in the night.

UGMA NATH: He walked all the way to Jahazpur [a distance of thirty-three kilometers]; he left the *rāvalo*!

SUKH DEV [as if justifying or rethinking his position]: What was here? I had no house, nothing at all. . . . I wasn't afraid of anything, and nothing attacked me! I didn't meet anyone at all, I went on foot. [To walk alone in the night requires a lot of courage.] In Jahazpur, at the place called Nauchokya, people were enlisting in the military; in the middle of the city.

There were hundreds of people there, who had come in order to enlist. . . . Carpenters, gardeners, iron workers, Minas, Rajputs, lots of people, all the *jātis*. And a Sahab came, a fair-skinned Sahab, an Englishman. There was just one: Dūk Sahab. [I assume this was a British military officer whose name was "Duke."] He arrived, sitting on a horse, and wearing a hat on his head. . . . People were lined up there in rows, three by three, and the Sahab walked in-between the rows, looking, looking. And then he put a mark on me.

[Ugma Nath explains that this mark was made on his shoulder, with something like chalk.[5]]

And the ones who had marks, they took them over to one side, so they put me on one side with them. On that day, in one day, in the same fashion, 150 people were selected; out of many hundreds who wanted to enlist.

After that he had us seated and he placed a guard over us [so they couldn't leave] and he told the rest to get out.

And they gave us food. And just as much food as we had eaten, they packed that much again in a cloth; and they said, "If a dog eats it, you won't get more, you'll stay hungry, so take care of it." So we slept, and then took this food with us.

From Jahazpur we walked to Bhilwara, on foot. When we crossed the Banas River, the regular soldiers were on either side of us, they wouldn't let us run away, they were herding us like animals. The old soldiers were set to guard the new recruits. There wasn't any [private] place to defecate in Jahazpur; there was a guard watching us even when we were going to the latrine.

Then, when we came back from washing our hands and faces [euphemism for relieving oneself], they counted us, "One, two, three." And they gave us water and said, "Eat your food."

So we ate, you ate, he ate, the cold, leftover *puri* from the night before, and we drank the water from the river, and they herded us along until we came to Dani ki Kotari. We spent the night there, before we got to Bhilwara. We traveled by foot from Jahazpur, and the sun set; so we rested there, and ate; food was ready there, like before.

So the next day, at dawn when the sun rose, they herded us again, to the railway platform* in Bhilwara, where the train from Ajmer came. They seated us [at the station], and the soldiers surrounded us, and they said, "If someone tries to run away we will shoot him!"

There too they gave us food, and after we had eaten, the train came. There were three special cars for the new soldiers; so they shut us up in the train cars, and the train went on to Ajmer.

The trained soldiers, in twos and threes, sat on top of the gates, and they closed the doors and windows, and said, "If anyone tries to run away we will shoot him!"

So from there our train went straight to Udaipur. There we had a medical test, in Udaipur. And those who were fit, in Udaipur, finally they joined the army. There we got food; but for fifteen days there were no uniforms available, so all we had to do was eat and sleep, and we were in great shape (*mast*). . . . After fifteen days the uniforms came. Meanwhile, we watched the experienced soldiers jumping and running. But after fifteen days we got our uniforms, and then they really started to push us.[6] Slowly, slowly, slowly—as with a new pair of oxen—they started to train us. Then people began to run away. Many were running away, but I thought, "If I run away, where will I go? What will I do? Because I have no home, no human beings, no one at all, nothing at all."

UGMA NATH [again prompting, doubtless on the basis of past tellings]: Some were crying, "Oh my women! Where is my house? Let's go back, where is my house? Where are my people?"

SUKH DEV: Some were crying, "Oh my wife, oh my mother, oh my children, oh my sheep and my goats!" But for whom would I cry? I had no one.

So the others noticed me—the experienced soldiers. One called me over and said, "Sit down."

So I said, "I didn't do anything wrong, why did you call me? Why did you sit me down?"

So he asked, "Who are you?"

"A Gujar."

"From where?"

"Gokulpura." At that time I didn't say Ghatiyali because I had no one there.

So he said, "What work did you do?"

"I grazed sheep."

"Belonging to your house?" (*gharūn*).

I gestured to my loincloth, and I said, "This is my house."

Then he congratulated me. He said, "Only you will be able to do this job, the rest will run away; only you will remain, nobody else will stay."

At that time my salary was seven rupees a month. At that time there were silver coins (*chandī kī sikkā*). So I lived well. To whom should I send it? So I got it and spent it.

. . . .

[Immediately after stating his absolute isolation, Sukh Devji turns to the subject of his marriage. As an orphan, he has remained a bachelor far longer than normal in Gujar custom. Any bride found for him was likely to be much younger. The details are a bit vague here.]

SUKH DEV: At that time, Bhoju's mother[7] had been betrothed to a boy from Gokulpura, to some other boy. But that boy got the disease *bāñy* [he could not walk].[8] So that boy's father came here and told her father he refused, because "my son can't do anything."

So then her father betrothed her to me. At that time I had some other relatives, so they talked, and they made this connection.

ANN [*wishing to confirm the name*]: With Raji?

UGMA NATH: With Raji.

SUKH DEV [His mind has turned to his marriage; he temporarily loses the thread of his army life]: Then for fifty years I stayed in this family. My father-in-law and me, all together, for fifty years; at that time I was doing agriculture and I had two hundred sheep, and four oxen. It was good. Together we earned a lot, and then we started to live separately. Then I bought this place. This used to be an adobe house [as I have seen in 1979–81; Bhoju rebuilt it after his first trip to America].

In this way I spent my sorrowful days (*dukh kā din*). In this way I left my Gokulpura. I fathered eleven children, and out of eleven there are two: Mohani and Bhoju.

UGMA NATH: Eleven were born, but only two remain.[9]

. . . .

[Sukh Devji now goes back to the early years of his own marriage.]

SUKH DEV: At that time we were happy, there were three brothers [Raji's younger brothers], but the Lord became angry with them; all the three brothers' wives died, and all three took second wives [*nātā*] which cost a lot of money.[10]

. . . .

SUKH DEV: So I sold my Gokulpura land, and bought land in Ghatiyali.

UGMA NATH: He sold his agricultural land, and bought land here.

SUKH DEV: But I still have a house there.

ANN: You still have a house?

SUKH DEV: Yes I do. There is one man living there now, but if Bhoju wants he can live there.[11]

[Sukh Devji returned briefly to his military life; his salary had gone up to twenty-five rupees, but his father-in-law, wanting him home in the village, had his name cut through some kind of ruse. Sukh Devji resented this, at least retrospectively, as it deprived him of a pension. Now, in his eighties, he continues against all entreaties, to work every day.]

SUKH DEV: My daughter-in-law says, "Stay at home," but I remember those days and that is why I don't stay at home. Today we have money, our condition is good, everyone gives us respect, but if it were all spoiled [their present good fortune], no one would ask about it.

Sukh Devji justifies his compulsion to go on working with his fear that those who now give his family great respect are "fair-weather friends"; in other words, he still feels insecure. At this point Ugma Nathji lectured Sukh Devji about how he ought to stay home and rest instead of going to the fields. Sukh Devji agreed, but obviously didn't mean it. He then concluded his story, strikingly, by returning to the memory of the Rajput who had supported him in his days of poverty, possibly as a parable about the uselessness of wealth without true kinship connections: "So that is how I spent my days of sorrow. . . . That *ṭhākur* I worked for had five wells, he was a millionaire [*karorpati*] in the village. But today there is no one to give him water [that is, no descendants to make water offerings to his ancestral spirit]. His wells were spoiled, his land was spoiled, nothing remains of his name."

Values that inform and motivate Sukh Devji's story seem to be the twinned aspirations to a flourishing family and economic self-sufficiency. Lacking both those, when he started as an impoverished orphan, only hard work sustained his dignity. Although devotion to Dev Narayan has been a major force in his household and personal life, he barely mentions this in the narrative Ugma Nathji and I elicited in 1997.[12] Rather, he presented himself as a self-made man, rejecting dependency on a high-caste patron to follow an unknown path: the British army.

As we have noted more than once, few of the farmers, herders, laborers, and craftspersons from whom we collected oral history narratives ever mentioned the colonial overlords in Ajmer. However,

Sukh Devji Gujar at work in his field (Ghatiyali, 1993).

Raji Gujar at the grindstone (Ghatiyali, 1997).

Sukh Devji—because of his unusual childhood and lack of prospects through ordinary channels—took advantage of the opportunity presented by the British army. It might well have led him to foreign lands or to an early death; but as things developed, it gave him the cash stake he needed to begin forging a new home for himself in Ghatiyali—not so far, after all, from his birthplace. His military experience surely broadened his horizons and his sense of the world's possibilities, hence influencing his parenting of Bhoju.

RAJI GUJAR (RECORDED ON 2 JUNE 1993)

In spite of living in their house for two months, and knowing them for almost two decades, I don't believe I ever saw Raji and Sukh Devji interact with one another. Sometimes I would hear that they had quarreled, but they did it out of my presence and hearing. In public each maintained the customary constraints traditionally practiced by village husbands and wives who will barely acknowledge one another's presence in the room. Bhoju's generation is far less concerned with these pretenses, but he and his wife, Bali, still follow the rules in the presence of Sukh Devji and Raji. Juxtaposing Sukh Devji's and Raji's narratives allows us to see some of the ways gender affects not only experience but its interpretation and representation.

In Raji's self-portrait, readers will observe points where her tale converges with, and diverges from, Sukh Devji's in meaningful ways. Certain areas elaborated by Sukh Devji are passed over very quickly by Raji; others that she elaborates he never mentions. The tragic consecutive deaths of Raji's three brothers' young wives take significance, however, in both accounts, although perhaps in different ways.

Raji, Bali, and I were lounging slothfully in the June heat, as my son and their children and grandchildren came and went, but not disruptively. The fan was turning, sporadically, when the power flowed. I was not especially seeking life stories, but Raji's emerged, almost spontaneously, with Bali's gentle promptings and my own sympathetic exclamations.

RAJI: My father was alone [*either without a brother, or living separately from his brothers*]. We were five children: three brothers and two sisters. I was the oldest, next came Shivji's father Bhairu [now deceased], and Ratan, and then Meva Lal. After that, one sister, Sausar; Sausar is married into Pander. I am the eldest, the eldest of all. My marriage was done alone.

[She means, she and her sister were not married at the same time into the same family. Sibling marriage is today still a common practice among Gujars and other Rajasthan communities (Kolenda 1994). However, Sausar must have been considerably younger than Raji.]

My first marriage arrangement was in Gokulpura; it was an engagement with someone from the lineage Lavara. That boy was sick. I was never married to him, I was only betrothed. He was sick, and he himself forbid it; he said, "I'll die soon and I don't want to give her sorrow." [Note that Sukh Devji had attributed this compassion to the groom's father, not the groom himself.]

BALI: He was unwell, so he willingly broke off the engagement.

RAJI: At this time, this one [Sukh Devji] was living in Ghatiyali.[13] His father died when he was small—his mother and his father. At that time he had an aunt here. . . .[14] So, when he was about as big as Eli [Ann's son] he came to Ghatiyali.[15]

And he did labor for anybody, and working, working, working like that he grew up, and went into the service.

[Raji omits all details of her husband's early years in Ghatiyali; the salient point is that he labored for others, and then joined the army.]

BALI: Did he go before the wedding or after?

RAJI: Before. Then my father, and my mother, and Sundarji's father [a close family friend, fellow devotee of Dev Narayan, and respected man in the Gujar community], they all three decided to give this girl in marriage. [Raji speaks of herself and her wedding in the third person here, perhaps to show her distance from the decision which was evidently not to her liking.]

ANN: Was he living in the *rāvaḷo* then?

RAJI: He was living there, at Bhavar Singhji's. He lived at Bhavar Singhji's for twelve years, and then he went into service. After that I was married to him. My father said, "He has no family, and I cannot send her into the *rāvaḷo*. If he has his own family, then I can get her married to him, but otherwise I cannot."

BALI: If there's no family, then from where will the wedding party [*barāt*] come?

[My understanding of the tape is a little unclear here, but the upshot is that Raji's father asks some Gokulpura relations of Sukh Devji if they are willing to come with a wedding party, and they agree.]

So he [Sukh Dev] went there, to Gokulpura, and the wedding party came from there, and that is how I was married. All I had was ankle rings on my ankles, no other jewelry.[16] My husband was like a pebble in a barren field [*chhāpar ko kokryo*]. That is the kind of place where my father arranged my marriage. Thus he married me. I went there once [to Gokulpura] at the time of my wedding, and after that I never went there, I stayed here.

ANN: About how old were you when you got married?

RAJI: About fifteen years old. So then, we had forty sheep, separate.

ANN: Like a dowry?[17]

BALI [quickly]: No, paid for with Sukh Devji's salary; he was in the army, and then he came back, and with his money he bought the forty sheep; he bought them with his own money.

RAJI [emphatically]: With our own money, earned ourselves! Then my brother Ratan was grazing the sheep; and then her grandpa [she gestures to Chinu, Bhoju's daughter, thus avoiding naming Sukh Devji], he and Bhairu [Raji's brother] were farming together. At that time we had camels too.

ANN: Oh-oh, camels!

. . . .

RAJI: We all lived together for twenty years. Then all three brothers were married, but alas! Bhairu's wife died and Ratan's wife died. First of all Meva Lal's wife died, then he got another in *nātā;* and then Ratan's wife died; and Ratan also brought another; and then Bhairu's died. . . . Then Ratan's wife died, and the one he has now, Gori, he brought her from Asan [near Devli].

ANN: Were any children born, before they died?

RAJI: No. Then Bhairu brought one from Abhaypur, Shivji's mother, Bhuri. It's near Banjari ka Devra.[18]

Up until then, I did all the housework; I ground five kilos of grain every day; I ground corn into flour [finely]; and I always kept a pot full of wheat flour [ready in case some guest should come].

ANN: At that time people ate little wheat?

RAJI: People ate little wheat—but barley, there was a lot of barley. And I kept a pot full of corn meal [a rougher grind] to make porridge.

At that time we would churn two days in a row and then leave off one, and then churn for two. There was more yogurt then. We had lots of milk.

ANN: So you had more butter?

RAJI: Yes. The churning pot was that big [she extends her arms in demonstration]. I couldn't lift it. It was so big that I couldn't reach the bottom easily; so I used a cloth to clean it, I put it in and pulled it out and put it in again. And at that time, the churning was very difficult, so Sukh Devji also did the work of churning buttermilk.

BALI: [who has obviously heard all of this before]: At that time two men would stand together, Sukh Dev and Ratan, one man on either side of the churning pot, women weren't able to do it. And the men did the milking too, Ratan and Sukh Dev: There would be fifteen kilograms of milk at one milking time.

ANN: You sold it all, sold the ghi, or ate it all?

RAJI: We churned, and the buffalo drank [the buttermilk]. We sold no milk; maybe we sold for a few days, but not much.[19] We sold ghi, and drank milk and ate yogurt, but we didn't drink buttermilk.[20]

Then my father died, when we were still living together. [Her voice sounds sad.]

Then we did his funeral feast, Gangoj, with one hundred maunds of grain.[21] We went to Hardwar. And whoever was alive, they gave his name too [including Bhoju, who born by this time].[22]

[The conversation continued, elaborating on a funeral feast held in Gokulpura that was important to Raji's sense of identity, and on other aspects of her relationships with members of an extended family. I asked her about her work in the old days.]

RAJI: Yes, I did housework; I churned, and on the days I didn't churn I did grinding, and I did sweeping, and lit the cooking hearth, and prepared tea, and vegetables, and cooked and fed everyone. And then I did the work of dropping cow dung. And if there was field work I went to the field; weeding cotton, and weeding corn; and after coming home, I went back to that food and drink work.

. . . .

BALI: In my time there is much happiness; in her time, imagine what it was like! She had to take out and dump twenty baskets of cow dung, and grind five kilograms of corn and ten kilograms of wheat, and made corn porridge and feed everyone—a stack of roti this high.

. . . .

RAJI: In the old days we had to bring twenty pots of water.

ANN: From the well.

RAJI: We had to water all the buffaloes and to water all the lambs; we would mix buttermilk in it and feed it to them. And now we don't have to bring water.

BALI: Now there is happiness. We have the tap for bathing, the water comes to the house. In the hot season, maybe we bring one or two pots of cold water [from the well] because the tap water comes warm, for that reason.

ANN: What about firewood? Did there used to be more wood?

RAJI: We used to bring so many bundles down from the hill. I used to go myself.

ANN: What kind of wood?

RAJI: It was *dhokaṛā*. Twenty women would go together.

ANN: Can you remember when the hill was covered with trees?

RAJI: There were *dhokaṛā* over the entire hill, but now it's finished. Besides *dhokarā*, there were *gurjaṇ* and *sālarā* and *jhījhā;* and one was *kharaṇī*, and *kharū* and *hīṅgoṭā*. There were *syāḷī, dhoḷī syāḷī,* and *chūṅrāṛā*.[23]

ANN: Was it easier to bring wood in those times? Was there a "closure" [reserved forest]?

RAJI: At that time there was no closure. When the *darbār* was alive he had guards who belonged to the fort.

ANN: Did he stop people from taking wood?

RAJI: They wouldn't let us bring wood, not even dry wood; neither wet nor dry, they would let us bring nothing! But sometimes they were staying here or there, and we took it quickly, secretly, we tied the bundle and brought it home.

ANN: Did the *darbār*'s workers bother you?

RAJI: [she doesn't quite understand]: The *darbār* didn't come, only the guard. When we were coming back with our bundles of wood, the guard would stop us and block our path, standing in our way; and we joined our hands and grabbed his feet and said, "Please let us go, we won't come tomorrow." And if it was a bad man he wouldn't give a bundle back [that is, he confiscated all their wood]; and if it was a good man he'd say, "O.k., now don't come again."

For three or four days we wouldn't go, and then we'd go back.

When we saw the chance, then we would go. And if we were twenty-five or twenty women all together, and the guard came to the jungle, and we pleaded, and he did not accept us, then we picked up stones [ready to fight, threatening him] and then he would run away.

. . . .

[After some further talk about the wild animals in the old days, mostly by Bali who knows I am interested in them, Raji resumed her reflections on her own life.]

RAJI: Now I have raised Madhu [she is about six], and now I am raising these children—Chinu, and now this black boy [she refers disparagingly but affectionately to the third disappointing girl-baby, Ghumar]. There is only one shortage, besides that I need nothing, I have no greed, no other desire. I keep nothing secret from Bali and I swear by Dev Narayan, I have given up everything.

BALI: Before, you were hiding something.

RAJI: But now, nothing at all. Since four or five years ago, I gave it up. I used to be greedy.

BALI: She used to have this selfish desire, "My Mohani should live here," but now Mohani has a house somewhere else, and she has sons, so now there is no trouble.

RAJI: I used to be greatly troubled [thinking] "after I die what will happen to my Mohani?" But now she is secured in her own place. God has put her in her own place, and she has two sons, and now she is responsible for herself. So now I have nothing to hide from Bali; and if there is anything lying around, I don't bother her stuff, and she does not bother my stuff.

[There follows an exchange between the two of them on domestic income sources, which I omit here.]

. . . .

RAJI: Now I have much comfort.

BALI: Comfort!

This did not quite conclude our taped conversation with Raji, but it meandered further from her personal experience at this juncture, as I pursued more broadly framed questions.

Raji's deep involvement in her daughter's welfare disturbs the stereotypes of a patriarchal and patrilocal kinship system, which says parents should let their daughters go once and for all to their marital fates. But if we are looking for feminist resistance we are disappointed, for Raji readily accepts the cultural rules and labels her own counteractions disapprovingly as "greed" rather than parental concern. Still, her acquiescence to the label never stops her from acting as she pleases. Her personal stance is one of defiance, but not revolution. She accepts the convention that a parent should not reduce patrimonial inheritance meant to be retained within the male line by transmitting it away from a son's household to a daughter's. Personally, however, she is unabashed in asserting that her love for Mohani is stronger than this cultural disapproval.[24]

The lives of Sukh Devji and Raji add to our understanding of the workings of power in Sawar, in part by revealing how much of importance to people living under it was not directly played out in reference to it. Sukh Devji encounters the colonial government in the form of the army and Duk Sahab. Yet for him, rather than the Raj having used or exploited him, he uses the British as stepping stones to his modest goals in life. Sukh Devji and Raji both tell their stories largely without reference to the Sawar Court. Of course, we meet with the forest guard in Raji's description of her household chores, but he is more of a joke than a fearsome figure of authority. Still, the Rajput neighborhood, to which their own was adjacent, was a major force in their lives. It was also read as a lesson by Sukh Devji that his Rajput benefactor, despite his high status, vast landholdings, and good wells, should be extinguished, forgotten, because of his lack of male progeny. This is a lesson on the importance of family. I interviewed Raji before the births of Bhoju's two sons, and that "lack" still simmered at the center of their lives. By the time I spoke with Sukh Devji, all his wishes seemed to have been fulfilled.

We turn now to still more fragmentary glimpses of domestic lives in the time of kings.

Domestic Economies and Ecologies:
Marriage, the Grindstone, and Other Learning Experiences

For Raji, not to have gone to an in-law's house was, as we have seen, a dominant part of her identity. In rural Rajasthan, women's lives, both past and present, are normally marked by the dramatic rupture of marriage. Narratives of a prolonged adjustment to a husband's home were often a starting place in our interviews. We shall listen to several women describe these difficult transitions and adjustments. From their tales we may gather some general impressions of patterns in domestic life, and especially women's work, in the time of kings. We also learn of government impingements, both gross and subtle, on domestic economies and ecologies.

Patterns are evident in these women's experiences, but I find that their strong individual voices also convey a striking variety of responses to and interpretations of such common experiences. We hear different women speak about their lives with a great range of emotions and attitudes including humor, anger, sadness, resignation, and defiance. We hear of relationships with husbands that include expressions of affection, of accommodation, or of strong distaste.

Some women's chores were daily and year-round. Although bringing water and dumping dung are also always enumerated among these chores, the task of grinding grain for flour and making bread seemed to be for all women the center of domestic duties in their marital home. In memories and in folklore, the predawn rising, the sound of the grindstone, the potential (at least in bawdy insult songs, or *gālī*) of trysts in the grinding room, infused this women's work with meaning and sometimes with double entendres. Women today still fill water pots (though more often from the neighborhood tap than the well), and still dump the cow dung. But these days the grindstone is usually silent.[25] If grinding at home for their husbands' families was the paradigmatic work for brides, grinding in the fort for horses was the paradigmatic conscripted labor, although it was only done by leather-worker women.

Among seasonal chores, the difficult labor women most often mentioned was that of directing water through irrigation channels by building temporary mud barricades in the fields—work called *pāṇṇat karṇā*, or "doing irrigation." Women performed this in coordination with men, who drove oxen back and forth to lift water from step-wells in leather buckets—a process referred to as *charas chalānā*, or running the *charas*. Many women—from relatively low-status Minas to high-caste Brahmins—recalling for us the difficulties of their first years as young wives in their husbands' homes, described irrigation as among the most difficult jobs they had to learn how to do. But some had trouble even with cooking.

Gopi and Jhamku talk about when they were brides (Ghatiyali, 1997).

Dai, a member of the barber caste, had prepared meals for my colleague Joe Miller and me in 1979. In 1997, Bhoju and I visited her home, where we had a long conversation with her, along with four elderly Brahmin women, all neighbors of hers. Although Dai's husband was still alive, all four Brahmins were widows. In the excerpt that follows, we hear from two of the Brahmin women: Jhamku, and her husband's younger brother's wife, Gopi. Jhamku did not know her age, but told us that she was five or six years old at the time of the plague (the same plague that killed Sukh Devji's parents, making her a few years his senior). We talked first about her earliest memories of life in her in-laws' place.

Jhamku was so young when she was sent to live in her husband's household that she did not know the difference between a mother and a wife. Probably she was sent at this early age because her husband's mother was deceased and there was a need for female labor. However, the lack of women in the house only increased the little girl's difficulties.

BHOJU: When you came here [from your birthplace] for the first time, how old were you?
JHAMKU: I was very small, I understood nothing. Once when I wanted to go back to my natal home and they didn't send me, I said to my

husband, "So, you bring your own damned mother, but you don't send her back!" (*ki apnī māṅ rāṇḍ ko le ātī ho lekin vapis nahīṅ bhejhtī ho*). And all the women started laughing at me, "You are not his mother, you are his wife."

When I came here the first time, I had no mother-in-law. But in my natal home I had my father's mother, and my mother. Here in my in-laws' place there were no women.

I wasn't able to grind flour, but I still had to grind because there was no power mill.

There was a neighbor, an old carpenter lady, and she would let me sleep next to her, and she would grind for me, and I learned how to grind from her.[26] My in-laws' grindstone was so big that when I sat in front of it [with legs on either side of it, the position for grinding], my hand would not even reach to the full extent of the wheel, so I couldn't grind.

At that time I had a lot of trouble, and I cried because I couldn't grind. In my natal home, people always helped me, and that is why I said, "So, you bring your own damned mother, but you don't send her back!"

The old carpenter lady said, "You are his wife, you are not his mother." And she used to tease me about what I had said.

BHOJU: So when you first came here what kind of work did you do around the house?

JHAMKU: First I got up early and ground the grain, and then I filled the water pots and made the food. And I did irrigation work (*pān-nat karna*) in the fields. My husband would run the *charas* and I would do this work. But because I had grazed cows and buffaloes in my natal home, I didn't know agricultural work. I didn't know how to do it, and the water would go here and there and the mud barricades would break and my husband would have to stop the *charas* and come and show me what to do.

I told the other women, "When I go back to my natal home, I will get five rupees from my father, and I will give it to my husband and tell him to hire someone else to do this irrigation work."

There was a carpenter, Bhura Khati's father [husband of the woman who befriended her], and I said to him, "Please take my silver anklet and sell it, but send me back to my natal home!"

I cried a lot. My natal home was Bangudar. They kept saying, "We will take you tomorrow, or the next day," but then they would say, "Today is not a good day."[27]

Jhamku remembers her hard times with a good deal of humor rather than sorrow; she was not beaten, not hungry, not widowed at an early age. All of this naturally affects the ways her memories are replayed—even memories of hard times.

Gopi, another Brahmin widow, married to Jhamku's husband's younger brother, told us of her own first years of marriage. She portrayed herself as similarly incompetent and disconsolate. In Gopi's story, Jhamku becomes a mentor:

GOPI: When I first came to my in-law's place, I said [imploringly], "Hey Balaji Maharaj [Hanuman], I will keep a vow (vrat) for you, but please have my brother come to take me. I won't eat any bread until my brother comes, only then will I eat bread."

My husband would say, "Eat bread! Eat bread!" [in a brusque tone], and I would say, "No I will eat when my brother comes."

JHAMKU: I would be inside grinding and Gopi would be outside scrubbing a water pot, but she didn't know how to do it. She would take a handful of ashes and put them inside the pot, and move her finger around and dump it out again. Then I called her in because I thought people would think it wasn't good to see a little girl out in the cold. It was winter, and anyway she didn't know how to do it.

BHOJU [to Gopi]: When you came here how old were you?

GOPI: I was thirteen years.

BHOJU [shocked]: You were that old and still didn't know how to wash the dishes?

GOPI: I didn't know anything, not even how much salt you needed to put in the bread dough, even that I didn't know. Right now, my granddaughter is only seven years old, and she can turn on the gas and cook vegetables. But I was thirteen and I didn't even know how much salt to use.

BHOJU: So what work did you do at home? In your natal home?

GOPI: In my natal home there were lots of women, so I did the work of grazing the calf, and I didn't do any housework. I never went near the cooking hearth.

We asked these women about the rulers, and Gopi immediately brought up the grain tax. Although the following chapter will treat these taxes in detail, we listen here to the ways Gopi and Jhamku speak of them as hardships—both in their natal homes, which were not part of Sawar, and in Ghatiyali.

BHOJU: At that time whose rule was it?
GOPI: The rule of *ṭhākurs* (*ṭhākuroṁ kā rāj*). They used to do the grain collection (*lāṭo*) in my natal home. It was the rule of *ṭhākurs*.

At that time they used a system of "fifths" (*panchvī*): Two to the government and three to the farmer. But from those three, the farmer had to pay the *kamīn* [client castes] and so forth, so we ended up with half. And the guard stayed there, when our grain was at the threshing ground. We had to take the [*ṭhākur's* share of] grain to the fort first, before we could take our own share home.

In our place, we used to roast grains in the well, but then a black mark [soot] would be left there from the fire.[28] So . . . we would hold it over the water and shake it so the soot would fall in the water; otherwise the guard would see the black mark and fine us.

. . . .

JHANKU: One-fourth went to the farmer, and three-fourths went to the master.
GOPI: If we took fodder stalks home, the guard would check to make sure we didn't have grain hidden underneath.

Nowadays, things are grand! [*mazā uṛ rahā hai,* literally "joy is flying"]. Whether someone has a hundred maunds or three-hundred maunds, it is all their own.

Note how the amount of the ruler's share escalates in these recollections. Jhanku first says the system gave three-fifths of crop production to the farmer. Gopi next says the farmer received only one-fourth of his crop. We address this mathematical fluidity and its causes in the next chapter. Note also that in these women's home villages, as in Sawar, the king's men jealously tried to prevent farmers from eating their own crops before the Court's share was safely removed.

Although they had genuine troubles, Jhanku's and Gopi's lives were relatively privileged, as has been the life—despite increasing poverty and disappointment—of Motiya Kanvar. She was the senior woman in the joint family household where I had lived for over eighteen months in 1979–81. She was called Elder Grandmother or Dark Grandmother—to distinguish her from her younger sister, Shobhag Kanvar, known to all simply as Grandmother.[29] As a member of the Rajput landowning caste, Motiya Kanvar's memories reveal some striking differences from those of other village women, whether Brahmins or farmers.[30] In other ways, including daily grain grinding, she shares experiences with the rest. Here she speaks about her marriage and her chores. She also recalls feasting on wild pig meat as a highlight of her youthful years. In this savory recollection we glimpse privileges only Rajputs dared to claim. I began with questions about the work she had to do after her marriage into Ghatiyali.

ANN: Was the work hard, grinding grain?

MOTIYA KANVAR: Yes it was very difficult; we got up at the time that the Ram-chanters come, or even earlier, at morning star-rise.[31] That was the time we started to grind corn and barley, and we made barley bread and corn bread and ate it.

ANN: You did that work?

MOTIYA KANVAR: Yes. And we had four oxen and two oxcarts [representing prosperity vastly beyond anything her household possesses today]; one of them was a *tangā* [a cart meant for human passengers, unlike the usual village oxcart, or *bailgārī*, which is used for agricultural hauling and on which people may ride, but decidedly not in comfort].

Whenever we [women] went out, then they hung a rug over the cart [to create a "curtained" environment, or *purdah*]. We produced a lot of grain, it filled the carts [at harvest]. My father-in-law stayed in the field, and we sent him his bread from the house.

ANN [surprised to hear this of a Rajput]: He stayed in the field?

MOTIYA KANVAR: He stayed in the field. Now there's a machine, but it used to be that our oxen did the threshing, both of wheat and of barley; and then we did the winnowing on the winnowing stool; and then we got it ready and filled the cart and brought it home.

[Just as Jamuni Regar did, Motiya Kanvar used the collective pronoun to refer broadly to a human, nongendered community as "we farmers." In other contexts, she says "we" meaning women. I was initially confused by this, as I knew Rajput women did not do agricultural work, and this led to my next foolish question.]

ANN: Did you go to the field, you Rajput women?

MOTIYA KANVAR: No no no! We did not go; our men went, my father-in-law and my husband's younger brother; I only had to do the housework. . . . I would ask my Bhabhasa (that is, her mother-in-law addressed by the same honorific kin term by which she and her sister are both now titled], "What should I cook today, my lady?"

And she would say, "There are such-and-such things, cook them, and make bread dough." Then the men would come, and eat, and after eating they went out, and then we [women] ate. . . . And after eating, we washed the dishes.

Then we put on our eyeshadow (*kajal*), and braided our hair and put on our auspicious forehead marks, and we sat there.

Here Rajput women's lives differ notably from peasant women's lives. Farmers' wives have the classic "double day"—working in the fields and doing the housework and cooking too. They hardly have the time or energy to beautify themselves in the evening. Of course, memory's selective quality is likely also at work here, and we may doubt this was a daily routine. Nonetheless, no woman from any other community ever mentioned such a practice.

MOTIYA KANVAR: So the *ṭhākurs* did farming all day, and in the evening they went to the jungle to kill pigs.

ANN: They killed pigs?

[I am astonished, having recorded scores of testimony to the Court's strict ban on hunting pigs.[32]]

MOTIYA KANVAR: In those days, if we had gone to sleep, they woke us up and said, "Get up and prepare the spices." We had a special pot, and we had to cook the pig's meat. We would all eat it, and then rest for a while, and then [in the morning] they went back to the fields [the men to resume their farm work]. . . . There were lots of pigs in the fields, and there were bushes next to the well. One time a sow with eight piglets fell into the well; and the goatherd looked in the well and said, "O there are pigs in it!"

And our father-in-law learned that there were pigs, so he called my husband, "Bharat, Bharat, there are pigs in the well!" So they went and got them out, and wrapped them in a cloth. He put them on his head, and carried them home. . . . Oh, Ainn Bai, I ate a lot!

In my son's time I have had much sorrow, but in my husband's time I have had much happiness. What I received here I'd like to get again in my next life. I have seen both sorrow and happiness. But no matter, sorrow comes in the world, and so it has come to me too. The roof and the wall never fall down together.[33] My man of the house [*ghar kā manakh*] went away and left me here; he never gave me any sorrow; in his old age he was blind, but still he gave me comfort.

I can well recall a period in 1981 when Motiya Kanvar was nursing Bharat Singh through an illness. She tried to keep him from eating foods the doctor had forbidden, and the cranky old man gave her "insults of the mother," causing her deep distress. More than fifteen years later, however, she chooses to recollect only comfort.

Kesar Gujar felt no similar compunction to speak well of her deceased husband. Kesar was among the most eloquent women with whom I spoke in 1993, with Bali Gujar's help. Kesar had a way with words that impressed even Bhoju, as we listened years later to the 1993 interview at which he had not been present. He was also justly proud of his wife's ethnographic acumen, for without Bali's help I would not easily have communicated on this frank a plane with Kesar.

I might well have chopped this interview into pieces and inserted them neatly and appropriately in several different chapters, for Kesar touches not only on domestic life but grazing land, deforestation, and the contrasts between past and present governments. I chose to keep it together, the better to let Kesar's character appear. I also hope to reveal the weblike quality of her memories, and hence something of the weblike nature of domestic ecologies in which woods and household are multiply connected.

The first topic we discuss is her early experiences in her marital home. Although I had found this topic to be the perfect starter with most women, in Kesar's case it almost shut down further talk:

ANN: Can you tell me about your life?

KESAR: One got married when very little, like two years old.

ANN: Did you go to your in-laws' home then?

KESAR: The first time I went to my in-laws' home, I was like that [points to an older girl, maybe ten]. They started to bring me here [to Ghatiyali].

ANN: Did you like it here?

Motiya Kanvar, Rajput widow (Ghatiyali, 1997).

BALI: Were you happy in Ghatiyali or in Devli [her natal home]?

KESAR: When I was happy in my natal home, would I be happy in fire [bādī]?

BALI: Don't say fire!

ANN: She means she was sorrowful?

BALI: In her natal home she was happy.

KESAR: [referring to Ann] She doesn't understand.

BALI: I will explain to her, but don't say "fire" and words like that. [Fire is often used as a curse, because of its association with death.]

ANN: Say whatever you wish, I need to hear the voices of women.

BALI: Those who write [meaning the men who will transcribe the interviews] what will they think?

ANN: Women's voices . . .

[Many mutual reassurances follow among the three of us, and the interview continues.]

ANN: When you were little what did you do in your in-laws' place?

KESAR: I ground flour, and I brought water, and I rolled bread, didn't I? And I dumped every kind of manure; and I swept; and they sent me to graze the goats and sheep; because I was not clever at other work; they were thinking, "This is easy work so she can do it." That's why they sent me.

In Kesar's case, speaking of the work she did as a young bride led the conversation to flow, without any manipulation, into a discussion of the changing landscape.

Kesar was one of the very few persons we interviewed to speak spontaneously of the earth as a goddess: Earth Mother (Dharti Mata). Of all the persons we interviewed, she was by far the most emotional when speaking of the loss of trees and grazing land. Perhaps this reverence and this grief are connected. Kesar identified strongly with herding work, and she also had a strong personality.

ANN: So, grazing, wandering, did you like it?

KESAR: It was good, good; in my time it was very good, the jungle was plentiful, for feeding the sheep and goats, and for this reason there was lots of milk. But now milk is like medicine [as hard to get, as costly as medicine; her voice sounds unhappy here. Kesar uses her voice expressively throughout the interview].

ANN: So this time is very different from that time?

KESAR: Yes.

BALI: So it was good before? the grazing land?

KESAR: At that time there was much more grazing land, because not that much land was under the plough. There was plenty of land lying there, Earth Mother was plentiful [Dharti Mata *mokalī thī*]; there was a lot of open space. So on their own, by themselves, the wandering animals could eat a lot, and in this way there was no sorrow. Because there was so much uncultivated land [*kānkaṛ*].

But now, all day, we have to stand with a stick in our hands [to keep animals out of the fields]. You didn't need sticks in the past to control them. They could wander where they wanted. Otherwise the farmers say, "Oh your mother's . . . [an insult, with the bad words unspoken]. Why did you let them come in my field!" That is what happens today [herders get cursed by farmers].

BALI: Why did the uncultivated land become less?

KESAR: People took over the land and started to farm it. . . . But in those days there was plenty of uncultivated land, and there was no obstacle in the way of grazing. Now in every direction there are obstacles; like the wall on the hill.[34] It is just as if they put our necks in a noose, as if we were hung! If we give them money then they let us graze, otherwise they will not.

[The conversation turned to gathering fuelwood in the past and present.]

KESAR: It used to be the rule of kings, and if we went to get wood, the king's guard was staying there; but now the government's guard— when they catch us they take money.

BALI: At that time there was much more woods.

KESAR: There was more woods but now there is nothing.

ANN: What happened, how was the jungle finished, what happened to the trees?

KESAR [in a weeping voice]: Alas, people took them, cutting, cutting, you took them, I took them, he took them, she took them, in this way everyone [cut trees]. After the king died, even in the night they took them, people were free, who was the one who would put an obstacle in their path? Here in Ghatiyali and in nearby villages people with saws cut in the night so no one could hear. Who was sitting there?

BALI: Under the rule of the great kings, people feared, but of today's government there is no fear at all.

Later in the conversation, I introduced a question that was frequently provocative: the difference between women's work and men's work. Kesar's reply was startlingly bitter.

ANN: Who does the most work, men or women?

KESAR [initially giving the ready, culturally approved answer]: Men work more; women have more different small works, like getting water, and sweeping and dung.

ANN: And what about men?

KESAR: What do they do? They sit on the curb outside and say, "Hey is the *roti* ready!" They eat. [She has changed her tune suddenly, from dogma—men do the big work—to her own sense of truth, speaking from her heart.]

BALI: And if you don't give it to them?

KESAR: They say: "Your mother's [insult] . . . what are you doing so late?" And then men get even more angry, then what do they say? "I'll beat you with a stick." They get more angry.

BALI: Did your husband talk like that?

KESAR: A whole lot, a whole lot, but now I have comfort. Your Nanaji, [she refers to her husband by the same kin term, mother's father, that Bali uses for him] gave me no comfort. Now my soul is happy; otherwise I was sorrowful. He gave me a whole lot of trouble, his temperament [*svabhāv*] was not good. I couldn't make jokes like you [Bali] and some other women, he didn't like it. He couldn't stand jokes, he was that kind of man.

ANN: He got angry?

KESAR: Now, after his death, I am happy.

BALI [cheerfully]: Now she has no troubles.

I had never before heard a Rajasthani woman boldly express happiness over the death of her husband, or critique his character while living or dead. The only exceptions were a few obviously amiable old couples who would joke around in one another's presence, as Kesar's husband clearly refused to allow. While Motiya Kanvar romanticized her relationship with her husband after his death, Kesar spoke bluntly, without any attempt to soften the truth.

Gauri Nath was a feisty, wiry woman whose many personal losses and constant hardships seem to have strengthened but not depressed her. Her identity as a member of the Nath community gave her a distinctive perspective on life. Naths are small farmers, like Gujars and Minas, but they are also performers, magicians, and temple priests. Moreover, they follow a religious teaching strongly focused on form-less divinity and liberation from rebirth; perhaps this in part gave Gauri her ability to joke gaily in spite of life's very hard knocks. Gauri had lost her only two children and had been widowed twice. She was the adoptive mother of Nathu Nath, who was one of my closest assis-tants in 1979–81. Her husband in Ghatiyali was cousin to Madhu Nath, from whom I recorded the tales of Gopi Chand and Bharthari (Gold 1992), and he too had once performed. Nath women do not perform publicly, but Gauri had a touch of theatricality in her speech style, and sometimes she used phrases with a ring of Nath performa-tive language to them.

Shambhu Nath went with me to interview Gauri. On this occasion my first questions were about women's lives in general, and later about personal sorrow. For her too, grinding grain looms large—especially as she remembers funeral feast preparations.

ANN: Tell me about women's lives, what's the difference for women between the past and the present?

GAURI: Lots and lots! We used to eat hot green peppers and bread, but now we don't even think about hot peppers.

And we used to wear cotton—thick, handwoven cloth; there didn't used to be any polyester, but now that's what we wear. Today there are so many kinds of cloth.

. . . .

ANN: Tell me about differences with veiling your face.

GAURI [she demonstrates]: When our face was totally covered we used to speak very softly, and if we had to call someone we whispered; but today we yell out loud, "Hey, kid!" Women used to speak . . . little, but today they speak directly.

ANN: What kinds of work did you do before?

GAURI: We used to grind all the grain, even for funeral feasts and weddings; we would grind five maund in fifteen days; at Madhu Nath's father's funeral feast, each of us women ground five maunds of grain. There were fifty maunds to grind; so we gave each woman five, and in fifteen days they did it. And sometimes we would grind for someone of another *jāti*. Once a *dhobī* [laundress] died, and other women ground for her.

ANN: Did you charge for that?

GAURI: All we got was fire [*bādī;* in other words, nothing]. One time there was a Gujar funeral feast, and they gave me ten kilos of grain to grind, and I gave them back flour. At that time, if there were one hundred maunds to grind, they would spread it out over the whole village. At that time there was no water tap, so we had to carry water.

ANN: Did you bring it to the house for bathing?

GAURI: No, we would bathe there [at the well]; no one bathed at home. But today we use soap, and we make warm water, and we bathe at home. At that time there was none of that. But for me, I don't like using soap, the same way I don't like poison for food.

. . . .

ANN [*knowing Gauri had been a seamstress in her day*]: Your skirts . . . when there was no sewing machine how did you make them?

GAURI: We sewed them ourselves by hand. Now my eyes cannot see well enough, but I used to be able to make good blouses and skirts by hand; I did embroidery. I made blouses so well, I embroidered them, put on silver trim, and the women who wore them [looked so beautiful] they were soaring![35]

At that time Gujar women didn't know how to make blouses, so they gave me one anna for making one blouse. The Gujar women would do wage labor (*mazdūrī*) and get one anna, and I would make a blouse (*kanchalī*) for them and they would pay me that one anna.

At that time after eating, I would sit by the lantern and make a whole blouse, every night.

SHAMBHU: She also did wage labor for one anna a day. And for sewing the blouse she got one anna.

GAURI: There was much sorrow, and the kind of sorrow I had no other woman could even stand to see.[36]

My husband lived with his elder brother, but one day my husband's elder brother's wife [decided to separate me] . . . There was another building in which the goats lived, so they cleaned up the goat house, and repaired it, and after that they put my water and my clothes there and they put some grain there. I didn't want to be separate but they put me there, and I cried. [This happened while her husband was alive, while she was young.]

Looking back on a life of serial losses, disappointments, and perpetual hard work, Gauri radiated vitality and resiliency of spirit. Although she spoke of limitless sorrow, her eyes sparkled, and I left the interview smiling.

We had a very different experience talking with Dhapu Mina, the mother of Hira Lal Mina in the village called Napa ka Khera.[37] There were three old women present, as well as Dhapu's granddaughter. Dhapu was the eldest woman there, and the one we had come to see. She was about eighty years old and—as Bhoju had not realized when he decided to call on her—very ill and weak. She had an old connection with Bhoju's family through their shared devotion to Dev Narayan at the Ghatiyali shrine of Puvali ka Devji. Unlike most interviewees, Dhapu was very reticent at first, almost monosyllabic. Bhoju eventually managed to draw her out to speak of her sorrows. We talked with her about women's work in the time of kings.

BHOJU: What kind of work did you [women] do at home [in your youth]?

DHAPU: We ground grain, and at that time we were growing cotton, so in the hot season we had to irrigate it. Cotton and corn, those were the crops we grew. We planted them, weeded, irrigated; and we did irrigation work for the barley crop too.

BHOJU: What time did you get up in the morning?

DHAPU: At the morning star-rise [around 4 to 4:30 A.M.].

BHOJU: What was the first thing you did when you woke up?

DHAPU: Grinding.

BHOJU: How much did you grind?

DHAPU: Five kilos.

BHOJU: And then?

DHAPU: At that time we had sixty cows and ten oxen, and we had to do the cow dung dumping.[38] When my grain-giver [the sun] was coming over here [she gestures at the sky] I finished that [Bhoju interprets her gesture as around 10:30 A.M.]. And my mother-in-law did the cooking.

There were no sisters-in-law. I was alone, and with me were my husband's younger brothers; so I was afraid all the time, because any of them would beat me [her father-in-law, her husband, her brothers-in-law].[39] So, I would do the irrigation ditch work all day. We had two *charas* on one well, so the water would flow more quickly, and we did this work all day.

BHOJU: Did you give the land to sharecroppers?

DHAPU: No we did all the work ourselves. At that time there were five brothers, one grazed the cows and some did farming, and one wandered around here and there. . . . I did the irrigation work. . . .

BHOJU: It seems as if you had a lot of trouble, from cock's crow to late at night, it was very hard work. When did you get any rest?

DHAPU: I never got rest in my whole life. Whenever I remember those times I am very sad, and I get tears in my eyes. Later two of my husbands' younger brothers' wives came and I got some help, but all my relatives beat me; my father-in-law, my husband's brothers, all of them. Sometimes my father-in-law wouldn't give me any food for five days, I swear by the sun [she looks up]: not even a seed of grain. The wind did not even blow a seed into my stomach.[40]

And even so I ground all the grain and did all the work, ground so much grain. Everyday I did all the grinding, the cow dung, and the irrigation. In Jeth [May–June, the hottest month], in the hot season, the days were so long, and the *lū* [hot wind] blew so hard, and even so I worked all day without eating anything.

BHOJU: It seems as if you would have produced a lot of grain, but still you remained hungry?

DHAPU: It all went out to pay debts. I don't know how much they had taken in loans, but as much as we earned it all went. Much did come, three or four carts of grain, but I don't know where it all went.

Dhapu frequently stresses the role of merchants and the oppressions of debt. One merchant, we learn, had served her family very ill by loaning them substandard grain for a funeral feast: "When my father-in-law died, then I didn't have grain. We took grain from the *baniyā*'s storage pit, but when we make it into bread it had a reddish color. When my father-in-law died, we borrowed grain from the storage pit, and people laughed at us." Dhapu's family was embarrassed because of having to use inferior, borrowed grain, thus losing face within the community. Continuing to speak of hard times, Bhoju asked her whether she ever received any help from the Court: "No, he didn't give us anything. We only took grain from the merchant. We were his debtors. People had to give their grain from the threshing ground to the merchant and then borrow it back with interest."

Dhapu was aware that her granddaughter Gita, a pretty young woman who was sitting with us, would not experience sorrow like her own. She turned the conversation away from herself, to the girl and her future. When we talked with Gita she actually expressed enough contentment with her marital home that Bhoju found it a bit unseemly and humorous, as complaint about living conditions in a husband's home is not only based on reality, but is a culturally enjoined attitude.

Both with and without Bhoju present, my conversations with women were often held in groups. I made one long recording in 1993 while sitting with women in the Ghatiyali neighborhood called the "Bazaar"—also known as Solahpuri (Sixteen-City) because of the sixteen different castes living together there, including Muslim, tailor, bangle maker, royal drummer, goldsmith, and merchant. The Bazaar's inhabitants are garrulous, always ready to order tea and gossip. Over my years in Ghatiyali I most often thought of this street as a hazardous slowing of whatever purpose I might have—a block of human speedbumps. I would go out of my way to avoid the Bazaar unless I wanted to sit and talk.

On this occasion I approached with recorder in hand, accompanied by Lila who would help me when my Rajasthani floundered. This was during the inchoate phase of our history project. Many themes and topics pursued elsewhere more diligently emerge here, especially some of the multiple ways the Court's rule impinged on the everyday economies of every single group: how even the grains a bangle maker might earn in trade for her services would be taxed on the road home.

I asked the women who rapidly collected around me about the time of the great kings. One answered, self-depreciatingly at the start, "What do we know about the great kings? They took *lāṭo*!" The noise level then rose considerably. In transcribing this conversation Bhoju and I were able to identify with certainty only Bhuri Lakhari among the group of six or seven women who gathered around me and Lila.

A BARBER WOMAN: They took *lāṭo*, but even so we were happy.
[The barber community, like some of the other smaller service castes closely associated with the Court, was among a distinct and small minority that recalled more advantages in the old days than farmers ever did.]

SECOND WOMAN: It was like this in the time of the great kings: whatever the grain harvest was, whether it was wheat or barley or chickpeas, they didn't let us bring it home.

ANN: They didn't let you bring it?

BHURI LAKHARI: And, if we go to another village to sell bangles, then we cannot bring the grain [received in payment for bangles] to our village from outside. They didn't let us bring it, they wouldn't let us bring home grain from other villages.

ANN: This too?
[This is the first time I heard about the Court's claiming not just grain from the fields but grain earned in exchange transactions by craftpersons.]

SECOND WOMAN: The tax collector was there; for food we died of hunger.

THIRD WOMAN: We could bring just a very little, secretly, secretly, in the basket. And on top of that we put cow pies [*phoṭā*, wet "cow pies"; not a substance in which the kings' bosses would enjoy poking around]. In this way we brought it, and then we could fill our stomachs. There was that much misery in that time.

And whoever accompanied the great kings to the field, he also took a share (*bāṅṭo*): one share to them [the king's men], and one to the rulers, and a third would be ours.

ANN: Only one-third!

WOMAN: That's the way it was in that time. Now the government's* time has come, so what is left? Nothing! Now everything is open.

The same speaker turns to the subject of eating in the fields, an important one:

But in the old times even if we boiled wheat berries (*gūgarī*) in the field, they snatched that away too.

BHURI: If they find out about it, they take it away. Once we were boiling wheat berries, and the tax-man came, so we threw the pot in the well. It was cooked, and ready to eat, but we weren't allowed to eat! If they see smoke, they come and check.

[This was obviously a vivid memory, of throwing out food ready to eat, for which your mouth was watering, in the lean time just before harvest.]

. . . .

The low castes were doing *begār:* some went to grind the grain, some went to drop the grain, some cleaned the grain. Others made bread. And this barber woman—barbers swept their kitchen and rooms and house and washed their dishes. And the barber,[41] her groom, he shaved them.

ANN: Yes, they shaved the Court people.

BHURI: The washerman did their washing and pressing, like that— that is what we call *begārī.*

ANN: That is *begārī.* So, what did the tailor do?

WOMAN: Sewed their clothes.

ANN: Without pay?

WOMAN: They paid, but only once a year; they didn't pay every time; just once a year, their manager, he would say, "Give them some grain. Give the grain to the washerman, to the *begārī* people." The managers hung around [the threshing ground] like that.

We see here ways in which the specific work of different communities was conscripted, and all earnings were taxed.

In this segment we have heard of personal and public sorrows, of hard work, and of the Court as a kind of constant drain—perpetually siphoning sustenance from household economies. It is hard to see any gainful work in the time of kings that did not pay its heavy toll to the Court. Other tolls taken were not measurable in goods.

"From Grinding, Grinding, Grinding, the Stone Wore Thin"

In chapter 4 Jamuni Regar gave one epitomizing example of conscription: "So in the day the Malis and Gujars took the beds, and made you sleep on the floor. And even if a woman was in childbirth labor, they would put her on the ground." Jamuni was one of many who told us that a woman in childbirth could be summarily removed from a cot required by the Court for guests.

In chapter 5, we listened to Polu Kumhar's expressive description of the king's men entering his kitchen, wearing their shoes, and taking the milk from the stove: "Sometimes we are boiling milk on the cooking hearth, and if someone in the fort needs the milk they will come with their shoes on, and walk in the kitchen, and take the milk and go, and we can't stop them." He also described the conscription of beds; this time from under children: "And suppose our child is sleeping on a cot and some guest comes [to the fort], they won't even wake up the child, they will just take it off the cot and take the cot. That's the kind of work they did. In this way all castes were sad, believe me." These examples of conscription clearly were deployed as paradigmatic images of the regime's callous brutality, epitomizing the cavalier fashion in which the king's managers and bosses intruded on village homes.[42]

Conscription takes many insidious forms. One subject I had never probed but often wondered about was whether the king's men had equally casually and brutally conscripted the sexuality of low-caste women—a cruel aspect of rural South Asian hierarchies acutely portrayed in painful fictional accounts.[43] For obvious reasons, these questions I would never ask, nor would Bhoju. Not a word had ever emerged alluding to such matters until late in my 1997 fieldwork, or so I thought. In concluding this chapter, I confront this other modality of conscription imposed by the king's men—of women, sexuality, and fertility. After I heard these stories, I wondered if other images such as the violent removal of beds with total disregard for persons were not screens for darker manifestations of courtly abuses.

No woman ever said anything to me directly on this subject, nor did any man in Ghatiyali or Sawar.[44] But in the more anonymous setting of Devli City, a male leatherworker broke silence and spoke of his community's trials, in blunt language. This man, Modu Lal, expressed sympathy for the helpless, assaulted women, but—with what struck me as a very male perspective—he laid far more stress on the resulting mix of Rajput and Regar blood. He saw this as productive of social change.

Leatherworker women were under the eyes of men in the fort when they went there to grind the horses' grain; opportunities for assault were built into the situation, especially in the Ghatiyali fort, which was used more as barracks than home in those days; no Rajput women were living there.

When later I reread interviews with Ghatiyali's Regar women I began to imagine hidden texts. Speakers may have alluded to this taboo subject without my realizing it. I shall open and close this section with women's words. The closing passage is a mythic narrative recorded from a Ghatiyali Regar woman who had only briefly done *begār* in the fort, in her early years, just months before the death of the Court. Retrospectively, her devotional tale became weighted with a new set of powerful meanings, after I had heard men speak about frequent rape of young *begārī* women such as she had been, in the time of kings.

I begin with a 1997 interview with Gori Regar, which had felt uncomfortable and seemed unsuccessful. The atmosphere was tense, Gori was visibly ill at ease and unhappy, her younger male kin seemed to be sneering, whether at her or at me I was not sure. On rereading this interview—filled with ellipses, allusions, and contradictions—I imagined it to hint at shame-evoking memories for Regar women. It was as if their sexual vulnerability in the fort were public, if unspoken, knowledge.

BHOJU: What kinds of work have you done in your life? farming?

GORI: I have done agricultural work and lots of dumping stones and dumping clay; I have done much of this clay-and-rock work. In this way I raised them [her children]. There was only one job I could do; otherwise there was no other source, I experienced sorrow.

BHOJU: What kind of work is best?

GORI [clicks her tongue]: Now [in old age] there is rest.

BHOJU: Do you remember the Sawar Court, the great kings' times?

GORI: Yes.

BHOJU: I have heard there was a lot of jungle. Do you remember it? [Gori tried to persuade us to interview a different old woman. One of her younger male relations then taunted her, "Why don't you tell it? Is it hard for you to tell? Are you afraid?"]

GORI: We were doing *begār*.

BHOJU: What kind of work did you do?

GORI: Oh *begār*. But my family really didn't do *begār*, we worked for the farmers. Then men did it, but the women didn't do it. Well, from other families, men and women both went [to the fort].

ANN: But you didn't go?

HER SON: She also used to go.

. . . .

GORI: We were grinding cracked grain for the horses.

HER SON: We ground it at home and sent it.

GORI: No, we were grinding it there. In the fort was a grinding mill, and we ground it there.

ANOTHER MALE REGAR: From grinding, grinding, grinding the stone wore thin.

I thought to discard this interview as incoherent: Gori denied going to the fort, her son contradicted her; then when she acknowledged going to the fort, he attempted to undermine that acknowledgment. This text began to haunt me. Why was Gori so reluctant to talk about *begār*? Why this tacking back and forth between agreement and denial? Such confusion was very rare in our interviews on the kings' times; most narratives were straightforward. What did the unidentified male voice mean: "From grinding, grinding, grinding the stone wore thin?"

It was about a month later (19 February 1997), in Devli City, that Modu Lal, a tailor, opened our eyes to a discourse about the king's men as sexual predators—practicing a violent form of conscription. A series of stories suggested that their eyes might be attracted to any females in the powerless untouchable communities—not just *begārī* women in the fort. Modu Lal initiated this discussion. He was speaking on a common theme: the king not being to blame for his men's ill doing. Suddenly, with no preamble at all, he brought up rape, using a direct word—*balātkār*. His chief theme, as I already noted, was less the anguish of women than the altered lineage within his community, to which descendants of Rajput rapists belong.

MODU LAL: If you rape my daughter, the blood of my lineage is changed in the coming generations; the coming generation, won't it fight with you? Someone born in a Regar family but not of the Regar patrilineage, he will quarrel of course.

This is the main reason the kings' rule went! The women from the small [low] castes didn't understand. They went to grind grain and cut grass for the horses, and to fill the carts with grass. And if someone's mind was spoiled, and he grabbed her and pushed her down, there was no one to help, or say anything, or object. There was no one to say or to hear anything.

BHOJU: They used to do that? . . .

MODU LAL: At that time we had many troubles.

[He moves into a storytelling mode.]

Once a Rajput soldier was coming along the river; and there was water in it [not always the case with the Banas]. A Chamar woman was working on the other side.[45] He told her to come and take his bedding on her head across the river; and at that time his mind went bad, and he did improper work with this woman; he raped her.

She became pregnant. Poor thing, what could she do? And she had a child.

And fifteen to twenty years later, the same soldier came by again with his bedding; and the child was in the field.

And he said to the child, "Come here and carry my bedding."

The child said, "Who are you?"

"I am a *ṭhākur*."

You may be the *ṭhākur* of your house but you are not my *ṭhākur*! I have a bundle of fodder, why don't you carry it to my house? I am the *ṭhākur* of my house!"

So the *ṭhākur* was angry and asked him his name and his father's name. In the evening the *ṭhākur* went to his house to complain to his father, "Your boy did this."

At that time the woman came out and said, "This boy is not his son, he's your son. Remember what you did. My son is not speaking as a Chamar; your blood is speaking" (*āpkā khūn bol rahā hai*).

That's why people [that is, leatherworkers] have changed their regard for Rajputs. They used to be afraid of *ṭhākurs* but they are not anymore because they are their descendants.

It used to be that they would say, "See, here is my fodder storeroom; go in and get some." And then they would rape them.

"Why do you make yourself equal with me?"

"Because I am yours!"

Blood won't stay hidden!

Modu Lal immediately began to narrate another event, which according to Bhoju is an old story, dating long before the period of our research. Several times in the course of this tale the narrator made asides concerning a particular Ghatiyali Regar man, Indar Jit, whose looks and demeanor were like a Rajput's. I had noticed this myself on my few forays into the Regar neighborhood. For Modu Lal, this man's existence and behavior proved his point. I recalled how encountering Indar Jit's presence and mannerisms among the Regars had startled me, and made me think about how used I had become to the subtle and not so subtle subservience we usually encountered in that community. Social position is encoded in body language, and, for whatever reasons, his was indeed not Regar.

MODU LAL: Once, in Devli Gaon, a *panchāyat* [council meeting] of the whole village was taking place; and there were some chairs for high people and the rest were sitting down; and a man of our community came, an intelligent man, and he sat on a chair, and at that time some young men, Rajputs, were laughing.

"Look at this Regar sitting on a chair in front of the whole village!"

The elders, who understood things, said "Leave him alone." But the young men objected.

He [the Regar on the chair] said, "Wait a second; who is this Rajput boy who was laughing at me? You are Dool Singh's son? Well, Prince, listen to what I have to say. In your fort, my mother went to do the work of dumping cow dung, and your father raped my mother and I am his progeny.

"And my father was your servant doing agricultural labor; and once your mother grabbed my father and you are his progeny.[46] So, you're the one who should sit lower. I may be a Regar, but I am Dool Singh's son so I will sit on the chair."

This is a true event of Devli Gaon.

The managers did this dirty work. And that's why people were ready to fight them, because they are their progeny.

. . . . .

The Regar who told Dool Singh he was his father's son was Nandalal. It is not good to have recorded this, because Dool Singh's descendants are still alive and so are Nandalal's, and they wouldn't like this. [He does not seem to be truly regretful.]

In the whole jungle, show me a tree that the wind doesn't strike and whose leaves don't move! There is adulteration everywhere; all have been mixed up and become equal. . . . People who are bumpkins [*guphā;* behind the times] still think we are leatherworkers, scheduled caste*; so we can't sit down or ride on mares, but the literate don't think this.

BHOJU: We still have our cultural traditions and you can't kill them all at once; you want to drink water at my house, but you can't. Maybe one hundred years from now it will be possible.

MODU LAL [not agreeing with Bhoju in the least]: Yes, change has happened!

Bhoju later told me that he had discovered in Modu Lal's words a different way of thinking about changes in social hierarchy. If young members of the leatherworker community were proud and bold, it might indeed be appropriate if it was their Rajput fathers' blood speaking.

Four years earlier I had first visited the Regar neighborhood, led by my drummer companion Lila, hoping to talk with old women. On that day, I had recorded a devotional story from an old woman named Gendi, and afterward I pretty much forgot about it. After our eyes were opened by the Devli interview, Bhoju and I returned to this tape and translated the story, which appeared in a new light, expressing the Regar community's resistance to sexual assault by Rajputs. That assault is lightly veiled here as a highly inappropriate marriage demand. This story is as fierce in its way as was Modu Lal's narrative of Dool Singh's son. Although some deny that devotional expressions within Hinduism can ever speak subversively against caste hierarchy, this tale offers a strong statement of psychological opposition to Rajput oppression.[47] In it the goddess Ganga—sometimes titled the "Mother of Purity"—destroys a lecherous Rajput and all his companions.[48]

Lila and I had been talking with a group of Regars of various ages. We had come particularly to interview Gendi, but spoke for quite a while with her grandson's wife, Sundar, who was in her thirties.

SUNDAR: We belong to the lineage of the devotee Raidas.

ANN [*knowing that Raidasi is the polite name for Regars, which nobody in Ghatiyali ever uses*]: That's why you take his name?

SUNDAR [and others]: Yes [they laugh].

LILA: The great devotee Raidas belonged to their community.
ANN: Yes, he is famous, and has arrived in our country![49]

Lila was always ready with a tale. She told a story of Raidas as a baby, first refusing to suckle from his untouchable mother's breast, but doing so after the midwife chastises him and instructs him, "Drink mother's milk; wherever you were born you are born, so drink happily, your name will be worshipped, you will be famed, no matter in which community you were born."

Lila followed this with another episode in which Raidas, now a grown man, is tanning hides when a group of pilgrims passes on pilgrimage to the Ganges River. Raidas pulls a bangle out of the dirty water in his leather tanning pit and sends it with them as an offering to Mother Ganges. The bad odor of the tanning pit is an ostensible reason for leatherworkers' untouchability.[50] Mother Ganges herself emerges from the river to accept Raidas's bangle. She simultaneously grants Raidas a vision (*darshan*) of her form, while he is sitting at home working. He is such a devotee that he has no need to go on pilgrimage to meet divinity, which is present in his "polluted" home.

I asked the Regars listening if they knew this story, and they were noncommittal. It is a story very much within the tradition of low-caste devotion—in which a great but simple-hearted untouchable devotee is recognized by a deity as more truthful and sincere and pure of heart than any high-caste devotees who perform appropriate rituals. But Lila's tales also hint that even Raidas was not very happy to be born a Regar.[51]

Gendi, the old woman we had come to see, now spoke up and told me that she did know this, and other stories too. She proceeded to tell another story, also about the pure goddess Ganges treating her devotee Raidas with favor. But this has a different and far more defiant ring to it.

One time Raidas had a wedding [in his family, of his daughter], so he brought Ganga [the goddess] to the wedding as a guest. In that village was a *thākur,* and the *thākur* went riding on his horse to the Regar's house. He said [to Raidas], "I want to marry this girl" [Ganga Mother].

The *thākur* was riding around on his horse, and came to the Regars, and said, "I will marry this girl."

[This is a realistic characterization of arrogant Rajput behavior; were it not that the "girl" is a goddess, and the proposal "marriage," this could sound very true to life: the Rajput on his horse looks over the untouchable women and demands that the most attractive be delivered to him.]

Raidas said, "This is my guest! How can I marry her to you?" Then Raidas beseeched Ganga Ma, "O Bhavani, this *thākur* is bothering me! He wants to marry you, so what should I do? I have brought you as a guest to the wedding, and he is acting this way."

She said, "It doesn't matter, if he wants to marry me, accept his wedding coconut; accept it as if you agree, and have me married in a very nice way."

The goddess continued, "When the *thākur*'s wedding party comes, then you should fill the *adha kī kundi* [the leather-tanning tank]—fill it with water and have them sit down near it. After that, I will take care of everything. That is all you have to do."
[Lila explained, in an aside, that he was to seat the Rajput and Regar groups separately.]

Well, Mother Ganga said all that. Then the wedding parties came. So, he filled the tanning tank, and he married his daughter to the Regar on one side, and he seated the Rajputs on the other [as if to marry Ganges Mother to the *thākur*; all Rajasthanis will picture the demure, veiled bride seated next to the groom]. Then Ganges Mother jumped into the tanning tank and the water rose up and washed away the whole wedding party! They were flooded away! She swept them away! [She didn't want to kill the Regars, Lila interpolates.] The whole Rajput marriage party just flowed away!

Gendi chortled audibly on the tape at the story's satisfying ending—merciless and thorough divine vengeance. The Rajput men did not just drown, they drowned in water from the leather-tanning tank: a fitting filthy end to match their filthy lust, an appropriate overwhelming of their imperious arrogance, evidence that the purity of Mother Ganges resides even in the evil-smelling hide-tanning pit.

This story appears to take up the theme of divine favor to Regars from the mother of purity, begun by Lila with her stories. However, Gendi's tale struck me as ringingly opposed to established social hierarchy in a different modality from the two Raidas tales Lila had offered. It was the difference between "God loves me even though I'm polluted" and "Those who prey on our seemingly disempowered and helpless community will be righteously destroyed by divine anger!" Versions of both stories Lila told are part of leatherworker lore throughout North India, but I have been unable to find Gendi's story within published accounts of devotional tradition.

Homes and families are where human beings begin, and are the places where—if anywhere mortal—we may stake our trust. Yet, as some of these narratives painfully expose, homes are not always dependable or stable. In Sawar as everywhere, death and sickness could decimate families. In Sawar, in the kings' days, rulers exerted pressures, both economic and psychological, that strained domestic resources in multiple ways. And the encompassing extractive ethos of British colonial power exacerbated local conditions. Under these prevailing systemic stresses, each home presents a unique configuration of personalities and circumstances.

Women like Kesar Gujar, Gauri Nath, Gopi the Brahmin, and her sister-in-law Jhamku all experienced hardships, but have lived into old age to recall them good-humoredly from times less difficult. Sukh Devji and Raji look back with satisfaction on their long struggle to create a prosperous home from a barren field. Only Dhapu and Gori Regar seem crushed in their old age by illness and domestic unhappiness endured over too many years. And Motiya Kanvar alone among the women recalls her youth with nostalgic longing.

Gendi Regar's story reveals that abjection of circumstance is not necessarily abjection of spirit. The rulers seemed to do all they could to keep members of the Regar community from feeling honor and pride in their homes, but in spite of ongoing crushing disadvantages, they retained not only faith but self-respect. Today, land reform and government programs have assisted Regar communities all over Rajasthan to move into living situations often better than those of the middle-level farming groups that look down on them—at least in terms of amenities such as water taps, electricity, and stone houses.

In this chapter we have seen the intermeshing of gender hierarchies with those of ritual purity and political power—and Regar women would have found themselves close to the bottom of all three of these (Dube 1998). I was hesitant to end a chapter on homes with stories of rape, when I had begun it with stories of fulfillment and success against great odds. My intention was not to give pride of place to suffering, still less to exploit its sexiness. Rather, I believe that in the Regar community's experience, worst case that it is, we are able not only to see the ways that power emanating from the fort penetrated even the most intimate aspects of life, but also to perceive that even abject communities are able to refuse that power psychologically, if not physically. Moreover, we see in some leatherworkers' views an envisioning of divine protection as justice, and an acceptance of the inevitability of mixed blood transformed into outspoken claims for radical social consequences. In chapter 8, as we look more closely at the severe economic crunch the great kings' extractive rule forced on every level of this agricultural and herding society, once again we will see both acquiescence and struggle.

8. FIELDS

Although the grievances surrounding land and land tax featured prominently in the peasant struggles of the early twentieth century in Rajasthan, . . . it was also the reproduction of a hierarchical culture with its myriad marks of social differentiation and cultural exclusiveness which imposed strains.—Parita Mukta, *Upholding the Common Life*

In shifting our focus from homes to fields we do not move very far from people's hearts. Sukh Devji, with whose life history chapter 7 began, was deeply in love with his land and crops. During my years in Ghatiyali I grew accustomed to requests for portrait photography, and I found it a small way to return the huge favors I owed to so many. But the only picture Sukh Devji ever asked me to take was of his flowering mustard field; to me it was indistinguishable from everyone else's flowering mustard field, but I was happy to record this splendor for him.

Today, farmers have deeds to their agricultural property, and taxes are negligible; no one complains of them. Farmers of unirrigated land pay nothing (and many who have successfully dug wells do not report the change). In the first portion of this chapter we listen to recollections of the Court's claims on agricultural production in the time of kings. The pre-Independence system of collection—complex, multifaceted, and exasperating—presents a direct intersection of rulers with ruled, of kings and their agents with farmers. Largely unseen colonial forces topped the system and drove it hard. Merchant moneylenders hovered close to the threshing ground. But it was the king's managers, bosses, and other retainers who were most vividly recalled.

Our chief aim in what follows is not to give an accurate account of fiscal matters under Vansh Pradip Singh; this we are not equipped to do as we chose not to pursue the actual revenue records of Sawar. Rather, our effort has been to find out from farmers, and to convey largely in their own words, the ways they retrospectively experience the collection system.

Writing about the "rules" governing economic arrangements between peasants and landowners in Bengal, Gautam Bhadra describes decision making as "a process of struggle" (1989:71). He goes on to say: "But there was no legally defined limit to how much the landlord could demand of the peasant: there was nothing written or definitive about it. It was kept vague and judged by the nebulous boundaries of 'custom'" (1989:71). Although Bengal's pre-Independence land-tenure system differed in significant ways from that of Rajputana, the combination of "struggle" and "vagueness" aptly characterizes the latter as well as the former.

Farmers' lack of control over their own crops was associated with lack of control over the trees in their fields. This evoked bitter recollections, as we shall hear in the second section. We relate there an important event in local history, predating Vansh Pradip Singh's reign, that highlights the passion a dispute over wood could arouse. Finally we look at the taxes the Court assessed on livestock. In this regard, popular folklore pits a holy man's magical power victoriously against the king's. Such contests between political and ascetic power have resounded vitally in Hindu traditions since before the common era.[1] Here, as is often the case in legend, the world renouncer is victorious. Tellingly, to the best of our knowledge, no miracle stories exist confronting the inexorable grain share collection.

Bitter Harvests: *Lāto-kūto* and the Liabilities of the Grain Pile

History books and oral testimonies converge in their accounts of the land-tenure and crop-taxation systems operating in pre-Independence Ajmer.[2] In the kingdom of Sawar, as in much of Ajmer, the prevailing system in the centuries preceding democracy was *jagīrdārī*.[3]

B. K. Sharma describes the *jagīrdārī* system as one that gives the *thākur* unlimited power:

The land held by the State grantees was known as Jagir. Before the British paramountcy the word Jagir was applied only to estates held by Rajputs on condition of military service. The Jagirs were also known as thikanas and the Jagirdars as Thakurs.

The Jagirdar was the Thakur or lord who held Jagir by grant (Patta) of his chief and performed service with specified quota (Tan) of military. The land under their possession was managed by them and the State had no right to intervene. (1990:14–15)

Later the *ṭhākur*'s military obligations to his overlord were replaced by fiscal ones, but his total authority remained.

As Vidya Sagar and Kanta Ahuja observe, such relatively unchecked power led to a proliferation of predatory exploitations, often petty but cumulatively oppressive: "The Rajasthan feudal land tenures suffered not merely from the well known maladies of an intermediary regime viz. lack of security of tenure, absence of fixity or fairness of rent, but suffered from arbitrariness of the kind that can exist only under a feudal regime. The cesses and obligations imposed on the tenants were extra-economic in nature and depended entirely on the personal and social hierarchies of the feudal regime" (1987:22–24). In his study of land reform in Rajasthan, D. Singh also confirms the rural population's extreme vulnerability under the *jagīrdārī* system, adding that it was "important to note that the procedure of collecting the rents and cesses was highly troublesome to the peasantry" (1964:33–34). Sawar narratives testify eloquently to arbitrariness in the royal regime's acts and requirements. Moreover, "troublesome" seems a mild term to describe the kind of power abuses villagers recall when asked to tell about those days.

In the pages that follow we delve more deeply into what Singh calls rents and cesses. The English "rent" is often used to refer to the fixed share of the crop paid by farmers to the Court, because the land farmers worked did not belong to them. However, "rent" never struck me as a satisfactory translation of the Rajasthani term *bāṇṭo*, which, according to the *RSK* means "the share of a farmer's agricultural production collected from the farmer for the king or landlord." I shall shorten this, context permitting, to "share."[4]

Some meanings of "cess" provided by the *Oxford English Dictionary* include "a local tax," "land tax," or "assessment." The literature on land tenure and taxation in pre-Independence Rajasthan uses "cess" to blanket a range of additional deductions taken from the farmer's share of the harvest, after the "rent" is paid or the royal share deducted. These are often labeled with the vernacular terms "*lāg*" and "*neg*," or alternatively *lāg-bag*. None of these Hindi words were used in common parlance in Sawar—they do not appear in a single interview text. But the multiple extractions to which they refer were all described to us in detail.[5]

Hira Singh's description of "cesses" in the same era with which we are concerned is particularly apropos to our findings, stressing as it does the indeterminacy of these fees. "In addition to the ground rent . . . the *kisans* had to pay a large number of cesses known as *lag-bag*. As with rent, only to a greater extent, it is extremely difficult to find out either the exact number of cesses covered by the term *lag-bag*, or the actual amount realized in lieu of a particular *lag*" (1998:104). Among the named *lāg*, Singh mentions one paid before the crop estimation "in the form of a part of the green crops for the landlord's horses" (104). In Sawar, many persons told us how the king's men would use the unripe grain crops for animal fodder—both by cutting them and by allowing their horses to feed right in the field. They had no specific name for these practices. As we will hear, they vividly described them as sheer insolent predation against which the farmers were bitter and helpless.

In 1993, Gopi Singh Ravat was Ghatiyali's government-appointed *paṭwārī*, or "revenue accountant" (a title that today as in the past denotes a village-level record keeper and tax collector). Gopi Singh contrasted the previous and present systems of landholding for us, evoking the dramatic magnitude of change that followed Independence and land reform:

> Here in Kekari tehsil it was *jagīrdārī*. The Sawar *darbār* and other *darbārs* were the real landholders. The farmers were not the real landholders.[6] They did all the work, and gave most of the crops to the landlord, and had only a little share for themselves.
>
> At that time the farmers feared much, because they didn't own their own land, but today they are owners: free [*azād*], independent [*svatantra*]; a person is himself master [*khud mālik*] of the

land he plants. There is no problem; he can produce two hundred maunds or fifty maunds and he is the owner of it.

But before, people paid tax in grain, not cash. Suppose total production is forty maunds, yet you have only ten maunds; the other thirty maunds you have to send to the fort of Sawar or Ghatiyali.

We never heard anyone cite an "official" rate of grain tax, or land rent, as high as 75 percent. However, the *paṭwārī's* statement concurs with many accounts of the reality for farmers: ten maunds out of forty would not be an inaccurate statement of the farmer's actual net yield. This was due to numerous smaller cuts—the above-mentioned "cesses"—taken by the king's agents and servants from the farmer's designated share.

Above the *jagīrdārs,* as related in chapter 3, a succession of British administrators in Ajmer, beginning in 1818, distinguished themselves by conceiving and implementing a series of different tax assessment systems. And, as chapter 6 showed, the Sawar Court managed to meet colonial demands and support its own considerable expenses by maintaining a well-organized staff of experts to extract revenue biannually from farmer subjects. At the conceptual center of these extractive practices were claims to the land and the grain heap.[7]

The collection process at harvest was a topic we pursued in more than a hundred conversations. Although the basic principles of this process are easily summarized, in practice it was fraught with uncertainties that for the farmers included the double miseries of economic losses and personal humiliations. There was no more poignant nexus of disempowerment than the system commonly called *lāṭo-kūṭo.*[8] This paired construction collapses two terms with different specific, but related, meanings. As pronounced together in the vast majority of our interviews, the phrase stands vaguely for a range of activities, but it is well to distinguish and clarify each term's specific import.[9]

According to the *RSK, lāṭo* means threshing ground, and the associated verb, *lāṭno,* means "for the landlord (*jagīrdār*) to take a specified portion of the farmer's grain."[10] Still following the dictionary, the very *kūṅtno* is explicitly defined as "to guess the number or amount of something without measuring, weighing, or counting." The definition of the noun *kūṭ* includes "a pile of grain," but I assume this is derivative. The primary meaning is "estimation," and the pile would then be the grain set aside as a result of that estimation.[11]

In Sawar, when people speak of the king's agents "doing *lāṭo-kūṭo*" they refer most often to the assessment. Still more generally, the term today evokes, unhappily, the whole process of assessment and collection in the bad old days. This process seemed designed to remind all farmers, through strategies ranging from merely arrogant to deliberately cruel, that their land and labor were not their own. Assessment was done on the ripened grain as it stood in the field before harvest. Interviews reveal that the unkindest cuts of all were not the king's actual share, but the many smaller "fees" that were most subject to abuses by rapacious agents of the Court. Of course the economic burden of the Court's share was greater, but the "fees" were described, and felt, as an addition of insult to injury.

Colonel W. J. Lupton (1908) writes of a "Variable System of Village Assessments in District Ajmer," arguing that the British intended with this system to effect a more just distribution of revenue burdens. However, Lupton complains, local officers had "consistently denounced" it. He goes on to elaborate: "this system was intensely unpopular with the cultivators who were supposed to be benefited by it; and . . . would still be unpopular no matter how it was modified" (119). He himself believed that the system had merits, and he expressed his opinions of peasant mentality with the utmost British scorn. From the present vantage, he sounds like a parody of the colonial voice: "The Indian peasant is not a person who will try to understand anything if he has otherwise a prejudice against it. And here the cultivators' one and general feeling was only that in some way or other, and always, he was being 'done' (if I may be pardoned the expression) over his assessment by the patwari and revenue officials" (120). In actuality, if the peasants felt they were "being 'done' " by the local officers, they had ample reason.

Among the most bitter accounts we recorded from farmers were of the royal agents nonchalantly grazing their horses on the ripe crops while performing the hated estimation at their casual leisure. What made this behavior even more obnoxious was that the peasants themselves were forbidden to sample the fruits of their own labors before the assessment took place, although (as we heard in chapter 7) people found various ingenious ways to resist this highly resented ban. These

Ripened wheat stalks ready to roast and eat in fields.

included roasting grains inside step-wells to prevent the smoke from rising visibly, and carefully hiding the tell-tale soot; or secreting grain stalks under other legitimate (and unattractive) burdens such as fresh cow dung to move them past the checkpoint guards posted by the Court around harvest time. These subterfuges were not merely symbolic claims on produce or a means of savoring relished treats. Sometimes they were the only way for farmers and their families to stave off hunger. People were often short of food by harvest time, and yet they were forbidden to eat the fruits of their own labors until the king had claimed his share and that share was deposited in his granary, transported there with conscripted labor by the farmers themselves.

Nowadays, to roast and eat newly ripened crops in the fields is anticipated with pleasure and joyfully performed in an easygoing fashion. I have personally relished many such spontaneous "cookouts" whenever I have been in Ghatiyali at harvest time. Only recently, however, did I realize that the incomparable sweetness of fresh wheat roasted in the open air was also the sweetness of freedom.

Even as they resented the behavior of the Court's agents, farmers had to wish for the manager and bosses to arrive, and to fret if the estimate were delayed. An angry agent could procrastinate, delaying the assessment until the grain was past its prime. He might then still assign to the Court a portion based on the field's full worth—had it been harvested at the optimal moment. In the presence of the agents, farmers had to pretend courtesy. Discourtesy on the farmer's part could up the assessment, or delay it even longer. Both parties would be fully aware that farmers were fuming and agents were trying to skim off whatever they could get. Understandably, fights broke out now and then.

In 1997 we asked the former tehsildar, Govind Singh, to explain the grain tax system to us. He had experienced it from above, as an administrator. It therefore seemed to me that he, if anyone, should have been able to clarify it—at least as a theoretical enterprise from an ideal perspective. Govind Singh only addressed himself to the official share collected for the government, the simple and straightforward part, compared with the confusing fees. Yet even this emerged as surprisingly murky. It began to strike me that the messiness of the *lāṭo-kūṭo*'s particulars was intrinsic to the game of exploitation it permitted.

BHOJU: So, what was the management system (*vyavasthā*) in Sawar state?

GOVIND SINGH: We used to do an estimation of the grain (*anāz kā kūṇṭā*) in all the tehsils. But, some paid in cash; sometimes if the crop was only fodder, the *ṭhākur* didn't want fodder so he took cash.

BHOJU: From what castes did you collect?

GOVIND SINGH: From all castes. He called this [that is, caste] his basis [*ādhār;* also defined as "criterion" or "foundation"].

BHOJU [looking for further clarification, and using Govind Singh's own language]: So, what exactly was the basis—for determining who would give how much?

GOVIND SINGH: Well, for one *bīghā*, fifteen *ser,* at the least. The maximum we were getting was half.[12]

BHOJU: So fifteen *ser* was minimum?

GOVIND SINGH: From Devli and Kalera he always took half; from Napa ka Khera and Nimera, from them also half. In Napa ka Khera and Kalera, always half.

BHOJU: Why?

GOVIND SINGH: Because in those places there were no "quarter-share" (*chauth vaṇṭā*) people. Those are Rajputs and Gujars.

BHOJU: Did all the Gujars give one-fourth?

GOVIND SINGH: No, but take the Jasvantpura Gujars, for example—those who were settled in Jasvantpura. . . . [He digresses to explain how this came to be.] There used to be Minas who were thieves, so to protect the road from them, Jasvant Singh brought these Gujars from Kuchalwara Mata. He took them from there, and settled them [in the place now called Jasvantpura] to protect the road from thieves. And for that reason they only paid one-fourth.

But the Gujars in Nadi and Kejari . . . they gave one-half like the other peasants [*kisān log*].

But from those Gujars who were wet-nurse brothers, and from those who were "settled" by the Court, he only took one-fourth.

Note that in this conversation fragment, Govind Singh evokes assessment on the basis of acreage, of caste, of profession, and of village. Sometimes these criteria merge—as with the Gujars of Jasvantpura who worked as guards—but sometimes they do not.

Bhoju sought out another Rajput official, Bankat Singh Kamdar, in order to clarify the collection system. Bankat Singh mentioned both caste and profession as affecting the tax rate, as well as the type of land—irrigated or not irrigated. Being on the side of the Court, he also noted that rates could be adjusted in the case of mitigating factors such as extreme poverty, but I must stress that no one else ever said this. Govind Singh also noted the institution of tax-free land donations to temples and shrines, a reality which—unlike royal charity to individuals—is common knowledge and well documented.

> In the tehsil, if there was irrigated land, then they did an estimate (kūntno) of it. . . . And, the Dhahai [Gujar wet-nurse lineage], Rajput, and Chaukidar [Mina and Gujar watchmen], from them he only took one-fourth; from whomever were watchmen, only one fourth.
>
> And the Mali [gardeners], Loda [farmers], from them he took half. But there were some from whom he only took one fifth—those to whom he was like a helper, they were very poor, and he only took one-fifth.
>
> And when he gave tax-free temple land, it was charity. . . . The authority was the king's, but he took no tax from them.

At whatever rate it was set, the king's official share, as described by Govind Singh and Bankat Singh, was only the largest among a series of cuts from the harvested grain a farmer could finally take home.

Gokul Mali of Ghatiyali offered us in detail one of the fullest and most realistically confusing descriptions of the *lāto-kūto* procedure in action. But even he, as we will see, left out a whole category of payments required of the farmer.

BHOJU: What about the *lāto-kūto*? . . . . Who came to your fields and decided how much grain would have to be given?

GOKUL MALI: At that time, there were Akkha Singh, Ukar Singh, Bhairu Singh, and the revenue accountant, Chandmal Jain. And the village crier—his name was Kalyan; and the land-record officer—he also came at the time of the *lāto-kūto*.

Gokul first gave us the names of three of the king's bosses, persons he recalled. Then, as he tried to clarify the process, he moved from named persons to roles. In his clarification we learn that at the time of the *lāto-kūto* one of these bosses would normally come to a given field, acting as leader of the assessment party, along with the other designated officials as Gokul now lists them:

So, there were four men, and each had a sickle (*dāntalī*). There were four sickles:

1) *gā̃v baḷāī* [village crier]

2) *paṭwārī* [village-level record keeper and revenue assessor; in general I will translate *paṭwārī* as "revenue accountant"]

3) *kānūngo* [land-record officer]

4) *hākim* [a term meaning any "official of status," and also "boss." It can be used for all of the above as the generic "king's agent"; or it can be used for the leader of the assessment party, as Gokul now uses it. I shall normally translate *hākim* as "boss"]

Before the farmer could harvest, they would use the sickles to cut the grain stalks and put them in a sack.[13] The agents would be riding their horses, and the farmer could not say, "stop."

So they would make a decision: "You will have eighty maunds," but they [the farmers] still have to give 25 percent.

Gokul's meaning here is that although the four men are doing the assessment, these "sickles" are reducing the crop. They pronounce the field's expected yield to be eighty maunds, but this figure includes grain they themselves have already pocketed. The farmer will have to give the Court twenty maunds, even though his actual harvest is less than eighty. These cuts are the first of many to be taken from the farmer's share. The Court's share is never reduced.

GOKUL: And there were approximately three or four horses; they sat on their horses, and if the horses ate the grain, no matter!

BHOJU: So did the agents ever get down off the horses?

GOKUL: How could they dismount? They were kings' agents! . . . . Why should they get down?[14]

They saw a field, and they roamed around the field, looking for where the grain was good, their horses were grazing, and the men cut, and then they would stop and go to the next field, having made their estimate.

. . . .

And suppose—when they arrive, there are four *bīghās*, they can write "forty maunds," or they can write "forty-five," as they please; and no matter how many [maunds] there really were, the farmer would have to give his share according to their estimate—not according to the real harvest.

And then these plants, the ones they cut from, they cut only the grain; they cut the grain tops, and put them in their sacks. All four could start, without waiting for permission from the leader. And when they finally wrote down the estimate, only then would they stop. And if the leader were angry, he could take even longer, and even more damage would take place.

And if there was garlic, they would take it; but if there was cumin, they took a cash tax; vegetables, onions, garlic they took [in kind], but for cumin they wanted cash.

. . . .

[Here, of course, Gokul speaks specifically as a gardener; other groups were not likely to grow these items.]

BHOJU: What about ginger?

GOKUL: Not then, it was not grown. But if you planted any fruit tree, the king was its master. The farmers could plant a tree, but they could not cut it down. If there are mangoes on the tree, first you have to take them to the fort, and ask permission, "There are some mangoes on the tree, can I eat them?" And then he says, "O.k., you can eat them." But the master of it all was the king.

This condition of disempowerment over trees in one's own field was a sore point and a flash point.

Pratap Regar, who had served as village crier in Ghatiyali, described the scene at the assessment in vivid language, stressing the farmer's helplessness by putting in his mouth an exclamation, "Oh, misery!" (*āre bāre*) appropriate to mourning.

PRATAP: At that time as many managers as there were, were riding horses. They rode in the fields, and the horses were grazing, and the workers wandered around breaking off the grain and putting it in their sacks.

BHOJU: What did the farmer do?

PRATAP: He cried, "Please don't destroy my crop! Oh, misery! Don't destroy it!"

BHOJU: Did you [as village crier] pay attention to him?

PRATAP: No. The land-record officer, the Brahmin, the government crier, and the village crier had sickles, and as long as the assessment lasted, they could keep cutting grain.

BHOJU: Could the farmer give insults?

PRATAP: No, he just pleaded.

The farmer in Pratap's description is a passive victim. But, as we know from Kalyan Mali's anecdote in chapter 5, this was not always the case. Some farmers did indeed insult the village crier.

Most people, looking back fifty years, did not distinguish between *kūto* and *lāto* but merged the two in their generalized recollections.[15] Gokul Mali, however, went on to clarify *lāto* for us—revealing that it was a different process. Here I follow his description for Ghatiyali, but there was a similar situation in other villages and kingdoms. *Lāto* was in effect only for the land nearest the village—fertile but unirrigated land called *māl*. The grain from this land, at the *kharīph* harvest, was all threshed by royal decree at a common threshing ground.

Then as now, many farmers worked several small pieces of land in different areas, including the *māl*. This might explain the merging of the two processes in memory, as most cultivators probably had to put up with both. Gokul stated:

Threshing mustard with oxen, 1993.

The land in the *māl* was designated *lāṭo*. You could not start to harvest until they gave permission. In the *māl* land, everyone would harvest at the same time, and the threshing ground was the same for the whole village: Ratya's Field. Even if your fields were far away from it, you had to bring your whole crop [from any *māl* land] to this threshing ground.

There, one man from the government was like a watchman; no one could eat roasted wheat or roasted chickpeas. During that time, a guard (*syāṇā*) lived in a shack there, and some villagers stayed with him. So the farmers were protected from the animals and the king was protected from the farmers.

They did all the threshing with oxen; the whole village had to do it all together; they waited for the order; everyone had to wait for all the farmers to be ready; then they tell the *darbār* "Everything is ready." Small farmers had to wait for the big ones and the guards kept them from starting. Say there were one hundred farmers; and ninety-eight have finished harvesting; those ninety-eight have to wait for the two who haven't finished.

They put the unthreshed grain in piles (*māḍ*), and they put ash on the piles, so if someone took some they would know—if the ashes had been moved. And when all the piles were complete, then they began winnowing. They called it "to start the winnowing basket" or "to start the *tuāv*" (the winnowing stool). But if there were no wind, they still had to sit there. And even when the pile of winnowed grain (*thāpā*) was finished, they couldn't take it home.

Note the repeated stress on waiting, as if he relives his impatience to bring home the fruits of his labors, and the many irritating delays to which this urge was subject. Unmentioned is the hunger at home, prolonged by the king's will.

Next would come the "sickles," as Gokul Mali continued to explain:

GOKUL: Until the king's agents took the Court's share, they kept an ash mark (*rās*) on the grain pile. And when the Court was ready, he would check this mark.[16]

Then after that, the whole teeam—the same four who had done the *kūṭo*—came here; and they all took grain in their sacks, before the king's portion was removed. First you have to give two handfuls to those dogs [the king's men].

And then the piles of grain were made, one for the government [*rāj*; he does not add "and one for the farmer," although it is implied]. First you have to take the king's grain to his place—either in Ghatiyali or sometimes in Sawar. If there was more than he needed for Ghatiyali we had to take it to Sawar.

BHOJU: So who transported it from the threshing ground?

GOKUL: The farmers who sowed it, they are the ones who transported it: Mali, Loda, Regar, all the farmers. Brahmins too had to transport it.

Then we can take our grain to our houses. And after this, the chaff, they didn't take that, they only took the grain. This is how the *lāṭo* took place.

Gauri Nath had a way with words. When she described the *lāṭo-kūṭo*, she explicitly compared the activities of the king's agents to those of the wild pigs: both rampant destroyers of farmers' prosperity.

GAURI: At that time the pigs ate the crops; the king ate and the pigs also ate. When they went to do the assessment in the fields, the *hākim* and the town crier, they took their sickles into the fields, and the barber too cut and ate. . . . When farmers were completely ready for harvesting, only then they [the king's agents] would come, and the farmers had to wait, and the grain would fall to the ground. A servant would bring a chair to the field for the *hākim,* and another would hold his horse.

From other speakers we gather further dimensions of the *lāṭo-kūṭo* process and the losses it entailed for farmers. Suva Lal Chasta, a Brahmin man, spoke of the *lāṭo-kūṭo* in strong language:

BHOJU: You were born in the British period. Which period was good, before 1947, or after?

SUVA LAL: The rule of the *rājā-mahārājās* was tyranny[17] for the public.

BHOJU: In what way?

SUVA LAL: The most important sorrow was that they did the grain estimate (*lāṭo-kūṭo*) whenever they wanted to do it. Sometimes the crop is ripe, but they might not come for twenty days, and until then the farmer could not even eat a cob of corn, or roasted wheat grains, or roasted chickpeas. And if he did and they found out they would punish him. And the grain could fall and 30 percent could be ruined, and they would still say, "This is a good crop." So, they say this much is 100 percent, and they take 50 percent—but if 30 percent is ruined that leaves only 20 percent for the farmers.

[In other words, having forced the farmer to let the grain sit too long in the fields, the kings' men still collected the Court's full share, thereby short-changing the farmer.]

From the remaining share left to the farmer, he had to pay the servants of the *rājā-mahārājās;* the farmers had to pay those servants out of their own share: like the Brahmin cook, the washerman, the stable keepers.

Suva Lal here introduces yet another set of payments required from farmers to the king's servants—the kamīn, or client castes.[18] These represent yet another category of demands on the harvest, quite separate from the "sickles" described by Gokul Mali.

In Sawar, as in many other localities in India, farmers gave a share of the harvest to their own client castes from whom they received services as needed during the rest of the year. The rub here was that they had to pay these groups not only on their own family's behalf, but for their services to the Court as well. Bhoju elicited the names of *kamīn* groups from many persons; usually listed, in various orders, were barber, carpenter, potter, ironworker, washerman, weaver, leatherworker, and sweeper. Ugma Mali counted drummers, whose service he described as "entertainment," among the *kamīn*. Ladu Loda distinguished between two groups of client castes. He told us that those called *kamīn* worked with tools, and did clean work: barber, carpenter, Brahmin, and iron worker. Those called *kārū* did dirty work: sweeper, washerman, weaver and leatherworker.[19] Most farmers, like Ladu Loda, included Brahmins among the various service communities, because Brahmins were attached to particular families and were paid for their ritual services in grain.[20]

When we talked with Bhura Mali, an old gardener, in his fields, he spoke of the taxation system from the farmer's viewpoint, clearly seeing through the stated share owed by the farmer to the state to the actual rate of predation. He merged the cesses introduced by Gokul with the payments to client castes mentioned by Suva Lal, speaking of them as all of a piece. Of course, members of artisan and service communities would have a different perspective on these payments. Bhura expresses an agriculturalist's experience:

> Everything belonged to him [the Court]. As much profit as we made from our fields, he took half.
>
> . . . .
>
> Suppose there will be ten maunds, so "Give us four," and from the six maunds left [to the farmers], they had to pay the barber, potter, leatherworker, village crier [*gāṅv balāi*], land-record officer [*kānūngo*], the priest, the royal crier [*rāj balāī*]—so maybe there was less than four maunds left them.
>
> Five kilograms to the town crier, five kilograms to the potter, and besides this the priest who cooks for the king; and besides this, the people doing the estimate (*kūtno*)—we had to pay them too.
>
> Yes, maybe they took four maunds, but all of their servants had to be paid by the farmer.

BHOJU: Was any caste most sorrowful?

BHURA: All the castes were sorrowful; even the *ṭhākurs* [Rajputs] were in difficulty. Only those who had some direct authority in their hands were happy.[21] The rest were all in difficulty.

Think about it! During this time we had to get grain from the shop just two months after harvest—we had no grain left to eat.

Today, if someone works hard, still he has five cents [that is, a little bit] left over, but before he couldn't have even that much.

At that time people were so troubled they sometimes went to bed hungry; sometimes we had no grain at home so we passed our time eating roasted wheat grains, and even that we had to roast inside old wells.

And when we planted chickpeas, when their leaves came out, we thought, "Oh good, we can keep our children alive!" That was how bad conditions were then.[22]

BHOJU: You were in such bad shape, but still the *rājā-mahārājā* paid no attention?

BHURA: No, from their point of view, we can die and they don't care.

Ugma Loda, a farmer of the same generation, perhaps slightly younger than Bhura Mali, also offered extensive descriptions of royal domination at work. He began with a favorable contrast of the quick dispute settlement formerly available from the royal Court versus the current legal system, which is as draining of time and money for residents of the Sawar Twenty-Seven as it is elsewhere in rural India.[23] But the rest of his description evokes many of the troubles of the past culminating in grain collections; his community was assessed half their crop.

BHOJU: Was the time of the great kings good, or the present?

UGMA: In that time dispute settlement was swift and good; suppose we quarreled and went to them to complain and they would call us both and ask what happened and effect a compromise and no one went to court, it was all solved right there.[24]

But the sorrow: suppose we are sitting on this cot and they had a guest they could just come and say, "You must give this cot."

And if it were our turn to send milk, even if we have a child, we have to send milk.

BHOJU: What castes had to give cots?

UGMA: Mali and Loda. And there was the conscripted labor [*begār kā kām*] for Mali and Loda. Now there is transportation, buses, but then everyone went by ox cart and if someone [wielding the

Court's authority] needed to go, he could just call us and say, "Its your turn to drive the cart."

. . . .

And the Malis and Lodas did all the work in the kingdom's fields but all the profit went to the fort, no share came to the workers.[25]

. . . .

BHOJU: Who in the village had the most difficulties?

UGMA: Malis and Lodas. Only two castes were at their ease, Gujar and Rajput. As much grain as I grew, they made two piles, one for me and one for them. But the Gujars and Rajputs, they had four piles, one for the great kings, and three for themselves.

. . . .

BHOJU: Are people happy now, farmers?

UGMA: Today it is the rule of farmers; because today we give very little tax. . . . For this reason, we are happy today.

Ugma Loda is a well-to-do farmer. Not everyone we recorded spoke so cheerfully of their present economic circumstances, but the apprehension that farmers were worse off under the kings is universal.

As noted in the preceding chapter, most speakers did not place the greatest stress on the role of merchants or moneylenders in Sawar farmers' sufferings. However, those who did bring up farmers' indebtedness spoke of it as endemic; for example, Dhapu Mina saw perpetual crushing debt as contributing to her personal hardship and hunger in her marital family. In the extract below, Rup Lal Khati notes the role of the merchant as yet another predator on the farmers' share of the harvest, but he also describes him as offering the only help available to families in financial distress. He shows that he was well aware of British power, but does not use the British presence to absolve the kings' exploitative behavior.

RUP LAL: In that time, the merchant (*seth*) would take all the grain from the farmers at harvest, because they were in his debt, and then they had to buy it back from him at a higher rate. The farmers were "hungry soldiers" (*bhūkha sipai*).

BHOJU: Did the kings help at all?

RUP LAL: No, they gave no help, only the shopkeeper (Baniya) helped [by giving loans, which the kings did not do]. In those days, if we borrowed in grain we would pay back in grain, but if we borrowed money we had to pay money.

At that time, we could not even roast grains in our own field; if our children came to the field and wanted grain we would tie some together and roast them in the well, holding them down with one hand, so no one would see.

BHOJU: When you were the ones who did all the work on the land, why did you fear the kings?

RUP LAL: It was their time, the great kings' time, and that's why we were afraid. We were not afraid of the English. At that time there was a double administration [*doharā śāsan*].

If the Rajputs did something bad you could complain to the English and they would do something about it, but no one would, because of fear of the Rajputs—because we had to live here, and complaining outside would only get them more angry.

The *darbār* sat in Sawar, and news did not reach him, but the village crier, the managers, and the other bosses, they could trouble people as much as they wanted.

It wasn't the fault of the English, their rule was forceful (*tagaṛā*). The confusion was caused by the great kings.

Not everyone among the minority who mentioned the British was so ready to exonerate them.

Gajanand Sharma Buvalia, a Brahmin, was one of the oldest men in the village; he gave his age as ninety-two. As a former activist against the Rajputs, and a follower of Mukat Behari Lal, he clearly identified the pernicious role of colonial power as it exacerbated the oppressions perpetrated by kings in the 1930s and 1940s:

At this time the Sawar *darbār* ruled and he took our grain; if we earned fifty maunds of grain he took twenty-five, and from what was left we had to give to the barber, potter, priest [who cooked for the *darbār*], and the town crier and the royal crier and the king's agent. . . . So after the harvesting and threshing they [the farmers] had nothing, as before.

. . . .

Before the English came, the kings would help the people, but at this time the British collected a fixed tax, and the *rājā-mahārājā* collected the grain tax, and no one took responsibility (*zim-medārī*).

. . . .

All the direct authority (*adhikār*) was with the kings. But after Congress came, their direct authority was finished.

We sought to learn if the *lāṭo-kūṭo* process had been experienced more or less in the same fashion in outlying villages of Sawar and in neighboring kingdoms, as it was in Ghatiyali and the nearby villages. The answers we received in various places confirmed that a similar level of harshness prevailed throughout the area.

Devli Gaon was at the edge of the kingdom of Sawar, on the far side of the Banas River; it was one of Sawar's *tehsīl* headquarters. We had a group conversation there with some elderly Gujars, but we never learned all their names. Bhoju asked a general question about the "sorrows" of the *lāṭo-kūṭo*. The collective response showed that conditions were very much the same in Devli Gaon as they were in Ghatiyali and its immediate vicinity. If anything, we heard more bitterness more bluntly expressed in outlying areas. Possibly, critiques from the margins were unmitigated by identification with the court's glories, as these were largely out of sight; while economic exploitations were the same.

WOMAN: At that time they took a share (*bāṇṭo*): one third for the government and two for the farmer.
BHOJU: How much did they take from the Gujars, a half or a third?
WOMAN: From the Gujars they took one-third.
[Note that the rate here is named as half from most farmers and one-third from the privileged; elsewhere we had heard it was either half or one-third from most farmers and one-fourth from the privileged.]
BHOJU: Could the farmers eat roasted chickpeas and roasted grain?
WOMAN: They could eat it in the fields, but they couldn't take it home. Even so, they brought it, secretly. The guard would sit on the road. They were not allowed to bring it home, because they had to wait for the *lāṭo* to take place.
BHOJU: Who lived in the fort? [Devli Gaon had its own fort.]
MAN: The manager, Raghuvir Singh, and the commandant of the fort (*kiledār*) also lived there.

BHOJU: What did the commandant of the fort and the manager do for the village?

MAN: They did nothing but come to the threshing ground and take the grain!

BHOJU: Was the rule of great kings a happy time, or is today happy?

MAN: Today we are very happy. It used to be we would farm and they would take half, but now no matter how much we earn we can keep it.

WOMAN: At that time the government took half, but out of the half that remained to us we had to pay the barber and the town crier and the leatherworker, and we were able to save nothing for ourselves. [Here as in Bhura Mali's account, client castes and government functionaries merge in recollection.]

That is why today we are happy. Then, if we were hungry and we prepared boiled wheat berries in the field, we could only eat in the field, we couldn't bring it home. So, if some were left over, we would eat it as we slowly walked because we had to finish it before we got home. But now, as much grain as there is, we can bring it home and there is no one to ask us about it. We pay tax to the government, but it is very little, like one rupee per *bīghā*.

ANN: When you saw the *darbār* in those days were you happy or angry? Did you think, "Oh, he's the one who takes our grain!"

WOMAN: We were sorrowful to look at him.

MAN: Today ordinary people can sit on a horse but at that time no one was allowed to sit on a horse.

WOMAN: Today the sweeper (Bangi) himself can sit on a horse and wander through the village![26]

The quick transition between the former glory of the Court on horseback and the present-day image of an untouchable on horseback is surely intended to be a powerful answer to my question. Respect and admiration were not the emotions aroused by the sight of the Court in the old days.

We pursued the topic of grain collection in another conversation in Devli Gaon, with Motil Lal Gujar:

BHOJU: What did the Court's manager do?

MOTI LAL: At the threshing ground when the grain was completely ready, first of all, he put it in piles: "This is the barber's, this is the village crier's." So they put it all into piles; and the king took his, and the kamīn took theirs, and then [last of all] the master of the field [khet kā mālik] took his.

[This expression, "master of the field" clearly calls attention to the injustice taking place as all those who did not work the land took from the fruits of his labor.]

The farmers also had to pay whoever worked for them out of their own share: they paid their own kamīn—their leatherworkers, barbers, and so forth, whoever worked for them.

. . . .

BHOJU: If there was famine did the government give?
MOTI LAL: In my time there was only one famine, in samvat 1996; but I did not see them giving grain to the farmers.

If there was a famine one year, but a good crop the year before, then people would borrow from their friends and relations, from here and there.

In the capital of the small adjacent state of Mehru, which was not under the administration of Sawar, a Mina man stressed the farmers' hunger, and the cruelty of not allowing farmers to eat before the king's claims were fulfilled: "In the months of Magh and Posh [about mid-December through mid-February], there was a shortage of grain, because they had eaten the old grain and the new harvest hadn't come and many were hungry; and if we ate roasted chickpeas and grains in the fields, he punished us and insulted us. And at the threshing ground they put marks on the piles of grain to make sure no one took any. And if the farmer was dying of hunger and took some grain home, they punished him." Thus even under another Court the farmers' situation appears to have been identical to that in Sawar under Vansh Pradip Singh.

Conflicts and Miracles

The heavy burden of lāṭo-kūṭo was evidently resented. Resistance in a "weapons of the weak" mode appears to have been a constant undercurrent. People defied the Court's ban on eating ripe foods in the fields, finding ways to keep the smoke from being visible to the guards, or of hiding food beneath other burdens and sneaking it home. There were also occasional fights between individual farmers and individual kings' agents—as related in chapter 4. But I heard no tales of heroic or of magical dissent.

In concluding this chapter, we turn to two overt if legendary conflicts between the people and the Court that are part of local tradition. One concerns a tree, and one concerns grazing tax. Both are said to have taken place before the time of Vansh Pradip Singh, and both express moments of outrage at the Court's high-handedness, but only one has a satisfying ending. Readers may wonder, as I did, why stories of confrontation focus on lesser oppressions, while the larger sorrows of conscripted labor and exploitative grain collection appear to be unchallenged in social memory—except in idiosyncratic acts of boldness or desperation. Fear of the shoe, with its threat of dishonor as well as damage, is the ready explanation. The shoe, as corporal punishment or imaginary shame, lay at the foundation of the system as it was told to us. At the same time, respect for the Court checked subjects' anger at the king's men. It also strikes me that the complexity of grain collection made it so thoroughly entangled with every aspect of peasants' lives that they could not (like battered wives?) easily find a separate cognitive space in which to articulate protest.

Elsewhere in the princely states of Rajputana, resistance to these deeply resented and insidious forms of oppression did take place. It may be a question of leadership, timing, and tinder. In chapter 9 we shall hear of one moment when Ghatiyalians effectively gathered in polite but steadfast protest against the Court's ban on pig killing. In the two legends recounted here, collective action and individual magic, respectively, alter the Court's behavior, but only magic seems capable of truly transforming the conditions of life.

THE MAUJA MINAS' EXODUS

Many conversations posed a direct link between the Court's power over the grain harvest and his power over the trees growing in farmers' fields. As Suva Lal Chasta put it, "At that time, as many trees as were at your house or in your field, they belonged to the *rājā-mahārājā,* and he could cut them and take them at any time. If the land isn't yours, how could the trees be?" Suva Lal went on to praise the present for its contrasting freedoms: "Nowadays the government gives authority to cut your own tree. You should plant another, but you can cut it if you want. Grow mango trees and eat mangos. Plant your own and eat your own! (*khud lagāo aur khud khāo!*)."

Given that arboriculture was not a major economic factor in this region, it is striking that it became a site of potentially explosive friction, as the episode of the Minas' exodus reveals. It seems that one tree could be a lightning rod, while forty maunds of grain was not. Because of my long-standing interest in shrine lore, I had learned during my first fieldwork period in 1980 about the Minas' goddess who had left Ghatiyali when her people decided to emigrate, but refused to return when they were persuaded to do so. Her Bhairuji had stayed behind.[27] While not every Bhairu in the village was located near a goddess, every goddess shrine would normally have a Bhairuji associated with it. The Mina goddess's Bhairuji happened to be the shrine closest to my first dwelling in Ghatiyali, just behind the *rāvaḷo* courtyard I shared with Shobhag Kanvar and Motiya Kanvar. Yet it was only in 1997 that I learned why the Minas had left the village en masse, at the time when Bhairuji refused to move. The reason was a dispute with the Sawar Court over a single acacia tree (*deśī bambūl*).

Once again, we hoped to tap Ganga Ram Mina's extensive oral historical and religious knowledge, but it was Shri Kisan Regar who filled in the details on the story of the Minas' exodus. I do not know why Ganga Ram, usually talkative, allowed his goddess's story to be told by a leatherworker. Perhaps the Minas are not at all proud of this incident, of which the denouement is their double subjection—first to the king and then to the goddess's curse of a dwindling community.

Ganga Ram himself informed us that there were once 350 houses belonging to the Mauja Mina lineage, while today there were only two and one-half—the half is a family with no progeny. Shri Kishan then began the tale:

SHRI KISHAN: They are cursed by this Mataji [goddess]: Ghanti ki Mataji (which translates literally as Ghatiyali Mother).
BHOJU: Why did they leave Ghatiyali?
GANGA RAM: In previous times, the Mina had a fight with the Court, and that's why they left.
BHOJU: Why, what was the fight about?

SHRI KISHAN: One time some Mina people had cut an acacia (*bambūl*) that was growing in their own field. And the king's manager caught them and rebuked them, "Why did you cut the *bambūl*? You will have to be fined!"

But they said, "We need shutters and plows! How can we pay fines for all the wood that we use? If we can't cut wood from our own fields, from where will we cut it?"

For this reason, they got into a fight. Then, the king's men took into the fort the *bambūl* they had cut; they took it away from the Mina. . . . And so they left, because of the *bambūl* tree.

You know the shrine—Dhunda ka Bhairuji. Previously both the Goddess and Bhairuji were there. The Minas wanted to take both deities along with them, but Bhairuji refused to go.

BHOJU: What do you mean, he "refused" to go?

SHRI KISHAN: They tried to dig it [the stone icon] out from the ground, but they were not successful; they were unable to do it. So they took Mataji, and still Bhairuji remains here.

When the Goddess's *bhāv* came [that is, when the shrine priest became possessed by the Goddess], she said, "You will return, but I will not return," and the Mina replied, "No, we will not return."[28]

When they were ready to leave, with all their things packed, a rider went to Sawar to inform the Court that the Mina were angry and ready to leave the kingdom. At this time the Court was Madhav Singh. He convinced them to return.[29] So after that, they did come back, because the Court called them back. But the Goddess would not come back with them, and she cursed the Minas: "Your lineage will not remain in Ghatiyali."

So from 350 houses, today there remain only two and one-half. Because of the Goddess's curse. . . . And she stayed there. [The shrine of Ghantiwala Mataji remains popular today as a local pilgrimage site.]

Soon after that, Minas started leaving Ghatiyali, and they settled in Mori, Vajta, Napa ka Khera. . . .

Sometime one, sometimes two families left at a time. All around this area, the houses of Mauja Minas are people who left Ghatiyali [following the curse].

In today's local exegesis, this story is hardly presented as a tale of political resistance. Rather it is a story about Mataji's *līlā*, or divine play, and the chief moral seems to be that one does not uproot a goddess lightly. As I have noted, the precipitating cause of the tree dispute had been left out of earlier versions encountered in my study of local shrines.

Reflecting back on this story after all we learned in our history interviews, I might reread it in its historical origins and imagine another message: the Minas betrayed their community and deity by weakening in their original resolution. The goddess predicted their weakness and disapproved of it. Presumably, the Court pacified them and returned their tree. But this small victory was not glorified, not even made explicit. And, most significantly, in accepting the Court's terms they broke a promise to their deity. She, whose power is superior to the Court's, determines that Ghatiyali is no longer her proper place, or theirs.[30]

The second legend we relate is more blatantly wholehearted in showing a divine power opposed to that of the Court as well as victorious over it.

COWS, MAGIC, AND TAX REFORM

According to Sawar residents, grazing taxes were collected by the Court, but they were neither a major source of revenue for the rulers nor a major source of complaint among the people. Bhoju, as a Gujar, was particularly interested in herders' memories. We questioned many of them about their lives in the kings' times, both for the experiences shared with other "peasant" communities and for the distinctive perspectives of herders. Although they certainly had no fondness for the king's men, herders generally expressed more regret for the past. Environmental deterioration has harmed them more than it has farmers, as Kesar Gujar so forcefully conveyed to us in chapter 7. Indeed, many former herders have turned to farming or other occupations.

Moti Lal Gujar told us he was two years less than eighty years old. He had spent his early years herding, then became a farmer, and finally, in his old age, he went into business as a liquor vendor. We talked with him in Devli Gaon, outside his store. He gave us this account, bitter enough:

Gujar youth posing in liquor store (Devli Gaon, 1997).

MOTI LAL: At that time [in his own youth] in the kingdom there was a one annā tax for grazing, due every twelve months. And out of one hundred goats, we had to give one goat; and if we had less than fifty, then one *khājarū* [special term designating a male goat destined to be consumed].

   Once a year they came to our house to count them. On that day they would take one, if there were under fifty; and if there were one hundred they'd take two; if there were two hundred, they'd take four. If there were sheep, they'd take a lamb. They would take them and herd them with the *gorelā* [the animals belonging to the rulers].[31] The king's men ate them.

BHOJU: Who were they?

MOTI LAL: The Court and those with him—the crows (*kāgalo*) and the eaters [that is, the Court's hangers-on].[32] They were munching the bones.

. . . .

BHOJU: So did the *darbār* always eat meat?

MOTI LAL: He never left off, the dark moon, the full moon, he never gave it up, that's why he had no children. He had two wives but no children; he left the world without progeny.

Moti Lal's dark innuendo here connects the Court's childlessness with his refusal to give up meat on sacred days, both of which are linked by an unspoken chain of causality to the tax on livestock.

Most questions about grazing tax yielded a response that included the information that there was no tax on cows, only on sheep and goats. Why were cows not taxed? By way of an explanation we heard from several sources a story about a holy man who flummoxed the grazing tax collectors by turning cows into lions. We recorded the most detailed version of the story in 1997 in Rajpura, just outside of Sawar. I heard another version that same year from Madhu Nath in Ghatiyali, but did not record it. It was about a different holy man and a different shrine, but it had the same plot. As a stock tale, this incident represents not just an objection to taxes, but draws on an ancient rivalry in India between royal power and ascetic power. Rajpura resident Chalak Dan Charan's telling, transcribed here, uses many localized details thus giving the narrative verisimilitude, much like an urban legend.

> There was a renouncer-sovereign [*nāgā mahārāj*]. He had ten- or eleven-hundred cows. He lived first in Nathun, but because of a fight with the Minas he left Nathun and came to Rajpura and halted here. . . . At that time there was jungle, and there was no village, but there was always water flowing. So it was a nice place, with jungle and water, and so he built an enclosed garden, and began to live here. [*This location is just on the outskirts of Sawar.*]
>
> At that time there was a grazing tax of one anna per buffalo, and two paise per cow, yearly. So some people told the Court, "There is a renouncer-sovereign here who has lots of cows, and you ought to tax him."
>
> The Court himself refused, and said, "I won't take any tax from him!" But the troublemaking bosses, the king's bosses, twisted things around. So these bosses came here to collect the tax. They got here in the evening, and the sovereign-renouncer asked them, "Why did you come?" and the bosses said, "We came to collect the tax on your cows."
>
> So the renouncer-sovereign told them, "The cows are in the cow pen. You come back in the morning, and when they go out to graze we can count them."
>
> But in the morning, the renouncer-sovereign took water from

the temple and sprinkled it on the cattle, and when they emerged from the pen there was one cow and one lion! One cow and one lion! Some of the king's bosses ran away, and some of the kings' bosses went mad.

Then, news reached the Court: "Your agents have done thus-and-so."

The sovereign-renouncer had a fever disease, black fever. He had a blanket and he would take it off and say to the fever, "Stay here, whore!" And it would stay there trembling. [In other words, by dint of magic powers he was able to transfer his fever from his body into his blanket.]

So, people thought there was a woman inside the blanket, because it was trembling. People got suspicious! So the people told the king that the renouncer-sovereign was wicked, and he kept a woman with him, and he ought to be driven away.

Then the Court himself came, riding on his horse. He came to the renouncer-sovereign. He saw the miracles, and he fell at the sovereign's feet. He saw there was nothing in the blanket!

The sovereign told the Court that he kept his fever inside the blanket. And the Court asked him to forgive him, and promised not to tax his cows: "I won't tax them!"

But the sovereign said, "You must forgive the tax on all the cows in all the twenty-seven villages, not just on my cows."

So that is why there was no tax on cows. At that time the king forgave the tax, and he also deeded eleven hundred *bīghās* of *dholī* [temple land] to the renouncer's temple. And it became a place of Mahadev [Shiva].

Cowed (pun intended) by the sovereign-renouncer's power, the Court grants him considerable agricultural land—from which there will be no royal share collected. The holy man does not attempt to use his magical clout to challenge the Court's general claims on crops. But he does make a smaller, token demand for the well-being of all. Because of the yogi's grace and political acumen the Sawar Court is forced to extend the grazing-tax boon—cows eat free—to all the people. The British overlords, as we saw in chapter 2, had no particular soft spot for cows, and they viewed unrestricted grazing as a broad environmental hazard that was necessary to check.

In the following chapter we continue to hear about ways the Court's powers circumscribed and limited ordinary people's lives, but we return to issues and conflicts revolving around the Court's protection of trees and wildlife. There we shall see some ways that the king's will and his agents' deeds, whatever their motivations, worked at times for the common good—in planting and protecting trees.

9 . JUNGLE

When the kings' rule was finished, the wild animals and the whole jungle was finished, and nothing at all is left.—Amba Lal Loda, interview in Ghatiyali, 1993

In the concentric architecture of these spatially articulated chapters, jungle encompasses fields, fields surround homes, and the Court is located at the heart of public space—central but elevated. Thus far I have written outward from the center, as well as topographically and hierarchically downward, building logically from ruler to people to land. But Bhoju's and my research trajectory, semiserendipitous as it was, commenced with the (absent) woods. The past of nature was our initiating interest. While probing about remembered trees, we gleaned narratives that stimulated our quest for political, economic, and social history. In this final chapter examining the kings' time, we return to these first preoccupations and visions: of deep jungle and wild pigs.[1]

Gazing upward once again, we look not toward the fort but rather to the surrounding hillsides where the Court's power was once so evident. Former hunting posts (*māḷo*) dot these hills today as material traces of the past when the king, his favored companions, and sometimes even the ladies of the court would shoot at wild game for sport, or, according to some accounts, just happily admire the animals. Today Sawar's hillsides serve villagers as grazing land (*charāgāh*). Some portions, officially designated "wasteland," have become sites for government reforestation projects and protected areas (called *klośur*).[2]

Jangal: *Preliminary*

The term most often used for uncultivated and unsettled land is *jangal* (in Sanskrit, Hindi, and Rajasthani). Our English word "jungle" derives from South Asian roots, but the equivalence after centuries of use in both languages and multiple contexts is not as straightforward as we might wish. As cognates, English "jungle" and Hindi "*jangal*" can be confusing. Arjun Appadurai notes "the radical rupture between our modern Western conception of jungle (as a dank, luxuriant, moist place) and the ancient Indian category, which referred to a dry and austere natural setting, which was nevertheless ideal for human subsistence practices" (1988a: 206). However, either English implications have slipped back into North India's vernaculars, or, as I suspect, the broader span of reference was already there. In any case, the semantic horizons of *jangal*, as it appears in our interview texts, may encompass both lushly wooded and arid, scrubby environments.³ The *RSK* reflects this span: the first definition for *jangal* gives *van* and *araṇya,* which are both Sanskrit terms for "forest"; the third definition is *registān,* or "desert."

In Sawar, *jangal* was the common colloquial term used casually and imprecisely by almost everyone with whom we talked to refer to uncultivated, uninhabited land—land where wild trees might or might not be growing. When people told us that in the time of kings there was "much jungle" or "very good jungle," while today "there is nothing" or "the jungle is finished," they used the term explicitly to mean dense forest and all it contained (plants and animals, an ecosystem rich in biodiversity). People sought phrases or metaphors which, in the current absence of trees, could make us grasp what "jungle" once had meant, visually and tactilely.

Dayal Gujar put it this way: "There were so many *dhokaṛā* trees that if we tossed a plate into them it would not fall to the ground! There were so many lions that were roaring, but we could not tell where they were [because the woods were too dense for human vision to penetrate] until they grabbed a goat or sheep."

Damodar Gujarati said: "The jungle was so thick that even if someone were close enough to slap you and run you still were unable to see or grab him. It was so dark you could not see from one hand to another."⁴

Ghatiyali's deforested hillside, village herd of cattle,
and new tree "plantation," 1993.

During a conversation with a group of older women, I asked if it
had been easy to gather fuelwood in the old days. One effusive response was typical: "We brought very wonderful bundles of fuelwood
(*baṛhiyā baṛhiyā mauḷī*). . . . The *dhokaṛā* trees grew so thickly, they
were like the fingers on our hand [that close together]. When you
were carrying a bundle of fuelwood, it was difficult to pass through
them."

Haidar Ali confirmed the difficulty of passage and evoked danger
along with beauty, telling us, "There used to be a very beautiful jungle;
and if someone were going to Ganeshpura he would be trembling
with fear, the jungle was so dense; there were thick trees and many
thieves and dacoits; but today you can go 'open account.' I remember
when I went into the jungle to get fuelwood, I couldn't even stand up,
I had to go in and out stooping.[5]

When Vansh Pradip Singh as a young prince exclaims in reported
speech, "I don't need villages, I need jungle!" he too explicitly evokes
this healthy, dense woods and its wildlife.

If we turn from oral history interviews to everyday speech in the
present, we hear people announce in a common euphemism, "I am
going to the jungle [to defecate]." By this they mean, "I am going
anywhere there are no people," and they do not by any means imply

the presence of trees (though one or two are helpful). Or people say, "That road goes through total jungle," meaning that it goes through uninhabited (therefore dangerous), but not necessarily forested, terrain. We could interpret this semantic slippage as a direct result of the very ecological devolution we are attempting to grasp: where there once was jungle there is now barren land, and old linguistic habits die hard. But I tend to believe the span of meanings contained in *jangal*— ranging from any uncultivated and uninhabited space to heavily forested areas—are inherent in the term itself and not attributable to anachronistic landscape memory.[6] When I asked Bhoju in a letter some years ago to define *jangal,* he wrote, "a deserted place, or a forest," and these I conclude are its two primary meanings.

In Sawar, there are other local language terms for land neither cultivated nor inhabited. These include *mangarā* and *kānkaṛ. Mangarā* is not in the *RSK.* Bhoju defined it as "that uninhabited place [*jangal*] where there is a lot of grass and shrubbery." The dictionary definition of *kānkaṛ* is "*jangal,*" or woods, but Bhoju gives a local definition as "that uncultivated field [*maidān*] where wild grasses grow." Here we might observe a distinction between *jangal* as possibly wooded, and the other two as grassy but definitely not wooded. If today, as Bhoju has observed, there is little difference among the three, this could well be a linguistic consequence of deforestation. Seventy years ago, Vansh Pradip Singh does not say in reported speech, "I want *kānkaṛ*"; when he says, "I want *jangal*" he means primarily trees and all they shelter. When Kesar Gujar praises a time when grazing livestock was easy work, she says, "There was so much *kānkaṛ,*" meaning grazing land but not necessarily dense woods.

Although the Court has nowhere been absent in the preceding chapters, Vansh Pradip Singh's distinctive personal presence is most vivid in the territorial extremes of Court and woods. He did not often intrude personally on ordinary folks' domestic lives, although as we have seen his managers and bosses did. Nor did he take a personal hand in grain tax collection, as that would have been beneath his dignity and unbecoming to his benign image. However, the Court's passion for wildlife and his strong sense of identification with his "jungle" render him an immediate presence in people's memories of the woods. Interpretations of present-day ecological deteriorations also habitually refer to Vansh Pradip Singh's stringent, unwavering vigilance, by way of contrast with the slack and corrupt government agents to whom the enforcement of today's forest conservation policies is entrusted.

Before considering the past of the jungle, and the ways the Sawar regime both protected and exploited natural resources, a few basic ecological factors are worth rehearsing. First, livelihood *at every level* of society was enhanced, and benefited from, healthy forest cover, both then and now.[7] Interdependence with the forest is not confined to herders or "tribals," but extends to those whose primary income is agricultural—the vast majority of Sawar's population. There are a number of reasons for this. Every household, then and now, from sweeper to king, needs firewood. If today the well-to-do have kerosene or even propane stoves, their use is severely limited by cost and by rationing. Dung and sometimes corncobs are used as cooking fuel, but they are insufficient for all household needs. Cotton stalks, we learned from interviews, were once a source of fuel and may still be a source where cotton is grown. However, where mustard has replaced cotton as cash crop of choice, as we find in Ghatiyali and environs, this source has also been eliminated. Moreover, all fuel sources are used in conjunction with wood, and at present there appears to be no substitute.

Wooded areas and shrubbery are major sources of fodder, and as such are enormously important for this mixed agricultural and herding economy. Grasses grow only in the rainy season. (As an urban child, imagining that "all cows eat grass," I did not realize until I went to Rajasthan that livestock fed on tree leaves.) Not just dairy animals but draft animals—precious oxen—need a constant supply of greenery.

Beyond the two primary uses of fuel and fodder, indigenous tree species and other forest plants have been until very recently important in numerous other ways to most villagers. Their fruits, saps, barks, and leaves were integrated into the everyday domestic economy. Although we collected this kind of information only incidentally, we have enough casual references to document its significance.[8] The jungle harbored sources of food (berries, seed pods, roots), medicines for humans and animals, and household utensils including pot scrubbers, brooms, and disposable leaf vessels. The latter provided supplementary income for families who gathered leaves and pinned them together into plates and bowls. This practice continues today, although the leaves of the *chūnrāṛā* tree are harder to find. This is far from an exhaustive list of "minor forest products" in Sawar.[9]

Kings' households share needs with peasants, albeit on a grander scale of consumption. Kings too keep livestock that require fodder, and in recent years the royal family's herders have taken the lead in defying government grazing limits, according to one source (Gold 1998a). In castles as in huts, cooking is done over a fire; if the royal diet is more elaborate it requires more fuel to prepare. However, in order to fathom the political ecology of pre-Independence Sawar, we must realize that the Court cherished the forest for reasons different from those of subjects: most evidently for hunting, and also for prestige. These factors are relevant to our understanding of the Court's motivations, as portrayed in living memories, to protect his jungle.

Cultural Dispositions and Colonial Agendas

A confluence of influences—religious, cultural, and political; Mughal and British colonial; familial and individual—flowed into Vansh Pradip Singh's regal concern for his jungle. Here, before going more deeply into the woods and sampling the many narratives of the Court's relationship with trees, pigs, and lions, I sketchily and speculatively contextualize Sawar's local landscape and its meanings—first in a broader Indic heritage and then in Rajputana's late colonial context.[10] I shall also touch on the administrative tactics of Ajmer's earlier Mughal rulers, as these are also probably in play, including the Islamic penchant for establishing ordered gardens. Persian terminology still dominates administrative language. *Zimmedārī*, an Urdu term with Arabic roots, is most frequently used in everyday language to characterize responsible and efficacious rule, including environmental protection.

There are cultural roots in Indian thought, accessible largely through Sanskrit texts, for a symbiotic relationship among kings, wilderness, and wildlife preserves.[11] The well-being of people, kingdom, and rulers is naturally bound up with sensible forest management; hence this topic has considerable historical depth as an explicitly political concern in the subcontinent. However, depending in part on ecological features, the relationship may be variously configured, as the environmental history of different subcontinental regions has revealed. As pointed out in chapter 1, sometimes a king's duty may be to clear and tame the forest, and to overpower its human and nonhuman denizens. Other physiographic contexts demand preservation and protection.

Edward Haynes observes a sequentially dual pattern in which the king would tame areas of wilderness and then control and protect limited spaces within them. Drawing on various textual sources from the Sanskrit epics, *puranas* and *dharmashastras,* he writes:

> The raja's duties toward this "jungle" were dual. First, he was to clear, control, and stabilize the waste, to reenact the deeds of the Pandava brothers and bring wild areas under his domination for the joint protection of his people and the manifestation of his royal order. . . . Second, portions of the woodlands were to be preserved and carefully maintained as royal "pleasure parks," hunting preserves, and managed commercial woodlands. These areas had both economic and symbolic value, for they represented institutionalized examples of the ruler's absolute sway over nature and the natural (1998:736–37).

Islamic rule in Ajmer has left its mark on Sawar, both on its bureaucratic organization and on royal interactions with the landscape. Both historians and art historians have noted India's Mughal emperors' penchant for constructing formal gardens, and they have interpreted these elaborate constructed spaces as visual statements of control. For example, John Richards writes: "Each royal garden was a metaphor for the formal symmetry of imperial rule imposed over the turbulent, multilayered, social landscape of India. Just as the physical landscape was disciplined by the emperor, so was society" (1993:261). Catherine Asher confirms this perspective, stating of the first Mughal emperor that "the manipulation of natural untamed landscape into a rational, ordered creation was for Babur a metaphor for his ability to govern" (1992:20).

Vansh Pradip Singh was also known as a builder of gardens. Indeed, the only two published sources on his life both stress this, even as both tellingly fail to mention his love for wild trees and pigs.[12] This omission may be tacit acknowledgment from local historians of farmers' hostility to the Court's conservation policies. In contrast to written sources, oral histories rarely mention gardens, but all speak, often ambivalently, of the ruler's obsession with protecting trees and wild animals. From the hindsight of present environmental degradation, this was appropriate and admirable. In recalling past deprivations, however, it was often resented. In protecting trees the king restricted the use of forest products his subjects needed; in protecting pigs he harbored and fostered the farmers' enemies. The king's small walled gardens, however, took nothing tangible away from the people, and were, like all shady places, categorically approved. They were not, however, open to the public.

Even today, the kingdom of Sawar is a place rich in revealed religious knowledge transmitted partially through texts but far more vividly and pervasively through oral traditions, performance, and ritual. Vansh Pradip Singh probably absorbed many such culturally available teachings from childhood. As noted in chapter 3, certain tree species figure frequently in Sawar folklore and festivals—most especially the pan-Indian religiously emphasized trio of *nīm, pīpal,* and banyan.[13] The *pīpal* tree, for example, is worshipped annually by women on the day of "Pipal Mother Puja" as a form of the Goddess (Gold 2000a). Both *pīpal* and banyan trees offer shelter and sustenance to wayfaring children in numerous folktales.[14] Gujars, the major herding community in this area, have special duties to respect and protect *nīm* trees, which are associated in several ways with the Gujar divinity Dev Narayan and his epic tale.[15] Sometimes Gujar goatherds lop *nīm* leaves to feed their charges, but almost always with pangs of conscience. Not coincidentally, these are the species Vansh Pradip Singh planted along the Sawar-Ghatiyali road, and attentively fostered. His subjects took him seriously regarding the protection of these trees, even though, as we saw in chapter 5, his threats were often worse than his sanctions.

Relatively close to Sawar, if not immediately local, is Rajasthan's famous, if small, Bishnoi community.[16] Bishnoi religion includes a particular reverence for trees. As one contemporary Bishnoi author puts it, "In trees is the breath of life. . . . Hundreds of years earlier, Guru Maharaj [the sixteenth-century founder of Bishnoi religion, Guru Jambheshvar]—knowing the importance of trees—established the religious practice of not cutting green trees, which today's world governments are only now beginning to establish" (Bishnoi 1991:22; my translation).

In Bishnoi lore the rural population, led by a woman, put their bodies on the line to protect trees *against* a ruler's wanton exploitation—quite the opposite of the situation in Sawar. Fisher suggests that Bishnoi tree protection is "a symbol of political resistance to the [ruling] Rajputs," but he also points to the local nobility's recent attempts to co-opt an identification with nature and establish themselves as allied with Bishnoi environmentalist values, which are globally admired (1997:64–70).

I have no evidence from Sawar that Bishnoi ideas about trees were common currency fifty years ago. However, the now internationally famous story of the Bishnoi heroine who led the first tree-huggers in fatal protest against Rajput lumber operations was well known when I began researching environmental folklore in the early 1980s.[17] In any event, Rajasthan's Bishnoi heritage highlights a nexus of religion and politics in tree protection.

Turning from cultural ambiance to closer specificities of history and politics, we can readily point to some explanations framing Vansh Pradip Singh's dedication to environmental responsibility. Most immediate and evident are the multiple pressures of colonialism with its constant economic and hierarchical jostlings. Small as Sawar was, it was a relatively big fish in the British pond of Ajmer-Merwara, which was surrounded on all sides by greater princely states.

As chapter 3 demonstrated, for about a century preceding the period we address, the British actively pursued forest protection and "reboisement" policies in Ajmer. As they did elsewhere in India, the British in Ajmer-Merwara wished, in their own self-interest, to assume the role of forest protectors. In 1908 Colonel W. J. Lupton, settlement officer of Ajmer-Merwara, noted in a document titled "Improvement of Agriculture" that he was "struck forcibly by the dearth of trees" in Ajmer-Merwara, as compared with the "well-wooded tracts in many districts of U.P." Tree culture, he continues, is "not an in-grained passion" among farmers in this region: "No tree which has leaves on it that cattle will eat is sacred from the devastating knife of the cattle-grazer and the tender of sheep and goats."[18] This was penned when Vansh Pradip Singh was a young prince, and his own passions were forming.

Chapter 6 showed that Vansh Pradip Singh held the British in contempt as impure barbarians, and he did all he could to keep them at arm's length. Nonetheless, he did attend the British-established Mayo College, and it is likely that he was fully aware of the importance set by British rulers on forest maintenance and enhancement. At least one interviewee, a Charan from Rajpura whose relations with the royal house historically were strained, suggested nonindigenous motives for Vansh Pradip Singh's tree passion, as he reminisced about former wildlife:

CHALAK DAN CHARAN: There were so many lions living here, at least two hundred; and rabbits, uncountable. But these days there is nothing. And Vansh Pradip Singh planted the trees on both sides of the road.

BHOJU: What was his reason for planting the trees, his motive?

CHALAK DAN CHARAN: He said that he wanted there to be shade, and they were beautiful to see, and the English had planted trees by the side of the road from Devli to Ajmer, and from Kota all the way to Ajmer—*nīm* and *baṛ*—so the *darbār* got the idea from seeing that.

Vansh Pradip Singh might well have been inspired in part by British example, but his tree-culture passion was arguably rooted in a set of ideas about people and nature that differed in origins and expressions from those held by the colonizers.[19]

Observing Vansh Pradip Singh's style of forestry operations, we find that besides placing guards in the forest and threatening offenders with shameful punishments, he steadily maintained a rhetoric of identification between himself and his woods, declaring, as we heard in multiple anecdotes, "If you cut a branch you cut my finger." Each person who quoted the *darbār* saying this would wag their right forefinger. The right hand is highly valued, pure, and indispensable. This gesture suggests that the royal person's best part is coextensive with the royal jungle. It was a forbidding trope—although, as we learned in many conversations, far from a perfect barricade to wood-hungry farmers and herders contemplating infractions of well-known rules.

A courtly passion for jungle is part of a familiar pattern during the last days of British paramountcy in Rajputana. Haynes, speaking of this era and general region, writes:

Thus, while there are certainly few aspects of the traditional jagirdari system of Rajasthan to which we would want to look back with wistful remembrance, it seems clear that, in those areas with stronger central administrations and higher jagir concentrations, woodlands were preserved from encroachment and degradation by "traditional" methods of resource preservation and allocation. This, of course, has two aspects. Not only were the trees conserved, but the peasants and pastoralists were prevented—frequently with extreme force—from utilizing the natural resources around them (1998:766).

This nicely describes the situation in Sawar and reveals it to be applicable to the period and area.

Other authors point to the colonial context as directly engendering rulers' particular attentiveness to their forests. Shail Mayaram describes matters concerning wild pigs in the native state of Alwar, not far from Sawar. "The Secretary of the Agrarian Grievances Commission recalls that the Meos complained vociferously of the ban on shikar [hunting], for pigs and deer ruined their crops. When the maharaja was told this he exploded and said: 'this is all that I have to show to the English, if this is finished what will I have?' The Commission's Report was buried" (1997:81). In Alwar as in Sawar, the farmers wanted to kill wild animals to protect their crops, but the king point-blank refused because of appearances. Ian Copland, in his recent reinterpretation of princely roles in the "endgame of empire," observes in similar vein that the princes of India, divested of military force, were left "with only the hunting-range to patrol" (1997:25).

Copland and Mayaram both speak of princes who were players in the broader arena of India's Independence struggle, but Sawar's Vansh Pradip Singh had very little part in the national drama. Unlike the Alwar maharaja, he professed no concern whatsoever for British opinion; indeed, as we saw in chapter 6, he scorned it. Nonetheless, he held his honor and reputation as the ruler of a high-ranking kingdom to be bound up explicitly with his capacity to succeed in conserving trees and wildlife within his kingdom's boundaries. By some accounts he deliberately sought to attract wild animals to his domain from neighboring and rival Bhinai by luring them with popcorn trails. One source even suggested that the popcorn was treated with opium water, to ensure that the boars, once arrived in Sawar, would have good reason to remain there.

In Sawar discourses, the term most often used to evoke the qualities of the Court's administrative care—especially for the woods—is *zimmedārī*. Many persons interviewed explicitly explained the massive deforestation following Vansh Pradip Singh's death as an absence of *zimmedārī*. Although the concept may have entered common parlance as part of precolonial Mughal administrative legacies, it has been locally reinterpreted and elaborated. In previous writings I have consistently translated *zimmedārī* as "responsible authority," attempting to add precision based on usage. However, according to dictionaries the term's primary meanings are the unembellished "responsibility," "answerability," and "accountability." The first Hindi word listed under "responsibility" in the English-Hindi dictionary is *zimmedārī*.[20]

The Arabic root of *zimmedārī—zimmā*—means "charge," "trust," and, again, "responsibility." My commonsense notion, based on random observations as an amateur linguist, is that words slip most easily from one language to another when they supply a nuance that did not preexist.[21] Thus *zimmedārī* entered Hindi and comfortably settled there. The twentieth-century Rajasthani concept of responsibility is part of shared Hindu-Muslim subcontinental culture. It is easily shared because it has more to do with governance and human interrelationships than with religion. Or, put another way, it has little to do with deities, or worship, or soteriology—where Hinduism and Islam may diverge fairly radically. It is profoundly concerned with morality and power, where we might expect to find common ground.

Zimmedārī does not involve disinterest. Rather, the source of *zimmedārī* as responsible authority has to do with personal identification, rootedness in place, and perpetuation over time. All of these concepts are unfortunately strictly incompatible with modern attempts to institutionalize a rational bureaucratic administration of forestry (as we will explore more closely in the closing segment of this chapter, as well as in the discourse of modernity with which we are most concerned in chapter 9).

By all accounts Vansh Pradip Singh was obsessively particular and personally vigilant in efforts to constrain both tree cutting and hunting within his domain. In reported speeches, the Court often verbalized a fear that ill reputation (*badnām*) would result were he to relax this vigilance. Although we cannot know the truth of Vansh Pradip Singh's inner motivations, it is telling that his former subjects regularly attribute such a fear to him. It means that they too participate in the belief that a king who allowed trees and wildlife to be devastated would not be able to sustain his good name, or his rule.

Years before, when Bhoju and I were researching sacred groves, people told us that gods had *zimmedārī* for the land around their shrines. Regional oral traditions hold that deities protect their shrines' environs, suffering desecrations intimately upon their divine persons. Deities too are said to have responsibility for the places belonging to them. Like kings, gods were and are reputed to be swift to punish offenders. There is, however, one significant difference between deities' responsible authority and kings' responsible authority. When a powerful deity's laws are broken, sanctions are automatically unleashed. Thus earlier research on sacred groves reported instant, miraculous retributions visited upon those who violated the boundaries and rules of shrines: tractors broke down, woodcutters vomited or fainted, polluters' tents spontaneously burst into flames (Gold and Gujar 1995).

Kings are to their territories as gods are to their shrines, merged physically or metaphysically. But a human ruler cannot govern responsibly without commanding effective power, or *adhikār*. In narrating Sawar's environmental history, people suggested that when responsibility was united with effective power—as was the case in the era and person of Vansh Pradip Singh—then protection (*surakṣā*) was insured. Vansh Pradip Singh delegated effective power through deploying guards to patrol and agents ready to punish. As legends have it, however, he was rarely far behind them in the pursuit of poachers. As Sawar's former subjects see the past, it is this personal concern and supervision by the Court that they deem most critical in determining his successful protection of forest life.[22] Looming behind them all, of course, was the shoe. In a way the Court's dominance, ambiguously with or without hegemony, becomes more explicable when likened to a deity's ineffable but effective power (*shakti*), rather than to a ruler's stick (*daṇḍa*). Subtler still is the darbar's claim to suffer pain along with trees and pigs.

According to popular accounts, even as a young prince Vansh Pradip Singh claimed that he *needed* jungle. He did not just protect what existed but actively sought to increase it. In a conversation with Ram Singh Shaktavat, a Rajput whose family is closely connected to the royal house, we heard of Vansh Pradip Singh in his youth decisively bent on fostering the forest, before he ascended the throne:

RAM SINGH: So Ummed Singhji [father of Vansh Pradip Singh] gave these two villages to Vansh Pradip Singh, but he [the young Vansh Pradip Singh] said, "I don't need villages I need jungle!"

BHOJU [startled]: What? At this time there was no jungle?

RAM SINGH: There were hills but less trees, not so many. So he set his special men—he had five men when he was prince—he set them as watchmen to protect the forest; he started to foster and protect it.

. . . .

And after that he brought animals here, from Bhinai, and from the neighboring jungles.[23] He had sweet potatoes and corn dropped on the road and they came here, eating, eating. And so, little by little, the animals came here.

So Vansh Pradip Singh made this jungle very good, and he created a Forest Protection Department [which didn't exist previously in Sawar].

. . . .

BHOJU: Is there an example of someone who tried to harm the jungle, and the *darbār* punished him?

RAM SINGH: No, because the horses [guards] wandered in the jungle and people were afraid of them.

Suppose you have an acacia in your field, you can't even cut that; so how would you cut from the jungle?[24] Suppose somebody complained [tattled] to him, "Bhoju cut a tree," then the *darbār* would say, *"My hand hurt all night, I feel pain in my hand, don't do it again."*

Note the unabashed rivalry with Bhinai, which extended to luring their pigs into Sawar's jungle. Another interesting implication here—beyond the king's claim physically to suffer the tree's pain—is that such pain would in itself be sufficient punishment and deterrent against future offenses.

Other interviews with persons at various levels of society vividly evoke the way in which the *darbār* asserted his intimate relationship with trees and other aspects of the natural world.

A Sawar Brahmin whose family had been domestic priests to the court (*rāj purohit*) told us: "The *darbār* paid a huge amount of attention to the jungle and whenever anyone cut a branch he would say, '*It is just as if my finger were cut.*' He allowed people to take the dry wood from any jungle, but he didn't let anyone take any green wood. If someone took green wood he became very angry, and he would say, 'O you good-for-nothing![25] Why did you do such a thing?' "

While answering a query about what projects Vansh Pradip Singh had pursued with passionate interest (*śauk*), Mul Chand Joshi, a Brahmin astrologer from a smaller village, Kalera, gave us this version of the Court's interest in trees.

MUL CHAND: He dug wells and step-wells and planted gardens, and he planted the shade trees by the side of the road between Ghatiyali and Sawar. He said, "*If you cut the smallest branch of a tree it is just as if you cut my finger.*"

BHOJU: So what was his motive for planting trees?

MUL CHAND: He wanted travelers to have shade. The road looked beautiful, there was shade, it was the beauty of the village, and he himself would wander in the gardens, and he could take any officer to wander in the garden.

Mul Chand's focus is the roadside trees rather than the jungle trees. Although the *darbār* protects both, he is particularly attached to the shade trees he himself caused to be planted. Mul Chand stresses the values of beauty, shade, and potential hospitality—all of which are traditionally associated with the religiously valued species of trees that once lined the Sawar-Ghatiyali road.[26] The eventual cutting and selling of these same trees was often evoked as an index of the community's moral decline (Gold 1998c).

We heard many stories about the *darbār*'s extremely vigorous and personal interventions to protect trees and animals. The following episode, narrated by Ram Narayan Daroga, is part of the teller's own family history.[27] Ram Narayan Daroga lives at a shrine to Lord Shiva on the road between Ghatiyali and Sawar.

Vansh Pradip Singh planted them [the roadside trees]. I myself, when I was young, I used to make the little walls around the *nīm* trees [to protect them]. And all the trees met together over the road, to make a canopy of shade.[28]

Well, once Sukh Dev Char[29]—he had forty or fifty goats, and one time, one of them ate . . . a branch of a sapling *nīm*. At that time my father was the watchman [*chaukidār*] of the *nīm*. And he got upset and said to Sukh Dev Char, "Uh oh! The *darbār* will make our skin fly off—yours and mine!"

At that time there was another guard, Chandra Singh, who was a bad man. So he went to the *darbār* and said, "Your Ukar Daroga [Ram Narayan's father] knowingly failed to protect the trees, and a goat has eaten a *nīm*. Then the *darbār* came to see the tree, and he said, "Where is Ukar? Summon him here."

And he [Ukar, the speaker's father] was scared shitless [literally, "he had to open his loincloth"]. But my father came to the *darbār*, and the *darbār* was upset [and demanded], "What are you doing, eating? or what?" [That is, are you destroying the trees or protecting them?]

My father said, "A lizard (*khaṅgetyā*)[30] ate it."

So the *darbār* said, "Find it!" And my father's luck was good, so he found a lizard, and at that time it just happened to be eating another plant.

So the *darbār* said, "Call the Bhils,[31] and kill all the lizards on the whole road!" And after that they killed all the lizards between Ghatiyali and Sawar. And the *darbār* rebuked Chandra Singh, "You are a liar, a lizard was eating and you made me angry, you good-for-nothing [*nālāyak*]!"

This anecdote reveals that the *darbār*'s protective attitude toward wildlife was neither indiscriminate nor necessarily ecological. He demands wholesale slaughter of a species of lizard in order to protect trees. Moreover, he orders this violence mistakenly, when duped by his subordinates. The trick, in their minds, appears well justified. The *darbār*'s rage over the loss of a single sapling branch is portrayed as excessive and almost childish. Through deceit, the guard is able to deflect this rage away from himself, goatherd, and goats, and on to lizards—about which presumably nobody cares. Yet this tale also

A Gujar and his goats defy the ban on grazing in a
protected area, outside Ghatiyali, 1993.

serves as a parable of the Court's righteous protection when contrasted with the post-Independence destruction of the same trees
which the *darbār* protected with such fanatic vigor.

Women's accounts of fuelwood-gathering expeditions in the time
of kings give a slightly different, gendered slant to the story of the
Court's power. Recall Raji's account of groups of women actually
feeling empowered to threaten the Court's guards with stones. More
usually, however, the tactics of women were evasion and, when
caught, servility.

Dhapu Mina, from the nearby hamlet of Napa ka Khera, told us
that she used cow dung cakes and cotton stalks for cooking fuel,
emphasizing the abundance of dung in the past due to larger herds of
cows and buffalo. When Bhoju pressed her, however, she too had
some wood-gathering adventures to tell. She tells of being harassed by
the guard just for gathering dry wood, which was according to all
accounts permitted even in Vansh Pradip Singh's heyday.

BHOJU: At that time where did you get fuelwood?
DHAPU: We made fuel from cow dung, dried cow dung cakes, and
from the dried stalks of the cotton crop.

BHOJU: Kantola was very near, couldn't you take wood from there, from the *dhok* trees?

DHAPU: No no no! The *darbār* wouldn't let us take it. After he died, people took it, we took it, but while he was living he didn't let anybody take it!

Once I went to the Ghatiyali jungle, along with Gattu and Panchi. We went and were gathering dry wood, and the guard came, and he said "Where is your ax?"

"No, we are just gathering dry wood."

But he said, "Let's go to the fort." We joined our hands and begged, "No we won't go to the fort," and he finally let us go.

But once when we had no fodder we came into Ghatiyali's jungle to get grass, and that time nobody stopped us.

As Gauri Nath explained it: "We got our firewood from the jungle and if we met a guard on the road he took it, and if not then we brought it home." As did all the other women, she described nostalgically a splendid abundance of *dhokaṛā* trees on the hills nearest the village. And she told of one encounter where she had failed to evade the forest guard: "Once we thought there was no one around in the jungle; I had taken off my wrap and tied it around my waist [village women supposedly never appear outside in public without their wraps properly arranged over their heads, even today; see Raheja and Gold 1994]. I was gathering wood and the guard came and said, 'Did your husband die, so you are taking this wood to burn him?' Then they rounded up all the women, and we had to bring the wood into the fort." The court controlled access to fuelwood strictly, with one exception: fuel for cremation pyres. It is this to which the guard rudely and inauspiciously alludes in Gauri's account.

This situation was corroborated by many tellers. Some present it straightforwardly, as a kind of charitable service of the Court. Gokul Mali, however, told about it with his usual wit and candor, and a strong sense of irony. Bhoju had asked him about help with life-cycle rituals—meritorious actions recommended to powerful persons in many Hindu prescriptive texts:

GOKUL: People were so poor that they couldn't get loans for weddings without a guarantor.

BHOJU: If there were some Brahmin or some other farmer, and he had three or four daughters, would the *darbār* help him?

GOKUL: No, not at all, he didn't help him at all.

BHOJU: So, if some poor man died, did he help with the feast?

GOKUL: No, but if a poor person died he gave wood for the cremation. He helped people after their deaths. If they took wood while alive he had them beaten with a shoe, but after they were dead he gave them wood to burn.

The Court's passion for tree culture and wildlife put him at cross-purposes with the farmers who hated the pigs (with good reason), as well as with the herders who wanted free access to forest grazing and forest products for their voracious charges. As we have seen in chapter 7, it also was modestly opposed by women who subverted the rules whenever they could, in order to bring home the cooking fuel that was a daily necessity. The opposition of royal interests to subjects' immediate needs led to conflicts and subterfuge concerning woods and wildlife, to breaking rules, and to poaching. The past achievement of environmental well-being in Sawar was evidently at the expense of some—for example, farmers whose crops were threatened by wild animals. It also opposed the needs of herders, and of women. But it resulted in recognizable ecological common good on which almost everyone would agree. Only from the hindsight perspective of the ecologically degraded present is everyone able to see what was lost with the loss of forest cover. Abundantly available and diverse forest products, natural beauty, and better weather are seen today as highly valued attributes of a past era. Nonetheless, few would wish to restore the political conditions that are understood to have sustained these.

Memories of wild pigs—*junglī suar*[32]—hold a special place in Sawar citizens' understandings of the political and environmental past. Pigs are emblems at once of royal power and nature's abundance. In Rajasthani courtly paintings from the eighteenth and early nineteenth centuries, boar-hunting kings, nobles, and ladies are common subjects.[33] What made sport for kings was a bane to farmers. We have seen in the preceding chapters how the king's assessment of grain tax and conscription of labor and household goods ravaged ordinary lives. Analogously, pigs—ranging unharmed by royal decree—ravaged the crops.[34] This conceptual and actual convergence in embittered memories of wild power and royal power has consequences evident today; environmental deterioration seems overdetermined by political developments. What follows here highlights those angry memories in which kings and pigs play out their parts on the Rajasthani landscape. Nothing better displays pre-Independence political ecology than pig stories. One of these gripped me from the first, and became the seed for this book.

KALYAN MALI'S WILD PIG STORY

Kalyan Mali was almost always to be found sitting on the stoop in front of his house, which was quite close to Bhoju's house. He wore thick glasses held together at the nose with soiled adhesive tape. In his eighties, he was a little deaf as well as dimsighted. The tale he told us on 3 January 1993 emerged with minimal probing, evoked by a simple question about the jungle that used to be. It was a spontaneous, free association on the topic of wild animals. And, judging from the way he spoke and the way his small audience responded, it was a story he had told more than once.

When Kalyan Mali began his tale of collective resistance to wild pigs, I at first mistook it for an anecdote rather than a personal memory because he lapsed into an oral performance style that was just like the style used by male and female storytellers, whether presenting worshipful tales of God's boons or legends of regional heroes. Not only did Kalyan Mali use the textured, rhythmic speech style of a storyteller, but one of the bystanders—his peer, Sukh Devji—spontaneously and rapidly assumed the role of *hūṅkar* or respondent, a role crucial to any nonmusical oral performance in the village (see Gold 1992:21–22). Sukh Devji's occasional promptings contributed substantially to the tale's lucidity. Kalyan Mali narrated the past as if he were watching or reliving it. To hear him was to experience with him abjection, rage, and a drama of defiance. At the same time his narrative was delivered with humor and evidently at times played for laughs.

I give nearly the full text, including Sukh Devji's interjections; Bhoju and Ann recede into the background almost immediately in this situation. If read attentively, Kalyan Mali's telling exemplifies the works of memory and oral history: to read it is like slowly turning the lens on a camera as images change from completely blurry to slightly fuzzy to startlingly sharp focus.[35]

Kalyan Mali and his family (Ghatiyali, 1980).

It is useful to summarize briefly the episode itself: The farmers of Ghatiyali are angered by their powerlessness to harm the wild pigs that are devastating their crops—a powerlessness imposed by the Court and the shoe. On the day of a religious fair in Ghatiyali, some exasperated village farmers—led by Kalyan Mali, the storyteller—gather in a large group and walk seven kilometers to Sawar to demand that the Court allow them to kill pigs. Unwillingly, under pressure, the Court acquiesces to this betrayal of his protective stance toward wild nature. Kalyan Mali's performed memories portray nuances of royal authority and peasant resistance with ramifications beyond the narrated event. Constructed retrospectively, these memories retain a vivid, pleasing taste of victory over power long banished.

ANN: Do you remember the wild animals, tigers and everything?
BHOJU: She is saying, did you see wild animals, tigers, wild pigs, lions, panthers? [Bhoju thus cues him to "pigs."]
KALYAN: I saw lots of them, I saw them and I chased them away.
BHOJU: Now where have they gone?

. . . .

KALYAN: There were so many wild pigs . . . and we made a complaint: "Come with me, to see." He went over there to see, and the pigs had eaten up everything.

[The unidentified "he" is named below as Jivan Lalji. I know now, although then I did not, that Jivan Lalji was the former *divān* or chief minister over all of Sawar. Why would someone of his status have been present in Ghatiyali? Could it have to do with the Tejaji Fair? It is also quite possible that this was some other, lower-ranking manager for whom Kalyanji substitutes the name Jivan Lalji, as it is one he retains in his memory.]

SUKH DEV: They ate up everything.

KALYAN: Our small piece of land near the village. . . .

SUKH DEV: A piece of land near the village. . . .

KALYAN: Yes, a fine piece of land, they ate everything up, and afterward he went along the road. Who? The king's agent [*kāmdār*], and he put his hand on my shoulder [this is rude, presumptuous]. . . . He put his hand on my shoulder, and I said, "All night, I chase them and chase them again, but they eat everything up, and aren't you ashamed, you? . . ."

SUKH DEV: He had no pity.

KALYAN: That Jivan Lalji. I spent the whole night guarding against wild pigs. "Aren't you ashamed? You don't listen to me." I got angry and shouted at him. I said, "Half the women in the village are widows!"[36]

SUKH DEV: Oh ho!

KALYAN: In my Ghatiyali.

SUKH DEV: They're widows!

KALYAN: And only the women who sleep in the fields with their husbands are auspiciously married [*suhāg*]. . . . . So, talking in this way we went and sat down at Four-Arms temple [the traditional gathering place for Ghatiyali's village council].[37] We gathered, and sat . . . the village people gathered in a group. We said, "Our bodies are suffering."

SUKH DEV: Yes, our bodies were suffering, and we gathered in a group.

KALYAN: We were suffering, and we were gathered, and then "Let us have our justice, this sorrow should be decreased."

SUKH DEV: Oh ho!

KALYAN: And just at this moment, Jaganath Lakaro came by, carrying his mattress.

SUKH DEV: On his head, Oh ho, good.

[This is now comical.]

KALYAN: And his wife was going with him, walking along behind.

SUKH DEV: She was going.

KALYAN: They were going to protect the crops. "Look!" And they looked.

SUKH DEV: Such was our condition.

KALYAN: Yes, such was our condition. [The agent, Jivan Lalji, said] "So, tomorrow, you come to Sawar."

SUKH DEV: Good.

KALYAN: Come to Sawar, and tell the Court [*darbār*]. On the next day . . . this was the tenth . . . Tejaji's tenth.[38] Next day was the eleventh, and they went over there.

SUKH DEV: They [a large group] went to Sawar.

KALYAN: They went, but [the king said] "How can I? Today is the eleventh, and I don't hold court, today, I have none."

[Here the *darbār* may seem briefly to hold the moral high ground with his fast on the eleventh, about which his subjects have forgotten; or is he just obviously stalling?][39]

SUKH DEV: "I can't see them, how could I see them?"

KALYAN: "I can't see you, so come tomorrow."

SUKH DEV: "Come tomorrow."

KALYAN: So, two hundred people were there, had come there. But later, the next day, just five or ten chief people, leaders. . . .

SUKH DEV: Went.

KALYAN: Went, and so they went, the next day, his tenants. And he said, "Let the public* stay below. . . . "

SUKH DEV: Oh ho.

KALYAN: "And five or seven leaders may come."

[Mistakenly, and naively, the *darbār* thinks the entire group of two hundred has come again. He is misled by the leaders so that he continued to believe this, and his being thus duped adds to their triumph.]

SUKH DEV: They came.

KALYAN: They came. So, five or seven leaders went, and he [the king] said, "I fell from the sky and the earth caught me, the earth caught me, and I have no children, nothing at all. . . . "[40]

SUKH DEV: Oh ho.

KALYAN: "And I am lame."[41]

SUKH DEV: Good.

KALYAN: "And . . . spreading from village to village, my . . . "

SUKH DEV: His bad name was spreading.

KALYAN: . . . was spreading. "What do you want?"

SUKH DEV: Oh ho.

KALYAN: "Go, ask the public.* You ask the others: 'What do you want?' Then I'll take food and water, but not before."[42]

So I went back for a little while, to the portal [pretending to consult with the nonexistent public], and then I went back and said, "The public has this to say, 'Let us kill them!' "

"Well, fine! These are my subjects. But don't give me a bad name, don't let my bad name be heard."

SUKH DEV: "My bad name would be heard."

KALYAN: "I would get a bad name. But all right, sure, kill! But don't harm the wood, for which I will punish, don't cut the trees or destroy anything else."

So the very next day, the people of the village rushed out in a hurry, and in one day they killed ninety animals.

SUKH DEV: Ninety.

KALYAN: Ninety, killed in one day. And those that were born in the rainy season.

. . . .

SUKH DEV: The newborn piglets, the babies. . . .

KALYAN: The babies couldn't be counted, but on the next day we went and killed sixty, and . . .

SUKH DEV: Good, everybody killed a pig.

KALYAN: We killed them, and our suffering was decreased. And the Chasta Brahmin said, "The pigs are our enemies," so even the Brahmin killed a piglet.

The nuances of this telling are rich and subtle. The characters and speeches reported from approximately fifty years back are surely stylized, but acutely so. The insufferable insolence of the king's agent is portrayed with a single brushstroke when he claps his hand familiarly on the angry farmer's shoulder. The kings' agents—we have seen in the preceding chapter—were very easy to hate.

As Kalyan Mali describes it, the *darbār*'s strategic and complicated pose of full authority, yet nearly abject humility, deserves some reflection. He speaks as if he inhabits "legend" rather than "history," describing himself in terms appropriate for a helpless orphan or a detached world-renouncer. He claims to retreat in devotional seclusion for his fast on the eleventh and fears for his reputation. Kalyanji's portrait of villagers' interactions with Vansh Pradip Singh seems to hold a mixture of gleeful trickery and genuine pathos. The *darbār* is not without dharmic majesty, yet he is palpably self-inflated, hypocritical, clearly dupable, and possibly pitiable.

The *darbār* wants to maintain a wildlife preserve to uphold his reputation and to secure his own hunting pleasure. The people want to save their crops and their own dignity. The farmer headed to sleep in his fields, with his mattress on his head and his wife trailing behind, is a vignette of utter indignity. Thus clashes are, as usual, not merely over power, nor means of subsistence (though both are evidently salient), but also over coded signs and the feelings they evoke (Guha 1983).

HIMMAT SINGH'S WILD PIG STORY

Kalyan Mali's wild pig story was the beginning of our sometimes halting and rarely linear attempts to understand the political, economic, social, and moral dimensions of environmental change. In 1993, we had deliberately avoided talking with members of the Rajput caste—the former power holders. The few attempts we made were disappointing; our interviewees were evasive and defensive. Worst of all, Bhoju felt our topic of inquiry inevitably saddened them, brought pain to their faces. He was reluctant to remind these still proud persons of their heavy losses.

However, at my urging one day at the end of June we went to visit Himmat Singh, a retired schoolteacher with whose family I had a history of amiable relationships. Himmat Singh's father and uncle were commonly understood to be the illegitimate sons of the tragically "childless" Vansh Pradip Singh. Moreover, they had been two of the Court's most prominent managers (*kāmdār*) in the last decades before Independence, and they figured prominently in some stories of those days. Their mother was a Daroga—a member of the "royal servant" caste whose women were traditionally sexually available to Rajput men, thus producing royal but disinherited children.

Bhoju felt a certain diffidence in this household, and I took a greater role in questioning than usual. Himmat Singh, in his precise schoolmaster Hindi so different from Kalyan Mali's evocative dialect, gave us the Rajput party line on the good old days: "The *darbār* and the farmers had a relationship just like that of father to son." Finally I came round to asking Himmat Singh about the wild pigs. And without excessive urging he began to narrate a story:

HIMMAT SINGH: So, the people were in great difficulty, the wild pigs were destroying the fields, so the people gathered together, and all went to the *darbār,* they went to the fort. [Around this point in his account, Himmat Singh fell into a performative, storytelling style, just as Kalyan Mali had done.] Having gone to the fort. . . .

The *darbār* said, "What's the problem, people?"

And they said [Himmat Singh drops his voice here, seems almost to whisper, perhaps evoking the extreme respect of subjects to ruler], "Well it's like this, there are many wild pigs . . . "

He called four or five men to him, and said, "What is the matter?"

"Sir, this is the matter. . . . "

He said, "People, if you didn't have me you wouldn't have pigs either, nor would the jungle remain."

. . . .

So he told them he would not count what was destroyed by the pigs [when assessing the grain tax on their fields].

[I suddenly realize I have just heard what began as the same story Kalyan Mali told, but with a different ending.]

ANN [excitedly]: What? He didn't accept what the people said, he forbade killing pigs anyway?

HIMMAT SINGH: Yes, he accepted dharma. Just like we give grain to pigeons, he gave grain to pigs. What he did was forgive two maunds.

ANN [still incredulous]: Forgive?

[I knew well this term which was used when royal grace decreed that certain taxes not be collected; Himmat Singh assumed incomprehension rather than amazement and substituted a different verb.]

HIMMAT SINGH: He removed two maunds. For some people two maunds, for some people three maunds.

. . . .

Yes, he was a good man. . . . In many places he built small water reservoirs.

For Vansh Pradip Singh, and for his heirs and kin, the protection of trees and wildlife was bound up with royal reputation and with dharma. Both stories make this clear. But the farmers' tale ends in a free-for-all pig slaughter, which assaults the ruler's dignity, religious status, and reputation even as it affirms the farmers' successful manipulative strategies. Himmat Singh's story very deliberately insists that such an outcome is unthinkable.

I left Himmat Singh's house dumbfounded, and when I reached home I blurted out to Ugma Nathji, who was working with my husband that day: "Himmat Singh says the *darbār* forgave the tax but didn't allow any killing of the wild pigs." Ugma Nathji—a man in his fifties—looked at me expressively and replied, "I was just a child then, but I remember what happened; I killed a pig myself."

These conflicting versions of the wild pig protest story framed my 1993 field research chronologically. In the intervening months we had tracked pigs through dozens of interviews; in 1997 we continued to follow their destructive trails. The *darbār*'s extraordinary affection and care for pigs was often evoked, almost in wonder as much as rage, by the farmers whose crops, income, health, and lives were at stake.

A 1993 interview with Pratap Regar, a leatherworker, encapsulates vividly this conflict of interests:

PRATAP: At that time there was much grass, and many wild animals, and people had to stay in their fields from the minute they planted seeds, because there were wild pigs and the *darbār* fostered them.

BHOJU: Did he let people kill them?

PRATAP: No no no! And in the hot season he built water tanks for them and made popcorn for them to eat where there was no appropriate food for them; I myself have come many times to scatter popcorn for them. And the *darbār* used to sit on the balcony in his hunting tower and talk about them, "Oh, there's a brown one! Look, there's a little one!" He was very happy to watch them.

BHOJU: If there were so many what happened to them?

PRATAP: Enough! When the *darbār* died their number was up. People came from all around and picked off every one of them.

Notice that the Court is portrayed here as somewhat obsessed and immature.[43] Note also Pratap's explicit linking of the death of the *darbār* to the death of the pigs—a convergence that echoes loudly through many accounts of the aftermath of the Court's death.

That the *darbār* wished to increase the pig population in Sawar was stressed by a number of people. Here Ram Narayan Daroga elaborates on one (possibly fictional) strategy:

BHOJU: Your father lived in the time of the great kings, what work did he do?

RAM NARAYAN: He was a watchman belonging to the forest division [he did *jangalāt kī chaukidārī*]. . . . We kept five to ten maunds of popcorn. One person was in charge of it; it was kept locked up. We would sprinkle it with drops of opium water.

. . . .

BHOJU: Why did he give them opium?

RAM NARAYAN: So it would become habitual and they would stay here and not go elsewhere. And the *darbār* would sit watching; and if the pigs didn't come, he would ask, "Why aren't the pigs here?" He didn't have that much zest for killing animals; he had more zest for nurturing them.

Gauri Nath told us: "There was a lot of trouble from the pigs. And there were tanks for them in the jungle, one for water and one for grain, the *darbār* fed them in the jungle. Even so, if we didn't sleep in the fields, then the pigs would clean them out totally. The Court didn't let farmers kill them but after he died they killed the pigs. Before that, if someone killed a pig, they would take him, call him, and take a fine from him."

Ganga Ram Mina presented a detailed description of the problems pigs caused farmers. He also mentioned another wildlife species, blue bull, as troublesome, along with wild boars.[44] In recent years blue bulls have returned to the Sawar area in numbers large enough to cause some farmers once again to sleep in their fields. However, few mentioned them in accounts of the past. I suspect this is because in collective memory wild pigs have become the emblem of "those days."

GANGA RAM: People were greatly troubled by pigs and by blue bulls. In those days, when we chased away the pigs, the blue bulls would come and when we chased away the blue bulls, the pigs would come.

Every night, all night, we would have to beat them with sticks; one man could guard only two *bīghās*. On the day before he planted his seeds, he had to build a shack in his field.

And when he was sowing the seeds, he would tie a cloth around the pipe [used for planting certain types of grain] so that not even one seed would fall out—because then the pigs would find out there was grain there, and they would all come.

BHOJU: If the farmer had to go home at night, and the pigs and blue bulls ate his crop, and he went to the *darbār*, would he help him?

GANGA RAM: No, not at all! The *darbār* wouldn't help him. He would say, "You should have kept watch."

BHOJU: And they couldn't kill the pigs?

GANGA RAM: No, they couldn't kill them. The *darbār* would say, "If you shoot a pig it is just as if you shot me!" He fed them one and one-quarter maunds of popcorn every day.[45]

BHOJU: Did he have guards to protect the pigs?

GANGA RAM: Yes he did, and if ever they heard the sound of a rifle they would immediately run in its direction.

· · · ·

One time there was a Mina named Hazari, from Mori, and he shot a pig in Mori Valley. The *darbār* heard the sound of the rifle all the way from Sawar, and he told his servant to ride to Mori Valley and find out who had shot something. But they had run away fast, so the horseman couldn't find them. But he knew that someone had killed a pig!

So, the *darbār* looked in Para, in Gurgao, in Sadara, and in Sankariya for Hazari Mina. Because he suspected that there must have been some *ṭhākur* who had hunted with him.

Well, they caught the Sadara *ṭhākur* while he was cooking the pig. They took the pot with the meat in it, and summoned him to the fort; and Vansh Pradip Singh said, "This is your last chance and if you do it again I will shoot you."

He called him "Good-for-nothing," and said "I will shoot you."

Intrigued by this tale of a known Mina hunter, we decided to seek him out in Mori. As it happened, Hazari had passed away years ago, but his younger brother Bhairu Mauja Mina told us the story as he recalled it.

BHOJU: We heard that Hazari Mina once killed a wild pig in Mori Valley.

BHAIRU: Yes, at that time even the *thākurs* were not allowed to hunt, and if they tried, we [the Minas, as guards working for Vansh Pradip Singh] would grab their rifles away from them. We didn't let them kill pigs.

But once the Sadara *thākur* came, and we killed it for him with our gun.

[Sadara was another small neighboring kingdom; apparently the *thākur*'s desire was not the thrill of hunting; he wished to eat boar meat, which was prized among Rajputs; it was apparently a practice to pay the local guards/hunters to kill a pig in this fashion, but Sawar's Court highly disapproved of this.]

Kalyan Mina and some other men, they told the *darbār* what happened.

[Note that Ganga Ram's idea, that the Court had heard the shot, is not subscribed to here, and this is possibly the more realistic of the two accounts.]

After that we sold our rifle; because people were complaining to the *darbār,* and then we could say, "Now we have no rifle and we won't kill anything."

While Ganga Ram's account stressed the *darbār*'s anger at the *thākur* who employed the Mina hunter, here the hunter's brother stresses, by contrast, his community's vulnerability to the Court's anger. Caught between the demands of different rulers, they take the wise strategy of ridding themselves of their weapon, thus assuring the Court of their innocence.

In the kingdom of Gurgaon we heard another story of a hunting conflict between the Sawar *darbār* and other Rajputs. This was told by the son of the current Gurgaon Court, who spoke authoritatively about a past that he was too young to remember. Clearly he had listened well to family stories. Unfortunately, I did not record his given name; I identify him here simply as Rathor.

BHOJU: What was your connection with Sawar? You are Rathor and they are Shaktavat. . . . [These are different Rajput lineages; Rathor comes out of Marwar and Shaktavat, as we know, is from Udaipur.]

RATHOR: We had a good connection, but sometimes it was spoiled. The reason was that sometimes we hunted in their area. Then our relations became bad.

. . . .

BHOJU: Can you recall an event?

RATHOR: One time . . . this is about our grandfather's brother, Giridhar Singh. Then, the Sawar Court thought Gurgaon people were hunting in this area, but he didn't know who the hunter was, only that someone was killing pigs. He wanted to search for him, so he set up a competition. He summoned all the rifle marksmen to the Sawar water reservoir.

And he had some clay water pots set up on boats in the water reservoir. Then he ordered all the marksmen to shoot the water pots.

At that time, the people from Gurgaon asked themselves, "Why did the Court decide to have this competition? Maybe he wants to catch us."

So, he [Giridhar Singh] was a good shot, but he deliberately missed all his shots. When the program was finished, Vansh Pradip Singh said to him, "I heard you were hunting in my area but it's not true, you are not such a great hunter."

So he saved himself, he escaped.

We had some further conversation with this man about the differences between Sawar and Gurgaon, and their respective rulers' attitudes toward pigs. He told us that in Gurgaon no one was beaten for killing pigs, but then again, he added, not very many people had rifles. In the end he summed up the Sawar Court's attitude: "In Sawar the Court cared more about the pigs because he fed them, and he counted them: How many males? How many adult females? He paid attention to them! He made a huge point of protecting pigs, he thought, 'As long as I'm here there should be pigs here!'"

Why Kings, Pigs, and Trees were Finished Off Together

The logical sequitur of Vansh Pradip Singh's desire—"As long as I'm here there should be pigs here!"—becomes his own self-fulfilling prophetic legacy. After his death, the pigs, and the trees that sheltered them, were finished. As we know, he died without progeny in 1947, and his widow's adopted "son," Vrij Raj Singh, was seated on the Sawar throne in 1951. Beginning during the four-year interregnum, and continuing unchecked under the new ruling family (and India's new regime), there was a rapid decimation of trees and wildlife. Within a single decade, as the tale was told, the densely wooded hills where tigers, deer, antelope, jackal, and destructive herds of wild boars once found sustenance and shelter were stripped almost bare.[46]

In this final section on the remembered jungle we trace and ex-emplify this logic: the convergences in people's minds of the end of trees, pigs, and kings. In a series of interview extracts, I have transcribed this thought in italic in order to highlight what strikes me as a remarkable identification with consequences that even today remain relevant, not just for understanding Sawar's past but for ecological recovery.

In 1997 Sampat Lal Purohit of Sawar town stressed the *darbār*'s own prophesy:

SAMPAT LAL: They didn't let the farmers kill pigs—even though they could kill deer (*hiran*) and rabbits (*khargosh*). But not pigs! Some people secretly killed them, but if the Court found out, it was very dangerous.

. . . .

BHOJU: The pigs did a lot of damage in Ghatiyali. Did they cause just as much destruction in other places?
SAMPAT LAL: Yes they did; it was bad in other villages as well.
BHOJU: Did the king assist the farmers when the pigs troubled them?
SAMPAT LAL: *The king said, "On the day that I die, the pigs will die too. All this will die, so don't worry!"*

Amba Lal Loda spoke of the sorrows of the past, spontaneously moving, as many others did, from the exploitations and abuses by the kings' agents to the ravages of the fields by wild pigs. This was recorded in 1993, before the return of the troublesome blue bulls.

BHOJU: Which castes were most sorrowful?
AMBA: Mali, Loda, Gujar.
[He gives examples of their trials.]
　　. . . if he [the Court] has a guest, then he would say, "Hey, I have

a guest, so bring me mattresses and cots!" And suppose we didn't do this work, what would happen? He would have the Bhangi apply the shoe to us.

. . . .

And when we planted our seeds, from that very day we had to take our mattress to the fields because of the wild pigs, and if we missed spending even one day, they would eat our crops.

From the very day we put in the seeds we had to put our cots there, but if we fell asleep at all, even for an hour, the pigs would clean out the field.

And besides that, they [the king's men] dropped grain for them in the jungle and fed them water; and if they heard the firing noise [of a gun] they would immediately come and see who fired; and they would immediately grab the person who did it and have him beaten with a shoe.

BHOJU: So how did all this come to an end?

AMBA: Little by little, as the *rājā-mahārājās*' rule went on, the *darbār* died, and their power became less; and on the other side the government's laws increased [that is, the Congress-led government of Independence], kept increasing, and people's understanding increased . . . and little by little the animals were finished and the jungle was cut. And today this is the condition; we have no fear of anything, we can plant our seeds and not go back to the field until the harvest, and there will be no destruction. Nowdays there are no such difficulties at all.

When the kings' rule was finished, so the wild animals, and the whole jungle was finished, and nothing at all is left.

Polu Kumhar embellished his accounts with details that brought home intensely and intimately the suffering of body and spirit under the *rājā-māharājās*: for example that the grass farmers were forced to carry in conscripted labor often included stinging nettles, or, as we saw in chapter 4, that the king's agent, when he commandeered a family's milk, wore his shoes into the kitchen, thereby adding insult (and pollution) to injury. Here Bhoju introduced the pigs theme, which Polu took up readily without an apparent break in his train of thought.

BHOJU: What about the wild animals causing trouble, didn't the *rājā-mahārājās* help you?

POLU: No, as many sheep and goats as there are today, there were that many wild pigs, and they lived in herds of two or three hundred.[47] And if we were planting seeds, if we didn't spend the night in our field to protect it, then the pigs would just follow the path of the plow, and go up one furrow and down the other eating the seeds.

BHOJU: Didn't the farmers herd them and chase them away?

POLU: If they were awake; but they worked hard all day and sometimes they fell asleep. So women were always waiting for their husbands to come home.

BHOJU: When there were so many pigs, how were they finished?

POLU: *When the* darbār *died, that was the end of the pigs;* people picked them off, and got rid of them. So Ghatiyali and all the people from nearby villages were satiated with pigs [that is, they hunted, killed, and ate them]. People came from other places and put them in buses and took them away; as soon as the *darbār* died.

Like Polu Kumhar, Rup Lal Khati equated the moment of Vansh Pradip Singh's death with liberation from the plague of wild pigs, stating bluntly, "*When the king died, there was no master and so all the pigs were finished, they killed them all.*"

We asked a ninety-two-year-old Brahmin, Gajanand Sharma Buvalia, to describe the end of the kings' era. It is telling that, just as did the nonliterate farmers, Gajanand spontaneously marks the end of an epoch of history with the killing of pigs. Different here is his reference to the intervention of an outsider, the deputy commissioner, not mentioned by any of the others: "The deputy commissioner came to Ghatiyali, and to Vajta [a nearby, smaller village, part of Sawar's kingdom] to listen to the people; the third time he came to Sawar. "*And then the Rajputs stopped bothering us; and the commissioner told the people, "If the wild pigs bother your crops you can kill them." And at this time* jagīrdārī *was over.*"

Wild pigs loom large in Sawar's memories as a rambunctious presence, and in these collective representations princely power and wild pigs died together. The stupendous abundance of pigs may appear to be an indication of wild nature's abundance a hundred years ago versus today, but socioculturally they were metonymous with brute political power and economic exploitation. The rulers fed, fostered, and protected them, reserving for themselves the privilege to hunt

Women rest their firewood bundles on what was
once a hunting tower (Ghatiyali, 1997).

them and eat their reputedly savory meat. The *darbār* loved the pigs,
and like him they were to graze unchallenged. In Kalyan Mali's narrative, resistance to royal power is violently acted out on the symbolically charged but very real bodies of wild pigs. That the recognized if unnamed heir to the former Court's symbolic status gave a
divergent account, replacing this violence with seemly restitution,
reveals the residual importance for princely identity, even today, of
the ability to protect wild nature and to soothe the subjects' protests
without allowing them to vent their fury.

Obviously, the landscape and its uses, like the past, has always been
multiply contested and continues to be multiply interpreted (Appadurai 1981). However, opposing accounts sometimes lead to converging conclusions. Himmat Singh's denial of pig slaughter is founded in
the same conditions as Kalyan Mali's revelry in it. Numerous accounts
from persons occupying a range of social positions bear witness that
similar predations of kings and pigs ended together, with the death of
Vansh Pradip Singh.

When Bhoju and I commenced our inquiries, both wild pigs and
the woods that sheltered them were notable only for their absence—
an absence nonetheless laden with meaning. Sticking up like proverbial sore thumbs on the now almost barren hilltops stand the

former hunting towers, proof in stone to doubters that once there truly was a tangled growth of forest to overlook, where regal hunters went to take their pleasure shooting. Although the selected memories assembled here are of an era proclaimed truly past, it is one that impinges in many ways—as our final chapter will show—on present and future material conditions and consciousness.

10. IMPORTS

LALU REGAR: Today there is no love-and-affection left; twenty or twenty-five years ago the whole village was unified.

BHOJU: What is the reason?

LALU REGAR: Father of a Daughter! [a common and mild expletive]. Today we have grain grown with white fertilizer, flour ground by the power mill, and water from the tap. So how can there be unity and love?—Interview in Ghatiyali, 1993

The end of princely rule and the climax of deforestation mark conceptually, if not necessarily precisely, the beginning of the narrative about imports explored in this final chapter.[1] This narrative coincides with numerous other momentous changes. In the early 1950s the political and economic disempowerment of Rajput rulers and landlords and the drama of land reform took place. Sawar's residents refer to the granting of "land to the tiller" with the English word "settlement": land titles were "settled" on the cultivators, written in the name of the farmer.[2] However imperfectly this project was accomplished, and despite all the efforts made by Rajputs to subvert its purpose or at least to cushion its devastating impact on their massive holdings, it was nonetheless transformative for rural society.

Such landmark institutional and structural change effectively eliminated, almost overnight, two out of the three major oppressions of the great kings' era: grain taxes and forced labor. Prohibitions were slower to go, but most have passed into memory. Now anyone may live in a *pakkā* (stone) house; wear shoes, and gold (if they can afford it); and serve fried treats made with sugar. A few privileges are still

contested, such as whether bridegrooms belonging to formerly untouchable communities should be able to ride horseback (as we saw in
chapter 8).

More gradual than land reform but cumulatively of tremendous
impact were various technological innovations of the 1950s and 1960s.
Farming today is dominated (at least in people's minds) by the use of
tractors to plow and by threshing machines at harvest; by the applica-
tion of chemical fertilizers; by the use of engine-driven pumps to
irrigate; and by the preponderance of new varieties of wheat as the
favored food grain (versus corn, millet, barley, and indigenous wheat
species) and oil seed or spices as cash crops (versus cotton).[3] Even in
the late 1990s, however, most forms of modernization coexist with
continuing, if waning, practices: for example fertilizing with composted manure, cultivating older varieties of grain, multicropping,
and plowing, threshing, and irrigating using oxen for power. Attitudes
toward these outmoded, if ongoing, practices name them as doomed.

Associated with changes in production are changes in lifestyle.
Improvements in economic conditions for small farmers have been
accompanied by increases in conspicuous consumption, particularly
in the form of stone and brick houses and furnishings for them,
motorcycles, electronic devices (radios, tape decks, and televisions),
and elaborate weddings and funeral celebrations. For the previously
severely disadvantaged—the "scheduled castes" of Regars, Chamars,
and Harijans—government programs have provided much, including
houses, land, wells, and electricity. In spite of the many material advantages acknowledged in the present, every person we interviewed
spoke at times of deteriorations both in individual and community
well-being. Such declines were located notably in the lack of good-
tasting food and its inherent power to nourish, which affects human
health, strength, and character, which in turn impact on social graces
and community harmony.

In the two decades of my own travels to and from Rajasthan, I have
witnessed much that would readily be named "modernization" or
"development." In 1979 the unpaved roads linking Ghatiyali with Kekari in one direction and Devli in the other were both impassable in
the rains. Buses therefore stopped running for the traditional four-
month monsoon season (*chaumāsā*, approximately mid-June through
mid-October), no matter what the weather really was. Today, the road

to Kekari is fully paved, and although the Devli road remains a rough ride the new bridge over the Banas River, completed in 1997, has, year-round, significantly shortened the journey from Ghatiyali to this regional transportation hub. By 1999 there were six buses daily passing through Ghatiyali, as well as several jeeps that carry passengers. It has become relatively easy (if not exactly pleasant) to leave by bus in the early morning and, changing only once, to be in the state capital of Jaipur by early afternoon; pushing it, a determined traveler can reach Delhi by night. Other villages in the Sawar Twenty-Seven vary in their transportation connections. Some, like Kushaita, are equally well linked; others, such as Mori or Vajta, do not lie on main, paved thoroughfares, and travel from these places remains more difficult. In Sawar itself, the bus stand is a fairly bustling place, complete with multiple fruit stands, tea stalls, sweet shops, a photostat service, and a dry cleaner.

Some enterprising Ghatiyalians have established stable outposts in Jaipur. Notably, the Anurag filling station in Moti Dungar is owned and operated by Gisar Phuleriya Mali of Ghatiyali. Most of its employees are from his village, and not all of them are Malis. Gisar himself is now at least half city man. He has a house in Jaipur and has expanded his business ventures to include a taxi service. When I asked one teenage boy from Ghatiyali if he was happy working at Anurag, he said casually, "Of course, everyone here is from our own (*apno*) village." Many poor workers from the Sawar Twenty-Seven have labored for months or years in the burgeoning suburbs of South Delhi, where distinctive Rajasthani dress is the most common apparel seen on construction crews. Other village men are interstate truckers, soldiers, and policemen—all occupations entailing considerable mobility. In addition to Bhoju, two men from Ghatiyali, both Brahmins, have traveled abroad—one, as a temple priest, to Pennsylvania and one to Saudi Arabia.

In 1979 there was one government school in Ghatiyali; today there are three, as well as a private-enterprise "English-medium" primary school that is profitable and crowded (a collaboration between a Brahmin and a Damami).[4] Although progress to total literacy in all of Rajasthan has been slow, the trend does continue upward.[5]

In general, local production of cash crops and sale of dairy surplus, along with salaries from outside jobs, have noticeably increased the flow of cash and of commodities through the villages. By the same token, staple grain scarcity and high prices can result, and less dairy products are consumed. For persons living in the villages, wages for labor in local quarries and road-building projects have increased, and this too increases participation in national and international markets. Evidence of the cash economy exists at every level—from plastic shoes and stainless-steel utensils to motorcycles and televisions. When I first reached Ghatiyali in 1979 there were no televisions; today there are over thirty. The flickering gray images of urban and foreign lives, as far as I have been able to observe, are truly gripping only to the young. Nor do regional broadcasts—whether focused on folk dances or fertilizer—seem to command a broad audience. Serials about mythological figures, however (it was Lord Krishna in 1997), hold four-generation families weekly in collective thrall.[6]

There has been a veritable construction boom. Bhoju estimates that the percentage of *pakkā* houses in Ghatiyali has increased from about thirty to over sixty in the past two decades. In Sawar itself elements of middle-class city life (I noticed indoor plumbing and breakfast as a meal, for example) are becoming increasingly common. The smallest, virtually monocaste and dominantly agricultural hamlets such as Napa ka Khera, Mori, and Jaswantpura would seem least affected by these changes. But they too participate in new circulations of ideas and goods. For example, a women's group (*mahilā mandal*) connected to a state-wide project is based in tiny Jaswantpura; however, Jaswantpura lies right on the Sawar-Ghatiyali road (Gold 1996).

These changes I have observed—increased access to transportation, education, communication, cash, and modern objects of desire—are part of a pattern of ongoing processes throughout rural Rajasthan, both in and beyond Sawar's twenty-seven villages. Interestingly, these basic "works" of modernity or "development" are almost universally understood either as welcome or neutral and are taken for granted; in interviews no one dwelt on them. A few select elements of the present are given far more attention, even though they may seem less fundamental than roads, schools, and cash flow.

If I try to characterize the problematic changes that with relentless frequency arose in our conversations, I would say it was changes having duplex natures, evoking mixed feelings. These were innovations alien in origin but insidiously intimate in usage; rooted in the land, ingested. Although verbally debated, these changes are essentially nonnegotiable in the sense that they may not easily, or even with some difficulty, be avoided or refused; they are perceived as inescapable and transformative. Not a single person complained about increased bus service as having altered the conditions of life, although it certainly has done that. But everyone complained about poisonous foreign trees (*vilāyatī*). People can choose not to take the bus, and many do choose not to send their children to school, but it would be difficult to avoid eating chemically fertilized and power-milled grain or drinking tap water, and it is impossible to avoid the sight of foreign trees, now the chief feature of the "natural" landscape.

In sum, the changes that dominated our conversations characteristically had to do with selected imports, ambivalently judged, whose penetrations are experienced as incorporated and nonreversible. While some changes are differentially evaluated from situated viewpoints, many reactions seem to cross-cut gender and class identities. Villagers' discriminating critiques of modernity highlight changes we may group heuristically into two sets of tangible nature and two of consequent insidious and less concrete impact. However, any and all of them are evoked in unison.

1. Changes in and related to the visible landscape to which changes in climate are attributed: foreign trees and strange weather. These include all changes in products available from nature as a result of environmental change, changes in irrigation practices, and changes resulting from population growth such as decreased grazing land and consequent reduction of dairy products.

2. Changes in and related to technologies affecting everyday life, particularly consumption. These include practices affecting the taste of grain and its nutritional content: chemical fertilizers, pesticides, and new species of grain and other newly introduced crops. Here I also group other consumable and wearable items, including water, medicine, liquor, and clothing. The triad of tap water, power-milled flour, and chemical fertilizer evoked by Lalu Regar in the epigraph to this chapter emerged frequently in interviews as the source not only of changes in workloads but also in personalities, families, and community well-being. Japanese sandals and polyester cloth were often mentioned as detrimental to health, and even to character. Discernibly

part of the same complex, discussed in the same breath, were western medicines and liquor.

3. Changes in and related to knowledge itself. Imported knowledge in the form of agricultural technology has altered ritual cycles and greatly diminished concern for astrological timings, hence the concern for traditional Brahminical learning and prescience. Threshing machines and tractors have virtually eliminated certain rituals. Although there are still those who administer herbal remedies for human and animal diseases, the experts have become reticent and embarrassed (at least before a foreigner and a schoolteacher) about this practice. The government-imposed and sporadically enforced laws against caste discrimination are also relevant here. Brahmins lament the loss of respect, while members of formerly disadvantaged groups are happy to leave such customs behind them (just as women would hardly wish away the power mill or the water tap).

4. Changes in human nature and community: a totalizing vision deriving from all the preceding conditions. Bob Dylan's hyperbolic words, "Everyone's dying today from the disease of conceit," echoed in my brain as eerily apropos to sum up village discourse on altered selves. The terms for this disease are varied and plentiful, and include self-interest or selfishness (*svārth*), jealousy energized by desire (*īrṣyā*), conceit (*abhimān*), egoism (*ahamanya*), pride or arrogance (*ghamaṇḍī*), superiority (*majāj*), and a charming local term for self-inflation that literally translates as "I'm big" (*hambaṛī*).[7] Many people say (as Jamuni Regar did in chapter 4) that such self-aggrandizement is increasing as a direct result of the three sets of processes summarized above. The disease of conceit itself is not understood as an import. All the words used to describe it have indigenous etymological and conceptual roots. According to the interpretations we recorded, in the past these human dispositions were checked by surrounding physiological and sociological pressures; but no longer. In Sawar, the disease of conceit is explicitly opposed to "village love" (*gāṅv kā prem*). People thus contrast the old days, when (according to memory) most interpersonal relations in the village were characterized by generosity and compassion, with modern times, when anger and selfishness prevail while community and personal moralities have dwindled. Changing roles in the family—upsetting both generational and gender hierarchies—are part of this story of modern times.

Village love in the form of carrots (Ghatiyali, 1993).

For me, village love was epitomized by the way gardeners, who had nothing to hope for from me, so kindly dug up masses of carrots on which my greedy children gorged themselves in winter 1993. When I wanted to pay, it was point-blank refused: "No, no, it's village love." This has something to do with an understanding of the bounty of the earth goddess (Prithvi Ma, Dharti Ma) as grace, and also with the acknowledgment (one we will hear Ajodhya Khati articulate forcefully later in this chapter), that nothing really belongs to human beings. Now and then, momentarily, such understandings may override the world of exchange or "give-and-take" (*lenā-denā*) that is all too much with us. Today village love emerges from time to time as spontaneous sparks, quickly extinguished. Collective memory says that in the past it was perpetual—like the "endless flame" that used to burn in temples. This may well be a trick or trope of memory, but memory is after all our subject here.

The Advent of Vilāyatī

It is risky to condense or flatten or epitomize a narrative as multidimensional and organically interdependent as this one. But I am tempted to find in the discourse surrounding "foreign" trees a poetic model of all imports and associated modernities, just as the legendary shoe epitomized past rule, and wild pigs the ambivalently constructed abundance of nature.

Thorny trees are not new to Rajasthan's Banas Basin. But the tree in question seems to escalate pernicious thorniness to a previously unknown degree. This now-dominant tree species in the Sawar-Twenty-Seven environment is an aesthetically unpleasing, stubbly plant locally dubbed "foreign *bambūl*" (*vilāyatī bambūl*), and often simply referred to as *vilāyatī* ("foreign").[8] This tree's Latin name is *Prosopis juliflora*, and it is not an acacia as the Hindi would imply but rather a kind of mimosa, native to Mexico. In the United States we are familiar with *Prosopis juliflora* as "mesquite," valued for its smoke's flavor. Significantly perhaps, I never once heard a Rajasthani resident exclaim that food tastes better when cooked over *vilāyatī*.[9]

M. M. Bhandari's survey of plants in western Rajasthan dates *juliflora*'s introduction into Jodhpur district (desert country far west of Sawar) as 1914. He notes that "it is a hardy plant, grows fast and is likely to be very useful for afforesting arid land" (1990 [1978]:137). In Ghatiyali and its environs, we were told, *vilāyatī* was introduced much later as an organic hedge to protect fields and mark boundaries. Farmers accepted it, but now claim that the trees have become unwelcome and hard-to-remove colonizers of agricultural land. Crops do not grow well in *vilāyatī*'s company. Puncture wounds and splinters from their thorns cause dangerous infections, and play havoc with bicycle tires. The presence of these foreign trees, however, has averted a severe fuelwood shortage.[10] Government planners continue aggressively to promote *vilāyatī*'s propagation in plantations on otherwise barren or unproductive land—largely because the young trees are not grazed and will therefore survive in quantity.[11]

Seedlings of almost every other kind of tree must be protected from livestock with elaborate improvised structures, as well as watered for several years, but *vilāyatī*—thorny and fast-growing—flourishes without human assistance. Goats and other livestock eat the seed pods, and new trees sprout from their dung; hence *vilāyatī* spreads quickly over the landscape (Bhandari 1990 [1978]:137).

Though because of *vilāyatī* I've snagged my skirt and hair, scratched my limbs, and flattened my tires more than once, I was frankly surprised at the vehement dislike this plant evoked from herders and farmers, in spite of their evident and acknowledged

The only way to protect a young tree from livestock.

dependence on it for cooking their daily bread. Our aim in this chapter is neither to champion nor debase the value of *vilāyatī* for reforestation of the Banas River Basin. Rather, Bhoju and I focused on people's emotional response to *vilāyatī* as a colonizer of their landscape.[12] I shall also go on to consider how this tree's eventual domination of the scenery intermeshes, conceptually and actually, with many kinds of gross and subtle invasions and replacements.

The term "foreign" implies a contrast with "local" or "indigenous." Among trees, another species—presumably indigenous to the region—is called *deśī bambūl,* or "local *bambūl.*"[13] People often contrasted *deśī bambūl,* used for medicine and furniture, to *vilāyatī,* which is good "only for burning."[14] While *deśī bambūl* has become scarce around Ghatiyali, *vilāyatī* is everywhere. A number of other verbally maligned but pragmatically incorporated elements of modern life in Sawar are, like foreign trees, opposed to indigenous, or local (*deśī*), things, but are either labeled "English" (*angrejī*), directly after the former colonizing power, or simply called by their foreign names. These include fertilizers, liquor and medicine, and synthetic fabrics and machinery. Like *vilāyatī,* these too are widely utilized, and are the subjects of an ambivalent discourse. All such linguistically marked imports are associated with, and emblematic of, far-reaching changes that have diminished some aspects of life, but that are by no means wished away.

A hierarchical evaluation of local as superior versus foreign as problematic, apparent in these tree appellations, is, however, context dependent. When it comes to ghi, or clarified butter, "pure *deśī*" is synonymous with "the best," hardest to procure and most costly.[15] Opposed to it is ghi that is adulterated or totally fake (that is, vegetable shortening). Regarding radios or tape decks, however (valued items notably foreign in their origins), people speak of *deśī* with derision, and the economics are also reversed. A *deśī* tape recorder may be cheap, people advised us, but its sound is bad and it breaks easily.

I cannot help but be reminded of Salman Rushdie's use of a popular Hindi film song to epitomize or celebrate the identity crisis for Indians in this era of transnational flow: "Mera joota hai Japani / Ye patloon Inglistani / Sar pe lal topi Rusi—/ Phir bhi dil hai Hindustani," which Rushdie translates poetically as "O my shoes are Japanese / These trousers English, if you please / On my head, red Russian hat— / My heart's Indian for all that" (Rushdie 1991:11). It seems that

the sense of being clothed in alien, transcultural fragments has penetrated not just the filmgoing urban populace, or the non-resident
Indians of whom Rushdie often writes, but rural minds as well. However, the cheerful assertion of a deeper Indian identity vocalized in the
song may be a cinematic fantasy of surface versus depth. While some
persons with whom we spoke expressed comparable thoughts (or
used similar strategies), others felt change had penetrated not just
their body chemistries but their souls.[16]

In chapter 3, I described the tree cover of the Banas Basin in the
nineteenth and early twentieth centuries, when the dominant species
was *dhokaṛā* (*Anogeissus pendula*). In interviews about the present,
vilāyatī is often compared negatively with *dhokaṛā*. When I spoke with
Kesar Gujar and Bali Gujar about fuelwood, both expressed their
disgust with *vilāyatī*:

KESAR: There used to be *dhokaṛā* and *khakheṛā* and the sheep and
goats ate them. And there was much *chūṅrāṛā* and the buffalo ate
them, and there was much grass for the cows, so there was no
problem at all, but what do we have now? *Vilāyatī!*

BALI: Women always cut it for fuelwood, and if you cut one then a
hundred grow back.

KESAR: So they leave the thorns behind, all over the jungle, and there are
so many thorns, no one can go inside, and this makes grazing sheep
and goats very troublesome; you cannot even walk in the whole
jungle. . . . Misery! *Gachaṛak gachaṛak* [sound, or feel, of thorns
going in] the thorns stick in their feet, poor things! [*Kesar's voice is
expressive with pity here.*] They get infected. This is today's hardship.

ANN: Of fuelwood, the hardship of fuelwood.

KESAR: I can't cut *vilāyatī* myself, I don't know how anyone can cut it,
I am not able to drop my ax on *vilāyatī*—because there are too
many thorns.

ANN [to Bali]: Don't you hurt yourself on *vilāyatī*?

BALI: You have to have shoes on your feet, leather shoes, not rubber
thongs. You put your foot on it and then you can cut it. In this way
women develop technique.

Bali, the younger woman, has pragmatically come to terms with the
import, but Kesar is unusually passionate in refusing to deal with it.

Gauri Nath described the introduction of *vilāyatī* on her own land.

The sense she conveys is similar to Kesar's: that its unexpected capacity to propagate was out of control and pernicious: "We once went to Devli, and from there we took seed pods of *vilāyatī bambūl,* and we put them in cow dung [to germinate]. We planted them around our fields to protect them from animals. But now there are so many of them in the jungle that there is no limit to them."

Dayal Gujar gave a more evenhanded account of the good and bad qualities of *vilāyatī:*

BHOJU: Today the government has planted *vilāyatī bambūl.* Is this harmful?

DAYAL: No, it's a very good thing because we have firewood, and if not for that no tree would remain at all. . . . It's good for burning, but it's bad for animals. If we get splinters, it's bad. And beneath it, in its shade, no grass or crops will grow. There is poison in its shade. It is very bad for the fields.

In many conversations we heard *vilāyatī* in opposition to all other tree species. Phrases such as, "all the trees were cut" and "all that's left is *vilāyatī*" or "there are no trees left, only *vilāyatī*" are common exaggerations. These phrasings suggest that in some ways *vilāyatī* is truly thought of in a fashion different from all other tree species. Even children who have no memories of the old forest share their elders' differential evaluations of *vilāyatī* versus all other trees.[17] Thus thirteen-year-old Satya Narayan, who is in the eighth grade, distinguishes *vilāyatī* from other sources of wood when discussing the moral dilemmas entailed by tree cutting. Although prompted by his teacher, Bhoju, to declare that it is sinful to cut trees because they have souls, Satya Narayan also frankly affirms that people need to cut them, no matter what the moral consequences may be. However, he exempts cutting *vilāyatī* from all sin.

BHOJU: Do you get sin from cutting trees?

SATYA NARAYAN: Yes.

BHOJU: Why?

SATYA NARAYAN: Because we shouldn't cut them.

BHOJU: Are trees and plants living things or nonliving things? [Note that the Hindi terms *jīv* and *nirjīv* for "living" and "nonliving" could also translate as "souls" and "nonsouls."]

SATYA NARAYAN: They are living things.

BHOJU: So when you know that trees and plants are living things, and that it is sin to cut them, why do you cut them anyway?

SATYA NARAYAN: To have wood to burn, that's why.

BHOJU: Are there any trees that it is no sin to cut?

SATYA NARAYAN: *Vilāyatī bambūl;* it is no sin to cut them, and it is no sin to kill a poisonous animal.

In terms of the local ecology, this truly is the one tree that it does the least harm to cut. But in thus isolating *vilāyatī,* and connecting it with poisonous snakes, Satya Narayan identifies the foreign tree with things that are dangerous to humans.[18]

As noted in chapter 3, one of my part-time employees in the village, Shambhu Nath, created for me three albums with descriptions of local trees, shrubbery, and crops, along with information on each plant's qualities and uses (Nath 1993). Shambhu was educated through the tenth grade, and was familiar with agricultural work. He wrote from his own knowledge, which I take as fairly ordinary knowledge for a literate villager in his thirties. Here is what Shambhu's book has to say about *vilāyatī bambūl:*

> This tree's thorns are very poisonous and dangerous. If one slips inside some human being and ripens there—that is, becomes infected—it [the wound] fills with pus and is very painful. Sometimes people have to go to the hospital. If you don't get the thorn out of your foot, it makes a knot in that foot and for your whole life it keeps hurting.
>
> *Vilāyatī bambūl's* wood has no special usefulness. . . . *Vilāyatī's* trunk is 90 percent crooked, and its wood has no work; all its wood goes for the work of burning. Among trees this tree can be said to have no special importance. Even so, nowdays the government is sprinkling this *bambūl's* seeds in all the jungles of the country, and raising plants, and planting them. The reason is that it is very thorny and even sheep and goats don't eat it.

Shambhu thus summarizes major popular complaints about foreign *bambūl*—curiously denigrating "the work of burning," although in village life such a fuel source is invaluable.

The crooked foreign trees with their dangerous thorns, in whose shade it is no comfort to crouch but on whose wood people are dependent, are but one element in a complexly configured vision of ecological change in postcolonial times. A number of other items, extremely important to the current village economy and lifestyle, are also linguistically denoted in various ways as alien imports. Although some of these are usually called "English" (*angrejī*) rather than "foreign," no consistent pattern is discernible in such variant usages.[19] Some of the most common and familiar items labeled "alien" include chemical fertilizer (*angrejī khād,* "English dung"), western medicine (*angrejī davāī,* "English medicine"), and liquor sold in government stores (*angrejī śarāb,* "English wine"), which contrasts with the bootleg home brew most often drunk in association with sacrifices and feasts in honor of goddesses. In the case of farm machines and synthetic fabrics, their alien origin is not explicitly labeled but is clearly marked by the use of foreign names, such as "thresher," "tractor," and "polyester."

Still other items of relatively recent introduction have standard Hindi names—notably *chakkī* for electric flour mill and *nal* for water tap. These equally contrast with previous practices both linguistically and physically. *Chakkī* contrasts with *ghaṭṭī*—the grindstone for daily flour and the former emblem of women's marital chores, as we saw in chapter 7. Now virtually silenced, these grindstones remain in a dusty corner of every home and are still worshipped by bride and groom as part of prenuptial rites. Use of the *nal* contrasts strongly with getting water from the *kuā* (well). Not only does the water taste different (to which I can testify) but the process of filling pots and buckets by those two modes is very different indeed. The power mill and the water tap are clearly perceived not only as innovations, but as dependent on the technical skills of outsiders. Most villagers are impotent when power failures disable these services; they have no recourse but to wait for help or return to the laborious manual alternative.

Both *chakkī* and *nal* are regularly cited as items that have changed the very fabric and rhythms of daily existence: externally, most particularly for women, in terms of reducing labor time and generally altering daily work schedules; internally, for everyone, in that electrically ground flour and tap water are both thought of as vaguely detrimental to health and strength. Men complain more of these losses, while women decry the inconvenience when the not infrequent power outages disrupt mill and tap functions. However, there is little active resistance from either gender to any of these foreign goods and devices, including *vilāyatī*.

Some persons tend to radicalize verbally today's transformations. Often I was told, rhetorically and hyperbolically, "Nobody plows with oxen anymore." In reality, about half the village farmland, made up of mostly small plots, is still worked by oxen pulling wooden plows that the carpenter caste still produces. But in people's minds, or at least in their public discourse, the future has arrived. Similarly, I interviewed one man who reputedly knew about herbal medicines. He said immediately, "Nobody uses them anymore. Everyone goes to the dispensary for English medicine." Later in the conversation it emerged that just a few days earlier he had successfully treated his granddaughter's skin problem with a plant remedy he prepared himself, after a drugstore cure had failed to help her.

I acknowledge that such verbal maneuvers are in part self-conscious responses to the inquiries of a foreigner and a schoolteacher, before whom some might wish to profess adherence to the trappings of modernity. Nonetheless, I shall not dismiss them as hypocrisy. It strikes me that such totalizing statements are ways of adjusting; people see their worlds changing so quickly that in their imaginations they seek to accelerate rather than resist the changes—as a way of learning to accept them. As with the herbal remedy, further inquiries usually elicit gradations of predominance for most elements of the brave new technologies. The interview texts that follow will highlight several key factors in the perceived complex of change, but even more vividly they show their intermeshing.

With Bhairu Phuleriya Mali, in 1993, Ugma Nathji and I discussed in detail gardening practices and crops. As a "flower-growing gardener" Bhairu was part of a community that took special pride in their knowledge and practice of produce cultivation. He began by telling us that every garden was like a shrine to Lord Shiva, in which one should never wear shoes.

When I bluntly turned the conversation to the subject of fertilizer, Bhairu's response, listing pros and cons, seemed to rehearse a familiar dialogue with himself.

ANN: Do you use "white" fertilizer or *deśī*?

BHAIRU: From *deśī* fertilizer we get more flavor, but from white fertilizer they [the vegetables] get large, but they don't taste good.

So if you want to earn a lot, then put on white; and if you want a good taste, then put on *deśī* fertilizer. It [*deśī*] weighs more, though. Or, you can put both together: first *deśī* and later white; then it comes out well. Without some *deśī* fertilizer, they [the vegetables] won't be good. Better to use both and the profits will be better.

Bhairu thus expresses measured, rationalized attitudes toward the use of foreign fertilizer in produce gardens, even while criticizing its effect on flavor.

The conversation then turned to grain crops.

BHAIRU: In the past there was no mustard and no *kalyāṇ sonī* [one of the new varieties of wheat]. There was *bājā gehūṅ* (indigenous wheat) and barley (*jau*).[20] Besides these grains, nothing.

UGMA NATHJI: And there was no English fertilizer, only *deśī* fertilizers? What were they?

BHAIRU: Goat dung and cow dung; besides them nothing. . . . And to make "green fertilizer" (*hariyā khād*) we planted *gauvar* and *sān* (hemp), if you couldn't afford cow dung and goat dung.[21]

. . . .

UGMA NATHJI: Which crops needed more water?

BHAIRU: Today's crops need more; today's, like mustard and red peppers. Like, *kalyāṇ sonī* drinks twice as much as *bājā gehūṅ* and *jau*; and *koṭā phārmī, sonā rekhī*—these new seeds need five to seven waterings, but previously it was only three.[22]

We used to harvest only twenty maunds from one *bīghā;* and now we harvest thirty to thirty-five; but fertilizer and all causes five maunds of expense [that is, the value of five maunds of grain must be spent]. Even so, there is some profit.

And in our field we never got more than twenty-five maunds. But my son is farming and he puts superphosphate, and then waters; and then he plants wheat together with D. A. P. [the three-letter abbreviation by which all farmers refer to diammonium phosphate], and twenty-five days later he irrigates with urea. Then he gets forty-five maunds of wheat in the same field where we used to get twenty-five—but with this much more fertilizer. And, he uses an engine* to water.

He gets forty to forty-five maunds of wheat, and has two thousand rupees expense [for everything]; so maybe he will receive thirty-five maunds profit. [*Bhairu here subtracts the expenses as if they were maunds of grain.*][23]

. . . .

UGMA NATHJI: And what kinds of sorrow did the farmers have long ago?

BHAIRU: It was very painful to water with the *charas,* and your feet would get cold standing in the water, and all day the oxen suffered, and so did we. But now, with an engine*: comfort!

Although he complained about the lack of flavor in vegetables cultivated with chemical fertilizers, when it came to grain produced largely for the anonymous market Bhairu perceived cost to be the main problem with chemical fertilizers. His praise for power irrigation, like most people's, is unmitigated.

A Mali woman with whom Ugma Nathji and I spoke in 1993 was emphatic in linking a good taste, and good business, with organic manures.

ANN: You don't apply "white" fertilizer for vegetables?

MALI: If we apply white fertilizer it spoils them, but these days people have began to use it, so we have to use it; in the past we didn't apply it, but now we [have to or we] will get nothing. But because of this the cooked vegetables don't taste good.

UGMA NATHJI: Were the vegetables that you grew without white fertilizer good or are these today good?

MALI: Those were good, the earlier ones, on which we didn't put white fertilizer. The vegetables today are bland and tasteless (*pīkī pīkī*); they aren't pleasing. With eggplants, the color becomes pale and it isn't good. But were we to put organic manure, composted manure, that vegetable would be delicious and then the buyers buy happily, and we can do better business; and those grown with white fertilizer don't sell well.

People say, "Oh this comes from pale-white (*saphed-dholā*) fertilizer, I won't take it, I'll take the vegetables fertilized with the other manure." Women today ask first before buying. With today's vegetables we can wander all over the village and sell nothing; but with the previous kind we could sell all our vegetables even in our own neighborhood [that is, in the Mali, Gujar, and Ravala neighborhoods]. . . . And nowadays, the rate has dropped 50 percent; we used to sell equally for grain, but now we sell double for grain, because these vegetables spoil the sauce. But sauce made with vegetables grown with organic manure is terrific.

UGMA NATHJI: It tastes good.

MALI: It tastes good.

Ugma Mali, a man in his early forties and thus younger than most of our interviewees, speaks of other deficiencies in chemically nourished grain. Bhoju was discussing the power mill with him, but Ugma's thoughts moved spontaneously to fertilizers.

BHOJU: Today's women don't do this [grind by hand]?

UGMA: Today all work is done with machines*; the flour-mill machine* exists, so who will grind by hand? But, from being ground in the electric mill, the grain loses its strength, and so we also lose our strength. . . .

Because of the flour-mill, and because of foreign (*videsī*) fertilizer, people have become weak.

BHOJU: Why?

UGMA: Because today is the era (*jamānā*) of machines*; all things are done with art [*kalā*, a term that in the village often implies not so much beauty as craftiness, artifice].

When people used to take a pilgrimage to the Ganges River they would go on foot, or they might walk four *koś* (eight kilometers) to visit their friends; and the sacred Ganges seemed as close as Four-Arms temple [the central temple in the village]. But now you need money in your pocket, and you need a bicycle just to go one kilometer.

Before there was no money and fewer people, so there was a lot of love. But today, everyone has money, and the population has grown, so there is no love; if anyone has work to do, they do it with money.

Ugma's free associations are worth noting here. Without prompting, he moves rapidly from the flour grinder to chemical fertilizer to general human weakness as exemplified by the abandonment of religiously valued foot pilgrimage. He concludes with a final flourish, opposing money and love in the context of crunching population growth. Such trains of thought are not unusual.

Our conversation with Lalu Regar, a leatherworker—conducted in Bhoju's own courtyard—also displays a characteristically interconnected way of thinking about various attributes of modernity. In this interview, Lalu supplied the epigraph for this chapter:

BHOJU: When you farmed, what crops did you mostly plant?

LALU: *Deśī* (indigenous) wheat and barley.

BHOJU: What's the difference between those crops and the present?

LALU: There used to be more production, today it is less. Because we used to put goat-dung fertilizer, but for the past five to fifteen years we've been putting "white" fertilizer.

BHOJU: And has white fertilizer changed the land?

LALU: It has made it alkaline.

BHOJU: If you put fertilizer this year and not the next what will happen?

LALU: There will be no production at all.

BHOJU: When we know that if we use white fertilizer the land will get alkaline, why do we use it?

LALU: Because we are crazy, that's why. Little by little the land has become like this; even if you put full goat-dung fertilizer and don't put urea you'll get no production, it has become an addict;[24] it needs urea.

BHOJU: So, the land has got a bad habit?

LALU: The land has begun asking a huge amount. The land has begun to collect rent from us.

. . . .

BHOJU: The village council used to meet at Four-Arms temple. Why don't they meet anymore?

LALU: People have stopped of their own accord. Today there is no love-and-affection left; twenty or twenty-five years ago the whole village was unified.

BHOJU: What is the reason?

LALU: Father of a Daughter! [a common and mild expletive]. Today we have grain grown with white fertilizer, flour ground by the power mill, and water from the tap. So how can there be unity and love?

This kind of fluid move from politics to fertilizer, from communal harmony to tap water, is not at all rare in the discourse on changes. Bhoju continued to question Lalu:

BHOJU: What shall we do? Go back and stop all these new things?
LALU: Sure [spoken with sarcasm].
BHOJU: Shall we tell our wives to grind flour?
LALU: Sure.
BHOJU: Mine would tell me to grind.
RAJI GUJAR [Bhoju's mother, who has been listening]: I used to grind five kilograms of grain in one morning but today's women couldn't do that.

Thus we see vividly how different elements of changed existence are mutually reenforcing. Because health is "down," many assert, today's women could not grind flour by hand even if they wished to do so, but universally they do not.[25] And one of the reasons health is down is that grain milled by the *chakkī* loses its strength-giving capacity.[26] Moreover, the reasons women's behaviors today are judged increasingly immodest include the inner heat caused by chemical fertilizer and the free time granted by the advent of the *chakkī* and *nal*—which has made it easier for many women, especially from poorer families, to become day laborers and thereby be exposed to the company of strange men.

Synthetic cloth is another epitomizing feature of the ambivalently construed modernity complex. It is also associated not only with poor health, but with a decline in women's good character. In the previous era daughters-in-law practiced perfect modesty and wore cotton; today they wear more revealing polyester coverings. Men's health, dispositions, and even their ritual actions are also said to be adversely affected by polyester.

In one interview focused on the neglect in present times of agricultural rituals, a farmer named Amba Lal Loda described an entire ritual, confessed that he had failed to perform it this year, mentioned that as far as he knew only one of his fellow Lodas had done it, and then was asked by Bhoju to explain this neglect.[27]

BHOJU: Why do people do this less today?

AMBA: Today people have forgotten everything.

BHOJU: What is the reason?

AMBA: The things that existed before don't exist today; people used to wear *rejā* [locally handloomed cotton cloth] and now they wear polyester.

The very conditions of everyday life, the ways gods are worshipped, and the cloth one wears next to one's skin—all have changed.

The final interview segment in this section moves from one topic to another with even greater fluidity than our talk with Lalu. This was a long conversation we had with a Brahmin, Gajanand Sharma. Gajanand is of the highest-ranking priestly community in the village, but he was a revolutionary leader against the Rajputs and the British in his youth. One of the oldest men in the village, now in his eighties, his memories reached back further than those of most other interviewees. He begins with historic moments—visions of imported machines:

GAJANAND: No one knew what an airplane was. One time I was on my way to my field with a cart of dung fertilizer, and we heard the sound of an airplane and we looked up and saw a "flying bed" (*uṛan khaṁṭolā*), and later we found out this was an airplane.

So in 1927 the first bicycle came to Ghatiyali. Jaganath Lakhara brought the first cycle to Ghatiyali in 1927. And the first time we saw a motorcar was when Vansh Pradip Singh married for the second time. He brought a motor car, and about one thousand people came to see it, they called it "the cart without oxen" (*binā bail kī gāṛī*).

Sonanath Khati, Moti Khati, they were great carpenters, but people said, "O they are great carpenters but who is the carpenter of this cart?"

[*At this point we discuss the details of land reform at length.*]

BHOJU: How much has changed from your times to these times?

GAJANAND: At least 50 percent. In those days, if a soldier came, nobody had courage to talk with him. But today even if the SP (superintendent of police) comes, anybody talks with them without any fear.

BHOJU: Is it because of education? But what about changes in nature (*prākṛiti*)?

[*Thus Bhoju steers him to our subject.*]

GAJANAND: It used to be that food and drink was good but today it is all spoiled. Take grains, wheat and barley, their portion (*ans*) [of goodness] is finished; because of medicines [*davāī*, that is, pesticides] and [chemical] fertilizers. Grains are no longer sweet and have no power (*śakti*).

When I was young I could single-handedly lift a sack weighing two and one-half maunds and put it in a cart; but today you need two people to pick up one of those.

At that time there was much rain, but from time to time there was famine too; even so people had a lot of strength to work; people had real *puruṣārth*. [This is the only time I recall hearing a villager use this Sanskrit term that Indologists translate as "human ends" or "life aims" but that seems here to mean both physical and moral strength.]

Because we were getting pure food; today food is impure so there are no *puruṣārth*. Today, whether people eat a lot of butter, or they eat dry bread, it doesn't even make a difference.

[In other words, even clarified butter, thought to be an extremely strengthening food, has no effect.]

BHOJU: Why are we losing our *puruṣārth*, and other things?

GAJANAND: It is because the earth's power (*śakti*) has been squandered. The reason is that in one field we used to plant only once in two or three years, but now we plant twice a year, and we also use chemical fertilizer; so we have plenty of food but no strength.

We used to plant sometimes only after four years, but now in one year we plant twice or even three times, because of population, we plant.

It used to be for two to three years the land would lie fallow. So, even without any fertilizer, even without manure (*deśī khād*), there would be good crops. But now the power of the earth has decreased.

BHOJU: Does the fertility power increase with chemical fertilizer?

GAJANAND: No, you can get more production but the land gets weak.

And besides this, the jungle is finished and for this reason eating-and-drinking things are finished. In my youth when we went to the jungle we never came back hungry.

BHOJU: What did you eat?

GAJANAND: Berries, fruits, roots—wild fruit. . . . There was much jungle and the cows and buffaloes gave much milk; without feeding them, they gave good milk. [That is, they flourished just on grazing.] And the price of clarified butter was one or two rupees per kilogram.

I have sold two kilograms of clarified butter for one rupee. But today you can't even find one kilogram for one hundred rupees; and even so, you can't find pure clarified butter.

. . . .

BHOJU: There is an old saying, *moṭā khānā moṭā pahanā* ("eat heavy, dress heavy"). What does it mean?

GAJANAND: Women's skirts used to be made of *rejā* and their wraps were also *rejā*.

BHOJU: Were there polyester things?

GAJANAND: We didn't even know the word.

BHOJU: Is our health affected by tericot [a synthetic blend] and polyester?

GAJANAND: Yes, of course. Local *rejā* is very good for the body; from wearing it the body stays cool.

At this moment Gajanand, with dignified drama, lifted his clean and pressed polyester *kurta* to reveal beneath it an old-fashioned garment made of *rejā*. Thus he acquiesces on the surface to the fashions appropriate for his rank, but follows his own beliefs concerning what is healthful.

This interview brings together many themes from this section and displays characteristically ambivalent evaluations of different aspects of modernity. Gajanand moves from the wonders of airplanes and bicycles to the deleterious effects of chemical fertilizers and pesticides, indicating that the latter cause deterioration of the earth as well as of human health.[28] Because of his advanced age, he was one among only a handful of persons interviewed who expressed nostalgia for wild foods. I presume these were pleasures not contained within the span of most living persons' memories. As a former activist against political oppression, Gajanand is pleased with modern democratic freedoms, but not with polyester clothing.

During my last weeks in the village in the early monsoon season of 1993, a "plantation scheme" administered by the much maligned "cattle guard" was underway. The scheme involved local elementary

Vilāyatī bambūl seedlings (Ghatiyali 1993).

school teachers who established a tree nursery in the schoolyard, raised funds for a watering system, and cared for what I was told numbered twenty thousand *vilāyatī bambūl* seedlings.

After the monsoon broke, these were planted in rows on village "wasteland"—well beyond homes and farmlands, in the hills toward Sawar. I photographed the planting of these trees shortly before leaving the village. Cheerful groups of women laborers were carefully setting each baby tree in the earth, while the forestry agent strutted among them, admonishing them not to be slack. No one to my knowledge opposed this project. Several people told me as a point of curiosity that it was funded by Japanese moneys designated for improving India's environment. Foreigners with motives villagers find hard to fathom thus finance the propagation of unloved foreign trees.[29]

Geographer Paul Robbins has studied ecological change in western Rajasthan. He is convinced that *Prosopis juliflora* (which he calls *angrezī*, following residents of the districts where he worked in the former kingdom of Marwar) is less advantageous for afforestation in those arid lands than the indigenous *khejarī* (*Prosopis cineraria*). Although Ghatiyalians hold no special brief for *khejarī*, they do, as we have seen, praise those species (notably *dhokarā* and *desī bambūl*) indigenous to the Banas Basin. Many of the faults Robbins identifies in *julifora* coincide with those I heard repeated often in Ghatiyali. He writes that *khejarī* has stronger timber, for example. And he notes that *juliflora* has no appreciable understory of grass and herb communities because its leaves contain germination inhibitors that limit the growth of other species. Recall Dayal Gujar's comment, "There is poison in its shade." Robbins concludes that "the choice of *juliflora* over *cineraria* therefore, leads to limits in both human and plant ecologies" (1996:279–80).

Thus an American scholar speaks strongly against the state government's seemingly stubborn promotion of *vilāyatī*, and confirms local perceptions of its alien perniciousness, contrasting it with an indigenous, traditionally valued species that strikes him as being more useful. Robbins has listened to both sides of the story, and comes down strongly in favor of indigenous species and local knowledge.

Some recent approaches to India's environmental crises critique "development," both in practice and ideology. For alternative sustainable strategies they propose to draw on traditional knowledge systems that originated in a remote precolonial past.[30] However, emerging countercritiques of tendencies to romanticize indigenous ecological harmony call for caution, if not full skepticism, when considering any return to "tradition," a dubious category, easily deconstructed.[31] As many point out, it is impossible to draw a clean line between foreign and indigenous—whether speaking of practices or species—let alone to label one wholly detrimental to environmental conservation and the other wholly beneficent.[32]

Strange Weather and the Disease of Conceit

In recent years the monsoon rains have often been inadequate. Although terrible famines were known in the past, it is a widely held conviction that in the past the good years were better, drought years fewer and farther between, and that in general there was more rain. It is beyond our scope to assess the validity of this conviction; our interests are in theories, not realities, of climate change.[33] Interviews evoked two pervasive explanations of why there is less rain today than there used to be. The most prevalent of these—one we heard from school children as well as nonliterate old men and women—poses a direct causal relationship between deforestation and drought. It asserts graphically that the trees now vanished from the hilltops had formerly "pulled" the rain clouds to the village. *Vilāyatī bambūl*, good only for burning, fails to do so. This, of course, is a village version of "desiccationism," which, as discussed in chapter 3, was in the colonial air in the nineteenth century.

The other theory, less widely held and sometimes offered with less conviction, has to do with the decay of social life, religion, and love among human beings—a decay understood as displeasing to God. As Ugma Loda put it, "In the days when God was happy, there was rain and the wells were full, but now God is angry." Reasons posited for divine anger include humans' lack of compassion, insolence toward elders and caste superiors, decline of community life involving disrespect for common property (including trees), and increasing indifference toward proper celebration of collective rituals.[34]

Obviously, the tree theory and the sin theory are not fully separable, for the destruction of the trees is part and parcel of current degenerate moralities. It is this discourse of moral and ecological decline that I have come to characterize in mental shorthand as "the disease of conceit." While discussing with residents of Sawar why there is less rain today—a situation about which everyone agrees—we heard causal factors of deforestation and sin articulated independently of one another, as well as complexly interrelated and counterpoised.

THE TREES PULLED THE RAIN

We heard a straight "less trees, less rain" explanation very many times from persons of all ages, all castes, and both sexes. It was usually stated in a remarkably similar fashion. I give just three examples from different social positions of the way people formulated this perception.

Pyarelal Mahajan is one of Ghatiyali's wealthiest men. His shop sells household staples and items for worship (oil, sugar, tea, incense, coconuts, and so forth), and he also lends cash at profitable interest rates. Pyarelal has only an elementary school education, but he knows sufficient writing and numbers for his bookkeeping needs. Now in his sixties, he was not born in Ghatiyali but moved there in his early youth.

PYARELAL: For the last fifteen years there hasn't been so much water.
BHOJU: Why has rain become less?
PYARELAL: Because of the trees not remaining. This is what I think: there are no trees, therefore there is no rain. When I first came here there were so many trees on Tikhya ["pointed"; the name of one of the hills surrounding the village] that you couldn't see the earth or the rocks. But now you can easily see livestock there. So, when the clouds come there is nothing to stop them.

Hardev Chamar, a poor, nonliterate leatherworker, probably in his fifties, also speaks of the connection between poor rainfall and fewer trees.

HARDEV: Rain is less, and population has increased. Forty years ago, we used to plant in the land near New Well.[35] Then from five maunds [of seed grain] we'd get two hundred maunds. The land was so strong, without fertilizer, the strength was in the water.
BHOJU: Why is rain less today?
HARDEV: Because the trees are less. The trees pulled the rain with the

wind, and now there are less trees. The wind pulled the rain. It was the effect of the wind. The trees pulled the wind, but now there are no trees.

Hardev here attributes the land's fertility to good well water, but today many of the old wells no longer yield sufficient water for irrigation.

Finally, Suva Lal Chasta, a Brahmin, was among a number who specifically contrasted the indigenous tree species with foreign trees in regard to their respective capacity to attract rain clouds:

BHOJU: Why has rain become less?
SUVA LAL: The biggest reason is that trees have become less. All the trees were cut and all that's left is *vilāyatī*, and it is not helpful in bringing rain, in drawing moisture. Other trees, like *nīm, deśī bambūl, dhokaṛā*, they pulled the monsoon and that is why there was much rain.

These and many similar statements offer a climate change theory based on a physical situation: tall trees engender wind and wind brings clouds to the vicinity of the trees. The trees also serve to block or hold clouds in an area, allowing precipitation to take place.

In explanations such as those cited above, sin is not evoked—but it is nonetheless implicit in the realities of deforestation. A certain embarrassment was evident when some villagers expressed to Bhoju as teacher and to me as foreigner a theory of divine causality. It may be that people who perceived their questioners' identities as rooted in secular modernity were more disposed to offer a theory they understood to be consistent with an "educated" worldview.

GOD IS ANGRY

Only a handful of people made no reference at all to trees when speaking of climate change—these sought direct reasons in God's anger at human beings' declining compassion. Polu Kumhar, a potter by birth, had through a riverbed gardening venture attained an economic status beyond most of his caste fellows. A reflective, articulate, successful man, Polu spoke thoughtfully of the lessening of rain and affection:

POLU: Just as the world's portion has decreased, so God too has become angry.

BHOJU: What do you mean?

POLU: We used to hug one another in greeting; we were happy. But today when a person comes, we say, "So what, he's come!" In this way, people's affection is reduced, and in the same way God doesn't love people, and so there is less rain.

Polu thus poses parallels between the dwindling of human affection and the dwindling of God's affection for humans—an analogy he was not the only one to articulate.

Rup Lal Khati spoke of how people today are richer in material things but poorer in spirit, as consumerism and the jealousies it provokes enters their lives. He sees this as one reason why God no longer hears human prayers for rain.

BHOJU: People used to have less money, but they still had love. But today? . . .

RUP LAL: Today there is no love at all.

BHOJU: Why?

RUP LAL: People are envious of one another (*apas mē jalan*). Like suppose somebody, like you, earns two cents—whether in sorrow or happiness—and then I see you and I feel envy, and I think, "Why should he earn money? He ought to stay like me." There is no progress, just envy.

Like, we see that he washes with soap, he washes his clothes with soap, and we feel envy, and try to do the same. But you have money and I don't, so I get even poorer [from spending money on soap].

So for this reason some farmers are in tight circumstances.

BHOJU: Before, when it did not rain, people used to worship all the gods, and perform the worship of Indra.[36]

RUP LAL: Yes, they used to get the drum and go to worship, and it used to rain even before they got back to the village.

BHOJU: But today they don't do it, why?

RUP LAL: Because people's lots have turned bad, and God too has changed toward people (*bhagvān bhī logoṅ se badal gayā*).

Rup Lal very explicitly identifies envy as the source of reduced love among villagers, leading in turn to divine displeasure. The decline of ritual is embedded in the decline of love and community through a circular causality that cannot be untangled. Ritual action has decreased because rituals do not work anymore. Rituals do not work anymore because God is angry or has turned away from people. God has turned away from people because people no longer worship as they once did.

DEFORESTATION, DIVINE ANGER, LESS RAIN ARE ONE STORY

Several interviewees expressed a completely merged understanding of environmental and moral deterioration. These to me are the most suggestive discussions—posing as they do a tightly knit moral ecology. Here is Ugma Loda's complex account:

BHOJU: Why is there less rain?

UGMA: Because of the trees being cut. . . . Nowdays there are no gardens and no forest.

BHOJU: Why?

UGMA: Literate people say there is no rain because of the trees.[37]

BHOJU: But what do farmers think about this?

UGMA: We think the same thing as the rest of the world. I think what you think and accept it. What could I say if I didn't?

[*He is silent and looks down, and then he looks up again and resumes.*]

It is God's manifestation in nature[38] that there is less rain. In the days when God was happy, there was rain and the wells were full, but now God is angry.

BHOJU: Why is God angry? With what things is God angry?

UGMA: People's behavior has changed. The biggest thing is that there is no longer compassion in any human vessel (*kisī ke ghaṭ mē koī dayā nahīn hai*). Before, if someone fell or was hurt, people would come and take care. But nowadays, nothing.

BHOJU: Before people worried a lot, were concerned, so what happened?

UGMA: Today our neighbor's son falls and is lying on the road and we may be crossing the road, but we are not going to help him.

BHOJU: Who is responsible for all these changes?

UGMA: No one is responsible. . . . People's behavior is less—their feelings, their love. Take my father [for example]: we never sat on a bed in his presence, never spoke before him. If we were playing and he came, we all became quiet. But my grandson, I can call him five times and he comes and says, "What is it?" [in the insolent tone of an irritated brat]. . . . Because cooking oil isn't pure, and grain is grown with chemicals, people's tempers have become hot like the food.

. . . .

It used to be that we had four or five buffalo at my house. So what did we eat? Milk and butter and yogurt. And we went out all day and weren't hungry. And in the afternoon we ate more butter and bread, and we were vigorous, and lived at our ease.

Today nothing is pure; food and drink are bad, and from this our behavior, compassion, love, have all decreased.

It is evident from Ugma Loda's reflections that he understands the many aspects of the changing world in which he lives to be causally interlocked. And this is realistic, not fanciful. As noted earlier, there are fewer dairy animals today because increased population and increased ambition have motivated farmers to put former grazing lands under cultivation. For the same reasons, dung is scarcer, causing farmers increasingly to rely on chemical fertilizers. Ugma further associates children's lack of respect and humans' generally reduced health, stamina, and good tempers with changed diets that directly result from these other transformations.

Damodar Sharma Gujarati, an elderly Brahmin about twenty years Ugma Loda's senior, offered the following vivid account of environmental and social history.

DAMODAR: In [*samvat*] 2004 [that is, 1947 C.E.] all the wells in the *goriyā* [fertile and irrigated land near the village] were so full that you could bend over and drink out of them with your hands. That's how much rain there was.

BHOJU: Why isn't there as much rain now?

DAMODAR: Because the jungle is destroyed. Because rain comes from trees. There is an area near Bundi . . . where the jungle is so dense that if a man goes in it he will get lost. So even today there are still trees in that place and there is still rain. That's why there is no rain [here, where there are no trees].

BHOJU: Why do trees cause rain?

DAMODAR: Scientists know.

BHOJU: But why?

DAMODAR: Farmers say that rain comes from the trees, and there used to be much dharma. For example, people used to feed Brahmins, and people used to do fire oblations (*havan*) for the goddesses and gods, and spread fodder for the cows.

But now the degenerate age [Kali Yuga] has come. The times used to be good. Men used to look on women as their sisters and daughters. But today, I am a Brahmin and my daughter could marry someone of any caste.

BHOJU: People don't pay attention to caste dharma?

DAMODAR: Now dharma is completely suppressed; but if you protect dharma then dharma will protect you. It is my dharma that I won't drink water from anybody's hands.[39] Then he [Dharma, now personified as a divinity] will protect me. But today, the sweepers, the leatherworkers, we have all become one; it used to be that sweepers and leatherworkers could not come near me, but now . . . it is as if God has forgotten us as we have forgotten him.

And today's politics are the worst of all. Today any low-caste person can lie to the police and say, "This person has insulted me." And they do not require a proof, they just come and grab us. For this reason I don't ever sit at the bus stand. Better for me to sit alone in the temple.

BHOJU: What change do you see in people's behavior?

DAMODAR: The Kali Yuga has come 100 percent. People used to be very happy and generous, but now they are misers. It used to be if I had grain and saw a hungry person I would give, and even if only women were home and one had no grain, she could borrow from another and clean it and grind it and make bread so no one could go to bed hungry.

And there was so much power in the grain that when you boiled it, it spit [literally, it "kicked"] so no one could stand near the pot. But today there is no such spitting, no strength in the grain. . . . Just as the strength of grain is finished, so is people's love.

BHOJU: O.k., people have changed because of selfishness, but there is no selfishness in grain, so what happened?

DAMODAR: It is because we don't use goat dung and cow dung fertilizer any more. From urea more heat grows in the grain, and from this people also have greater heat. And that is why people have much more anger and egotism. People today get angry very quickly at everything.

I have quoted Damodar at length in order to show just how fluidly he moves among changes in the environment, changes in religious behavior, intercaste relationships, sexual morality, agricultural technology, and human character. From his decidedly positioned perspective as a Brahmin he understandably deplores the reduction of Brahminical ritual status and political clout. Concerning other elements in the situation, his views are identical with farmers' views. Damodar uses the ancient Hindu cosmological model of a dark and degenerate age, the Kali Yuga, to encompass and account for all these changes. Although this was not common, he was not the only one to speak of Kali Yuga.[40]

In a long four-way conversation in which Bali Gujar (in her early thirties), Ajodhya Khati (mid-forties), Kesar Gujar (mid-sixties), and I (late forties) all participated, ideas unfold about the ways conceit, technology, the decrease of love, and human dependence on God are interwoven in contexts of radical change. This conversation begins with me introducing the topic of climate change but quickly spins off in several other directions. It is worth attending to carefully especially for the way it captures the fine points of why and how love is lost as modern goods spread unevenly. These fine points are depicted at an interpersonal level, but affect the whole village, the times, perhaps even the rain.

ANN [addressing Ajodhya]: I have heard that a lot of change has happened in the village in the last twenty years—like the crops are different and the weather has changed; there used to be lots of rain and now there is less; and people say that there is less love.

BALI: There used to be more rain and now there is less.

AJODHYA: As are the people, so is the rain, and so are the times (*jamānā*), and so is production.

ANN: Some other people said that dharma is less, love is less. . . . Do you also think this?

AJODHYA: Yes, all of it has happened.

ANN: Why? How?

AJODHYA: In all matters, just as human beings behave, so the times are. . . . The times are deteriorating, going from bad to worse.

BALI: This is the situation, human beings have become free (*ajād*). [*According to Bhoju, she uses "free" to mean "lazy."*]

AJODHYA: They have become free.

ANN: So is that what you think?

KESAR: Now we have water taps (*nal*) and electricity.

AJODHYA: Yes, and we used to have to grind grain in the hand mill. So, yes, we have water taps, and electric pumps [for irrigating fields], and flour from the power mill . . . and wheat grown with English fertilizer. There is no local (*deśī*) fertilizer [that is, composted manure] left. Where is the local fertilizer?

We used to make our bread from stoneground grain and drink well water, and there were lots of dairy products. But now? Today there is not even any water in the well. We used to keep ropes, and we had head pads (*chūmarī;* in Hindi, *iddūnī*) [to carry home the water pots], but now you cannot find these in the house.[41] We used to haul the water out from the well and bring it home.

KESAR [attempting to squelch what sounds like a tendency to nostalgia]: And we used to say, "Misery! I'm worn out. The well is too deep, let it burn! [cursing]."

But today? We get our water from nearby, and we still feel tired. In the old days we had to bring it from much farther [implying that today women have become weaker]. These days we have even turmeric and pepper ground in the power mill; salt, chickpea flour; everything. Even if all we need is a quarter kilo of turmeric we take it to the power mill. For this reason we are getting weak.

ANN: Your body is weak, but what about your soul? Is there a difference in your soul, in your heart?

BALI [quickly]: There is no difference in the soul. It is just as before, except that people get puffed up, [thinking] "Oh, I have a water tap connection!" [As Bali and Bhoju have a tap in their home, she may be anticipating criticism of herself here.]

AJODHYA: People [these days] are feeling so proud [*ghamaṇḍ*]: "I have the power mill! I'm not going anywhere, I'm sitting here!"

People put up fans. If I have a fan in my house why do I need to go out for the wind? If I feel hot, I will turn on the fan. It is freedom! (*ajād*).

I was generally puzzled by the ways these women used the word freedom in a fashion that seemed simultaneously approving and critical. With the same word they could evoke relished liberation from hard labors brought by new technologies and the resulting laziness of body and spirit that seemed to accompany such convenience. I tried to elicit more clarification.

ANN: So, is this good? Is there rest and comfort for women today?

AJODHYA: I had comfort in the past too, but now it has doubled! Now we are really comfortable. It is God who gave us this comfort, what belongs to me? Sometimes we are proud, [thinking] "Oh, I have this much wealth, this many different kinds of things." But none of it is ours, it all belongs to God. Nothing is our own.

Like, "Oh, I have a grandson" or "My grandson just got married!" So you feel proud, but it is nothing at all! Who knows to whom they belong? In my fate nothing is written; maybe it is from someone else's fate.

BALI: The people from old times, they were not so proud as they are today.

AJODHYA: I don't know where these children came from. It used to be we were not self-inflated (*hambaṛī*)—but today there is too much of it! Like you are talking with me, but I am not talking with you properly, because I feel I am a big person, I feel proud. . . . And if I talk with you happily, but you don't answer, then I'll stop talking. So love has become less.

ANN: People today are more proud? They don't talk with each other?

AJODHYA: They don't talk with each other.

ANN: But I have heard that people care less about caste these days.

BALI [explaining why she disagrees with this]: If I were doing something, they all used to come, previously: Minas came, Malis came too, Baniyas came too, Brahmins came too. Like a funeral feast, or Gangoj, or a wedding, or any feast: they all came. But today: it's shut down with Malis, it's shut down with Minas, and as for the carpenters [Ajodhya is a carpenter and a good friend of Bali's]— some come and some do not come.

ANN: How did it shut down?

BALI: Love has dwindled.

ANN: Today, you said there was lots of ease, so why is love less? When you're not grinding and you're sitting under the fan, why aren't you happy?

KESAR: Today if we grind we will get blisters.

BALI: You sit under the fan and you are happy, but others are not happy with you [because they are jealous]. These others come and they say to themselves, "Oh, they have a fan, the fan is running, maybe they are sleeping," and they don't come in [to socialize].

ANN: This is jealousy?

BALI: They don't think, "Oh, they have a fan, let's go in and sit down," but instead they are jealous.

[Bali's explanation shows that the definition of jealousy has divisiveness built into it.]

AJODHYA: If there are good people, they think "Oh, he's become a teacher, that's good, let's go over there and see him." But we [that is, ordinary people] think badly, "Oh, he's a teacher, he will be proud, let's not go there." So some might think, "Oh, he had a hard time, and now he's got a job, let's share his happiness." But no, this is not the way most people are thinking.

[This is obviously a direct reference to Bali's home, to her husband Bhoju's professional status and the jealousy and hostility it had aroused in some.]

If I get something good, then you go that far away from me; because you are jealous; if you have something, then I will cross from that far away [to avoid you].

KESAR GUJAR: If you have the flour mill at your home you are so proud: "I have a power mill in my home, me and only me!" [*mūṁ to mūī*].

[According to Bhoju, these references to the power mill are specific criticisms of a neighbor woman, a fellow Gujar who now has a mill in her home and has consequently become snooty.]

ANN: So there is much difference because of machines.

BALI: Yes, superiority! People get to feel superior when they have a power mill.

KESAR: It is not [necessary to be in] competition with other people; some might not even have a *lākh* bangle [an inexpensive ornament] and someone else can have a diamond! We should live our own lives. [In other words, we should not pay attention to these differences.]

. . . .

ANN: So, there is electricity, the power mill, polyester cloth—what else has changed?

BALI: All things have changed, today nobody likes cotton.

KESAR: No, people like me wear cotton.

AJODHYA: Bhil, Chamar, Regar, Baniya, Brahmin, they are all wearing good clothes. Gujar, Thakur [that is, Rajput], Nai (barber), Kumhar (potter), Balai (weaver)—as many castes as there are, they all wear polyester! Each and every community.

After some quarreling over the virtues of cotton, about which Bali and I have an ongoing debate, she turned the conversation to the future.

BALI [addressing Ajodhya]: You have a son and grandson, and your son is working as a carpenter, but what about your grandson? Will he be a carpenter, or a farmer, or a government servant?

AJODHYA: Lord knows! That is his fate. Isn't it so? Whatever is someone's fate, that's what he will do. It is like the saying: "Rolled in the dung pile, afterward lives in the palace."[42] So we should not be proud of this.

ANN: What will happen to carpenters' work if people don't use wooden plows but tractors, and all the trees are finished?

AJODHYA: Yes, where are the trees? There aren't any trees! People sold them to the machine* [the saw mill] and ate [the profits].

BALI: Where do you get them from?

AJODHYA: Sometimes we can buy some acacia (*deśī bambūl*) and sometimes we can buy a dry piece of wood, but sometimes it is very hard to get a piece of wood because there are no trees left, it is very expensive.

[A conversation about the relative price of wooden items follows; we then return to trees.]

ANN: You don't use any trees from around here?

AJODHYA [emphatically]: There are no trees around here! [That is, there are no trees good for carpentry work; once again *vilāyatī* is not counted as a tree.]

. . . .

ANN: But in the old times, you got wood from here?

AJODHYA: Huh?

ANN: I mean twenty years ago?

AJODHYA: Previously, oh yes, so many!

Thus we circle back to environmental deterioration, to the negative evaluation of the present landscape compared to the past.

This conversation moved fluidly from climate change to human pride and its association with new machines, implying that convenience, comfort, and freedom take their toll on sociability and humility. The women point to increased caste exclusiveness at feasts, a trend that seems to go against other homogenizing changes in everyday life. Factory-produced cloth, for example, has homogenized appearances. In the past each *jāti* was virtually identified by the clothes they wore: women by distinctive woven skirts and tie-dyed wraps, men by turbans. This is no longer so, but the result does not seem to be greater mixing among different communities. From Ajodhya we also learn how ecological forces make some social and professional changes seem inevitable: how can a carpenter expect her grandson to work with wood if there are no trees?

Postcolonial Landscapes of the Heart

In concluding this chapter, and our book, we speculate on the tenuous links between a perceived absence of responsibility at the top, where the Court once ruled, and the articulated deterioration of love and landscape. Sawar narratives present a merged vision of human morality with nature's bounty or depletion. Some imply that nonadherence to dharma—lack of compassion, avariciousness, and other moral and social deficiencies—has far-reaching geophysical consequences. I have more than once encountered skepticism when presenting these interview texts to American audiences. Surely, people say, nostalgia or a good-old-days mentality is at work in Ghatiyalians' memories of verdure and social harmony. Certainly the current discourse on environmental and moral degradation must be put in perspective as cultural construct: the past always paradisiacal, the present shadowed and corrupt.

Nostalgia, however, is highly selective; much that once was—autocracy, forced labor, smallpox, for example—is by no means missed. Moreover, we are convinced that changes in landscape and in society witnessed in Sawar (and much of the subcontinent) over the past fifty years are truly unprecedented. Population increase as well as deforestation are statistically documented, as discussed in chapter 3. Old people with whom we spoke were well aware of demographic swelling, to which a few explicitly attributed constricted space and social graces. As one of them put it succinctly: "Love is less. Why? Because people are more."

No one sees or seeks a way back to past circumstances. In spite of negative assessments of current social life and interpersonal relationships, when asked to compare personal well-being in the past with the present, nearly everyone praises the present. This has to do not only with improvements in the quality of material life, but also with the lifting of oppressive control. Bali uses the word "free" to evoke a kind of independence from previous constraints, which may result in less self-discipline; Ajodhya uses it to mean the lovely breeze from an electric fan that frees people from discomfort (but arouses jealousy in the have-nots). The same ambivalent constructions exist at the level of government where freedom describes relief from the twinned tyrannies of kings and colonizers, but also entails the perceived irresponsibility and corruption that stereotypically characterize today's government agents.

We may summarize dissatisfactions with moral ecology as they point inward at social life and neighborliness—so clearly exposed by Kesar, Ajodhya, and Bali; and as they point outward at the government (*sarkār*).

The inward-directed critique, as we have seen, says that in the old days maybe we were poor and oppressed and without freedom, but we had love, generosity, mutual respect, and good will within the community. We shared burdens, sorrows, small pleasures of civility, and our mutual good behavior pleased God. Somehow, the Court's encompassing responsibility fostered this. His control, even when it was viewed as oppression and exploitation, unified rather than divided the people—at least in their memory.

But today, by contrast, simple sociability is moribund; for the same reasons, traditional community government (the village *panchayat*) has lost its potency. There is no king, and God—displeased—has become remote.

Looking outward, the narrative says that in the old days the Court's rule was harsh, exploitative, bitter; people were perpetually in debt, verging on hunger, and subjected to demeaning laws. But the commons was preserved, the forest was dense and alive, disputes were settled swiftly, and rulers—however rapacious and selfish—were responsible to this place. They belonged to it, and it belonged to them: the two sides of *zimmedārī*.

But today, by contrast, there is the "rule of votes" (*voṭ kā rāj*), or "people's power," or simply the government—an ill-defined, bloated, and alien entity. This regime lacks consistency and responsibility. Imposed from without, government today is shifting, impersonal, and corrupt. The freedom and independence that followed the removal of the British and the collapse of princely power, whether referred to by the Urdu *āzādī* or the Sanskrit *svatantratā*, are well understood as proud achievements and modern realities. But to these are also attributed the destruction of the natural environment. A slippage of meaning extends freedom from oppressive rulers to freedom from social constraints, from moral conscience, and from hard work.

Responsibility is difficult to locate today, as many told us when we pressed them to speak on the subject.[43] Bhoju asked several men directly where responsible authority resided now that there is no king. Here is one response from Haidar Ali, a senior and respected member not only of the Muslim minority but of the entire village community.

> The public* has responsibility, but no one listens to them because there is corruption everywhere and even the ministers at the state level, they are also in on this.
>
> Step by step, they [anonymous government officials] are consuming [the commons, bribes, etc.], so who has responsibility? There is no one at all who has responsibility! (*koī zimmedār nahīṁ*).
>
> The ordinary public* is suffering, but then too the public* is greedy; we too are killing ourselves for the sake of our self-interest.

Selfishness is located, on the one hand, in today's irresponsible and diffuse government and its corrupt, "consuming" politics; on the other, it has permeated ordinary folks and replaced unifying, unacquisitive "village love." Thus, whereas in the past the king's responsible authority was connected with a moral community, today the government's corruption is connected with the ascent of individualistic self-seeking acquisitiveness.

In the village of Gorada, an elderly man, Chandra Mina, explained the lack of responsibility following the end of kings' rule similarly as a process of diffusion and dilution: "In the twenty-seven villages [under kings' rule] there was one master [*mālik*]; it was the Court who was master. But today there is nobody. You have come, so we think you are our master; after you go, another officer will come and he will be the master, and he goes and another comes."

Ladu Loda, a thoughtful, successful farmer in his sixties, began by characterizing the general decline in unity and community: "Today the rule is the people's. So people think, 'What is useful to us and what is useless?' So people think about themselves, each one differently, and they are not together—like, literate people think differently from uneducated people. So now people are not all together; now they have lots of knowledge, and they learn lots of things, and they are free." As is evident from the way Ladu expresses this, he does not judge today's liberties—both material and cognitive—as necessarily negative. They are, however, definitely understood to have undermined earlier forms of responsible moral authority.

Probing this issue further, toward the end of a very long conversation, Bhoju evoked from Ladu Loda a strong condemnation of present institutions:

BHOJU: Before there was a king, God was the protector. And after that, the king was the protector. Who is it now?

LADU: First of all, today, the protector is oneself; we are responsible for ourselves. The next thing is, if there is a problem in the village then responsibility rests on the village headman and on the village council.

BHOJU: It used to be that when illegal things happened we would go to the king and we would get an immediate judgment. What about today?

LADU: Today the system is corruption.[44]

In sum we find that many persons directly equate today's multiple freedoms with today's moral decay and laziness. All this is subsumed under an absence of responsibility at every level, in government and in homes. The results of this absence affect people's inner lives, but are also visibly evident in the barren hills. The trees have been consumed. The system is corruption.

One of the main tropes for loss of community is that people no longer sit all night by fires in the winter telling stories, exchanging knowledge. That these fires of community no longer burn eloquently unites ecological and social losses. One reason the practice has nearly died is the lack of spare wood to fuel fires kindled purely for sociability, but lack of wood is, as we have heard throughout these pages, indicative of a decline in community morality in general: the greedy, imprudent, and selfish stripping of trees from the village commons to which climate change is also attributed.[45]

Jamuni Regar, whose words we reported at length in chapter 4, expressed just such complex circularity.[46] By returning to her words, we circle round in closing. Asked why the rain was less, Jamuni replied, "I don't know why. . . . Well, there used to be more dharm; people's behavior was good. There was love, conviviality (*baiṭh uṭh*). But now there is conceit (*abhimān*). Today you do your work, and I do my work. [That is, people don't help one another as in the past.] In the cold season we used to make a fire and sit around it all night. The way that humans have changed, the Lord also has changed. [She implies that for this reason there is less rain.]" A moment later in the interview, when asked what happened to the trees, she answers, "The kings and the trees both went, they were all consumed."

This now familiar tale of lost community feeling, lost trees, and an absence of responsibility, which is also an absence of tyranny, is evidently a social construction of the past, a shared story. It has its unexamined internal contradictions. If the village community were once united by love, mutual respect, and ecological forbearance (albeit under tough sanctions), why did it all dissolve so quickly when the feared ruling power was replaced by a constitutionally chartered "people's power"?

One explanatory possibility is to pose a causal relation that links the valued traits people locate in the past—of love, generosity, and mutuality—with sufferings endured in those days. As we have just heard, some speakers equate today's freedom with today's moral decay and laziness. However, no one directly attributed past generosity within the community to past oppressions from rulers; at least not in so many words. Earlier in this chapter we compared love in the old days to an endless flame, while today it is only manifest in sporadic sparks. In the time of kings, endless flames burnt before important deities, funded by ample largesse from the Court, whose own wealth of course was extracted from the people. Now temple committees must raise money through volunteer donations within the community; this rarely yields enough cash to support endless flames; lamps lit at twilight may burn but a few hours. Sustaining the metonymy with fuel and flame, we have seen that literal firewood, plentiful in the days of efficacious forest protection, fueled conviviality, which today people believe is reduced to embers.

Why should it be that community deteriorates along with nature, and as a function of the advent of freedom? Why did "people's power" turn out to mean not self-rule but self-interest and self-inflation? Why is decreased love predicated on increased autonomy and comfort? Bhoju and I do not have answers to these questions. Nor do we have prescriptions for the future. How do Sawar's youth find their footing, and conceive their own futures, in the altered physical and social landscape that is all they know?

In January 1997, as described in chapter 7, we interviewed a group of grandmothers in a spacious courtyard belonging to a Nai family—traditionally barbers. The mistress of the household was Dai ("midwife")—who had cooked unappetizing meals for Joe Miller and me in 1979. Her family had very old bonds—both hierarchical (patron-client) and egalitarian (shared devotion to Dev Narayan)—with both households I have inhabited in Ghatiyali. Dai's son Mahavir operates one of Ghatiyali's barber shops, but earlier in his life he had worked as censustaker and mapmaker for Joe Miller and me. Mahavir was not around this day, but his son, about age ten, had quietly joined the group of old women, as Bhoju and I were conversing with them.

The boy sat there, alertly, as the conversation about past times began to peter out. We raised the topic of the future, of education, and of children's goals. Bhoju unexpectedly addressed this bright-eyed child and asked him if he planned to be a barber when he grew up. My usually clumsy camera captured a quizzical look as it traveled slowly across his face—during the slight pause before he announced, with full conviction, that he expected to get a job. The look seemed to say (as I imagined his thought), "Me, a barber? well, yeah; but then again—no way!" When pressed by Bhoju the teacher as to which job he desired, he declared, "I will become a teacher."

His grandfather had shaved and coifed hereditary patrons at their homes in exchange for a share of their harvest; and both grandmother

Barber youth thinks about his future (Ghatiyali, 1997).

Gujar schoolgirl being interviewed about her
aspirations, Gandher school, 1997.

Children planting trees, Gandher school, 1997.

and grandfather had served the Court in various ritual and mundane functions. His father runs a barber shop where customers pay cash. There is no predicting what the outcome will be for this child, but from where he sat in 1997 his gaze turned resolutely away from the past. Schoolgirls from cowherding as well as priestly and merchant communities announced with just as much firmness their plans to become teachers or, even more frequently and doubtless even less realistically, doctors.

Jamuni Regar, along with many others from the farming and laboring communities, was ambivalent about the values of education. She prayed to the goddess for her son not to get the job that all who have been to school desire. But she is willing to consign her grandsons, with a blessing, to a brave new world that she herself will never know. For persons "on their way to the cremation ground," as Jamuni Regar so forthrightly described herself, children and grandchildren face an unpredictable future for which deforestation is a visible and ominous sign.

Bhoju's real life, in which doing ethnographic history forms only a strange interlude, is to work as a government middle school teacher, and since 1998 as a headmaster. He spends his days with children. One of his projects as a professional educator has been to make the subject of "environment"—nominally part of the elementary curriculum—a genuinely meaningful topic for children. One of the ways he does this is with tree-planting projects in the schools.[47] He goes to unusual lengths to obtain indigenous species, some of them particularly attractive to children with the promise of flowers and fruits. I had the opportunity to participate in one of these projects, and found the excitement and energy with which the schoolyard buzzed to be intoxicating. My own youngest son, then about to enter fifth grade, joined in with a will, and later said plaintively to me—without any sense of irony—that he wondered why his school didn't ever do anything that neat. And this when he had seen and taken in the stark, chairless, unadorned boxlike classrooms of a rural elementary school without bathroom facilities, water taps, or electricity. The intoxication of that day came perhaps from the melding of children's hopes with the new life of young plants.

Bhoju has two students share responsibility for a single tree, from planting it to making sure it is well protected from livestock through a long season of watering. Thus on a very small scale he helps to rebuild an identification with nature's growth and beauty that was seriously damaged, in the last years of kings and the first years of Independence, for complex reasons we have attempted to articulate. Bhoju's efforts for environmental regeneration have been strongly influenced by all he heard during our research on the time of trees and sorrows. In this and many other ways, these forests of memory branch into the future.

APPENDIX

Selected Trees and Plants Mentioned in Interviews

Local linguistic variations and the failure of botanical reference books to use diacritics in transliterating vernacular names make the task of definite identification a difficult one. Moreover, in interviews people tended to speak of trees, shrubs, and vines without differentiating among them. We have only included Latin identifications here (at the end of the entry) when we are reasonably certain of them. We supply the sources of identifications only for lesser-known species.

baṛ: banyan tree; *Ficus bengalensis*

bor: any kind of berry; small red berries that grow on low thorn bushes, and also the fruits of the *boraṛī* tree

boraṛī: Rajasthani for the Hindi *ber*, "the jujube tree, and its small plum-like fruit" (McGregor 1993); *Zizyphus jujuba*

chūṅrāṛā: Rajasthani for the Hindi *ḍhāk*, a tree whose leaves are used for making disposable cups that regularly appear at all feasts and picnics; grows in association with *Anogeissus pendula* (Joshi 1995: 9, 54); *Butea monosperma*. Also identified as a common tree whose leaves are used as plates, used instead of paper to wrap up parcels, and given as fodder to buffalos; its flowers (*kāsu*) are collected and made with alum into the impermanent yellow dye used in the Holi festival (Brandis 1972 [1874]: 142); *Butea frondosa*

deśī bambūl: indigenous acacia; *Acacia nilotica*

dhokaṛā (also called *dhok*): the dominant tree in the Banas Basin in the first half of the twentieth century (see chapter 3); *Anogeissus pendula*

gaṅgair, gangeraṇ, Sanskrit *gāṅgerūkī:* a special plant, used in Ayurvedic medicines (*RSK*); "the fruits are edible and often sold in the market; decoction of wood is used as a remedy against cough; walking sticks are made of the wood; pencils used in village schools (Bhandari 1990:77); see also Brandis 1972 [1874]: 38; *Grewia populifolia*

gulmohar: a beautiful shade-giving tree with red flowers, small leaves like tamarind, and fruits (Nath 1993: vol. 1); "the large flowered gulmohar, one of the trees which make Bombay compounds so beautiful in the cold weather, called by the French . . . 'Fleur de Paradis'" (Nairne 1894:97); *Poinciana regia*

hīngoṭ, hīngoṭo: "a very large tree found in the jungle with fruits like the lemon, a little long and round; it has thorns . . . its fruit is tasty but bitter" (*RSK*); "a scraggy shrub, in favourable situations a small tree, 30 feet high, wood yellowish white, moderately hard; thorns sharp . . . [found] chiefly in the drier parts of India and Burma (Brandis 1906:124–25); see also Shetty and Singh 1987:177; *Balanites roxburghii, Balanites aegyptiaca*

jhāl: "a kind of tree whose fruit is green" (*RSK*; see also Brandis 1906:453); probably *Salvadora persica*

kāṭhūṇī: Rajasthani for the Hindi *kaṭhūmar,* a tree with small fruits like wild figs, only more sour (McGregor 1993); identified in Brandis (1906:606) as *Ficus hispida*

khair: a source of gum, timber, and the astringent extract used with pan leaves (McGregor 1993); "common in the Aravalli hills. . . . The bark is very astringent, rather bitter, in places used for tanning. The most valuable product of the tree, however, is Catechu . . . [which is] extensively consumed in the East with the Betel-leaf, and largely exported to Europe for dyeing and tanning" (Brandis 1972 (1874):186–87); *Acacia cathecu*

khakheṛā, also *kanker, kankeṛo:* "a kind of thorny tree of middle height" (*RSK*); "a much-branched thorny bush or small tree" useful for fodder (Joshi 1995:228); "a large shrub, under favourable conditions a moderate-sized tree, with a short trunk and thorny branches, wood tough, close-grained (Brandis 1906:40); *Flacourtia indica, Flacourtia ramontchi*

khaḍū, khaḍḍū, mīṭhā khaḍū: "a special kind of medium-sized tree" (*RSK*)

khejarī: see Joshi 1995, Robbins 1998, and many other sources; *Prosopis cineraria*

kikar: Acacia arabica

nīm: known for its bitter fruit, for the medicinal and antiseptic properties of its leaves, and for its use in ritual (McGregor 1993); *Melia azadirachta*

pātaṛī, also *pātaṛau:* the fruit of the *babūl* tree (*RSK*)

pīlavaṇ: a thick-stemmed vine that climbs on trees

pīpal: the "holy fig-tree" (McGregor 1993); *Ficus religiosa*

sālar: a special kind of tree with uses in Ayurvedic medicine (*RSK*); "a species associated with the mixed deciduous forests dominated by *Dhokaṛā*" (Shetty and Singh 1987:22); *Boswellia serrata*

śīśam: planted as a roadside shade tree and along the boundaries of fields and gardens; its bark is used medicinally, its wood is good for furniture (Bhandari 1990:104; Shetty and Singh 1987:224); *Dalbergia sissoo*

syālī: a type of bush whose branches are used to make the roofs of *kachchā* houses

vilāyatī bambūl, Hindi *babūl:* "foreign acacia," actually a mimosa (see chapter 10); *Prosopis juliflora*

NOTES

Preface: "There Are No Princes Now"

1 See DeNeve 1997 for an illuminating discussion of image work in Indian tourism advertisements, including some for Rajasthan.

2 Each year I lecture students in my introductory course on Hinduism about the alien and improper imposition of the Portuguese-derived term "caste" on the two distinct South Asian concepts of *varṇa* and *jāti*. I have nonetheless found it impossible in writing this book to do anything but employ the term "caste"—with all of its historical inaccuracy—to refer to and translate inadequately all that is comprehended by *jāti* in village discourse. The term "birth-group" is always awkward; "community" is often misleading. Moreover, Rajasthanis possessing even a smattering of English knowledge freely substitute "caste" for *jāti* in the same fashion I have. I have thus followed colloquial convention, and I do not imply with my use of this word any particular approach to society or hierarchy, let alone signal complicity with essentializing orientalist constructions of India. For critiques of such constructions see, for example, Dirks 1992 and Inden 1990. Interestingly McGregor (1993) does not surrender to common practice, and he glosses *jāti* first as "birth" and second as "position fixed by birth; community or [last of all] caste group"; Chaturvedi and Tiwari (1975), on the other hand, begin with "caste" before listing "community; race; sect; genus; type; kind; breed."

3 See Gold 1988:11–22 for a personal account of my first fieldwork experience; see Raheja and Gold 1994:164–181 for more about this household and its dominant female.

4 For this genre of songs, called *keśyā*, and their performative contexts, see Gold 1988:130 and Raheja and Gold 1994:39–47, 62–67. An alternative version of this line substitutes "prostitute" for "she-buffalo."

5 Ishita Banerjee (personal communication) reports a similar practice in the past at the great temple of Puri when ladies of the royal family came for *darshan*.

6 "The implication of the king's question is: Are my men abusing their privileged place by giving the populace a hard time, extracting bribes and so forth?" (Gold 1992:86–87, n.37).

1. The Past of Nature and the Nature of the Past

1 In Sawar the most common way to refer to the former rulers and their kind was to speak of them as "great kings" (*rājā-mahārājā*). It follows, for me, that if the rulers are kings, the place they rule must be a kingdom, however small. Thus in speaking of kings and kingdoms I follow the conventions of local language. It could be more appropriate to refer to Sawar's former rulers and similarly situated potentates as "princes" or "petty princes," or even as "chiefs" or landlords, for their small dominions were not even numbered among the "princely states." However, local history books call them kings and speak of their ascension to thrones (see chapter 6).

The British practice of labeling Rajput rulers "princes" or "chiefs," it seems to me, intentionally diminished them. The English word "chief" has, of course, tribal, uncivilized connotations. And although Rajput, the name of the ruling caste, means "king's son," the common word for prince in Rajasthani—*banā*—in no way bears the masterful, divine connotations of "king" or of several other respectful titles used for the rulers of small kingdoms, including *ṭhākur* (master), *darbār* (Court), *mahārāj* (great king), and *anndātā* (grain-giver)—all of which are also regularly used for God. There are, of course, context-dependent shades of meaning for all these terms.

Although the terms "princes" and "princely" enter this work via other published sources, when faithful to oral history I retain local usage—believing that, even if it is employed merely as convention, it ought to be taken seriously.

2 As explained in the preface, the first-person singular in this book is normally Gold's voice. Gold writes of Gujar in the third person, and uses the first-person plural deliberately when speaking of both authors' shared work, aims, strategies, and experiences.

3 As an adjective *jabānī* (derived from *jabān*, "tongue") may mean unwritten or traditional, but as a noun it refers to transcribed oral testimony, such as an affidavit. In that sense Bhoju hit upon the perfect word for what we have compiled here.

4 In introducing his book, Amin makes a similar point, juxtaposing but not opposing memories with other records: "But for me it was not a question of counterposing local remembrance against authorized accounts: the process by which historians gain access to pasts is richly problematic, as is the relationship between memory and record, and the possibilities of arriving at a more nuanced narrative, a thicker description, seem enhanced by putting the problems on display" (1995:4).

5 At least this tradition would stretch from Malinowski (1961) on the "imponderabilia" of everyday life to Geertz (1983) on "local knowledge."

6 See Chakrabarty 1997a for lucid reflections on the several predicaments of Indian historiography at the present juncture.

7 For a few of the numerous explorations of dialogue and collaborative research, see Clifford 1988:55–91; Humphrey and Onon 1996; and Tedlock and Mannheim 1995. See Marcus on the "uses of complicity" (1998: 105–31); he offers a valuable critical perspective on this entire enterprise. See also Jackson (1998) on the fundamental importance of intersubjectivity to ethnography, not only in fieldwork practice but in philosophical underpinnings and textual expressions.

8 For measured theory, see Abu-Lughod 1991; for experimental praxis, see, among others, Hajj, Lavie, and Rouse 1993; Lavie 1990; and Pandolfo 1997.

9   Comaroff and Comaroff (1992) remains my favorite account. Other discussions and exemplifications of the project of ethnographic history or the wedding of history and anthropology that were particularly helpful in the conceptualizing stages of our work include Cohn 1987; Dening 1991; Dirks 1987; Hastrup 1992; O'Brien and Roseberry 1991; Ortner 1989, 1994; R. Price 1990; and Roseberry 1989. Adenaike and Vansina (1996) present historians doing fieldwork. Stevens (1993) deals with ethnographic history of environmental transformation. More recently, Abercrombie (1998) and Sutton (1998) offer fine examples of ethnographically based and politically alert memory work in the Bolivian Andes and the Greek Islands, respectively. Of special value is Dube (1998), who not only insists that the splits between history and anthropology, archival research and fieldwork, myth and history, and orality and textuality are deeply ideological ones, but in his own study of "untouchable pasts" beautifully exemplifies the multiple virtues of transcending these splits.

10 There are now ten volumes in the *Subaltern Studies* series, published by Oxford University Press, Delhi, along with two selected essay collections published in the United States (Ranajit Guha and Spivak 1988 and Ranajit Guha 1997). Of course, historians associated with the project have also published numerous monographs. The work of the subaltern collective has had an extraordinary impact on theoretical writing in history and anthropology that goes well beyond South Asian area studies. For critical appreciations and appreciative critiques, see O'Hanlon 1988, 1997 and Ortner 1995. Sarkar (1997) is rather more critical, especially of the collective's more recent work.

11 I am thinking, among others, of Gupta (1994, 1998); Khandelwal (1996); Lavie (1990); Narayan (1993, 1997); Tsing (1993); and Visweswaran (1994).

12 For some preliminary work on children's perceptions of environmental change, see Gold and Gujar 1994.

13 Ranajit Guha's landmark book *Elementary Aspects of Peasant Insurgency in Colonial India* (1983) offers an insightful and beautifully exemplified discussion of such decontextualization and its causalities in historical writings.

14 See Gupta and Ferguson 1997 for a discussion of fieldwork-based knowledge and its limitations; and of location as crucial in anthropology.

15 The discussion of language that follows here owes much to conversations held by the Working Group on Governance and Nature, at the Mario Einaudi Center for International Studies at Cornell University, in which I was fortunate to participate for about two years (1997–1998). I am especially indebted to Ron Herring, the group's convener, for much of my understanding of terminological matters.

16 Brian Greenberg (personal communication, 1991).

17 These works are too numerous to list exhaustively. I have found illuminating Glacken's 1967 classic in cultural geography; Simmons 1993, a modern geographer's exploration; and Soper 1995, a philosophical approach. More recently Coates 1998 offers complex literary and political vistas. Bell 1994 offers a sensitive sociological study of the meanings of nature to residents in rural England, an ethnographic work that reveals ambiguities in European understandings as they mesh with self-conscious country life.

18 For a positioned primer on attitudes toward nature and their political consequences,

see Merchant 1992. Peet and Watts 1996 contains more complex discussions of theory for political ecology, and a number of case studies in scattered world regions. For a wide-ranging exploration of one issue—the "wilderness debate" on an international scale—see Callicott and Nelson 1998.

19   Relevant here is a large body of literature concerned with the "death of nature" (for example, Merchant 1990), which is also construed as the "disenchantment of the world" and possible routes to "re-enchantment" (for example, Berman 1981).

20   Virtually countless ethnographies exist from many different localities; see, for a few examples, Brightman 1993 (North America); Devisch 1993 (Africa); Reichel-Dolmatoff 1996 (Amazonia); Rose 1992 (Australia); and Roseman 1991 (Malaysia). There are also numerous works focused on religions and the environment that expand on these contrasts; for examples of a textbook and an anthology, see, respectively, Kinsley 1995 and Tucker and Grim 1993.

21   Ortner's provocative essay (1974) and the many subsequent objections to it (for example, MacCormack and Strathern 1980) are relevant. Ortner later takes these critiques into account and updates her own position (1996:173–80).

22   The inversion of this proper pattern—for nature to invade, co-opt or unseat culture—is delightfully horrifying to western imaginations. Such inversions tend to be associated with tropical climes and have pervaded invidious imagery of Europe's colonized others (Inden 1990). The episode in Kipling's *The Jungle Books* titled "Letting in the Jungle" is a dramatic representation of the power of untamed tropical flora and fauna in the South Asian setting that its author knew so well. This florid scene of devastation seems at once to represent an absolute battle between wild and tame (relentlessly stressed in the movie version). At the same time, reflecting perhaps Kipling's own multicultural perspectives, the wild jungle actors are all speaking, conscious companions of the half-wild wolf-boy Mowgli, whose hatred of the village is the source of their enacted fury; see Mowgli's "Song against People" in Kipling 1895:85.

23   In anthropology this is part of the specific legacy of structuralism and its binary vision of all human thought. As recently as 1996, Descola and Palsson devote the first major segment of their introduction to an anthology of anthropological perspectives on nature and society to arguing that "nature-culture dualism" is inadequate (1996:2–9). That they feel the need to belabor this conceptual inadequacy is proof of its stubborn persistence in anthropological ideation.

24   For *prakṛti* in the theology of the Hindu goddess, see Coburn 1996.

25   See Agarwal 1991 and Sinha, Gururani, and Greenberg 1997.

26   "Landscape" may also offer a bridge to modernity, if we follow Appadurai's more recent discussion of various "scapes" in global culture. He proposes several neologisms sharing the suffix "scape": "These are not objectively given relations that look the same from every angle of vision but, rather, that they are deeply perspectival constructs, inflected by the historical, linguistic, and political situatedness of different sorts of actors" (1996:33).

27   Ingold says: "The environment, as distinct from nature or the 'physical world', is the same reality constituted in its relation to a subject, or group of subjects, in their active engagement with it. . . . It is by their action in the world that people know it, and

come to perceive what it affords" (1992:48). Ingold goes on to argue against the cultural construction of the environment in a fashion I find unconvincing.

28 But see A. Gupta's interrogation of the term "ecology" as applicable to North Indian "peasant understandings of the relationships between the soil, plants, air, water, and humans" (1998:235).

29 Kothari and Parajuli in "No Nature without Social Justice" (1993) make the case with powerful rhetoric; see also Gadgil and Guha 1995; Gold 1998c; Ramachandra Guha 1989; and Guha and Martinez-Alier 1997. See Harvey 1996 for insights into the union of morality and environmentalism in some American activist positions on environmental justice. Harvey evidently sees this union as strategic rather than intrinsic, but nonetheless finds virtue in "a nonnegotiable position of intense moral rectitude untouchable by legal, scientific, or other rationalistic discourses." He also points out, using the famous Indian case as an example, that "the very grounding of the discourse in a language of sacredness and moral absolutes creates a certain homology between, say, struggles over exposure to environmental hazards in urban areas, nativist beliefs on the relation to nature and peasant movements through the developing world such as that of the Chipko" (389–90).

30 Bhoju and I occasionally tried to elicit definitions of *prakṛti* in some early interviews, but most often met with blank responses. Memorably, one younger man said, without hesitation, "God's grace."

31 See Grove, Damodaran, and Sangwan 1998 for a fairly measured alternative account of the debate.

32 Grove's aim (1995, 1998) has been to document the interrelations between colonial power and environmental changes in colonies on a broad scale, arguing that the processes he has called "ecological imperialism" require a less localized scope because of a "fateful globalisation" resulting from the widespread nature of colonialism's impacts (1998:4). In this sense, his work could be viewed as a valuable complement to the smaller-scale studies.

33 Besides Skaria's wonderfully executed study based in western India, Ramachandra Guha's own *The Unquiet Woods* (2000) chartered this rich field of historical research in the Himalayan region. Other recent illuminating works on India's environmental history and politics include Murali 1995 on Andhra; Rangarajan 1996 on the central provinces; Samaddar 1995 on the region of eastern India called Jangalmahal. Sundar's book on Bastar (1997) unites ethnographic with archival work, considers oral traditions vis-à-vis colonial records, and gives attention to the meanings of nature. Sumit Guha offers a fascinating history of environment and what he calls "ethnogenesis" in central and western India "on the margins of agriculture" (1999:1). A study by Sivaramakrishnan (1995) helpfully discusses colonial forest policy and its self-interested appraisals of indigenous practice; his 1999 monograph expands in detail the Bengal case. For Rajasthan, see Mayaram 1997:75–82 for a detailed and incisive account of late-nineteenth and early-twentieth-century interactions among colonial government, princely states, and environment in Alwar and Bharatpur.

34 The highly charged, ongoing conflicts over large dams such as the Sardar Sarovar project would be one huge example; Baviskar 1995 offers a sensitive ethnographic

account of some aspects of this struggle; see also W. F. Fisher 1995. Conflict over land use in parks is another major area of contest; for attempts to steer a path, see Kothari, Singh, and Suri 1996 and Kothari et al. 1997.

35 Chapter 9 takes up the theme of royal forest protection, but note that we have neglected to treat the Bhils of Sawar, a very small remnant of a forest people who live as laborers, almost in bondage to the Court, even today. See McGee 2000 for kings and trees in Sanskrit texts on governance.

36 David Arnold distinguishes environmental history from ecological history in that the former is "more often understood as the story of human engagement with the physical world, with the environment as object, agent, or influence in human history" while the latter would avoid such an "unashamedly" anthropocentric approach (1996:4).

37 The problem of subaltern speech has always had to do with who was listening and what competing voices filled the air (Spivak 1995).

38 Witness Kaali's chapter in the most recent volume of the series where he refers to "subaltern spatial manipulations" in Tamilnad as "the expression of a not-for-a-moment silent subaltern politics" (1999:164). For a particularly fine example of combing rulers' records for a subaltern voice, see Ranajit Guha's "Chandra's Death" (1987). For an insightful exploration of subaltern views in vernacular literature, see Bhadra 1989.

39 Of course, historians also question giving priority or special validity to archival sources. See Amin for a moderating perspective on the uses and value of archival documentation for social historians for whom, he writes, "there is no running into the comforting lap of hard evidence" (1994:9). For insights into historians' attitudes toward oral sources versus documents, see also Wallot and Fortier 1998. For archives, Spivak 1999:203–5 is provocative.

40 One person says to Dube: "What could a poor man do? The orders had to be followed. A rich man may have done otherwise. He was in a position to withstand pressure. But a poor man? And our caste people have been poor. Ninety-five out of one hundred are poor. Our ancestors were poor. Our caste was oppressed. One Brahman *malguzar* could take care of a large Satnami population. Why? Because they had the weapon [of writing]" (1998:94).

41 Two recent books go a long way in improving this imbalance: H. Singh's *Colonial Hegemony and Popular Resistance* (1998) and K. L. Sharma's *Caste, Feudalism, and Peasantry* (1998). Both volumes deal, as we do, with power in Rajasthani states in the years before and after Independence; both discuss conscripted labor, grain collection, intercaste relationships, and other topics overlapping and intersecting with some major themes in our Sawar accounts. But even in these fine works the space given to the actual voices of farmers and herders is very limited. Other works focused at least partially on the same historical period have illuminated power structures in Rajput-dominated kingdoms; these include Tambs-Lyche 1997 and Vidal 1997.

42 I state the obvious to acknowledge that anthropology has had to relearn history, embarrassingly late in its own game (as did I embarrassingly late in my own work).

43 From the chapter "History" in her most recent book, I gather that Spivak has shifted

to emphasize the need to listen, but she also stresses that "the decision that we can hear the other" is a risk; "anguish" might result from listening (1999:198–99).

44 This situation has its parallels in gender hierarchies; see Gold 2000a and Raheja and Gold 1994 for discussion of issues and literatures.

45 See Comaroff and Comaroff for a discussion of hegemony as "that order of signs and practices, relations and distinctions, images and epistemologies—drawn from a historically situated cultural field—that come to be taken-for-granted as the natural and received shape of the world and everything that inhabits it" (1991:23).

46 Bhadra (1989) has written of a "process of struggle" in which neither dominance nor subordination are complete. See also Wadley 1994.

47 See Sullivan 1995 for a religionist's discussion of these issues and the admonition not to forget "sociocultural origins and contexts" when writing about memory.

48 For carefully surveyed approaches to the relationship between memory and history, I found Hutton 1993 most helpful. Other articulations of this juncture from which I have gained understanding include Burke 1997:43–59; Connerton 1989; Dening 1991; Fentress and Wickham 1992; Halbwachs 1992; and Irwin-Zarecka 1994. Lambek nicely captures the anthropologist's fascination: "It is this kind of opposition between history (the dispassionate representation of the past) and memory (the subjective continuity with it) to which the experience from non-Western historical fields, such as that of the Sakalava [his research community], invites alternatives" (1998:111). See also Bloch's healthy cautions against the loose ways memory is used in recent historical and anthropological literature (1998:114–27).

49 In recent years important critiques deconstruct the ways much colonial and postcolonial historiography and anthropological discourse have denied or flattened other peoples' histories by positing timeless traditional cultural worlds. For the big picture, see, of course, Fabian 1983 and Wolf 1982. Roseberry 1989 helpfully rethinks Wolf. Both A. Gupta 1994 and Chakrabarty 1997b offer important discussions of time and history in orientalist, colonial, and postcolonial representations of India.

50 This intimacy has been the subject of countless ruminations in the last fifteen years or so, stimulating another vast discussion to which no footnote can do justice. See Behar 1996 for one attempt to synthesize it, confessionally. Also, I have found Abu-Lughod 1993 to be encouraging.

51 See Appadurai 1981:202–3 for cultural organization of debate about the past; see also Sahlins 1985 for culture, history, and contact situations depicted with meticulous scholarship and theoretical flair.

52 On enslaved women's narratives, see Fleischner 1996; on Jewish history and "Shoah," see Boyarin 1991, 1992; Irwin-Zarecka 1994; LaCapra 1998; Langer 1991; and Videl-Naquet 1996. Spiegelman's comic book rendering of the process of eliciting memory from his father rings true (1986). Other recent cultural histories of displacement based on memories include Jing 1996 on a case of forced dislocation in China, and Slyomovics 1998 on a Palestinian village. See Sturkin 1997 for the politics of memory, especially in relation to forgetting, in American culture. Less directly relevant to our Sawar project, but nonetheless germane to gathering oral history from the disempowered, are debates

Notes to Chapter One ❧ 333

in psychology on the truth of childhood memories (made compelling in the context of American public culture's revelatory searchlight on childhood sexual abuse).

53 On landscape and memory see, of course, Schama 1995. Casey also discusses the mutual formation of the two: "Landscape contributes to place's memorial evocativeness in three primary ways: by its variegation, its sustaining character, and its expressiveness" (1987:198). Other important works of environmental history include Basso 1996 on Apache; Cronon 1983 on New England; and Peluso 1992 on Java.

54 See, however, Krishna 1997 and Poffenberger and McGean 1996 for work on recovery and regeneration in South Asia and elsewhere.

55 Pandey sums up important results of the turn to memory: "To take account of other, different kinds of articulations of the past is to open up the area of historical enquiry: to accommodate the malleable, contextual, fuzzy, 'lived' community (and this should now include the 'nation'), and to recognize how the community (the subject of history) is forged in the very construction of the past—in the course, one might say, of a historical discourse" (1999:49).

56 See also Daniel 1996:194–212 and Mayaram 1997:192–208.

57 See Lowenthal 1985 on the translation of distance in time to distance in space.

58 Chapter 4 selectively reviews recent literature on memory, history, and landscape.

59 I shall follow local semantics in using the English word "Court," as Rajasthanis use the word *darbār,* to refer both to whatever individual person is current ruler as well as to the institution of royalty and its collective personnel. As a term of reference Court may be applied to rulers of large or small kingdoms in Rajasthan.

60 See Zonabend 1984 on how the remembered past—in a French village—is by definition in contrast with the present. Other European village-based ethnographic studies of past and present include Behar 1986 and Sutton 1998.

2. Voice

1 For Gujars in Rajasthan, and in Ghatiyali, See Miller 1994, especially pp. 18–72.

2 See Raheja 1988 for Rajput-like Gujars in Uttar Pradesh; see Gooch 1999 for nomadic Gujars.

3 Kavoori in his study of the pastoral herding communities of western Rajasthan writes that Gujars have a closer relationship with agriculture than do Raikas. "They tend to own more land and are more integrated into the sedentary village community" (1999:5). For more on western Rajasthan herders, see Agrawal 1998 (largely on Raikas); Kavoori 1999 (on several groups); and Srivastava 1997 (on Raikas).

4 For example, Jaswanatpura, a small village that lies on the road between Sawar and Ghatiyali, was explicitly "settled" as a Gujar community by the king, Jaswant Singh, as a strategy to keep the road safe. Elsewhere in the Sawar Twenty-Seven, as in Mori village, Minas also worked as guards. For a critique of typing by caste as a colonial project, see Raheja 1996; Raheja demonstrates the colonizers' selective and manipulative use of proverbial speech and shows that many stereotypes were often contested within oral tradition. Given all this, I must acknowledge that I often heard Gujars typed as proud fighters (and Baniyas as tricky wheelers and dealers, Balais as stupid, and so forth).

5 This was Bhanvar Lal, the son of Shri Lalu Ram Gujar; his term as *sarpanch* ended in 1999 and, as this book goes to press, the local "rule of votes" has returned a Rajput to power, a development we are not able to examine here.

6 See chapter 7 for an account of Bhoju's father's impoverished childhood; he was a self-made man in Ghatiyali; Bhoju lacks paternal lineage support.

7 Although 1993 was a longer fieldwork period than that of 1997, the majority of it was not focused on the oral history project. Of approximately 110 interviews, 45 were conducted during two months in 1997, while 65 were scattered over eight months in 1993. Approximately 70 percent of our interviews over both fieldwork periods were in Ghatiyali, including virtually all of the 1993 recordings. The other 30 percent were conducted in seventeen other villages, with Sawar, Gorada, and Devli Gaon slightly predominant among them. We recorded interviews with approximately fifty persons who were probably over sixty years old, and of those about 25 percent were women. We spoke with an additional sixty persons who reported or estimated their ages between forty and sixty; about one-third of these were female. About 45 percent of all of our interviews were with two *jāti*s—Gujars and Malis—groups numerically dominant in the region as well. Regars made up about another 10 percent; Brahmins, Rajputs, and Minas were around 5 percent each. The remaining 30 percent of the interviews were sparsely distributed through another twenty *jāti*s.

8 Mani Raj Singh Shaktavat is appropriately called "prince" (*banā*), not Court. The actual current "Court," his eldest brother, is Dev Raj Singh. However, Dev Raj Singh lives away from Sawar and is somewhat estranged from his family.

9 See Jodha 1985, 1990. For deforestation and its domestic consequences in South Asia, see Agarwal 1986.

10 In the case of agricultural rituals, for example, farmers directly attribute the decrease in ritual activity to the increasing use of machine power (Gold 1999a).

11 These topics are treated in Gold with Gujar 1997; Gold 1998c; Gold 2002a and Gold 1999a.

12 Simultaneously with broadening the geographic scope of our historical research, we had also initiated a project on education that demanded a different kind of work from both of us. Most of our work on education remains unpublished, but Gold 2002b presents a small piece of it.

13 See "Gloria's account" in Raheja and Gold 1994:xvii–xxvi; see Lamb 2000 for a beautiful portrayal of an intense experience of incorporation into a Bengali family and community.

14 Out of approximately 65 interviews in 1993, fifteen were with women. Of these fifteen interviews, Bhoju had participated in only one.

15 While, as noted above, Mani Raj is not the present Sawar *darbār,* he is for all purposes the senior male authority in the fort.

16 Rashmi is one who may well read and judge this book; I trust that she, having showed me the vistas from the royal roofs, will agree that the view from below is also worth having.

17 Bhoju had a black helmet with a visor that could be pulled down completely to cover his face; once when I was riding behind him without any headcover and he was

wearing this item, he overheard a man comment on our appearance in one of the smaller villages: "Now we know the Degenerate Era (Kali Yug) has arrived; men veil their faces and women go around bare-headed."

18 See Gujar and Gold 1992 for Bhoju's description of this awakening of anthropological curiosity in a young man, under twenty, whose previous passion was volleyball.

19 Skaria's brilliant discussion of the "multiplicity of truth" in oral narratives is relevant here (1999:28–33).

20 The king's agents—his "bosses" described below—are the "sinful squirrels" who have destroyed the tree of state. Gold 2001a explores related aspects of tree imagery in Indic kingship and Sawar folklore. See also Rival 1998 for a wonderful compilation of nuanced case studies revealing cross-cultural propensities to use trees symbolically to think about human life.

21 The Hindi word, *hākim* may be glossed as "ruler" or "boss." The Rajasthani variant is *hākam,* and can also mean "king," according to the *Rājasthānī Sabad Kos* (Lalas 1962–1978), hereafter *RSK.* I believe that "boss" is a colloquially appropriate translation for *hākim* because it can work at many different levels of power and always includes a kind of authoritative pushiness. It strikes me that the most salient feature of *hākim* is their ability to order others to do things. In Sawar the term was used loosely, and sometimes more or less as an equivalent to *kāmdār*—which I consistently translate as "manager."

22 It is noteworthy that Bhoju states that freedom was realized under the "rule of Indira," which began in 1966 almost twenty years after the death of Vansh Pradip Singh.

3. Place

1 According to Shetty and Singh, the Banas Basin includes "the eastern part of Udaipur, western Chittorgarh, Bhilwara, western Ajmer, Tonk, Jaipur, western Sawaimadhopur and southern part of Alwar district" (1987:22–23). This would exclude Sawar, which is located in the extreme southeast of Ajmer. However, none of the other units the authors define would include eastern Ajmer, and I must conclude that they, like Misra (1967), would place Sawar in the Banas Basin.

2 See Dirks 1997 for religious interpretations of sporadic rainfall in South India; I have found similarly based explanations in Sawar (Gold 1988).

3 Misra locates the Banas Basin within the Eastern Agro-Industrial region, one of seven geographic regions in Rajasthan characterized by sociological as well as ecological features. This region "lies east of the Aravalli range and the western boundary of the region is marked by 50 cm rainfall line. The northern boundary is marked by the state boundary of U.P. and Punjab and the eastern and southern boundary by the Chambal ravines and the southeastern agricultural region. It is mainly drained by the Banas river and its tributaries" (Misra 1967:174–75). On Narain and Mathur's (1990) map of "agricultural regions," Sawar and much of the Banas Basin appear to be in an area labeled "East Rajasthan Uplands."

4 Speaking generally, the most recent *Census of India* states that crop patterns in Ajmer district have "remained largely unchanged over the years." Its list of crops for the two growing seasons is similar to Shambhu's for Ghatiyali; the document states: "This

district does not grow enough grain to feed the increasing population and therefore, the emphasis must be maintained overwhelmingly on food crops" (1994:lxv).

5   Each new wheat has been given an attractive name by its promoters. *Kalyāṇ* means prosperity, well being. *Sonī* is derived from *sonā*, meaning gold, and is probably an affectionate diminutive; Shambhu Nath lists this variety as *sonā kalyāṇ*, "golden prosperity." See A. Gupta 1998:194–97 for farmers' seed selection in Uttar Pradesh; on responses to new grains, see also Vasavi 1999.

6   Dhoundiyal (1966:161–62) charts crop production in Ajmer district. Although not all of his trends match those in Ghatiyali, he shows a dramatic increase in oil seeds from 31 tons in 1956–67 to 176 tons in 1960–61, evidence that this trend was well underway more than four decades ago. Chouhan has charts on all of Rajasthan's crops, which show increases in just about everything except for barley and the two millets—confirming at least the dramatic shift in grain taste. Cash crops vary most radically from district to district. Chouhan's chart shows an approximate doubling of rape seed and mustard seed production between 1957 and 1979, but tells us that in terms of the whole state cotton has also vastly increased (1987:242).

7   Panagariya and Pahariya note a dramatic rise in Rajasthan's production of oilseeds between 1950–51 and 1994–95. The authors conclude that "this trend has to be watched carefully lest Rajasthan may not again become an importer State in foodgrains" (1996:269).

8   A Divali story recorded from multiple sources in Sawar tells of the goddess Parvati seeking to worship the "greatest" entity and finding that it is not the ocean, not the earth, not the serpent on which the earth rests, but the ox—foundation of all life.

9   See Appadurai 1990 for calculations connected with this practice in Maharashtra.

10 For a classic anthropological study of Hindu understandings of food, see Khare 1976.

11 For a fine ethnography of Rajasthani pastoral life, with a focus on religion, see Srivastava 1997. For a helpful discussion of pastoralism in India, and specifically in Saurashtra, see Tambs-Lyche 1997:147–73.

12 See Dhoundiyal 1996:172 for migration of herding communities in Ajmer district's history.

13 Using *Census of India* data, we find consistent population increases between 1971 and 1991 in large and small settlements among the Sawar Twenty-Seven. For example, the capital, Sawar, shows an increase of 33 per cent (5,166 to 6,891), Ghatiyali of 46 per cent (2,390 to 3,484), Vajta of 39 per cent (1,238 to 1,720), Kushaita of 40 per cent (905 to 1,265), Jasvantpura of 40 per cent (473 to 661), and Mori of 65 per cent (281 to 463).

14 See, for example, Gandhi on banyan (*Ficus bengalensis*) (1991:53–57) and *pīpal* (*Ficus religiosa*) (135–41); Santapau on banyan (1966:39–44) and *peepul* (46–48); Joshi on *nīm* (*Melia azadirachta* or *Azadirachta indica*) (1995:199) and *pipal* (200). Gujars have special duties to respect and protect *nīm* trees, which are associated in several ways with the Gujar divinity Dev Narayan and his epic tale (Miller 1994).

15 See Shetty and Singh 1987:22–23 and Brandis 1906:315. The *Census of India* in listing the "main species found in the district" puts Dhokra first and includes, among many others, *salar* (*Boswellia serrata*), *khejri* (*Prosopis spicigera*), *khair* (*Acacia catechu*), *ber*

(*Zizyphus jujuba*), *kalia* (*Albizzia onoratissima*), and *khirni* (*Wrightia tomentosa*) (1994:lxiv–lxv).

16 Misra, for example, writes: "The wood of this tree is hard and strong and has a certain amount of elasticity. It provides good firewood and makes excellent charcoal. The wood is also used for making agricultural implements and big trees produce good rafters" (1967:56–57). See also Sharma and Tiagi who add its appeal to goats to the list of multiple causes for the loss of *dhok* trees: "This tree is worst affected by the goats, overgrazing reduces it to a tuft of green shoots only 6–9 cms high" (1979:155).

17 The appendix lists by Rajasthani name those species named in interviews that I have been able to locate and identify in other sources.

18 An Ajmer archives document of 1869 notes that "on most of the Ajmere hills the roots of the former trees and bushes still remain and the natural growth will therefore gradually spring up if properly protected." File no. 983 (Q88), 1869, Bikaner; document file titled "Establishment of Forest Reserves in the Ajmer-Merwara Districts and Proposed Appointment of a Deputy Conservator of Forest for the Purpose."

19 I borrow this apt phrase from Herring's "Embedded Particularism" (1999) and Nagarajan's "Embedded Ecologies" (1998); if lacking originality, it still suits my purposes.

20 Temples and inscriptions would doubtless take us back much further.

21 As far as I could tell, intervillage marriage connections cross-cut the boundaries of kingdoms (as they do today of tehsils and districts); so do performance and patronage routes of local bards and many other kinds of cultural networks.

22 For Minas, see M. H. Singh 1990 [1894]:51–56 and *Imperial Gazetteer* 1989 [1908]:36. On the relations between Rajputs and tribal peoples, the work of N. Sinha (1993a, 1993b) on Bhils in southern Rajasthan is illuminating, as is that of Unnithan-Kumar (1997) on Girasias in Sirohi. Weisgrau 1997 is a study of Bhils in Udaipur district in modern times, but includes a helpful discussion of "Bhil-Rajput relations," both historical and contemporary (71–77).

23 Sumit Guha discusses similarly fluid categories in the seventeenth century (1999:55).

24 In M. H. Singh we read: "The Minas for generations were wholly given to robbery and general lawlessness, their national weapons being bows and arrows. From their very childhood they practised crime" (1990 [1894]:55). Singh goes on to note that the "course of time has now refined the character of Minas, and they are more and more being persuaded to adopt peaceful habits" (56). See Mayaram 1991 for an incisive critique of colonial uses of "criminality" applied to particular groups.

25 According to the *RSK*, *khaiṅrau* may mean a small village, or a field near the village. Here it seems to mean a group of small villages.

26 Kantola is the name of a large hill between Ghatiyali and Sawar where the cave and other shrines are located. One person we interviewed glossed the name as "where there once was deep jungle." The term appears to derive from *kāṇṭo*, meaning thorn.

27 "In Bundi State and in the rugged country round Jahazpur and Deoli, which is called the Kherār and belongs to Bundi, Jaipur, and Udaipur, are found the Parihar Minas, who claim descent from the Parihar Rajputs of Mandor. They are a fine athletic race, formerly notorious as savage and daring robbers; but they have settled down to a great

extent" (*Imperial Gazetteer* 1908:36). Possibly there is a link between this Kherar and the Khera of which Bhairu Mina spoke.

28 Contrast this with a story I heard for the origin of the name Mina, set in the time when Parasurama was pursuing his slaughter of Rajputs: those who were cowardly cried out "*maiṁ nahīṁ hūṁ*" (I am not one), which eventually contracted to Mina.

29 Personal communications from David Roche and Maxine Weisgrau, who have both done field research in Udaipur district, were my initial sources for Gavri, treated in Weisgrau 1997:194–96. See Erdman 1985 for the importance of Gangaur in Jaipur.

30 I had intended to catalog and possibly photograph these papers, which Mathur's son, although hospitable and helpful, would not allow removed from his premises. However, my time was short and in the end I preferred to spend it doing interviews with nonliterate people rather than examining documents. Interesting items there were lists of birthday presents presented to the Court by people of all communities; lists of salaries for the Court's paid workers; records of production amount in the different villages; and records of where daughters from Sawar's royal family were married and where in-married brides were born.

31 Udaipur was the capital of the princely state of Mewar; see Tod 1978 [1914]; and Ray 1978.

32 See Wolpert 1989:152 for confirmation of dates.

33 Some of the other villages granted to Gokul Das were in Bengal. In one interview we were told of Sawar people on pilgrimage to Bengal who happened to visit a temple where they heard the names of Sawar and its rulers praised as patrons; the temple had some association with the old Shaktavat dominion.

34 Of course, others ruled Sawar before the Shaktavats. Kishan Lal Gujar, an unusual farmer-historian, told us that the lineage that preceded Gokal Das was Solanki, and that preceding Solanki were the Diya Rajputs (whom he dated around the time of Dev Narayan, or about 1000 C.E.). There are Sati stones in the gardens near the Sawar fort that are said to be that old or older.

35 For a masterful and illuminating overview of distinctive patterns in Rajasthan's political history, see Narain and Mathur 1990.

36 For a brief discussion of Sawar's paintings, see Beach 1992.

37 Sarda's focus is largely on Ajmer city; R. Joshi 1972 is an excellent Hindi source for social and political history of nineteenth-century Ajmer.

38 For Mughal administration of rural Rajasthan, see S. Gupta 1986; for an argument for continuities from the Mughal system of revenue collection to that of Rajput princes in Jaipur state, see Bajekal 1990.

39 A *tāzīmī* chief is one on whose coming the king or *badshah* gets up and stands, or a chief in whose court there is special prestige (Sundardas 1965).

40 According to the *Imperial Gazetteer* 1908, La Touche's Settlement Report for 1875 contains "complete genealogies" of all the *tāzīmī* states.

41 For Rajputana during paramountcy, see Copland 1997; Rudolph and Rudolph 1984; Ramusack 1978; Ray 1978; and Stern 1988.

42 I am grateful for kind assistance received in both the Bikaneer and Ajmer archives.

Notes to Chapter Three ❧ 339

43 Several historian colleagues have been kind enough to read my book manuscript; all of them have included in their comments a wish that I had or would consult the revenue records.

44 For Ajmer-Merwara, see especially Stebbing 1922–28, 2:553–59; Stebbing 3:103–13; and Champion and Osmaston 1983:359–64 (Stebbing's vol. 4, published posthumously).

45 See Shivaramakrishnan for insights into the causes of such contention that lie in the ways colonial foresters disengaged forest landscapes from "regional agrarian economies" (1999:186).

46 On the history of famines in Rajputana, see Kachhawaha 1985 and Maloo 1987. For an illuminating discussion of colonial famine policy, see Raheja n.d.

47 Haynes (1998:749) reports on the long-term process in Gujarat and Rajasthan where between 1880 and 1900, areas under forest, interrupted woods, and grassland declined, respectively 59.1 percent, 60.5 percent, and 35.1 percent. See also Haynes 1999:58–75 for detailed discussion and documentation of deforestation in Rajasthan between 1780 and 1980.

48 File no. 983 (Q88), 1869, Bikaner.

49 Pandey (1998) comments on this from a present-day "ethnoforestry" perspective: "Brandis found that in the territory of Bednor, the hills were wooded. Brandis was told that it was the tradition in the State to protect the Birs. Knowing well that the grass, which, even in dry seasons, maintained itself under the shade of the trees, and the branches of the trees themselves, had saved the cattle of Bednor in years of drought, and more than this, that the water supply in those tanks, upon which the fertility of the country depended, was maintained by the forest growth upon the hills. This is a remarkable finding on the local knowledge on forests that existed then" (42–43).

50 *Bīr* according to the *RSK* is an alternate form of *bīrau* (Sanskrit); meaning "3) a field of protected grass in which others are not allowed to graze; 4) grazing land; 5) *jangal*." See Gold and Gujar 1995 for sacred groves.

51 File no. 983.

52 Mayaram discusses and documents what she describes as an "expansion of state rights and colonization *vis-a-vis* the local community" in both Alwar and Bharatpur. Village commons become "reserved" and "protected" forests, the result being access denied to farmers and herders and made a privilege for "royal consumption" (1997:78–80).

53 On village commons in Rajasthan, see Brara 1992; Jodha 1985, 1990; and Robbins 1996.

54 File no. 983.

55 For more on this theory, see Grove 1995, especially pp. 380–473; Grove 1998:5–36; and Grove, Damodaran, and Sangwan 1998, especially the introduction and essays by Rangarajan and Skaria. Spooner and Mann 1982 is also relevant. Ramachandra Guha points out that this theory was highly motivated in that it was "designed to further the claims of the Forest Department over territory otherwise under the control of the Civil or Revenue Department" (personal communication, 19 June 2000).

56 File no. 67.3443 (Q43), 1908, Ajmer; document file titled "Influence of Forest on Water Supply."

57 File no. 1028 (Q61), 1880, Bikaner; document file titled "Orders Regarding Light Grazing in the Forest Reserve and Note on Grazing in Forest Reserves in Ajmer Merwara," and signed by the assistant commissioner in Beawar, a captain whose name I am unable to decipher.

58 File no. 8.3384 (Q30), 1892, Ajmer; document file titled "Formation of Village Birs and Appointment of Forest Guard."

59 File no. 45.3421 (Q16), 1902, Ajmer; document file titled "Opening of Reserved Forest to Grazing."

60 Ramachandra Guha 2000 is a pioneering source on colonial power in conflict with local ecologies. See Murali 1995 for a wonderfully detailed account of protests against forest control in Andhra with much use of oral testimony; see also Sivaramakrishnan 1995. Hill 1997 offers a carefully documented study of the intertwined history of colonialism, powerful landlords, and general ecological deterioration in North Bihar, in the Purnia district of eastern India.

61 Here I must express gratitude to Saurabh Dube for kindly suggesting to me that I would be well advised to avoid this fraught mare's nest. I refer readers to thoughtful discussions in Mukhia 1993; H. Singh 1998:23–27; and Stern 1988. Earlier treatments particularly concerned with marxist categories include Thorner 1956 and Critchley 1978. Vidal, without too much concern for the term "feudal," offers an interesting interpretation of Jagirdar, or "the nature of Rajput kingdoms," based on a tension between hierarchical superiority of the prince and an egalitarian concept of "shared kinship within the clan" (1997:54–55). See also Rubin 1983.

62 It is interesting that the term comes to refer in popular sayings to work done improperly or halfheartedly, or to any meaningless, profitless work. In the context of shrines, however, "*begār* signifies labor freely given to please and honor a god. . . . It is also a recognition of the deity as ruler and a statement of humble surrender to that divine authority" (Gold 1994:88). Negi 1995 is the only (slim) book-length study I have seen of *begār*.

63 For *lāg* and *neg* as "payments for ritual services" in rural Uttar Pradesh, see Raheja 1988:212–18.

64 The colonial government attempted to establish some rather complex, refined assessment policies in Ajmer, but in Sawar, in any case, these do not appear to have trickled down (Lupton 1908).

65 Dube 1998:55–56 discusses a similar set of restrictions on a disadvantaged group in Chhattisgarh in the late nineteenth century.

66 The phrase "hewers of wood and drawers of water" is formulaic in protests of the plight of poor villagers; for an example from Central India, see Dube 1998:151.

67 For land reform in Rajasthan, see D. Singh 1964; Yugandhar and Datta 1995; Rudolph and Rudolph 1984:38–78; Rosin 1987, who focuses on Marwar; and Vyas 1976. For succinct accounts of the unification of the former princely states, and the British joint province of Ajmer-Merwara into the state of Rajasthan, see *Rajasthan State Gazetteer* 1995, 2:80–89; Panagariya and Pahariya 1996:75; and Misra 1967.

4. Memory

1 In 1980 while on a bus pilgrimage fostering an ethos of detachment, one old gentle-man rejected an invitation to speak of the past when he held land and power, saying, "People sit and talk about past times, but it's no use." Instead, he launched into a story about the fruits of a life given over to devotion. This is the sole instance I can recall of such dismissal of the value of recollection, and of course at the time I had no interest in the past.

2 See Bloch 1998:116–17 for an excellent discussion of the relationship between so-cial memory and autobiographical memory, including an appreciative critique of Halbwachs.

3 Not all of the recent works on memory and history explain the link between the two in ways that converge with our project. See, for example, Pierre Nora writing in the context of a massive project on French social history. He opposes the two endeavors rather dualistically: "Memory is always a phenomenon of the present, a bond tying us to the eternal present; history is a representation of the past. Memory, being a phe-nomenon of emotion and magic, accommodates only those facts that suit it. . . . History, being an intellectual, non-religious activity, calls for analysis and critical discourse. Memory situates remembrance in a sacred context. History ferrets it out; it turns whatever it touches into prose" (1996:3). As Hutton (1993) points out, Nora's project is in some ways a celebration of memory and in others a recognition of that magic's vanishing (8–10).

4 For a different set of four important themes in memory studies, in a work I encoun-tered after I originally composed this chapter, see Lambek and Antze 1996. They speak about memory as moral practice; memory as claims; memory as essentially incom-plete; and memory as part of selfhood. All these characterizations are valid for and applicable to Sawar and to this book.

5 For other approaches to material traces vis-à-vis collective memory as sources for history, see Dening 1991; Hutton 1993; and Le Goff 1992.

6 See chapter 9 for a discussion of terms for uninhabited areas, including *mangarā*.

7 See Jodha 1985 on the ongoing depletion of common property resources in Rajasthan.

8 This might remind some readers of religion, but religion is perhaps more evidently constructed and sustained through institutions. It may also remind us, more par-ticularly, of folklore. In 1999, someone had to be making up those Clinton and Lewinsky jokes—but they lived and breathed in the public domain of voice, print, and ether, and were surely a clear indication of collective mentalities at work.

9 See Ingold 1996:201–28 for a "key debate" in anthropology on the proposition that "the past is a foreign country." Lowenthal himself is among the speakers who treat the intersection of memory, history, and ethnography from varied angles.

10 See Cohn's "The Pasts of an Indian Village" (1987:88–99), first published in 1961, for acute insights well before their time into multiple and positioned understandings of pasts coexisting in a single community; see also Dirks's landmark monograph (1987). For ethnographic history Price's prologue to her work on kingship and colonialism in Tamilnad (1996) is helpful.

11 Vansh Pradip Singh died in *samvat* 2004 (1947 c.e.); Vrij Raj Singh ascended the throne in *samvat* 2008 (1951 c.e.) and died in 2033 (1976 c.e.). Vrij Raj Singh ruled for twenty-five years, during twenty of which Sawar was part of the modern state of Rajasthan. It is remarkable, or perhaps not so remarkable, how little we hear about him and how much we hear about his predecessor.

12 This neighborhood was constructed between my 1981 and 1993 fieldwork periods, and many Regar families had moved there by 1993. When I asked how to say "colony" in the local language I was told by a somewhat baffled respondent, "*kālonī.*"

13 I am not sure why Bhoju put the question in this way because he did not usually bring up the English. Perhaps he was curious to what degree someone like Jamuni would be aware that the English ruled over the great kings. *Rāj* means any "rule" or "rulers." Many in the West associate the word with the British presence in India (perhaps best known through *The Raj Quartet* novels and TV series). However, in our interviews it is used more often to refer to Rajput royalty than to the British.

14 Note that Jamuni begins with apparently pleasant memories of royal pomp and largesse, feasts and song.

15 Note the inclusive "we" as in "we Regars"; it was for the most part men who did long distance transport work while women ground grain within the fort and transported fodder and dung within the village.

16 Many interviewees in and around Ghatiyali recalled Akka Singhji as a particularly notable *hākim.*

17 As noted in earlier chapters, Gujars belonging to *dhābhāī* lineages had a privileged status due to their female relations working as wet nurses to the royal family.

18 *Bāvaṛī* is a kind of a well that is open on all four sides and has a wide mouth with stairs leading down to the water.

19 Collecting each morning's dung from the livestock pen, heaping it in baskets, and carrying it on their heads to the compost pile is a regular task performed by women at every level of village society. This not-relished chore is always mentioned by women when they are asked to recount their daily routines, and it appears in women's songs as well. Regar women had to do this work for the rulers as well as for their own households.

20 *Gālī* translates as "insults," but may connote greater violence. *Gālīs* are "given" like a beating, or a "tongue-lashing"; they are also emitted, perhaps something like lava.

21 Yule and Burnell tell us that "maund" is "the authorised Anglo-Indian form of the name of a weight . . . which, with varying values, has been current over Western Asia from time immemorial" and whose value has varied "even in modern times" from "little more than 2 lbs. to upwards of 160" (1990 [1886]:563–64). In Ghatiyali by the 1980s people stated confidently that one maund was equal to forty kilograms (Gold 1988:160).

22 Seer came into Indian English from the Hindi *ser* as a measure of weight of about one kilogram, equal to one-fortieth of a *maṇ*, or "maund" in Indian English (see Yule and Burnell 1990).

23 These are both untouchable leatherworking *jāti*s.

24 Jamuni was probably married as a small child; note that she merges her birth with her marriage in memory/identity.

25 This is Vrij Raj Singh, the successor to Vansh Pradip Singh. He is rarely referred to by name; and I did not hear him referred to as *darbār*. Brought in as an outsider, legally adopted by Vansh Pradip Singh's queen only after her husband's death, and rejected by popular opinion, he is labeled by his outsider origins—the Chausala-wala. Chausala was once part of the Sawar Twenty-Seven, but was separated from it quite some time before the adoption of Vrij Raj Singh.

26 Bhils are a "tribal" community who were closely affiliated with Rajputs and who did various kinds of gathering work in the woods.

27 See Scott on "petty theft" as "self-help" (1985:265–72). In Sawar to have trees on one's "own" farmland but be forbidden their fruit or the use of their wood was another recurrent, bitter memory (chapter 8).

28 Unripe mangoes—small, hard, green, and sour—are even today eaten raw by children, and also are cooked as vegetables into a rather tasty dish.

29 In interviews in this and the following chapters a number of terms are used for merchants, each having a nuanced shade of meaning. *Baniyā*, *bohrā*, and *seth* all refer to the role of shopkeeper and money lender; *mahājan* is the term most commonly used in Sawar to speak of merchants as a *jāti*.

30 Gold 1998b has another example of a former untouchable speaking of equality while acting out the old forms of deference in terms of seating arrangements. In Ghatiyali, no Regar ever seated themselves beside us, but in other villages this did happen, somewhat to Bhoju's surprise.

31 Here I translate *dukhī* as "badly off," whereas elsewhere I translate it more literally as "sorrowful." In English "sorrowful" sounds rather ponderous and emotional and is not always appropriate. Note here that from interview to interview, appraisals of who is badly off will vary enormously. Brahmins will claim that they too suffered, although Regars would not usually identify Brahmins as suffering, and so forth.

32 Literally this term means "sitting down and getting up," but it is used idiomatically to refer to pleasant social interactions including conversation. I might note that from my own experience this is a very appropriate idiom. If one does not ask someone to sit (as happened to us only once), it is a very pointed mark of disdain or discourtesy.

33 This noun from the Sanskrit translates as pride, arrogance, vanity, or conceit.

34 The theme of past winter socializing around all-night fires was a common one in our interviews and we return to it in chapter 10.

35 *Vilāyatī bambūl* is literally "foreign *bambūl*"—the Latin name is *Prosopis juliflora*. Chapter 10 discusses foreign trees at length; for the "new wind" see David 1976.

36 *Savāmaṇī* means literally one-and-one-quarter maunds; such a feast would use that much wheat flour, with a matching amount of other ingredients (see Gold 1988:160).

5. Shoes

1 The *gāṅv balāī*, which I translate as "village crier," was an official employee of the Court. His work included delivering announcements and calling workers to conscripted labor. He also attended the process of grain assessment and collection, and

was one of the predators on the farmer's crops (chapters 6 and 8). The position of village crier was appointed within particular lineages of the "untouchable" leather-worker communities. Because of his birth-given low status, the respect due to the village crier as "king's man" can become a particular focus of resentment, as described in interviews such as this one. See also M. H. Singh on the caste and position of Bhambi, which is similar: "One Bhambi in each village is granted by the Raj a *pagri* or turban and a *lathi* or stick. He is considered the head village-Bhambi, and arranges for every kind of *Begar* work. . . . The Bhambis are also called Balais, and cultivate land, though only to a small extent" (1990:196–67).

2   Literally: whoever ate shoes, ate shoes and kept on eating them. Initially I deliberately gave this a literal translation, but every native Hindi speaker who encountered it corrected me, and I defer. Nonetheless, I would like to point out that *khānā*, "to eat," is used idiomatically in a number of other contexts to refer to internalization: for example, "to take the sun" (*dhūp khānā*); to spend a lot of energy in a fruitless, or circular, fashion (*chakar khānā*, literally "to eat dizziness"); and in Rajasthani weddings, to culminate the marriage ritual by circling the sacred fire (*phere khānā*, literally "to eat rounds"). I think the locution *jūte khānā* implies that shoe blows are internalized, thus demeaning and stigmatizing.

3   On "key" or "epitomizing" symbols, see Schneider 1976. It also strikes me that Turner's characterization of the bipolarity of symbols, understood as a dynamic exchange of energy between the physical-individual and symbolic-cultural (outdated as this sounds today) could well be applied to shoes in Sawar, with one important amendment. Turner writes: "[Ritual symbols'] essential quality consists in their juxtaposition of the grossly physical and the structurally normative, of the organic and the social. . . . Norms and values, on the one hand, become saturated with emotion, while the gross and basic emotions become ennobled through contact with social values" (1967:29–30). In another essay he expresses it this way: "At one pole of meaning . . . the significata tend to refer to components of the moral and social orders—this might be termed the ideological (or normative) pole of symbolic meaning; at the other, the sensory (or orectic) pole, are concentrated references to phenomena and processes that may be expected to stimulate desires and feelings" (1977:184). The amendment, therefore, is that the social order invoked by shoes is neither noble nor moral.

4   For critical and insightful commentary on our common anthropological fascination with resistance, see Abu-Lughod 1990 and Ortner 1995. For tropes as an anthropological (or cultural) device, see Clifford and Marcus 1986; see also Boon, who wisely warns: "Yet these tropes are just that—tropes—and are not to be generalized as a culture's tacit creed or central doctrine. . . . 'Tropic' as well is the scholarly privileging of evidence that reinforces such metaphors and rounds off a consolidated world view" (1990:71). H. Singh critiques other historians of South Asia for their tendency "to exaggerate and unrealistically glorify the elements of resistance and struggle in peasant culture, eschewing acceptance, conformity, and consent on the part of the subordinate classes" (1998:38).

5   For example: a Mali (or Gujar or Balai, meaning a "moron" or a "Polack" in compara-

ble western folklore) is hurrying somewhere and is eating as he walks because he has no time to waste. On the road a passerby points out to him that he is eating with his shoes on—improper behavior by merged rules of purity and etiquette. The Mali (or Gujar or Balai) ponders this a moment and then figures out a solution: he removes his shoes, places them on his head, and continues to walk along eating. Get it? Note also that shoes are ritual sponges for inauspiciousness (see Gold 1988:277). In 1993 Bhoju's wife Bali weekly balanced her underweight baby girl against a scale full of shoes—to absorb the inauspiciousness that afflicted the child's growth probably because unwittingly in her early pregnancy Bali had been present at the death of her husband's younger brother's wife, a young woman taken mortally ill quite unexpectedly.

6 See Wadley (1994:96–102) for a helpful and lucid discussion of honor in a North Indian village. She writes: "A male gains honor, then, by having land and wealth, by being kind to others, by keeping his word, and by having virtuous women who maintain purdah. Families can lose honor through their women . . . by having daughters or daughters-in-law who elope, become pregnant prior to marriage, or are seen outside too often. Men may bring dishonor to a household by stealing, gambling, drinking, and eating taboo foods, and by being unkind or miserly" (99).

7 For persons of the "servant" rank as created from the Cosmic Man's feet, see the famous "hymn of creation" from the *Rig Veda* (for example, in O'Flaherty 1975:27–28). Many anthropologists of India have written about pollution and dirt, especially dirt accumulated on or within human bodies, as one source of low rank in Hindu hierarchies. For two quite different approaches, see Dumont 1972 and Marriott and Inden 1976. For a critique of the enterprise of identifying India with a hierarchical caste system, see Appadurai 1988b.

8 For the different, but symbolically connected, slant on feet in devotional religious discourse, see Kripal 1995. He writes that "feet in India" are the "bridge" uniting the world of the gods and the world of human beings: "Accordingly, that which is lowest on the body of God or the guru . . . is the very highest that humanity, caught in its sufferings and delusions, can ever hope to reach: at the sacred feet, the highest of the low may touch the lowest of the high" (201).

9 Disputed dates locate *Arthashastra*, the famous text on governance, somewhere between 321 B.C.E. and 150 C.E. See also *Laws of Manu*, chapter 7, for still earlier recommendations on rule and punishment (Doniger and Smith 1991).

10 I have found scattered published references to shoe-beating, shoe bans, and other elements of shoes as power in other regions of Rajasthan and India. Examples are found in Moore 1998, and in Dube 1998. Moore, writing of Alwar district in Rajasthan, witnesses an incident involving shoe-beating and shoe-kissing. She sees "a police inspector . . . parade a suspected thief, his hands tied and his face chalky with ash, through the bazaar. The inspector stopped in crowds of shoppers to proclaim the man's crimes and to invite the onlookers to strike him with their shoes. The parade ended at the jail, where the man kissed his captors' polished shoes and pleaded forgiveness" (192). Dube cites an incident described in an interview text from his oral history work in central India. A villager attempts to refuse a demand for a load of grass from the landlord: "The malguzar would say, 'Bastard, you can keep so many animals

in your house but can't bring me grass. Bahen chod [sister fucker] if you don't bring it tomorrow then I will beat you with my shoe' " (91; see also 93).

Ramachandra Guha notes that in the north "peasants would dishonour . . . a grasping official or a corrupt merchant by putting a garland of shoes around his neck" (personal communication, 19 June 2000). Weaver, a journalist, describes a rural Rajasthani women's movement, ending with an account of a village *panchayat* (council) session where an abused woman is awarded by male elders the right to strike her husband and father with a shoe. The article ends: "Sonia walked toward them, calmly and deliberately, and she picked up a shoe and hit both of them on the head. Then she walked away, her honor restored" (1999:61).

11 On caste names for sweepers, see Gold 1998b.

12 See Gold 1988:151, n.24, on the measure of one and one-quarter and its associations with removing inauspiciousness.

13 There was a ready free-association that surprised me, though it shouldn't have, between the display of power hierarchy ranking ruler over peasant, and that ranking men over women; conversationally, from the happier vantage of the present, women especially slipped easily from one to the other.

14 Dube describes something very similar to *pratibandh* in Chhattisgarh, where "shoes, umbrellas, and turbans became focal signs of contest." He quotes one member of the leatherworking community recalling that "if we wore shoes and crossed a Rajput he would say, 'Bastard Chamar, take off your shoes.'" Dube finds that these accounts "underscore that relationships of power and the privileged position of the malguzar [landlord] in Chhattisgarh involved an intermeshing of the ritual hierarchy of purity and pollution, the culturally and ritually constituted dominance of landholding castes, and the forms of power derived from colonial administration" (1998:97).

15 Bourdieu's (1996) insight for Kabyle honor—that the challenge itself involves "the recognition of honour"—is relevant here. It is not dishonoring to be threatened but only to submit; riposte is a major part of the game. However, as Dube (personal communication) correctly observes, the Rajasthani situation is also different because of the caste order in which hierarchy differentiates players in the game. Honor may nonetheless be negotiated at any level of the hierarchy.

16 See Roberts 1989 on trickster lore in the context of slavery for some interesting parallels.

17 The exact nature of this man's misconduct was not divulged.

18 Such generalization of shame is characteristic of "honor and shame" societies according to the anthropological literature. For the now old-fashioned but classic work, see Peristiany 1966. Peristiany and others writing in his mode have been critiqued for essentializing, and have been deconstructed; see, for example, Herzfeld 1987. I nonetheless find some of their observations relevant to Sawar. For example, Peristiany writes: "Honour and shame are the constant preoccupation of individuals in small scale, exclusive societies where face to face personal, as opposed to anonymous, relations are of paramount importance and where the social personality of the actor is as significant as his office. . . . The behaviour of the individual reflects that of his group" (1966:11).

19 The Bhils were, and remain, a disadvantaged tribal group; Weisgrau 1997 offers some insightful perspectives on Rajasthani Bhils today.

20 Bhoju checked on this story again in 1998, and Gokal Mali confirmed that Bhura, son of Bhagirath Mali, was called into the fort and beaten.

21 Charans were sometimes rewarded for service, or poetry, with villages over which they ruled as kings. This Charan ruler now lives in Udaipur; Choti Mehru was within his estate.

22 "You are like a Regar" is, of course, close to home, as the crier was from a lineage of leatherworkers. By "this and that" Kalyan Mali obviously employs a euphemism for whatever strong "insults of the mother" were actually emitted on this occasion.

23 For Shri Kalyanji, see Gold 1988:143–46.

6. Court

1 See Hardiman 1996 for an excellent discussion of merchants and their relationship with kings and peasants; see also Tambs-Lyche 1997 who poses for Kathiawar an alliance between kings and people, and against merchants, that I did not find in Sawar's memories.

2 For the British institution of the Court of Wards in Bihar, see Yang 1989:78–89.

3 See Schomer et al. 1994 on the "idea of Rajasthan," especially the essays by Erdman and Loderick; see also Panagariya and Pahariya 1996.

4 For other scattered details on Mayo College, see Allen and Dwivedi 1984:118–24.

5 I did hear from several oral sources that Vansh Pradip Singh had collected a fine library that unfortunately was sold quickly after his death. At the home of Mathur's sons we saw the original handwritten version of his history of Sawar, as well as a collection of crumbling documents including letters and account records. My interest remained so strongly focused on oral histories that I never went back to catalog those items, although I had initially planned to do so.

6 In my experience, people who were comfortable with English would speak it with me by preference, even if I attempted to speak with them in Hindi. For different reasons, people at ease in Hindi would speak Hindi to me rather than Rajasthani—my comprehension of Rajasthani being evidently less than perfect. However, another explanation is possible in the standoffish pride we see displayed by the Court in bygone days, especially toward foreigners.

7 I have inserted paragraphs for readability. Omitted portions are punctuated by ellipses; brackets indicate my short explanatory insertions, with longer explanations in footnotes. Material in parentheses is Mathur's own.

8 These hunting posts are still there, see chapter 9. When I reported after 1993 on stories of lions in Sawar in living memories, scoffing colleagues convinced me that the terms śer and bāgh—terms that Chaturvedi and Tiwari 1975 translate as "lion" and "tiger," respectively—must both refer only to tigers, or possibly leopards. No lions have inhabited Rajasthan in recent centuries. I went back in 1997 prepared to argue this, but found several persons adamant that there had indeed been lions.

9 This Arabic term for "revenue district" was inherited from Mughal administrators by Rajputs and it is still used today by the present state government.

10   In the pamphlet, which has several other obvious typographical errors, the figure reads 2,500; but there is also a number written out in letters: *ḍhāī sau*, or 250. I must assume—comparing it with the oral accounts—that this lower figure is correct.

11   This was the location of the garden house where we lived in 1997 (see chapter 2).

12   *Niyam* is variously glossed as "rule," "habit," or "regimen," but also includes, unlike those terms, a strong measure of self-restraint (Gold 1995b:437). *Śauk* implies something rather more passionate than interest; glosses in the Hindi-English dictionary include desire, yearning, predilection, fancy, eagerness, pleasure, hobby—all of which are relevant.

13   See Waghorne (1994) for a very interesting study of kingship in South India from colonial, indigenous, and intersecting perspectives; especially relevant is chapter 9, "The Iconic Body of the King." The author describes a photograph: "There is nothing solid, nothing stable, about this picture. Even the raja's royal dress is so ornate, so intensely glittering, that it appears surreal. If this king were the center of society, the nature of that very society would be a study in relativity. . . . Neither flesh nor spirit, this royal being sits quite visible to the eye . . . a sensual being without a solid body. He remains a most interesting theo-logical proposition" (225).

14   McGregor 1993 defines *tehsīldār* precisely as a "subcollector of revenue."

15   See Kautilya 1987:147–48 on the king's daily schedule; see also Rudolph and Rudolph (1967:216–25) on Gandhi's daily regimen, compared with that of Benjamin Franklin. Dube (personal communication) suggests that the implication of the Court's *niyam* may be a "regimentation of time itself" and thus an extension of royal authority.

16   L. P. Rangarajan (1987) writes: "There is extensive evidence in the *Arthashastra* on Kautilya's concern for the welfare of animals. Regulations for the protection of wild life, a long list of punishments for cruelty to animals, rations for animals, regulations on grazing and the responsibility of veterinary doctors are some of the major topics. . . . Killing or injuring protected species and animals in reserved parks and sanctuaries was prohibited. . . . Rations are laid down for horses and elephants, including special rations for tired horses" (96).

17   On the importance of oxen and of treating them well, see the Rajasthani oral epic tale of Lord Dev Narayan, recorded by J. C. Miller in Ghatiyali. Near the beginning of the tale is an episode where a white ox appears in the court of God, demanding a boon, which is granted: "The white (ox) who (is kept) hungry, his owner will remain hungry. And he who keeps the white (ox) satiated, his owner will remain satiated" (Miller 1994:360).

18   Following a precedent set, I believe, by Kirin Narayan (1989), I use here and throughout the book an asterisk after any term within a translation from Hindi or Rajasthani that was originally English. The English word "public" is often used by nonliterate speakers who do not regularly pepper their Hindi or Rajasthani with English words. It is understood as part of the local language.

19   See, however, Kalyan Mali's story about wild pigs in chapter 9 for the *darbār* in memory at least claiming to fast on the eleventh. Note also that in Kalyan Mali's tale the *darbār* succumbs to his public's petition; but in this Daroga version he fakes them out and does what he pleases, as usual.

20 The term used here is *nār*, a variant of *nāhar*, which according to the *RSK* is equivalent to *sinh* and *śer*. McGregor 1993 tells us that *nāhar* is Brajbhasha and Avadi for either "tiger" or "lion"—which doesn't help our quest for zoological precision.

21 For Mewar's pride and glory, see Tod 1978; Allen and Dwivedi write of the Udaipur ruler in 1874 that he is "proudest of all the Rajputs: the Maharana of Mewar" (1984:57).

22 Allen and Dwivedi (1984:284) includes a 1937 photograph of Bhopal Singh, the last ruling Maharana of Mewar.

23 Apparently he wishes to watch them mating.

24 Bankat Singh Kamdar, for example, told us: "In the stables there were fifty-three horses, all in Sawar, Ghatiyali, and Devli; and three elephants. One of the elephants came to him from Suhava (village) in dowry; and one he bought from a party of holy men. And one elephant the Maharana of Udaipur [Mevar's capital], Bhopal Singh, gave him because he liked his hunting."

25 See Vidal 1997 on hierarchical and egalitarian relations among Rajputs.

26 This topic is one area where my foreign identity inhibited people who did not wish to offend me but hinted that the repugnance for shaking hands had to do with the well-known deficient and repellent sanitation habits of English people—that is, their failure to clean with water after defecation. See, however, Mayaram who reports on the reputation of the Alwar *rājā* who wore gloves when shaking hands with the British. She suggests that his "refusal to shake hands with Europeans unless he was wearing gloves seems derived from rituals reversing colonial protocol as much as from notions of pollution" (1997:59–61).

27 On the role of Charans in the courts of Rajasthan, see, for example, Kathuria 1987: 206–17; for some of the legendary attributes of Charans, see M. H. Singh 1990:114–18. Ujwal (n.d.) is a Charan's own account that is focused hagiographically on the community's goddess Karni Ma, but it is also revealing of the Charan role in Rajput politics.

28 At present the sharecropping, or *sīrī*, system is pervasive in the Sawar area, but it was not practical in the days of kings because not enough would be left to divide after the Court took its "lion's share."

29 See Yang 1989:123–29 for a description of "estate bureaucracy" in Bihar in the late nineteenth century, where we see the roles of *tehsīldār* and *paṭwārī* in action.

30 This interview was disrupted by a drunken Rajput, laughing insanely, another member of the royal Shaktavat lineage. In all my years in Rajasthan I had never seen a man out of control, publicly drunk, in broad daylight. Bhoju and Bankat Singh attempted to ignore him, but the interview suffered from his wild interjections and general hilarity.

31 Devli Gaon should not be confused with the nearby city of Devli. The latter was set up during the British administration as a military base, which it remains today as well as being a thriving commercial center in Bhilwara district.

32 According to the *RSK*, *kāmdār* is a manager working for a king, landowner, or merchant.

33 This Sanskrit term means a deputy, an assistant, lieutenant, or vice-regent (like a vice-president, who takes over if the president is away or sick).

34 According to McGregor 1993 this comes from the English word "number," with the persian suffix *dār* added to give it the meaning of a village headman responsible for the government revenue.

35 *Rasālat* is not in any of my dictionaries; it may be a vernacular form of the Sanskrit *aśvashālā*, meaning "stables."

36 On a cash economy, markets, and trade in rural areas under colonialism, see Fuller 1989; S. Sen 1998; and Yang 1998.

37 According to Mathur (1977), Jasvant Singh adopted Madho Singh in 1856. Madho Singh lived until 1936 and was the father of Ummed Singh, who was the father of Vansh Pradip Singh.

38 Ramachandra Guha writes: "In common with other chiefdoms/kingdoms, Sawar seems to have started its forest department in imitation of the British. The British showed them the political and commercial benefits of state reserves. State forests were a genuinely colonial contribution. The detailed rules you describe—what villagers and their cattle could and could not do in the forest—would be a product specifically of the late 19th century" (personal communication 2000).

39 According to the RSK, *bīṛ* is an alternate form of *bīṛau*, from Sanskrit. Its meanings include "a field of protected grass in which others are not allowed to graze"; grazing land; and *jangal* (see chapter 9).

40 See Raheja and Gold 1994:61.

41 From the Persian, meaning "heap, pile, store, storehouse, granary."

42 *Mahuā* is "the tree *Bassia latifolia* and its flower, from which an intoxicating drink is distilled" (McGregor 1993); I suspect *mahuā* flowers were imported, as I never heard this tree listed among those indigenous to the Banas Basin.

43 *Jhupara* means hut, and *kherā* means hamlet. The village called Tikhalya listed here is probably different from the one Govind Singh named as within Sawar tehsil.

44 I am unsure about the intention of Gendi's insult; usually these particular words have attached "*kā*," so that the meaning is actually "of penis-eaters" and the implication, as with most bad insults, reflects on the mother—that she is sexually voracious. Here we did not hear the *kā*; nonetheless, the implication does not, I believe, have anything to do with oral sex but rather with sexual hunger.

45 The Charan of Rajpura told us this about the end of the dogs: "The *darbār* had five to seven dogs. So there was a sweeper named Harbura, he took the dogs [after the *darbār*'s death] but a few days later they died . . . because they were used to eating halva, so they died in the sweeper's house."

46 Although Suva Lal makes it sound as if Suraj Karan did this work of awakening the people almost singlehandedly, other evidence shows that he was part of a larger movement (see Pande 1988).

47 At Mathur's home was a lengthy typescript in English with full details of this case.

48 For princes, see Allen and Dwivedi 1984; for epic kings, see Gold 1992; Miller 1994; and Smith 1991.

49 For varied strategies, personalities, and politics of Rajasthan's princes in the late nineteenth and first half of the twentieth century, see Vidal 1997 on Sirohi; Mayaram 1997 on Alwar and Bharatpur; Stern 1988 on Jaipur; and Copland 1997, where the

argument encompasses more than a dozen kingdoms that were major "players" in the "endgame" of empire. On the lesser princes of Ajmer we do not have many detailed studies; see, however, Joshi 1972.

50 For the resistance movement (*āndolan*) in Bijoliya, see Pande 1974, 1988 and H. Singh 1998:126–56. On protests within Ajmer itself, see Pande 1988:1–74. Ray 1978 documents agrarian unrest in Mewar.

51 See Bhadra on a Bengali text that critiques the "bad agents" of the king, while the king himself is "necessarily more just, more responsible and kinder" (1989:82).

7. Homes

1 *Gharū* ("belonging to the home") is an adjective used to describe land and livestock that are one's own; a critical distinction as emerges in the first interview.

2 See Gold 2000a for an extensive discussion of this literature.

3 For the double homes and single lives of women, see Raheja and Gold 1994; for women's strategic uses of multiple kin relationships, see especially pp. 73–120.

4 This is *samvat* 1996, or 1939–40 C.E.; according to Kachhawaha 1985 there was severe famine in Ajmer-Merwara in 1939–40, corresponding with the famine commonly referred to as the "'96 famine" in Ghatiyali.

5 Michael Ondaatje's novel *The English Patient* includes a reference to the British marking Indian recruits with chalk (1993:200); thanks to Gloria Raheja for calling this to my attention.

6 *Ghasbā lagyā* means, literally, "to rub us"; idiomatically, "to overwork us."

7 No person utters their spouse's name. Sukh Devji refers to his future wife as "Bhoju's mother."

8 I cannot find this disease in the RSK; it could be a variant of *vāyu*, or "wind," which would not be a disease name but, as one of the humors in Ayurvedic medicinal theory, implicated as a cause of disease.

9 Infant and child mortality rates at that time were very high. Unfathomable as this series of losses sounds to modern American readers, these numbers are not unusual for this era.

10 *Nātā* is a very common practice among Gujars and other farming communities; both Bhoju's and his sister's current happy unions are *nātā*. Nonetheless, it is culturally devalued, and I believe this, plus the expense that fell in part on his shoulders, is what Sukh Devji is lamenting here—on top of the acute human tragedy of losing three young women in a short space of time.

11 Note the importance of patrimony, as unlikely as it is that Bhoju would ever move to Gokulpura, which is a small and remote Gujar village. However, when Bhoju was posted as a teacher to Gandher it was clearly a plus that Gujar children from Gokulpura were in his classes. He too feels the paternal connection.

12 Joe Miller has recorded Sukh Devji speaking of the importance of Dev Narayan in his life (personal communication).

13 In her interview Raji employs a variety of circumlocutions in referring to her spouse. Women play a game of teasingly trying to get one another to pronounce their hus-

band's name, and they were always both enchanted and scandalized by my own shameless readiness to do so.

14 Raji says *mausī*, meaning "mother's sister"; in Sukh Devji's account, his Ghati-yali connection was his father's brother's wife's mother. According to Bhoju, this person was not immediate kin of any description, but rather a "distant relation" (*dūr riśtā*).

15 Eli Gold was then five years old; recall that Sukh Devji said he was ten. There is a general carelessness in reporting age; no one among this generation kept track of birthdays. But it is also true that Eli was much larger than Ghatiyali children; at age five he probably looked at least eight to Raji.

16 At weddings today, Gujar girls ideally should have a full set of silver ornaments for wrists, ankles, neck, and waist; all of this Raji now possesses.

17 This was a thoughtless question; Gujar marriage customs have always stressed gifts from the groom's side to the bride's. Dowry has entered the picture only in recent years in the process earlier anthropologists dubbed "Sanskritization," however inade-quate the concept.

18 This is the Dev Narayan shrine that has blessed this family with the births of sons: not only of Bhoju, but of Bhoju's first son Kuldip (who is called Monu). The shrine is located not far from Gokulpura.

19 As we relisten to this interview Bhoju tells me that, according to Lord Dev Narayan, Gujars should sell neither milk nor sons. That is, they should not give their sons into service jobs, and they should not peddle milk.

20 *Chhāch* is a nutritious byproduct of churning that might be given to the poor or returned to the livestock. It actually makes a delicious, cooling drink with spices and salt, but people think of it as cheap or poor.

21 There would be matching amounts of sugar, oil, etcetera to make a full feast, but the size is measured by grain.

22 See Gold 1988:190–261 for the Rajasthani practice of taking the bones of deceased kin to the Ganges River at Hardwar, returning home with Ganges water, celebrating this water in a festival called Gangoj, and feasting the community afterwards. It is perhaps increasingly common to hold collective funeral feasts in advance for persons still living because of the expense and the risk of legal penalties involved each time.

23 See the appendix for plant identifications.

24 This is not only a mother's perspective; Sukh Devji himself has expressed anger about his daughter's first husband's ill treatment of her, and satisfaction at her current successful marriage.

25 When the power was out in Ghatiyali for over a week, and getting wheat ground was rather difficult, Raji took to rising at 4 A.M. and grinding grain—in spite of many protests from family members about the nerve-grating noise and about her needlessly taking on this extra work. The grain could have been sent by cycle or bus to a place where the power mills were running. Raji, however, was evidently enjoying herself as well as making a statement.

26 Bhoju explained to me later that the little Brahmin bride's family had for her benefit

established with the carpenter family the fictive kin relationship called *jholī rakhnā* or *jholī bhāī*. Such relationships are established when a family marries a daughter into a village where they have no relations. She is adopted, literally "kept in the pouch" or *jholī*, by a family in her marital village (often of a different caste) in whose house she has the status not of bride but daughter. The male members of the household that shelters her in this way become *jholī* brothers to males of her natal home. Thus women find comfort and support in their marital homes from at least one household. This certainly provided Jhanku with an important refuge.

27 To tell soothing lies to children, promising them whatever they are weeping for, whether they will ever get it or not, is a regular practice still in Ghatiyali. Although I never got used to it, it is a completely routine part of adult interactions with children.

28 To roast newly ripened wheat grains on the stalk and eat them in the fields is a pleasure savored by farmers. The special term for grains roasted on the stalk is pronounced *dhāṇgī* in Ghatiyali, but appears in the RSK as *dhāṇī*.

29 Shobhag Kanvar was subject and heroine of the only life-history narrative I have previously published (Raheja and Gold 1994:164–81).

30 For a detailed discussion of gender in Rajput ideologies and practices, contrasted particularly with those of Girasias (a group identified as tribal), see Unnithan-Kumar 1997.

31 Here she uses a current time indicator—Ram Dhuni. As part of recent Hindu revival efforts instigated by the Hindu nationalist movement following the troubles in Ayodhya in the early 1990s, a Ram Dhuni group was formed in Ghatiyali. They march through the village every morning in the predawn hours, drumming and singing of Ram. This has become an alarm clock for the village. Morning star-rise (*tārā ugtā*) is an old-fashioned way to name an early morning hour; that time of day is also called "the time of grinding."

32 Other Rajputs told me, and we will see in chapter 9 as well, that the Sawar Court did not look with favor on anyone's hunting or eating pig meat, whatever their birth or rank. However, Motiya Kanvar's account makes it clear that some favored Rajputs must have had some immunity. The Court himself had assisted in Motiya Kanvar's marriage arrangements, as she related in another part of the interview that I have not included here.

33 This is a saying meaning that although they are so mutually dependent, husband and wife do not often die at the same time.

34 Kesar refers to the wall built as a boundary to a designated protected area that is patrolled by the local forestry agent.

35 See Gold 1992 for a similar phrase in describing a beautiful woman in Nath oral performances.

36 On the trope of sorrows in South Asian life-history narratives, see Grima 1992 and Wilce 1998.

37 A recent issue of *India Today* features an article set in Sawar's little hamlet of Napa ka Khera. The author reports on bride selling and the general disempowerment of women among the Minas there (Parihar 1999).

38   This strikes me as a very high number of livestock, given the poverty and hunger she claims afflicted her in this family.

39   To be married into a family of unmarried males is a fabled disadvantage; see the women's worship tale titled "The Brahmin's Daughter and the Five Bachelors" in Gold 1995b.

40   *Ūṛra ann ko kuṇ ko bhī mārā peṭ me na diyo.*

41   She uses *kuvās*, an old-fashioned and polite word for barber.

42   See H. Singh (1998) for a protest song, addressed to farmers, against Rajput abuses recorded during the movement in Bijoliya, which includes the line, "You let your relatives and guests sleep on the floor, while the *thikana* functionaries grab your cots and beds" (105).

43   See especially the stories of Mahasveta Devi for powerful visions of the subjection of low-caste women to high-caste males—stories of seduction, corruption, and abandonment (Bardhan 1990; Devi 1995). On a possible medieval European counterpart, *droit de cuissage* ("right of the lord to spend the first night of the wedding with the bride"), see Boureau 1995, who claims this "custom" is a myth. The Hindi film *Mirch Masala* ("Spices") is a gripping story of village women's collective resistance defending one of themselves against a high-ranking male who desires her sexual favors.

44   From rumors of rumors I gather that women from other communities were also procured for Rajput pleasure.

45   Chamar is a caste name for leatherworker communities throughout North India, while Regar seems more regionally limited (Briggs 1920). In Sawar the two are distinct communities, with Regars more numerous. Both were traditionally occupied with tanning hides, sewing leather goods, and disposing of dead livestock.

46   This passing, shocking reference to a Rajput woman sexually aggressive with a Regar man was so beyond the pale that we did not discuss it at all. Bhoju did not ask Modu Lal about it, and I did not ask Bhoju about it.

47   For various approaches to devotional religion viewed both as complicit with and subversive of caste hierarchies, see Dube 1998; Gold 1998b; R. Guha 1989; Apffel-Marglin 1995; and Zelliot 1992.

48   For an association of the Regar community with the Ganges River in a nearby region of Rajasthan, see K. L. Sharma, who writes, "Raigars have great faith in Gangamai" (1998:135).

49   On Raidas, see Callewaert and Friedlander 1992 and Hawley 1988:9–32.

50   Today the Ghatiyali Regars are farmers and herders and none perform any of their traditional "degrading" tasks. Someone has to be called from another village when an animal dies, and the smelly practice of tanning hides has completely ceased. Even so the Regars still have a very low status.

51   Variants of these stories are found in Briggs' study of Chamars from the first half of the twentieth century (1920:208–10). Callewaert and Friedlander, in their study of Raidas's life and work (1992:28–29), also report a version of the Ganga offering story, although it does not include specific reference to the tanning pit.

8. Fields

1 Gold 1989 reviews some classic literature on royal and yogic powers.

2 In a letter to me in 1998, Bhoju summarized those elements of the taxation system that he found most critical—synthesizing salient features from all we had heard in scores of interviews. I believe he hoped to staunch the stream of questions I was mailing him with this admirably succinct account. Bhoju's words gave the jist of our findings elaborated in chapter 8.

> The Sawar Court used to take one-fourth [of the crop] from the Rajputs and the Dhabhai (who were Bajar Gujars). So for this reason, Rajput and Dhabhai used to be called "quarter-givers." For the rest, from all the *jātis*, the Court took one-half. And whatever land the Court had granted to temples or to deities' places was called *ḍolī*; from this he used to take nothing at all.
>
> They did the *kūṁtā* on irrigated land—an estimation of the amount of maunds of production. Until the estimation took place, nobody was allowed to eat roasted chickpeas, or roasted grain, or any kind of grain—nor could they take any of this home. When the estimation was done, at that time the bosses, the village crier, the revenue accountant, the land-record officer—all those "sickles"—used to go to the fields, and they took their *lāg*. So, these were called *lāg*: "the town crier's *lāg*," "the manager's *lāg*," and so forth.
>
> In some parts of this area, where the land is not irrigated, there is only one crop a year, watered only by rain. On this they used to do the *lāṭā*. All the harvesting was done at the same time, and all the grain was brought to one threshing ground. The *lāṭā* was done in that single place. The government's watchman stayed there. And until the distribution of grain was performed, the farmers could not take any kind of grain to their homes. Here too, at the time of the *lāṭā*, the village crier, the managers, and the land-record officer used to take their *lāg*. They took from the farmer's grain share, not from the ruler's grain share.

3 On *jagīrdārī* a great deal has been written: D. Singh 1964:31–50 thoroughly details the system; see also, for example, Rudolph and Rudolph 1984:50–53 and B. K. Sharma 1990:11–18. See also Neale's (1969) still suggestive discussion of the meanings of "land control" (rather than land ownership) in nineteenth- and twentieth-century India. And for a lucid discussion of Rajput dominance as based on "rights in the produce of the land," see Unnithan-Kumar 1997:48.

4 Other more general meanings for *bāṇṭo* include "the action of dividing something" and simply "share" or "portion."

5 Dictionaries help us to understand the merging of meanings in these terms. *Lāg* is defined in McGregor as, among other things, "due expenditure, cost, ground-rent." In the RSK the Hindi glosses for *lāg* include *neg, dakṣiṇā,* and *lagān;* the latter translates as "rent payable or accruing on land, or assessment on land;" *neg,* on the other hand, means "presents given at marriages and other auspicious occasions." *Dakṣiṇā* is usually an additional respectful donation to a Brahmin who has rendered priestly services. Hence there is a peculiar and meaningful merging here of honorific gift, charity, tax, and land rent—and that is more or less the way it was in Sawar. Raheja (personal communication, 30 May 1998) suggests that "the language of *lāg* and *neg* here might

have been a language used to cast a blanket of legitimacy, so to speak, over these practices, and that this language and perspective might not have been shared by those from whom the 'payments' were extracted." In marriage transactions, *lāg* and *neg* are gifts that the recipient has a right to claim. Colonial ethnographers gleaned these terms from high-caste mediators not from farmers, who likely felt that many who squeezed such fees out of them had virtually no right to take them.

6 Literally "masters of the fields."

7 For the "grain heap" as an organizing political metaphor in rural North India, see Neale 1962:21. He draws from Bennett's "Final Settlement Report on the Gonda District," in which Bennett describes the "basis of the whole society" as "the grain heap, in which each constituent rank had its definite interest" (cited in Neale 1962:21). See also Fuller's critique of Neale (1989).

8 B. K. Sharma refers briefly to "lata and Kunta" as "another method" of assessing the royal share in Rajasthan, "under which the produce was estimated by the officials of the standing crop" (1990:16). K. L. Sharma speaks of "the system of *lata* and *kunta*," observing that "the kunta was assessed on the estimated yield of the standing crops. Generally, it was 50 per cent of the estimated yield, but at times it was even more" (1998:99). See also Mukta 1994:84. Fuller notes that "already, possibly by the fourteenth century, a system (*kankut*) had been introduced which relied on making estimates of the harvest beforehand, so that the royal assessors did not need to visit each and every village to collect their dues at harvest time." His chief point is that in North India by the sixteenth and seventeenth centuries millions of cultivators were taxed "according to an assessment system which in practice (if not in its originating logic) had ceased to depend on shares in the actual harvest at all" (1989:44–45). However, although an estimation system was in practice in Sawar by the early twentieth century, it neither kept the royal agents out of the villages nor dissociated land revenue from harvest share.

9 In this it differs slightly from a Hindi "echo" construction such as *roṭī-voṭī* (bread and everything you eat with it), where the second term is a nonsense term and the echoing implies "and so forth." It is more like the conventional pairing of two differentiated items, such as *kamīz-salvār* (top and pants, a matched two-piece woman's outfit), that together form a unit.

10 See, however, S. P. Gupta, who suggests that *lāto* meant "estimate of the sheafs" in the eighteenth century (1986:177 n.69).

11 See Appadurai 1990 for estimation versus precise measurement in modernizing Indian agriculture.

12 Govind Singh alternates confusingly here from a specific weight amount to a proportionate amount.

13 The term *jholī* is the same for the bag in which a bard, holy person, or beggar collects grain charity. I have heard this word used in derogatory import in modern times, but I am unsure whether the "sickles" having *jholī* is deliberately meant to liken them to aggressive beggars.

14 See Yang (1989) for a very useful historical discussion of the local operations of "*qanungo*" (*kānūngo*) and *paṭwārī* in Bihar under British rule. Yang traces transfor-

mations of the roles of these two as the British and the gentry both tried to enhance their own control over revenue records. From Yang we learn that "in the Mughal administrative system . . . the *qanungo* . . . was the government agent and the *patwari* . . . spoke for the village" (97–103). For *qānūngo* in Rajasthan under Mughal rule, see S. P. Gupta 1986:174–76.

15 See Pande for a moment in 1949 when this distinction becomes a matter of dispute in the kingdom of Bhinai; the grain has been threshed but farmers insist that not "lat" but "koonta" (for which it is now too late) is the only acceptable form of assessment (1988, 3:51–55). By 1949, in neighboring Sawar, no one was paying either *lāṭo* or *kūṭo.*

Gyan Prakash reports two systems in operation in nineteenth-century Bihar called *batai* and *dānābandi,* which appear to be exactly equivalent: "Under batai, the actual produce was brought to the threshing floor and was divided between the landlord and the peasant. In danabandi, however, the division was based on the estimate of the ripe crop in the field." The latter method, he notes, defeats "the peasant practice of pilfering from the crop before it was brought for division," but could only work if the landlord "possessed a reliable bureaucracy which would not collude with peasants in estimating the crop" (1990:113–14).

16 See Raheja 1988:163 for an elaborate marking of the grain pile in an Uttar Pradesh village, before ritual prestations to Brahmin priests are made by Gujar landowners.

17 He uses the strong Hindi term *atyāchār,* which translates as "atrocity, tyranny, excess, outrage." This is a literate Brahmin's language, and not a term I heard from farmers.

18 A patron-client or "*jajmani* system" existed in Sawar's villages before Independence and land reform. Today only residual elements remain, as the cash economy grows rapidly more powerful. See Wiser 1988 for a classic study; see Raheja 1988:204–5 for distribution of grain to client castes at the threshing ground in an Uttar Pradesh village. In Ghatiyali usage, Kamin meant generally those castes taking shares of the harvest in exchange for services. However, McGregor gives "low, base; a base person, a person belonging to a community of low status" as a definition.

19 According to the *RSK, kārū* means "Bhil, Chamar, Mina and so forth; a person of the castes that are counted as 'small,' " that is, as "low."

20 See Raheja (1988:162–63), however, on the way that grain donations to Brahmins at harvest are qualitatively different from those to other client castes.

21 *Adhikār* means "rights, power." This important term recurs frequently in our interviews and is most often used when the exploitative aspects of rule are evoked. By contrast, another word, *zimmedārī,* meaning "responsibility" or "responsible authority" tends to describe another aspect of rule that combines involvement and identity with protection and care. See Gold and Gujar 1995; Gold 2001a; and chapter 9, this volume.

22 Today chickpea leaves are not considered appropriate food for human consumption.

23 For coexisting multiple legal systems in another region of present-day Rajasthan, see Moore 1998.

24 I have translated as "dispute-settlement" the word *nyāy,* which could also be rendered as "justice"; however, justice as a word is so heavily laden in English that a colleague

has advised me to avoid it. The process to which Ugma refers is above all a process of mediation rather than one of abstract judgment.

25 That is, besides working their "own" land for only half of the harvest, they had to work the crown lands and receive minimal pay.

26 As we wrote notes on this interview, Bhoju felt impelled to inform me that even today any sweeper who wishes to ride a horse requires police protection. He said that at one recent wedding there were "more police than wedding guests" to protect a sweeper; and at another a Chamar was forced to make his horseback procession around the village after 11 p.m. so that everyone would be asleep and no one would come out to see him.

27 Bhairuji (Bhairava) is a form of Shiva, always present near any goddess (see Gold 1988).

28 For oracular possession by deities, called *bhāv* in Sawar, see Gold 1988:95, 154–86.

29 Madhav Singh is Vansh Pradip Singh's grandfather. See Gold 1992 for a legendary episode similar to this in the tale of King Bharthari.

30 On the strategy of flight, see Dube: "Chamars, along with other day laborers and ploughmen, adopted the desertion of villages as a mode of resisting officeholders, landlords, and rich peasants. . . . We should not underestimate the difficulties in-volved in the strategy of flight . . . but it offered poor ploughmen and farm servants a feasible way to resist and retain their bargaining power" (1998:32–33).

31 The village herd is called *gher;* the king's herd is called *gorelā.*

32 *Khāvaryā* is derived from *khāvno,* "to eat." This insulting term means, according to Bhoju, "those who live only to eat."

9. Jungle

1 Because my writing also began with trees and pigs, many but not all of the materials in this chapter have been previously published; fragments appear in Gold with Gujar 1997, Gold 1998a; Gold 1998c; Gold 1999b; Gold 2000b; and Gold 2001a. Each of these writings was shaped for particular audiences and publications. Needless to say, my understandings have developed and changed not only with additional fieldwork but with readings in secondary literature.

2 Today, uncultivated common lands are subject to a variety of competing claims, includ-ing encroachment by farmers, and enclosure for government and non-governmental forestry projects. There is a cognitive gulf involved in the category "wasteland" as applied by the British, as well as by the present state government, to areas users understand as pastureland (*charagāh*). For both popular and governmental ap-proaches to uncultivated land in Rajasthan, see Brara 1992.

3 For further elucidation of "jungle" and *jangal* in South Asia, see Dove 1994. On the basis of fieldwork in Pakistan, Dove argues persuasively that a dialectical "linkage between cultural and natural systems" is at work in linguistic transformations and, moreover, that this linkage "has implications for the political relationship between local communities and central governments" (91–92). Although the Pakistani situa-tion is slightly different from the Rajasthani case, Dove's apt conclusion that "how

Notes to Chapter Nine ❧ 359

society views nature is in part a function of how society has affected nature and how nature has affected society (110)" is certainly germane to Sawar.

4 Bhoju says that the expression used here, *hāth se hāth nahīṁ dikhnā*, may be employed to describe a very dark night or a dense sandstorm.

5 For memories of abundant forest in Bengal as adding to life's difficulty and dangers, see Sivaramakrishnan 1997.

6 Many place names in Sawar record vanished landscape features, as we saw in chapter 3. For discussions of the ways that language and oral traditions—including place names—contain ecological memories, see Basso 1996 and Lambek 1998.

7 See the most recent *Census of India* handbook for Ajmer district, which states: "The forests play a very important role in the economy of the district. They meet the requirements of villagers in respect of agricultural implements and timber for their hutments and provide grazings. The wood is used as fuel in towns and villages" (1994: lxv).

8 Gold and Gujar 1994 contains some discussion of the uses of wild plants in Ghatiyali; see also Appadurai 1991a.

9 On "minor forest products" under colonialism, see Sundar 1997:110–12. Joshi 1995 provides an extensive survey of the wide variety of plant uses by tribals in Rajasthan. Many items he documents are also found in agricultural villages.

10 See Gold 2000b for a considerably more speculative but less sketchy discussion of these matters.

11 Falk 1973 offers a thoughtful conceptual survey drawing on Hindu and Buddhist sources; McGee 2000 presents an illuminating discussion of kings and trees in Sanskrit texts. For strong associations between kingship and environmental well-being in precolonial Tamilnad, see Ludden 1984:51–99 and Ludden 1995:35–73. Waghorne, also writing on South India, gives some insights into the relationship between kings and wild animals and forest lands, both in Pudukkottai, the location of her study, and in the broader literature on Hindu kingship. She writes: "These strong suggestions of a special relationship between the Pudukkottai raja and the domain of the forest appears to be part of a broader South Asian motif" (1994:176–88).

12 For example, in his brief account of the life of Vansh Pradip Singh, Goyal notes: "He was so concerned about the protection of the gardens that if he saw a tree branch cut he would become extremely angry" (1987:7; my translation).

13 A number of references to their uses and lore found their way into my earlier writings. See, for example, Gold 1988:134–35, 163–64, 248–50 and Gold and Gujar 1995. References include *pīpal* tree weddings; divine punishments for harming *nīm* trees; and cures involving "sweeping with *nīm* leaves." In my years living in Ghatiyali I saw banyan leaves used for curing stomachaches, and I tried *nīm* leaf cures on my own skin afflictions.

14 In Gold and Gujar 1994 is a children's story of a poor boy who finds shelter under a nurturing banyan tree; in Gold 1995a is the story of a girl, expelled from her mother's house, who takes refuge in a *pīpal* tree and is magically nourished there.

15 See Miller 1994.

16 For Bishnois and their religion, see Fisher 1997:64–70 and Khan 1997:187–208.

17 One version is retold in Gold and Gujar 1995.

18 W. J. Lupton, "Improvement of Agriculture" (Ajmer: Rajasthan State Archives, Ajmer Branch, 1908, unpublished document).

19 On colonial ideas about nature, Arnold 1996 gives a lucid and illuminating historical account; and Grove 1995, 1998 offers a contextualized synthesis.

20 Dictionaries consulted include Bulcke 1971; Lalas 1962–1978; McGregor 1993; and Sundardas 1965.

21 Sanskritist Gary Tubb writes of *zimmedārī*: "It is also a Persian legal term, from the Arabic 'zimma,' responsibility. It refers to a person who is legally responsible for something in any of a number of ways, which to my knowledge are not spoken of together in Sanskrit law, and therefore as far as I know there is no Sanskrit term that is remotely equivalent to it" (personal communication, 1998).

22 Evidently there is a scale factor here; personal vigilance such as Vansh Pradip Singh's simply would not be possible in a much larger domain. Even in Sawar, our interviews in remote areas revealed far less remembered hypersensitivity to the Court's will.

23 Bhinai, a kingdom larger than Sawar, also was under the British in Ajmer.

24 This is probably a reference to the Mina's dispute with the Court over an acacia tree (described in chapter 8).

25 "Good-for-nothing" (nālāyak; a relatively mild expression) was reported by many to have been the *darbār*'s strongest insult—yet was an insult feared by his subjects. Given the rich and earthy imagery of everyday insult language in the village, this reflects the court's gentility.

26 These are *nīm, pīpal,* and *baṛ*.

27 Darogas were attached as high-ranking servants to royal families. Daroga women were often concubines to the Rajput rulers; their offspring, within three generations, may be granted Rajput status.

28 This man's memories seem to merge the time when the shade trees were newly planted and the time when they were fully grown.

29 Char is a Gujar lineage.

30 *Khaṇgeṭyā* is a word in local language, and I have not located it in any dictionary. According to Bhoju, *khaṇgeṭyā* is the Rajasthani word for *giragiṭ*—Hindi for chameleon. Chameleons, however, have a diet of insects, not greenery. Possibly the lizards were chewing or clawing the seedlings without eating them.

31 Bhils are considered a "tribal" group; they are sometimes hunters. In Sawar they were bonded laborers to the court.

32 Although it would be zoologically more proper to use the English "boar" for the nondomesticated species, I believe it is truer to Rajasthani usage to translate "*janglī suar*" as "wild pig." In spite of a strong distinction made between domestic and wild pigs in terms of the animals' eating habits and the relative desirability of their meat for human consumption, they share significant elements in the semantic domain of piggishness, and the term *suar* is normally used for both. Wild boars figure in Hindu mythology; for an in-depth study of the Sanskritic deity Vishnu's majestic "boar incarnation," see Nagar 1993. For ritualized and comic boar hunt episodes in South Indian regional epics and religious dramas, see Beck 1982 and Hiltebeitel

1991:225–26. I cannot pursue here the intriguing but tenuous connections with mythic boar lore.

33 See Gold with Gujar 1997 for examples of hunting paintings that depict boars.

34 For wild pigs as threats to crops in Rajasthan, see MacKenzie 1988:187 and K. Singh 1977:497. Writing about all of India, Sukumar states that "damage by wild pig is probably the most widespread" and notes that "pigs are commonly killed for this reason but this is not a major conservation issue anywhere" (1994:304–5). Seshadri says of the wild boar: "The farmers consider it a particular enemy and set upon it, but it is a survivor, and does not deplete easily" (1986:76). For ritual and political signifi-cance of boar hunts in Maharashtra, see Sontheimer 1997:286–88.

35 See Tedlock 1983 for "oral history as poetry," "ethnography as interaction," and other illuminating insights into fieldwork, recorded memories, and transcribing performed narratives.

36 The term translated as widow is *rāṇḍ*. The implication is that women are "widowed" because the men have to sleep in the fields in order to protect their crops from pigs. There may also be a hint that women alone in the house are tempted to infidelities, the other common meaning of *rāṇḍ* being "slut."

37 See Gold 1988:41–44.

38 Although there is no further reference to this fact, this day is even now the occasion of Ghatiyali's largest religious fair. This might explain why a significantly large group could gather thus, spontaneously, without being summoned by the crier as they would be for a regular village council meeting. Four-Arms temple is very close to the Tejaji shrine where the fair takes place and where many men would have gathered anyway for the celebration. This reference also tells us that the event in question took place in the bright half of Bhadrapad, well into the rainy season, when the crops would have been growing nicely and the depredation of pigs all the more detestable.

39 When I originally published this text (Gold with Gujar 1997), I accepted the *darbār*'s fast at face value. As chapter 6 revealed, however, interviews conducted afterward informed us that Vansh Pradip Singh was notorious for *not* fasting on the eleventh, which makes it likely that Kalyan Mali and everyone involved perceive the refusal to meet the complainants as a ruse on the Court's part.

40 This is a phrase straight out of epic poetry; it may mean that one is detached from families in a religiously superior way, like a renouncer; or it may mean that one is pathetically alone, as helpless as an orphan, without recourse (Gold 1992:196).

41 Recall that the *darbār* once received a bullet wound in the foot.

42 Refusing food is a time-honored strategy to establish both sympathy and power. Here again, as with the fast on the eleventh, the *darbār* is represented deploying his religious virtue to control an unruly populace, but they are evidently not impressed.

43 In India in this era, wildlife protection was not necessarily a high moral enterprise. Even Gandhi did not take an absolute stand on nonviolence toward troublesome animals; the Mahatma wrote in 1946: "If I wish to be an agriculturist and stay in the jungle, I will have to use the minimum unavoidable violence in order to protect my fields. I will have to kill monkeys, birds and insects which eat up my crops. . . . To

allow crops to be eaten up by animals in the name of ahimsa, while there is a famine in the land, is certainly a sin" (Gandhi 1946:60).

44 To my surprise, blue bull (*Boselaphus tragocamelus;* in Rajasthani, *roj;* in Hindi, *nīl-gāy*) is not listed among the mammals to be found, either in the *Ajmer District Gazetteer* (Dhoundiyal 1966) or in the *Rajasthan State Gazetteer* (1995). Haynes, however, lists blue bull along with wild boar and blackbuck as animals that "posed special problems to cultivators throughout Rajasthan" during the late nineteenth and early twentieth centuries (1998:755). Blue bull is a kind of antelope described by Seshadri as the biggest of the four antelopes in India, and "traditionally left alone by rural people being regarded as a near relative of the cow and therefore sacred" (1986:53).

45 It is no accident that the amount the Court is said to feed the wild boars daily is the amount traditionally pledged for feasts dedicated to deities as thanks offerings. See Gold 1988:151 and Raheja 1988 for ritual meanings and uses of the amount of one and one-quarter.

46 See Richards, Haynes, and Hagen 1985 for the large picture of expansion of arable lands and the consequent decrease in forest and grazing land throughout North India, including Rajasthan.

47 Wild pigs usually live in herds of twenty to thirty individuals, so this may be an instance of considerable exaggeration.

10. Imports

1 Various portions of chapter 10 have appeared in other publications, including Gold 1998c, Gold 1999b, Gold 2002a.

2 For land reform in Rajasthan, see D. Singh 1964; Rosin 1987; and Yugandhar and Datta 1995. Herring 1983 provides a comparative study of the process in other regions of South Asia.

3 See Narain and Mathur, who agree with Ghatiyalians on the superior nutritional quality of what they call the "coarse grains"—previously but no longer the "staple diet of the rural Rajasthani." These authors comment that "the rural people of Rajasthan have no effective means to articulate their grievances at the all-India down-grading of their nutritionally rich diet" (1990:10). The village discourse, however, treats this situation differently: wheat is in style, and stomachs have lost the ability to digest bread made of barley.

4 The Damami, or royal drummer, *jāti*—although untouchable in ritual terms—has historically pursued education, at least in this area.

5 According to statistics drawn from the 1991 *Census of India,* the statewide literacy rate in Rajasthan was 38.55 percent. Broken down by gender, for males it was 54.99 percent and for females it was 20.44 percent. According to Sharma and Retherford 1993 and Sharma 1994, of the total rural population only 30.37 percent was literate, and the literacy rate for rural females in 1991 was a startlingly low 11.59 percent. In Ajmer District, where most of Sawar's villages are located, the rate for rural females is somewhat higher, at 13.96 percent. Neighboring Bhilwara district, where Bhoju teaches, however, was, according to Sharma 1994, well below the state average for both sexes, with only 9.61 percent of rural females educated and rural males at 38.36 percent.

6 For media and religion, see Babb and Wadley 1995.

7 My selection of particular English words to translate the words in this paragraph is a somewhat arbitrary attempt to represent semantic nuances and to convey the range of vocabulary involved in this discourse. For example, *ahamanya* is most literally "egoism" as it derives from the Sanskrit root for "I" (*aham*).

8 As a noun, the primary meaning of *vilāyat* is the land belonging to another, a foreign land. Most dictionaries also give England, Europe, and Iran or Turkistan, in that order. The *RSK*—beyond a general definition of *vilāyatī* as "foreign"—lists eleven entries of nouns qualified by this adjective. Several of these are plants, although *bambūl* is not among them. The entries also include items such as "foreign blue"—a dye or color from China. Clearly, imports may become commonplace but remain explicitly not native. Memory eventually fades, we may presume. Corn and tomatoes—both brought to Rajasthan in some distant century from the Americas via Europe—are thought to be indigenous.

9 Thanks to Amita Baviskar for pointing this out to me. Maheshwari and Singh 1965:129 confirms the identification with mesquite of *vilāyatī bambūl*.

10 In the rainy season of 1993, economist Bina Agarwal of the Institute for Economic Growth in Delhi administered survey questionnaires to women in Ghatiyali as part of her multiregional study of the effects of environmental change on Indian women. One of the questions she asked of relatively older women (mostly above age 45) was how much time it took at present to collect firewood, compared with some twenty years ago when they first came to the village as daughters-in-law. She found that in most cases they spent less time now. Despite evidently severe deforestation, firewood procurement was no longer a serious problem because of the proliferation of *vilāyatī*. Some twenty years ago in large parts of semiarid India there was a severe "fuelwood crisis" with a significant impact on women's work schedules (Agarwal 1986). In many regions, the crisis persists (Agarwal 1997).

11 See Shiva 1991:123–80 on conflicts over afforestation and the appropriation of so-called wastelands for social forestry. See also Brara 1992 for important ethnographically informed insights into conflicting government and village perceptions of the uses of "wasteland" in Rajasthan.

12 See Crosby 1986 for the colonialism of plants.

13 Although foreign and local *bambūl* are superficially similar in appearance, local *bambūl* is a true acacia: *Acacia nilotica*. Sharma and Tiagi report of this tree "known as Bahool locally and Babbul (Sanskrit), the decoction of the bark and fruits is used medicinally in Ayurveda. Incisions made on the stem yield a gum which carries medicinal value" (1979:105). Botanically, *vilāyatī* is more closely related to the indigenous *khejarī* (*Prosopis cineraria*) than it is to local *bambūl*. Some *khejarī* grow around Ghatiyali, but it was never predominant. People are aware of its high religious value for the Bishnoi community, but grant it no special importance.

14 See, however, Rajendran, who—based on observations in South India—claims that *juliflora* is a gold mine. He states that its charcoal is highly valued, that it can restore saline soil, and that it is even good for making furniture (1995:20). The latter two claims are denied vehemently by Ghatiyalians. Thanks to Roger Jeffery for sending me

this reference. Robbins 1996, 1998 offers a nuanced perspective on the virtues and flaws of *juliflora* based on ethnography in western Rajasthan.

15 It is beyond our scope to contemplate the politics of *deśī* as they have evolved and changed in the past century in India, from Gandhi's *svadeshi* movement and the struggle against colonialism to the current resurgence of Hindu nationalism. For an incisive, critical discussion of the use of "indigenous" in various literatures and discourses, see Gupta 1998:179–83, 227–33.

16 Sahlins's discussion of hybridity is relevant here. He critiques some inappropriate uses of the term, writing, "Hybridity is a genealogy, not a structure. . . . It is an analytic construal of a people's history, not an ethnographic description of their way of life. In their way of life, externalities are indigenized, engage in local configurations and become different from what they were" (1999:412). See also Vasavi's poignant discussion of "hybrid times, hybrid people" as portrayed by farmers in Karnataka (1999:11–124).

17 See Gold and Gujar 1994 for a discussion of Ghatiyali children's attitudes toward, and knowledge about, the environment, where the following interview is included among many others.

18 Snakes are beaten to death on sight in Ghatiyali.

19 The trees called *vilāyatī* in Ghatiyali, for example, are called *angrejī* in Jodhpur district (Robbins 1996).

20 I have been unable to locate this particular wheat variety in any source except for Shambhu's survey, which lists a *bajyā gehūṅ* (Nath 1993). It should not be confused with millet (*bājrā*). A number of persons spoke generally of *deśī* wheat, opposing it to native species on two counts: better flavor and less need for water.

21 I have identified these green manures as Hindi *gavar, Cyamopsis tetragonoloba* (Bhandari 1990 [1978]:104); and Hindi *san* or "hemp," *Crotolaria juncea*, whose uses as described by Maheshwari and Singh include "making ropes, mats, cordage and paper. The flowers and fruits are eaten as vegetable and the green stem and leaves make good manure" (1965:49).

22 These are local language variants on other new wheat species promoted in Rajasthan; probably their names can be interpreted as "Kota farming" and "golden furrow." Kota is an important city in the region.

23 Only a fairly prosperous farmer would follow this complex and expensive fertilizing and irrigation strategy.

24 Lalu uses a term for opium addict.

25 Ideas of decline are prevalent in South India as well. See, for example, Van Hollen, who writes: "I frequently heard women comment that 'in those days' women's bodies were stronger and healthier than they are today. . . . 'In those days' women were healthier because they ate food that was not tainted by pesticides" (1999:7).

26 Other interviews I am unable to include here contrast the strength obtained from the old grains, especially barley, with that from wheat bread. For thorough discussions of farmers' ideas about changing grain and changing people, see Gupta 1998 and Vasavi 1999.

27 In Gold 1999a I discuss, somewhat speculatively, the discourse on why agricultural rituals were in the 1990s so suddenly dropped by many Sawar farmers.

Notes to Chapter Ten ❧ 365

28 See Gupta, who writes: "Chemical fertilizers were also blamed for the poor health of the population. It was believed that eating grain grown with chemical fertilizers failed to provide the nourishment necessary to ward off disease" (1998:282).

29 Thanks to Anirudh Krishna, I was able to look at one of the documents produced by the Japanese group (SAPROF 1991). From it we learn that the project organizers, with all good intentions, assume villagers to "mismanage" so-called wasteland. The recommended strategy for field personnel is to engage villagers' self-interests, but never to tap their knowledge—a familiar development mentality (see also Brara 1992).

   Between 1993 and 1997 a new, unpredicted, and exciting development began to manifest. In the shelter of the imported and despised trees planted through government reforestation projects, which had produced an area of thick brambles impenetrable even by goats, *dhok* were coming back. Once alerted, even my untrained eyes perceived their distinctive dark color, which had changed the face of the hillsides in just four years. However, I did not hear much talk about this. Regeneration had not yet become part of the story.

30 For one of the earliest and influential statements along these lines, see Shiva 1988 on "maldevelopment." Other sources include Banuri and Marglin 1993; Gadgil and Guha 1992; and Kothari and Parajuli 1993.

31 See, for example, Agarwal 1991; Greenough 2001; Gupta 1998; Sinha, Gururani, and Greenberg 1997; Jeffery 1998; and Pedersen 1995.

32 Discussion of these complexities is well beyond my purpose here; see Gururani 1996 and Gupta 1998 for these and related issues.

33 See Bhara 1982 for a study of the startlingly accurate memories of some other Rajasthani farmers for good and bad rainy seasons. See also INTACH 1989 for connections between deforestation and "desertification." According to Bhoju, the monsoon of 1994 brought the heaviest rains seen in this part of Rajasthan for at least one hundred years. But in 1997, interviewees claimed, as they did in 1993, that rainfall was not as abundant as it had been in the past; another drought was witnessed in 2000.

34 Wadley 1994 reports on similar perceptions from a different North Indian region with a different local history.

35 This land is behind the school, very close to the village dwellings. It belongs to Gujarati Brahmins and was once tax-free temple land. Chamars were probably laborers on this land; today they may be sharecroppers (*sirī*) for Brahmin landowners.

36 See Gold 1988:53–58 for a description of a collective ritual performed in Ghatiyali in 1980 to entreat the Vedic rain god, Indra, who has no temple.

37 As the interview with Hardev Chamar cited above indicates, the "no trees, no rain" theory is hardly exclusive to literate villagers. Whether these theories emanated from nineteenth-century colonial forest agendas in Ajmer, or evolved spontaneously in the local context based on observation, I would not venture to guess. Moreover, as an account of a recent campaign for environmental restoration in another district of Rajasthan suggests, environmental activists today consciously and strategically reinforce ideas about the importance of trees for climatic well-being (Saint 1989).

38 This is an awkward but deliberate translation of *bhagvān kī kudarat;* it might be more simply rendered as "God's nature" or "God's being."

39 Damodar's subcaste, the Gujarati Brahmins, hold themselves to be ritually superior to all other communities and take no cooked food or water from any other castes.

40 In Gold 1998c I explore the Kali Yuga theme in interviews and texts more fully.

41 This is once again an exaggeration. Due to frequent if erratic shutdowns of the tap, most women still have the equipment on hand for bringing home water from the well or hand pump. As noted earlier, a rhetorical device we frequently encountered was the hyperbolic statement that things prevalent in the past were totally finished, when actually they still existed but were less dominant. Head pads are ritual items as well as utilitarian ones, and are celebrated in women's songs and used in the many rituals involving water pots. Not only do most households have these pads, but a number still possess some that are beautifully decorated with colored cloth and cowry shells.

42 *Roṛyā meṁ loṭā ar pāchhalā mahalā meṁ revai;* the import of this saying is not an "American dream" of rags to riches through self-help, but rather that one's situation in life is in the hands of God, and pride in achievement is therefore inappropriate. Note, however, that far from declaring a rigid vision of birth-given status, this saying anticipates the most radical possibilities for change.

43 For one interesting slant on why this should be so, see Garg and Parikh, who write:
Unless the individual in our society vests authority in himself, the systems in our society will continue to be one-person empires. It is only with the discovery of authority within the self that an individual can learn to treat himself as a representative in the system. Such an acceptance can generate a sense of responsibility toward the self and the system. Freedom from the fear of authority outside and acceptance of the authority from within can alone generate the responsibility for being a representative in the system. The agrarian ethos prevalent in India today denies the simultaneity of authority within and without. This simultaneity of location of authority is a dire need today. (1995:203)

44 For an insightful theoretical discussion and case study of forest management corruption in Rajasthan, see Robbins 2000. On North Indian villagers' perceptions of government corruption, see Gupta 1995.

45 One fairly familiar pattern is that under conditions of increasing scarcity old rules of communal self-restraint are jettisoned, resulting in a free-for-all commons "tragedy." For a helpful discussion of commons situations, see Herring 1990.

46 See Bateson 1972 for resonant ideas about ecology and circuitry.

47 Funding from the Spencer Foundation and the Cornell University branch of ASHA have made these projects possible.

GLOSSARY

abhimān: conceit

adhikār: authority; command; entitlement; authority that is efficacious because it is backed by power

ahamanya: egoism, from the root *aham*

anna (ānā): one-sixteenth of a rupee in the old Indian currency; thus four *ānā*s is twenty-five *paise*

bājrā: small millet; *Holcus spicatus* or *Pencillarian spicata*

baniyā: merchant, shopkeeper

bāṇṭo: a share or portion; the share of a farmer's agricultural production collected from the farmer for the king or landlord

begār, begārī: forced and unremunerated labor, conscripted by rulers from their subjects

Bhangi (bhangī): a *jāti* whose traditional occupation is to be sweepers and herders of pigs; associated with sanitation work considered highly polluting, *Bhangis* are at the bottom of the ritual hierarchy and were formerly "untouchable"

bīghā: five-eighths of an acre, the standard measure for farm land in North India

bīṛ: a field of protected grass, an area off limits to public grazing

Chamar (chamār): a *jāti* associated primarily with leatherwork, formerly "untouchable"

charāgāh: common grazing ground, pastureland

charas: large leather bucket used in irrigation

dāṃtalī: crescent-shaped iron tool used to cut crops in the fields; sickle

darbār: Court; refers both to whatever individual person is the current ruler of a kingdom, and to the institution of royalty with its personnel and functions; Court is used for small and large kingdoms

deśī: local, indigenous

dhābhāī: the son of a Gujar wet nurse to royalty; hence, a privileged lineage among the Gujars *dhāṅgī, dhāṇī:* grain on the stalk roasted with fire, usually eaten in the fields before harvest

dharma: morality, virtue, duty, righteousness

dīvān: chief minister

gāṅv balāī: village crier; a village-based man appointed from among the formerly untouchable leatherworker communities (*Regar* and *Chamar*) to make announcements and do other work on behalf of the rulers; this work included calling workers to *begār* and accompanying the higher-ranking kings' men on their grain tax assessment work

ghamaṇḍī: pride, arrogance

gūgarī: boiled wholewheat berries

Gujar: a *jāti* associated with herding and dairy production

hākim (*hākam* in Rajasthani): an official of status; a ruler or boss; in Sawar the term was used loosely to refer to the kings' agents or anyone with authority, delegated from above, to give orders to other people

hoḷā: green chickpeas roasted on the plant with fire; usually eaten in the fields before harvest; often paired with *dhāṅgī,* as in "we ate *hoḷā-dhāṅgī*"

jāgīr: an estate, given by the government in earlier eras in return for services; *jāgīrdār* is the holder of such an estate; *jāgīrdārī* is a land tenure and revenue system based on such estates

jangal: forested land; scrubland; wild, unpopulated and desolate territory

jangalāt: (Sawar variant of *jangaḷāyat*) a government department concerned with forest maintenance and protection

jāti: group to which a person, plant, or animal belongs by birth; caste

jvār: large millet; *Holcus sorghum*

kachchā: an adjective with multiple significations including incomplete, unfinished, uncooked, unripe, and crude; when applied to houses, it means adobe as opposed to brick or stone

kāmdār: a manager for a king, landowner, or merchant; in Sawar, a generic term for high-ranking agents of the Court

kamīn: client castes; those castes who formerly took shares of the harvest in exchange for various services

kānūngo: land-record officer

kharīph: the crop cultivated from July to October, grown with monsoon rains and requiring no irrigation; in Rajasthani, *siyālū*—meaning the crop harvested in the cold season

kuḷī: a tool attached to the plow, used for cultivating the soil

kūṅtno: the act of making an estimation without counting, measuring, or weighing; specifically, in Sawar, the king's men's estimate of the vaue of the ripened crop in the field before harvest; the government's share was taken on the basis of this estimate, rather than of the actual yield

lāṭno: to take a fixed portion of grain from the threshing ground for the landlord's share; *lāṭau:* that fixed portion of grain taken by the landlord from the threshing ground

lāṭo-kūṭo: in Sawar, the Court's system of assessing and collecting its share of farmers' agricultural labors

Loda (lodā): a *jāti* associated primarily with farming

māl: agricultural land belonging to a village or community; in Sawar, the valued, fertile land nearest to village houses

Mali (mālī): a *jāti* associated primarily with gardening

māḷo: hunting tower; a raised platform used for shooting wild animals or for scaring beasts away from farms

maṇ: (Rajasthani): forty kilograms

maund: (Indian English): forty kilograms

Mina (mīnā): a *jāti* sometimes labeled "tribal," understood to have been among the original inhabitants of Sawar; today settled agriculturists

nāḍī: a small water reservoir

Nath (nāth): a *jāti* of householder yogi magicians, religious performers, and Shaivite priests; today largely agriculturists

nauharā, noharā: an enclosure separate from the main house, often roofless, where fodder is stored and livestock are penned; when belonging to royalty, living quarters for the kings' agents

paise: one-hundredth of a rupee, a cent

pakkā (houses): made of bricks or stone—complete, finished, well made

panchayat (panchāyat): a village council; a caste council; a community meeting called to address a particular question

pāṇṇat: the action of irrigating fields through small channels

pāṇṇat karnā: to manipulate mud barricades in order to send water through desired irrigation channels

paryāvaraṇ: the environment

paṭwārī: revenue accountant; recordkeeper and revenue assessor

prakṛti: nature, the natural world; active, proliferating female cosmic principle

pratibandh: restriction, prohibition, ban

rabī: the crop cultivated from October to March; requires irrigation; in Rajasthan called *unyāḷū*—meaning the crop harvested in the hot season

rājā-mahārājā: kings and great kings; the most common term used in Sawar for *Rajput* nobility in pre-Independence times

rāj balāī: royal crier; like the village crier, the royal crier is appointed from among the formerly untouchable leatherworker communities, but the royal crier is based in the capital and moves around the kingdom in the company of the Court's managers and bosses

Rajput (rājpūt): "member of a loose grouping of Hindu communities equated ritually with the ancient *kṣatriyas* or 'warriors' " (McGregor 1993); literally "king's son"; today in Sawar a *jāti* to which belong members of the former ruling class

rāvaḷo: the neighborhood where the *Rajput* live, usually near the palace or fort

Regar: a *jāti* associated primarily with leatherwork; formerly "untouchable"

samvat: an era, often identified with King Vikramaditya, beginning shortly after 57 B.C.E.; Sawar's elderly, when they spoke of dates, usually used the *samvat* reckoning

śauk: passionate interest

ser: (Rajasthani); *seer* (Indian English): a measure of weight of about one kilogram, equal to one-fortieth of a *maṇ* or "maund"

siyālū, syāḷū: the crop harvested in the cold season (Hindi *kharīph*)

sīrī: a shareholder in agricultural land; someone who shares the work, expenses, and harvest with a landowner

svārth: self-interest, selfishness, seeking one's own advantage

syāṇā: forest guard, sometimes called in English "cattle guard," meaning someone who keeps cattle from destroying trees; a low-level position in the era of kings, today *syāṇā* refers to a government-appointed forestry agent assigned to oversee reforestation programs

tehsil (*tahsīl*): a revenue district

tehsildar (tahsīldār): subcollector of revenue

ṭhākur: a lord or chief; a person of rank or position; the master of a village; a glorious person; God

ṭhikānā: abode; a portion of land in a state that is under the authority of a major landholder (*jāgīrdār*); a small kingdom like Sawar may be referred to as *ṭhikānā*

unāḷī, unyāḷū: the crop harvested in the hot season (Hindi *rabī*)

vilāyatī: foreign

zimmedārī: responsibility, answerability, accountability; from Arabic *zimmā*, meaning charge, trust, responsibility

REFERENCES

Abercrombie, Thomas A. 1998. *Pathways of Memory and Power: Ethnography and History among an Andean People*. Madison: University of Wisconsin Press.

Abu-Lughod, Lila. 1990. "The Romance of Resistance: Tracing Transformations of Power through Bedouin Women." *American Ethnologist* 17 (1): 41–55.

——. 1991. "Writing against Culture." In *Recapturing Anthropology: Working in the Present*, ed. Richard G. Fox, 137–62. Santa Fe: School of American Research Press.

——. 1993. *Writing Women's Worlds*. Berkeley: University of California Press.

Adenaike, Carolyn Keyes, and Jan Vansina, eds. 1996. *In Pursuit of History: Fieldwork in Africa*. Portsmouth, N.H.: Heinemann.

Agarwal, Bina. 1986. *Cold Hearths and Barren Slopes: The Woodfuel Crisis in the Third World*. New Delhi: Allied Publishers Private, Limited.

——. 1991. "Engendering the Environment Debate: Lessons from the Indian Subcontinent." CASID Distinguished Speaker Series, no. 8. East Lansing: Center for Advanced Study of International Development, Michigan State University.

——. 1997. "Environmental Action, Gender Equity and Women's Participation." *Development and Change* 28: 1–44.

Agrawal, Arun. 1998. *Greener Pastures: Politics, Markets, and Community among a Migrant Pastoral People*. Durham: Duke University Press.

Allen, Charles, and Sharada Dwivedi. 1984. *Lives of the Indian Princes*. London: Century Publishing.

Amin, Shahid. 1994. "Some Considerations on Evidence, Language, and History." *Indian History Congress Thematic Symposium, "Language and History."* Aligarh: Symposia Papers no. 10.

——. 1995. *Event, Metaphor, Memory: Chauri Chaura 1922–1992*. Delhi: Oxford University Press.

Apffel-Marglin, Frédérique. 1995. "Gender and the Unitary Self: Looking for the Subaltern in Coastal Orissa." *South Asia Research* 15: 78–130.

Appadurai, Arjun. 1981. "The Past as a Scarce Resource." *Man* (New Series) 16: 201–19.

——. 1988a. "Comments on 'The Jungle and the Aroma of Meats: An Ecological Theme in Hindu Medicine.' " *Social Science and Medicine* 27 (3): 206–7.

——. 1988b. "Putting Hierarchy in Its Place." *Cultural Anthropology* 3 (1): 36–49.

——. 1989. "Transformations in the Culture of Agriculture." In *Contemporary Indian Tradition,* ed. Carla M. Borden, 173–86. Washington, D.C.: Smithsonian Institution Press.

——. 1990. "Technology and the Reproduction of Values in Rural Western India." In *Dominating Knowledge: Development, Culture, and Resistance,* ed. Frederique Apffel Marglin and Stephen A. Marglin, 185–216. Oxford: Clarendon Press.

——. 1991a. "Dietary Improvisation in an Agricultural Economy." In *Diet and Domestic Life in Society,* ed. A. Sharman et al., 205–32. Philadelphia: Temple University Press.

——. 1991b. "Global Ethnoscapes: Notes and Queries for a Transnational Anthropology." In *Recapturing Anthropology,* ed. Richard G. Fox, 191–210. Santa Fe: School of American Research Press.

——. 1996. *Modernity at Large.* Minneapolis: University of Minnesota Press.

Ardener, Edwin. 1975. "Belief and the Problem of Women." In *Perceiving Women,* ed. Shirley Ardener, 1–17. New York: John Wiley and Sons.

Arnold, David. 1996. *The Problem of Nature: Environment, Culture, and European Expansion.* Oxford: Blackwell Publishers.

Arnold, David, and Ramachandra Guha, eds. 1995. *Nature, Culture, Imperialism.* Delhi: Oxford University Press.

Asher, Catherine B. 1992. *Architecture of Mughal India.* Cambridge: Cambridge University Press.

Babb, Lawrence A., and Susan S. Wadley, eds. 1995. *Media and the Transformation of Religion in South Asia.* Philadelphia: University of Pennsylvania Press.

Bajekal, Madhavi. 1990. "The State and the Rural Grain Market in Eighteenth-Century Eastern Rajasthan." In *Merchants, Markets, and the State in Early Modern India,* ed. Sanjay Subrahmanyam, 90–120. Delhi: Oxford University Press.

Banuri, Tariq, and Frédérique Apffel-Marglin. 1993. "A Systems-of-Knowledge Analysis of Deforestation." In *Who Will Save the Forests? Knowledge, Power, and Environmental Destruction,* ed. Tariq Banuri and Frédérique Apffel-Marglin, 1–23. London: Zed Books.

Bardhan, Kalpana. 1990. *Of Women, Outcastes, Peasants, and Rebels.* Berkeley: University of California Press.

Basso, Keith H. 1996. *Wisdom Sits in Places: Landscape and Language among the Western Apache.* Albuquerque: University of New Mexico Press.

Bateson, Gregory. 1972. *Steps to an Ecology of Mind.* New York: Ballantine Books.

Baviskar, Amita. 1995. *In the Belly of the River: Tribal Conflicts over Development in the Narmada Valley.* Delhi: Oxford University Press.

Beach, Milo Cleveland. 1992. *Mughal and Rajput Painting.* Cambridge, Eng.: Cambridge University Press.

Beck, Brenda E. F. 1982. *The Three Twins.* Bloomington: Indiana University Press.

Behar, Ruth. 1986. *Santa Maria del Monte: The Presence of the Past in a Spanish Village.* Princeton: Princeton University Press.

——. 1996. *The Vulnerable Observer: Anthropology that Breaks Your Heart.* Boston: Beacon Press.

Bell, Michael Mayerfeld. 1994. *Childerley: Nature and Morality in a Country Village.* Chicago: University of Chicago Press.

Berman, Morris. 1981. *The Reenchantment of the World.* Ithaca: Cornell University Press.

Bhadra, Gautam. 1989. "The Mentality of Subalternity: *Kantanama* or *Rajdharma.*" In *Subaltern Studies VI: Writings on South Asian History and Society,* ed. Ranajit Guha, 54–91. Delhi: Oxford University Press.

Bhandari, M. M. 1990 [1978]. *Flora of the Indian Desert.* Jodhpur: MPS Repros.

Bharara, L. P. 1982. "Notes on the Experience of Drought: Perception, Recollection, and Prediction." In *Desertification and Development: Dryland Ecology in Social Perspective,* ed. Brian Spooner and H. S. Mann, 351–61. London: Academic Press.

Biersack, Aletta, ed. 1991. *Clio in Oceania: Toward a Historical Anthropology.* Washington, D.C.: Smithsonian Institution Press.

——. 1999. "Introduction: From the 'New Ecology' to the New Ecologies." *American Anthropologist* 101: 5–18.

Bishnoi, Shri Krishna. 1991. *Bishnoī Dharm-Sanskār.* Bikaner: Dhok Dhora Prakashan.

Bloch, Maurice E. F. 1998. *How We Think They Think: Anthropological Approaches to Cognition, Memory, and Literacy.* Boulder: Westview Press.

Boon, James A. 1990. *Affinities and Extremes: Crisscrossing the Bittersweet Ethnology of East Indies History, Hindu-Balinese Culture, and Indo-European Allure.* Chicago: University of Chicago Press.

Bose, Atindranath. 1942. *Social and Rural Economy of Northern India, cir. 600 B.C.–200 A.D.,* vol. 1. Calcutta: University of Calcutta.

Bourdieu, Pierre. 1966. "The Sentiment of Honour in Kabyle Society." In *Honour and Shame: The Values of Mediterranean Society,* ed. J. G. Peristiany, 191–241. Chicago: University of Chicago Press.

Boureau, Alain. 1995. *The Lord's First Night: The Myth of the Droit de Cuissage.* Chicago: University of Chicago Press.

Boyarin, Jonathan. 1991. *Polish Jews in Paris: The Ethnography of Memory.* Bloomington: Indiana University Press.

——. 1992. *Storm from Paradise: The Politics of Jewish Memory.* Minneapolis: University of Minnesota Press.

——. 1994. "Space, Time, and the Politics of Memory." In *Remapping Memory: The Politics of TimeSpace,* ed. Jonathan Boyarin, 1–37. Minneapolis: University of Minnesota Press.

Brandis, Dietrich. 1874. *The Forest Flora of North-West and Central India: A Handbook of the Indigenous Trees and Shrubs of Those Countries.* London: W. H. Allen and Company.

——. 1906. *Indian Trees: An Account of Trees, Shrubs, Woody Climbers, Bamboos, and Palms Indigenous or Commonly Cultivated in the British Indian Empire.* London: Archibald Constable and Company.

Brara, Rita. 1992. "Are Grazing Lands 'Wastelands'? Some Evidence from Rajasthan." *Economic and Political Weekly,* February 22, 411–18.

Briggs, George W. 1920. *The Chamārs.* London: Oxford University Press.

Brightman, Robert. 1993. *Grateful Prey: Rock Cree Human-Animal Relationships.* Berkeley: University of California Press.

Bulke, Phadar Kamil. 1971. *An English-Hindi Dictionary.* Calcutta: Rupa and Company.

Burke, Peter. 1997. *Varieties of Cultural History.* Ithaca: Cornell University Press.

Butalia, Urvashi. 2000. *The Other Side of Silence: Voices from the Partition of India.* Durham: Duke University Press.

Callewaert, Winand, and Peter G. Friedlander. 1992. *The Life and Works of Raidās.* New Delhi: Manohar.

Callicott, J. Baird, and Michael P. Nelson, eds. 1998. *The Great New Wilderness Debate: An Expansive Collection of Writings Defining Wilderness from John Muir to Gary Snyder.* Athens: University of Georgia Press.

Carstairs, G. Morris. 1985. *The Death of a Witch: A Village in North India 1950–1981.* London: Hutchinson.

Casey, Edward S. 1987. *Remembering: A Phenomenological Study.* Bloomington: Indiana University Press.

Census of India 1981. 1984. Series 18, Rajasthan, parts 13a and 13b, District Census Handbook, Ajmer District. Jaipur: Census Operations, Rajasthan.

Census of India 1991. 1994. Series 21, Rajasthan, parts 12a and 12b, District Census Handbook, Ajmer District. Jaipur: Census Operations, Rajasthan.

Chakrabarty, Dipesh. 1988. "Conditions for Knowledge of Working-Class Conditions." In *Selected Subaltern Studies,* ed. Ranajit Guha and Gayatri C. Spivak, 179–230. New York: Oxford University Press.

———. 1997a. "Postcoloniality and the Artifice of History: Who Speaks for "Indian" Pasts?" In *A Subaltern Studies Reader 1986–1995,* ed. Ranajit Guha, 263–93. Minneapolis: University of Minnesota Press.

———. 1997b. "The Time of History and the Times of Gods." In *The Politics of Culture in the Shadow of Capital,* ed. Lisa Lowe and David Lloyd, 35–60. Durham: Duke University Press.

Champion, Professor Harry, and F. C. Osmaston, eds. 1983. *E. P. Stebbing's 'The Forests of India' Volume IV being the history from 1925 to 1947 of the forests now in Burma, India, and Pakistan.* Delhi: Periodical Expert Book Agency.

Chapple, Christopher Key. 1993. "Hindu Environmentalism: Traditional and Contemporary Resources." In *Worldviews and Ecology,* ed. Mary Evelyn Tucker and John A. Grim, 113–23. Lewisburg, Pa.: Bucknell University Press.

Chatterjee, Partha. 1989. "Caste and Subaltern Consciousness." In *Subaltern Studies VI,* ed. Ranajit Guha, 169–209. Delhi: Oxford University Press.

———. 1993. *The Nation and Its Fragments: Colonial and Postcolonial Histories.* Princeton: Princeton University Press.

Chaturvedi, Mahendra, and B. N. Tiwari, eds. 1975. *A Practical Hindi-English Dictionary.* New Delhi: National Publishing House.

Chouhan, T. S. 1987. *Agricultural Geography: A Study of Rajasthan State.* Jaipur: Academic Publishers.

Clifford, James. 1988. *The Predicament of Culture: Twentieth-Century Ethnography, Literature, and Art.* Cambridge, Mass.: Harvard University Press.

Clifford, James, and George E. Marcus, eds. 1986. *Writing Culture: The Poetics and Politics of Ethnography.* Berkeley: University of California Press.

Coates, Peter. 1998. *Nature: Western Attitudes since Ancient Times*. Berkeley: University of California Press.

Coburn, Thomas B. 1996. "The Great Goddess." In *Devī: Goddesses of India*, ed. John Stratton Hawley and Donna Marie Wulff, 31–48. Berkeley: University of California Press.

Cohn, Bernard S. 1987. *An Anthropologist among the Historians, and Other Essays*. Delhi: Oxford University Press.

Comaroff, Jean. 1985. *Body of Power, Spirit of Resistance: The Culture and History of a South African People*. Chicago: University of Chicago Press.

Comaroff, Jean, and John Comaroff. 1991. *Of Revelation and Revolution: Christianity, Colonialism, and Consciousness in South Africa*, vol. 1. Chicago: University of Chicago Press.

——. 1997. *Of Revelation and Revolution: The Dialectics of Modernity on a South African Frontier*, vol. 2. Chicago: University of Chicago Press.

Comaroff, John, and Jean Comaroff. 1992. *Ethnography and the Historical Imagination*. Boulder: Westview Press.

Connerton, P. 1989. *How Societies Remember*. Cambridge, Eng.: Cambridge University Press.

Copland, Ian. 1997. *The Princes of India in the Endgame of Empire, 1917–1947*. Cambridge, Eng.: Cambridge University Press.

Critchley, John. 1978. *Feudalism*. London: George Allen and Unwin.

Croll, Elisabeth, and David Parkin, eds. 1992. *Bush Base, Forest Farm: Culture, Environment, and Development*. London: Routledge.

Cronon, W. 1983. *Changes in the Land: Indians, Colonists, and the Ecology of New England*. New York: Hill and Wang.

Crooke, William. 1989 [1879]. *A Glossary of North Indian Peasant Life*, ed. Shahid Amin. Delhi: Oxford University Press.

Crosby, Alfred W. 1986. *Ecological Imperialism: The Biological Expansion of Europe, 900–1900*. Cambridge, Eng.: Cambridge University Press.

Daniel, E. Valentine. 1996. *Charred Lullabies*. Princeton: Princeton University Press.

Darda, R. S. 1971. *From Feudalism to Democracy: A Study in the Growth of Representative Institutions in Rajasthan, 1908–1948*. New Delhi: S. Chand and Company.

Das, Veena. 1995. *Critical Events: An Anthropological Perspective on Contemporary India*. Delhi: Oxford University Press.

Das, Veena, and Ashis Nandy. 1986. "Violence, Victimhood, and the Language of Silence." In *The Word and the World: Fantasy, Symbol, and Record*, ed. Veena Das, 177–95. New Delhi: Sage Publications.

David, Kenneth, ed. 1976. *The New Wind*. The Hague: Mouton.

DeNeve, Rose. 1997. "Tourism and the Imperial Gaze." *Seminar 453* (May): 21–24.

Dening, Greg. 1991. "A Poetic for Histories: Transformations that Present the Past." In *Clio in Oceania: Toward a Historical Anthropology*, ed. Aletta Biersack, 347–80. Washington, D.C.: Smithsonian Institution Press.

Desai, Kiran. 1998. *Hullabaloo in the Guava Orchard*. New York: Atlantic Monthly Press.

Descola, Philippe, and Gisli Palsson. 1996. "Introduction." In *Nature and Society: Anthropological Perspectives*, ed. Philippe Descola and Gisli Palsson, 1–22. London: Routledge.

References ❧ 377

Devi, Mahasweta. 1995. *Imaginary Maps: Three Stories by Mahasweta Devi*. New York: Routledge.

Devisch, René. 1993. *Weaving the Threads of Life: The* Khita *Gyn-Eco-Logical Healing Cult Among the Yaka*. Chicago: University of Chicago Press.

Dhabhai, Shri Ramkumar. 1987. "Khairāṛ kshetra: bhaugolik evaṁ ārthik pṛiṣṭhbhūmi," [Khairar District: Geographic and Economic Background]. In *Tridaśābdī Samāroh* [Thirtieth Anniversary Commemoration], ed. Chitarmal Goyal, 2–5. Savar: Khairar Gramoday Sangh.

Dhoundiyal, B. N. 1966. *Ajmer*. Alwar: Sharma Bros. Electromatic Press.

Dirks, Nicholas B. 1987. *The Hollow Crown: Ethnohistory of an Indian Kingdom*. Cambridge, Eng.: Cambridge University Press.

———. 1992. "Castes of Mind." *Representations* 37: 56–78.

———. 1997. "The Policing of Tradition: Colonialism and Anthropology in Southern India." *Comparative Studies in Society and History* 39 (1): 182–212.

Doniger, Wendy with Brian Smith. 1991. *The Laws of Manu*. New York: Penguin Books.

Dove, Michael R. 1994. " 'Jungle' in Nature and Culture." In *Social Ecology*, ed. Ramachandra Guha, 90–115. Delhi: Oxford University Press.

———. 1999. "The Agronomy of Memory and the Memory of Agronomy: Ritual Conservation of Archaic Cultigens in Contemporary Farming Systems." In *Ethnoecology: Situated Knowledge/Located Lives*, ed. Virginia D. Nazarea, 45–70. Tucson: University of Arizona Press.

Duara, Prasenjit. 1995. *Rescuing History from the Nation: Questioning Narratives of Modern China*. Chicago: University of Chicago Press.

Dube, Saurabh. 1998. *Untouchable Pasts: Religion, Identity, and Power among a Central Indian Community, 1780–1950*. Albany: State University of New York Press.

Dumont, Louis. 1972. *Homo Hierarchicus*. London: Paladin.

Eaton, Richard M. 1993. *The Rise of Islam and the Bengal Frontier: 1204–1760*. Berkeley: University of California Press.

Erdman, Joan L. 1985. *Patrons and Performers in Rajasthan*. Delhi: Chanakya Publications.

Fabian, Johannes. 1983. *Time and the Other: How Anthropology Makes Its Object*. New York: Columbia University Press.

Falk, Nancy E. 1973. "Wilderness and Kingship in Ancient South Asia." *History of Religions* 13: 1–15.

Feld, Steven, and Keith H. Basso, eds. 1996. *Senses of Place*. Santa Fe: School of American Research Press.

Fentress, James, and Chris Wickham. 1992. *Social Memory: New Perspectives on the Past*. Oxford: Blackwell Publishers.

Fields, Karen E. 1994. "What One Cannot Remember Mistakenly." In *Memory and History: Essays on Recalling and Interpreting Experience*, ed. Jaclyn Jeffrey and Glenace Edwall, 89–104. Lanham, Md.: University Press of America.

Fisher, R. J. 1997. *If Rain Doesn't Come: An Anthropological Study of Drought and Human Ecology in Western Rajasthan*. Delhi: Manohar.

Fisher, William F., ed. 1995. *Toward Sustainable Development? Struggling over India's Narmada River*. Armonk, N.Y.: M. E. Sharpe.

Fleischner, Jennifer. 1996. *Mastering Slavery: Memory, Family, and Identity in Women's Slave Narratives*. New York: New York University Press.

Fuller, C. J. 1989. "Misconceiving the Grain Heap: A Critique of the Concept of the Indian Jajmani System." In *Money and the Morality of Exchange*, ed. J. Parry and M. Bloch, 33–63. Cambridge, Eng.: Cambridge University Press.

Gadgil, Madhav, and Ramachandra Guha. 1992. *This Fissured Land: An Ecological History of India*. Delhi: Oxford University Press.

——. 1995. *Ecology and Equity: The Use and Abuse of Nature in Contemporary India*. London: Routledge.

Gandhi, Mahatma. 1946. *Daridra-Narayana: Our Duty in Food and Cloth Crisis*. Karachi: Anand T. Hingorani.

Gandhi, Maneka. 1991. *Brahma's Hair: On the Mythology of Indian Plants*. Calcutta: Rupa and Company.

Garg, Pulin K., and Indira J. Parikh. 1995. *Crossroads of Culture: A Study in the Culture of Transience*. New Delhi: Sage Publications.

Geertz, Clifford. 1983. *Local Knowledge: Further essays in Interpretive Anthropology*. New York: Basic Books.

Glacken, Clarence J. 1967. *Traces on the Rhodian Shore: Nature and Culture in Western Thought from Ancient Times to the End of the Eighteenth Century*. Berkeley: University of California Press.

Gold, Ann Grodzins. 1988. *Fruitful Journeys: The Ways of Rajasthani Pilgrims*. Berkeley: University of California Press.

——. 1989. "The Once and Future Yogi: Sentiments and Signs in the Tale of a Renouncer-King." *Journal of Asian Studies* 48 (4): 770–86.

——. 1992. *A Carnival of Parting*. Berkeley: University of California Press.

——. 1994. "*Yatra, Jatra,* and Pressing Down Pebbles: Pilgrimage within and beyond Rajasthan." In *The Idea of Rajasthan: Explorations in Regional Identity,* vol. 1, eds. Karine Schomer, Joan L. Erdman, Deryck O. Lodrick and Lloyd I. Rudolph, 80–108. New Delhi: Manohar Publishers.

——. 1995a. "The 'Jungli Rani' and Other Troubled Wives in Rajasthani Oral Traditions." In *From the Margins of Hindu Marriage: Essays on Gender, Religion, and Culture,* ed. Lindsey Harlan and Paul Courtright, 119–36. New York: Oxford University Press.

——. 1995b. "Mother Ten's Stories." In *Religions of India in Practice,* ed. Donald S. Lopez Jr., 434–48. Princeton: Princeton University Press.

——. 1996. "*Khyal*: Changed Yearnings in Rajasthani Women's Songs." *Manushi* 95: 13–21.

——. 1998a. "Authority, Responsibility, and Protection: A Fieldwork Report from Rural North India." In *Governance Issues in Conservation and Development,* ed. Goran Hyden, 25–34. Gainesville, Fla.: Conservation and Development Forum.

——. 1998b. "Grains of Truth: Shifting Hierarchies of Food and Grace in Three Rajasthani Tales." *History of Religions* 38 (2): 150–71.

——. 1998c. "Sin and Rain: Moral Ecology in Rural North India." In *Ecological Concern in South Asian Religion,* ed. Lance Nelson, 165–95. Albany: State University of New York Press.

——. 1999a. "Abandoned Rituals: Knowledge, Time, and Rhetorics of Modernity in Rural

India." In *Religion, Ritual, and Royalty,* ed. N. K. Singhi and Rajendra Joshi, 262–75. Jaipur: Rawat Publications.

———. 1999b. "From Wild Pigs to Foreign Trees: Oral Histories of Environmental Change in Rajasthan." In *State, Society, and the Environment in South Asia,* ed. Stig Toft Madsen, 20–58. Richmond, Eng.: Curzon Press.

———. 2000a. "From Demon Aunt to Gorgeous Bride: Women Portray Female Power in a North Indian Festival Cycle." In *Invented Identities: The Interplay of Gender, Religion, and Politics in India,* ed. Julia Leslie and Mary McGee, 203–30. Delhi: Oxford University Press.

———. 2000b. " 'If You Cut a Branch You Cut My Finger': Court, Forest, and Environmental Ethics in Rajasthan." In *Hinduism and Ecology: The Intersection of Earth, Sky, and Water,* ed. Christopher Key Chapple and Mary Evelyn Tucker, 317–36. Cambridge, Mass.: Harvard University Press.

———. 2001a. "Rooted Responsibility: Locating Moral Authority in North India." In *Taking Responsibility: Comparative Perspectives,* ed. Winston Davis. Charlottesville: University Press of Virginia.

———. 2001b. "Story, Ritual, and Environment in Rajasthan." In *Sacred Landscapes and Cultural Politics,* ed. Philip Arnold and Ann Grodzins Gold, 151–37. Aldershot, Eng.: Ashgate Publishing.

———. 2002a. "Foreign Trees: Lives and Landscapes in Rajasthan." In *Imagination and Distress in Southern Environmental Projects,* ed. Paul Greenough and Anna Lowenhaupt Tsing. Durham: Duke University Press; Delhi: Oxford University Press.

———. 2002b. "New Light in the House: Schooling Girls in Rural North India." In *Everyday Life in South Asia,* ed. Diane Mines and Sarah Lamb. Bloomington: Indiana University Press.

———. n.d. "Beyond Water and Stone: Remembered Journeys from Rajasthan." In *Memory and Movement: The Mastery of Displacement in South Asian Experience,* ed. Paul Greenough (unpublished manuscript).

Gold, Ann Grodzins, and Bhoju Ram Gujar. 1994. "Drawing Pictures in the Dust: Rajasthani Children's Landscapes. *Childhood* 2: 73–91.

———. 1995 [1989]. "Of Gods, Trees, and Boundaries: Divine Conservation in Rajasthan." In *Folk, Faith, and Feudalism,* ed. N. K. Singhi and Rajendra Joshi, 33–54. Jaipur. Rawat Publications.

Gold, Ann Grodzins, with Bhoju Ram Gujar. 1997. "Wild Pigs and Kings: Remembered Landscapes in Rajasthan." *American Anthropologist* 99 (1): 70–84.

Gooch, Pernille. 1999. "The Van Gujjars and the Rajaji National Park." In *State, Society, and the Environment in South Asia,* ed. Stig Toft Madsen, 79–112, Richmond, Eng.: Curzon Press.

Goyal, Chitarmal. 1987. "Shrī ṭhākur Vanśpradīpsingh kī sāvar ko den," [Shri Thakur Vansh Pradip Singh's Legacy to Sawar]. In *Tridaśābdī Samāroh* [Thirtieth Anniversary Commemoration], ed. Chitarmal Goyal, 7–8. Sawar: Khairar Gramoday Sangh.

Greenough, Paul. 2001. "*Naturae Ferae:* Wild Animals and Mortal Risks in South Asian Environmental History." In *Agrarian Studies: Synthetic Work at the Cutting Edge,* ed. James Scott. New Haven: Yale University Press.

Grima, Benedicte. 1992. *The Performance of Emotion among Paxtun Women: "The Misfortunes which Have Befallen Me."* Austin: University of Texas Press.

Grove, Richard H. 1995. *Green Imperialism*. Cambridge, Eng.: Cambridge University Press.

———. 1998. *Ecology, Climate, and Empire: The Indian Legacy in Global Environmental History, 1400–1940*. Delhi: Oxford University Press.

Grove, Richard, Vinita Damodaran, and Satpal Sangwan. 1998. "Introduction." In *Nature and the Orient: The Environmental History of South and Southeast Asia*, ed. Richard Grove, Vinita Damodaran, and Satpal Sangwan, 1–26. Delhi: Oxford University Press.

Guha, Ramachandra. 1989. "Radical American Environmentalism and Wilderness Preservation: A Third World Critique." *Environmental Ethics* 2: 71–83.

———. 1990. "An Early Environmental Debate: The Making of the 1878 Forest Act." *The Indian Economic and Social History Review* 27: 65–84.

———. 2000 [1989]. *The Unquiet Woods: Ecological Change and Peasant Resistance in the Himalaya*, expanded edition. Berkeley: University of California Press.

Guha, Ramachandra, and J. Martinez-Alier, eds. 1997. *Varieties of Environmentalism: Essays North and South*. London: Earthscan Publications.

Guha, Ranajit. 1983. *Elementary Aspects of Peasant Insurgency in Colonial India*. Delhi: Oxford University Press.

———. 1987. "Chandra's Death." In *Subaltern Studies V: Writings on South Asian History and Society*, ed. Ranajit Guha, 135–65. Delhi: Oxford University Press.

———. 1989. "Dominance without Hegemony and Its Historiography." In *Subaltern Studies VI: Writings on South Asian History and Society*, ed. Ranajit Guha, 210–309. Delhi: Oxford University Press.

———. 1996. "The Small Voice of History." In *Subaltern Studies IX: Writings on South Asian History and Society*, ed. Shahid Amin and Dipesh Chakrabarty, 1–12. Delhi: Oxford University Press.

———. 1997. *Dominance without Hegemony: History and Power in Colonial India*. Cambridge, Mass.: Harvard University Press.

Guha, Ranajit, and Gayatri Chakravorty Spivak, eds. 1988. *Selected Subaltern Studies*. New York: Oxford University Press.

Guha, Sumit. 1999. *Environment and Ethnicity in India, 1200–1991*. Cambridge, Eng.: Cambridge University Press.

Gujar, Bhoju Ram, and Ann Grodzins Gold. 1992. "From the Research Assistant's Point of View." *Anthropology and Humanism Quarterly* 17 (3): 72–84.

Gupta, Akhil. 1994. "The Reincarnation of Souls and the Rebirth of Commodities." In *Remapping Memory*, ed. Jonathan Boyarin, 161–84. Minneapolis: University of Minnesota Press.

———. 1995. "Blurred Boundaries: The Discourse of Corruption, the Culture of Politics, and the Imagined State." *American Ethnologist* 22 (2): 375–402.

———. 1998. *Postcolonial Developments: Agriculture in the Making of Modern India*. Durham: Duke University Press.

Gupta, Akhil, and James Ferguson. 1997a. "Discipline and Practice: 'The Field' as Site, Method, and Location in Anthropology." In *Anthropological Locations: Boundaries and*

Grounds of a Field Science, ed. Akhil Gupta and James Ferguson, 1–46. Berkeley: University of California Press.

———. eds. 1997b. *Culture, Power, Place: Explorations in Critical Anthropology.* Durham: Duke University Press.

Gupta, S. P. 1986. *The Agrarian System of Eastern Rajasthan.* Delhi: Manohar.

Gururani, Shubhra. 1996. "How Much Milk and How Much Water?": Practices of Fuel, Fodder, and Forests in Uttarakhand Himalayas, India. Ph.D. diss., Syracuse University.

Hajj, the, Smadar Lavie, and Forest Rouse. 1993. "Notes on the Fantastic Journey of the Hajj, His Anthropologist, and Her American Passport." *American Ethnologist* 20 (2): 363–84.

Halbwachs, Maurice. 1992. *On Collective Memory,* trans. Lewis A. Coser. Chicago: University of Chicago Press.

Haraway, Donna J. 1991. *Simians, Cyborgs, and Women: The Reinvention of Nature.* New York: Routledge.

Hardiman, David. 1996. *Feeding the Baniya: Peasants and Usurers in Western India.* Delhi: Oxford University Press.

Harvey, David. 1996. *Justice, Nature, and the Geography of Difference.* Malden, Mass.: Blackwell Publishers.

Hastrup, Kirsten. 1992. "Introduction." In *Other Histories,* ed. Kirsten Hastrup, 1–13. London: Routledge.

Hawley, John S. 1988. *Songs of the Saints of India.* New York: Oxford University Press.

Haynes, Edward S. 1998. "The Natural and the Raj: Customary State Systems and Environmental Management in Pre-integration Rajasthan and Gujarat." In *Nature and the Orient,* ed. Richard H. Grove, Vinita Damodaran, and Satpal Sangwan, 734–92. Delhi: Oxford University Press.

———. 1999. "Land Use, Natural Resources, and the Rajput State, 1780–1980." In *Desert, Drought, and Development: Studies in Resource Management and Sustainability,* ed. Rakesh Hooja and Rajendra Joshi, 53–119. Jaipur: Rawat Publications.

Herring, Ronald J. 1983. *Land to the Tiller: The Political Economy of Agrarian Reform in South Asia.* New Haven: Yale University Press.

———. 1990. "Rethinking the Commons." *Agriculture and Human Values* 7 (2): 88–104.

———. 1991. "Politics of Nature: Commons Interests, Commons Dilemmas, and the State," Harvard Center for Population and Development Studies Working Paper Series, no. 106. Cambridge, Mass.: Harvard University.

———. 1999. "Embedded Particularism: India's Failed Developmental State." In *The Developmental State in Historical Perspective,* ed. Meredith Woo-Cumings, 306–34. Ithaca: Cornell University Press.

Herzfeld, Michael. 1987. *Anthropology through the Looking-Glass: Critical Ethnography in the Margins of Europe.* Cambridge, Eng.: Cambridge University Press.

Hess, Linda, and Shukdev Singh. 1983. *The Bijak of Kabir.* San Francisco: North Point Press.

Hill, Christopher V. 1997. *River of Sorrow: Environment and Social Control in Riparian North India, 1770–1994.* Ann Arbor, Mich.: Association for Asian Studies.

Hiltebeitel, Alf. 1991. *The Cult of Draupadī: on Hindu Ritual and the Goddess.* Chicago: University of Chicago Press.

Hitchcock, John T. 1959. "The Idea of the Martial Rajput." In *Traditional India: Structure and Change,* ed. Milton Singer. Philadelphia: American Folklore Society.

Humphrey, Caroline, and Urgunge Onon. 1996. *Shamans and Elders: Experience, Knowledge, and Power among the Daur Mongols.* Oxford: Oxford University Press.

Hutton, Patrick H. 1993. *History as an Art of Memory,* Hanover, N.H.: University Press of New England.

Hymes, Dell. 1981. *"In Vain I Tried to Tell You."* Philadelphia: University of Pennsylvania Press.

Imperial Gazetteer of India. 1989 [1908]. *Rājputāna.* New Delhi: Usha Rani Jain.

Inden, Ronald. 1990. *Imagining India.* Oxford: Basil Blackwell.

Ingold, Tim. 1992. "Culture and the Perception of the Environment." In *Bush Base, Forest Farm: Culture, Environment, and Development,* ed. Elisabeth Croll and David Parkin, 39–56. New York: Routledge.

———, ed. 1996. *Key Debates in Anthropology.* London: Routledge.

INTACH (Indian National Trust for Art and Cultural Heritage), ed. 1989. *Deforestation, Drought, and Desertification: Perceptions on a Growing Ecological Crisis.* New Delhi: INTACH.

Irwin-Zarecka, Iwona. 1994. *Frames of Remembrance: The Dynamics of Collective Memory.* New Brunswick, N.J.: Transaction Publishers.

Iyer, K. Gopal. 1995. "Agrarian Transition in Rajasthan: Role of Tenancy Reforms." In *Rajasthan—Feudalism and Change,* vol. 2 of *Land Reforms in India,* ed. B. N. Yugandhar and P. S. Datta, 63–105. New Delhi: Sage Publications.

Jackson, Michael. 1998. *Minima Ethnographica: Intersubjectivity and the Anthropological Project.* Chicago: University of Chicago Press.

Jeffery, Patricia, and Roger Jeffery. 1996. *Don't Marry Me to a Plowman! Women's Everyday Lives in Rural North India.* Boulder: Westview Press.

Jeffery, Roger, ed. 1998. *The Social Construction of Indian Forests.* New Delhi: Manohar Publishers.

Jing, Jun. 1996. *The Temple of Memories: History, Power, and Morality in a Chinese Village.* Stanford: Stanford University Press.

Jodha, N. S. 1985. "Population Growth and the Decline of Common Property Resources in Rajasthan, India." *Population and Development Review* 11 (2): 247–64.

———. 1990. "Rural Common Property Resources: Contributions and Crisis." *Economic and Political Weekly,* June 30, A65–78.

Joshi, Prabhakar. 1995. *Ethnobotany of the Primitive Tribes in Rajasthan.* Jaipur: Printwell.

Joshi, Rajendra. 1972. *Unnīsavīśatābdī kā ajmer* [Nineteenth-Century Ajmer]. Jaipur: Rajasthan Hindi Granth Academy.

Kaali, Sundar. 1999. "Spatializing History: Subaltern Carnivalizations of Space in Tiruppuvanam, Tamil Nadu." In *Subaltern Studies X: Writings on South Asian History and Society,* ed. Gautam Bhadra, Gyan Prakash, and Susie Tharu, 126–69. Delhi: Oxford University Press.

Kachhawaha, O. P. 1985. *Famines in Rajasthan: 1900 A.D.–1947 A.D.* Jodhpur: Hindi Sahitya Mandir.

Kane, P. V. 1974. *History of Dharmasastra*, 2nd ed. Poona: Bhandarkar Oriental Research Institute.

Kathuria, Ramdev P. 1987. *Life in the Courts of Rajasthan.* New Delhi: S. Chand and Company.

Kautilya. 1987. *The Arthashastra*, edited, rearranged, translated, and introduced by L. N. Rangarajan. New Delhi: Penguin Books.

Kavoori, Purnendu S. 1999. *Pastoralism in Expansion: The Transhuming Herders of Western Rajasthan.* New Delhi: Oxford University Press.

Khan, Dominique-Sila. 1997. *Conversions and Shifting Identities: Ramdev Pir and the Ismailis in Rajasthan.* New Delhi: Manohar.

Khandelwal, Meena. 1996. "Walking a Tightrope: Saintliness, Gender, and Power in an Ethnographic Encounter." *Anthropology and Humanism Quarterly* 21 (2): 111–34.

Khare, R. S. 1976. *The Hindu Hearth and Home.* New Delhi: Vikas Publishing House.

Kinsley, David. 1995. *Ecology and Religion: Ecological Spirituality in Cross-Cultural Perspective.* Englewood Cliffs, N.J.: Prentice Hall.

Kipling, Rudyard. 1895. *The Two Jungle Books.* Garden City, NY: Garden City Publishing Company.

Kishwar, Madhu, and Ruth Vanita, eds. 1984. *In Search of Answers.* London: Zed Books.

Kolenda, Pauline. 1994. "The Joint-Family Household in Rural Rajasthan: Ecological, Cultural, and Demographic Conditions for Its Occurrence." In *The Idea of Rajasthan*, vol. 2, ed. Karine Schomer et al., 64–116. Columbia, MO.: South Asia Publications.

Kothari, Ashish, Farhad Vania, Priya Das, K. Christopher, and Suniti Jha, eds. 1997. *Building Bridges for Conservation.* New Delhi: Indian Institute of Public Administration.

Kothari, Ashish, Neena Singh, and Saloni Suri, eds. 1996. *People and Protected Areas: Towards Participatory Conservation in India.* New Delhi: Sage Publications.

Kothari, Smitu, and Pramod Parajuli. 1993. "No Nature without Social Justice: A Plea for Cultural and Ecological Pluralism in India." In *Global Ecology: A New Arena of Political Conflict,* ed. Wolfgang Sachs, 224–41. London: Zed Books.

Kripal, Jeffrey J. 1995. *Kālī's Child: The Mystical and the Erotic in the Life and Teachings of Ramakrishna.* Chicago: University of Chicago Press.

Krishna, Anirudh. 1997. "Participatory Watershed Development and Soil Conservation in Rajasthan, India." In *Reasons for Hope: Instructive Experiences in Rural Development,* ed. Anirudh Krishna, Norman Uphoff, and Milton Esman, 255–72. West Hartford, Conn.: Kumarian Press.

Kumar, Amitava. 2000. *Passport Photos.* Berkeley: University of California Press.

LaCapra, Dominick. 1998. *History and Memory after Auschwitz.* Ithaca: Cornell University Press.

Lalas, Sitaram. 1962–1978. *Rājasthānī Sabad Kos* (Rajasthani Dictionary), 9 vols. Jodhpur: Rajasthani Shodh Sansthan.

Lamb, Sarah. 2000. *White Saris and Sweet Mangoes: Aging, Gender, and Body in North India.* Berkeley: University of California Press.

Lambek, Michael. 1996. "The Past Imperfect: Remembering as Moral Practice." In *Tense*

Past: Cultural Essays in Trauma and Memory, ed. Paul Antze and Michael Lambek, 235–54. New York: Routledge.

———. 1998. "The Sakalava Poeisis of History: Realizing the Past through Spirit Possession in Madagascar." *American Ethnologist* 25: 106–27.

Lambek, Michael, and Paul Antze. 1996. "Introduction: Forecasting Memory." In *Tense Past: Cultural Essays in Trauma and Memory*, ed. Paul Antze and Michael Lambek, xi–xxxviii. New York: Routledge.

Langer, Lawrence L. 1991. *Holocaust Testimonies: The Ruins of Memory.* New Haven: Yale University Press.

Lansing, J. S. 1991. *Priests and Programmers: Technologies of Power in the Engineered Landscape of Bali.* Princeton: Princeton University Press.

Lavie, Smadar. 1990. *The Poetics of Military Occupation.* Berkeley: University of California Press.

Le Goff, Jacques. 1992. *History and Memory.* New York: Columbia University Press.

Lévi-Strauss, Claude. 1985. *The View from Afar.* New York: Basic Books.

Lodrick, Deryck O. 1994. "Rajasthan as a Region: Myth or Reality?" In *The Idea of Rajasthan: Explorations in Regional Identity*, vol. 1, ed. Karine Schomer et al., 1–44. Columbia, Mo.: South Asia Publications.

Lowenthal, David. 1985. *The Past Is a Foreign Country.* Cambridge, Eng.: Cambridge University Press.

Ludden, David. 1984. "Productive Power in Agriculture: A Survey of Work on the Local History of British India." In *Agrarian Power and Agricultural Productivity in South Asia*, ed. M. Desai, S. H. Rudolph, and A. Rudra, 51–99. Delhi: Oxford University Press.

———. 1995. "Archaic Formations of Agricultural Knowledge in South India." In *Meanings of Agriculture in South Asia*, ed. Peter Robb, 35–73. Delhi: Oxford University Press.

Lupton, W. J. E. 1908. *Report on the Question of the Assessment of Land and Water Revenue in Ajmer-Merwara.* Ajmer: Scottish Mission Industries.

MacCormack, C., and M. Strathern, eds. 1980. *Nature, Culture, and Gender.* Cambridge, Eng.: Cambridge University Press.

MacKenzie, John M. 1988. *The Empire of Nature: Hunting, Conservation, and British Imperialism.* Manchester: Manchester University Press.

Magier, David. 1992. "The Language of the Bard." Appendix to *A Carnival of Parting*, by Ann Grodzins Gold, 335–50. Berkeley: University of California Press.

Maheshwari, P., and Umrao Singh. 1965. *Dictionary of Economic Plants in India.* New Delhi: Indian Council of Agricultural Research.

Malamoud, Charles. 1989. *Cuire le Monde: Rite et Pensée dans l'Inde Ancienne.* Paris: Editions la Découverte.

Malinowski, Bronislaw. 1961 (1922). *Argonauts of the Western Pacific.* New York: E. P. Dutton.

Maloo, Kamala. 1987. *The History of Famines in Rajputana.* Udaipur: Himanshu Publications.

Marcus, George E. 1998. *Ethnography through Thick and Thin.* Princeton: Princeton University Press.

Marriott, McKim. 1976. "Hindu Transactions: Diversity without Dualism." In *Transaction*

and *Meaning: Directions in the Anthropology of Exchange and Symbolic Behavior,* ed.
Bruce Kapferer, 109–42. Philadelphia: ISHI Publications.

——. 1990. "Constructing an Indian Ethnosociology." In *India through Hindu Categories,*
ed. McKim Marriott, 1–39. New Delhi: Sage Publications.

Marriott, McKim, and Ronald B. Inden. 1976. "Toward an Ethnosociology of South Asian
Caste Systems." In *The New Wind,* ed. K. A. David, 227–38. The Hague: Mouton.

Mathur, Jivanlal. 1977. *Bṛj-Bāvanī.* Sawar: Mani Raj Singh.

Mayaram, Shail. 1991. "Criminality or Community? Alternative Constructions of the Mev
Narrative of Darya Khan." *Contributions to Indian Sociology* 25: 57–84.

——. 1997. *Resisting Regimes: Myth, Memory, and the Shaping of a Muslim Identity.* Delhi:
Oxford University Press.

McGee, Mary. 2000. "State Responsibility for Environmental Management: Perspectives
from Hindu Texts on Polity." In *Hinduism and Ecology: The Intersection of Earth, Sky,
and Water,* ed. Christopher Key Chapple and Mary Evelyn Tucker, 59–100. Cambridge,
Mass.: Harvard University Press.

McGregor, R. S. 1993. *The Oxford Hindi-English Dictionary.* Delhi: Oxford University Press.

Mead, Margaret. 1970. *Culture and Commitment: A Study of the Generation Gap.* Garden
City, N.Y.: Doubleday.

Menon, Ritu, and Kamla Bhasin. 1998.*Borders and Boundaries: Women in India's Partition.*
New Delhi: Kali for Women.

Merchant, Carolyn. 1990. *The Death of Nature: Women, Ecology, and the Scientific Revolution.* San Francisco: Harper and Row.

——. 1992. *Radical Ecology: The Search for a Livable World.* New York: Routledge.

Miller, Joseph C. Jr. 1994. *The Twenty-Four Brothers and Lord Devnārāyan: The Story and
Performance of a Folk Epic of Rajasthan, India.* Ph.D. diss., University of Pennsylvania.

Misra, V. C. 1967. *Geography of Rajasthan.* New Delhi: National Book Trust.

Moore, Erin P. 1998. *Gender, Law, and Resistance in India.* Tucson: University of Arizona
Press.

Mukhia, Harbans. 1993. *Perspectives on Medieval History.* New Delhi: Vikas Publishing
House.

Mukta, Parita. 1994. *Upholding the Common Life: The Community of Mirabai.* Delhi:
Oxford University Press.

Murali, Atluri. 1995. "Whose Trees? Forest Practices and Local Communities in Andhra,
1600–1922." In *Nature, Culture, Imperialism: Essays on the Environmental History of
South Asia,* ed. David Arnold and Ramachandra Guha, 86–122. Delhi: Oxford University Press.

Myerhoff, Barbara. 1992. *Remembered Lives: The Work of Ritual, Storytelling, and Growing
Older.* Ann Arbor: University of Michigan Press.

Nagar, Shanti Lal. 1993. *Varaha in Indian Art, Culture, and Literature.* New Delhi: Aryan
Books International.

Nagarajan, Vijaya Rettakudi. 1998. "The Earth as Goddess Bhu Devī: Toward a Theory of
'Embedded Ecologies' in Folk Hinduism." In *Purifying the Earthly Body of God,* ed.
Lance Nelson, 269–96. Albany: State University of New York Press.

Narain, Iqbal, and P. C. Mathur. 1990. "The Thousand Year Raj: Regional Isolation and

Rajput Hinduism in Rajasthan before and after 1947." In *Dominance and State Power in Modern India: Decline of a Social Order,* vol. 2, ed. Francine R. Frankel and M. S. A. Rao, 1–58. Delhi: Oxford University Press.

Narayan, Kirin. 1989. *Storytellers, Saints, and Scoundrels: Folk Narrative in Hindu Religious Teaching.* Philadelphia: University of Pennsylvania Press.

———. 1993. "How Native is a 'Native' Anthropologist?" *American Anthropologist* 95 (3): 671–86.

———. 1997. *Mondays on the Dark Night of the Moon.* New York: Oxford University Press.

Narayanan, Vasudha. 1997. "One Tree Is Equal to Ten Sons": Hindu Responses to the Problems of Ecology, Population, and Consumption. *Journal of the American Academy of Religion* 65 (2): 291–332.

Nath, Shambhu Natisar. 1993. *Prakritik Vanaspati Paudhe* (Natural Vegetation), 3 vols.: *Per* (Trees); *Ādhunik Phasaleṅ* (Modern Crops); *Jhāṛiyā, ghās, pūs, chārā* (Bushes, Grasses, Weeds, Fodder). Unpublished manuscript, files of the author.

Neale, Walter C. 1962. *Economic Change in Rural India: Land Tenure and Reform in Uttar Pradesh, 1800–1955.* New Haven: Yale University Press.

———. 1969. "Land Is to Rule." In *Land Control and Social Structure in Indian History,* ed. Robert Eric Frykenberg, 3–15. Madison: University of Wisconsin Press.

Negi, Jaideep. 1995. *Begār and Beth System in Himachal Pradesh: A Study of Erstwhile Shimla Hill States.* New Delhi: Reliance Publishing House.

Nora, Pierre. 1996. "General Introduction: Between Memory and History." In *Realms of Memory: Rethinking the French Past,* vol. 1, ed. Pierre Nora, 1–23. New York: Columbia University Press.

O'Brien, Jay, and William Roseberry, eds. 1991. *Golden Ages, Dark Ages: Imagining the Past in Anthropology and History.* Berkeley: University of California Press.

O'Flaherty, Wendy Doniger. 1975. *Hindu Myths: A Sourcebook.* Baltimore: Penguin Books.

———. 1988. *Textual Sources for the Study of Hinduism.* Chicago: University of Chicago Press.

O'Hanlon, Rosalind. 1988. "Recovering the Subject: Subaltern Studies and Histories of Resistance in Colonial South Asia." *Modern Asian Studies* 22 (1): 189–224.

———. 1997. "Cultures of Rule, Communities of Resistance: Gender, Discourse, and Tradition in Recent South Asian Historiographies." In *Identity, Consciousness, and the Past: Forging of Caste and Community in India and Sri Lanka,* ed. H. L. Seneviratne, 147–76. Delhi: Oxford University Press.

Ondaatje, Michael. 1993. *The English Patient.* New York: Vintage Books.

Ortner, Sherry B. 1974. "Is Female to Male as Nature Is to Culture?" In *Woman, Culture, and Society,* ed. M. Z. Rosaldo and L. Lamphere, 67–87. Stanford: Stanford University Press.

———. 1989. *High Religion: A Cultural and Political History of Sherpa Buddhism.* Princeton: Princeton University Press.

———. 1994 [1984]. "Theory in Anthropology since the Sixties." In *Culture/Power/History: A Reader in Contemporary Social Theory,* ed. Nicholas B. Dirks, Geoff Eley, and Sherry B. Ortner, 372–411. Princeton: Princeton University Press.

———. 1995. "Resistance and the Problem of Ethnographic Refusal." *Comparative Studies in*

Society and History 37: 173–93.

———. 1996. *Making Gender: The Politics and Erotics of Culture.* Boston: Beacon Press.

———. 1999. "Thick Resistance: Death and the Cultural Construction of Agency in Himalayan Mountaineering." In *The Fate of "Culture": Geertz and Beyond,* ed. Sherry B. Ortner, 136–63. Berkeley: University of California Press.

Panagariya, B. L., and N. C. Pahariya. 1996. *Rajasthan: Polity, Economy, and Society.* Jaipur: Rawat Publications.

Pande, Ram. 1974. *Agrarian Movement in Rajasthan.* Delhi: University Publishers.

———. 1988. *Peoples Movement in Rajasthan (Selection from Originals),* vol. 3. Jaipur: Jaipur Publishing House.

Pandey, Deep Narayan. 1998. *Ethnoforestry: Local Knowledge for Sustainable Forestry and Livelihood Security.* Udaipur: Himanshu Publications.

Pandey, Gyanendra. 1999. *Memory, History, and the Question of Violence: Reflections on the Reconstruction of Partition.* Calcutta: Centre for Studies in Social Sciences.

Pandolfo, Stefania. 1997. *Impasse of the Angels.* Chicago: University of Chicago Press.

Parajuli, Pramod. 2001. "No Nature Apart: Adivasi Cosmovision and Ecological Discourses in Jharkhand, India." In *Sacred Landscapes and Cultural Politics,* ed. Philip Arnold and Ann Grodzins Gold, 83–113. Aldershot, Eng.: Ashgate Publishing.

Parihar, Rohit. 1999. "The Bride Price." *India Today,* March 8, 36–38.

Pedersen, Poul. 1995. "Nature, Religion, and Cultural Identity: The Religious Environmentalist Paradigm." In *Asian Perceptions of Nature: A Critical Approach,* ed. Ole Bruun and Arne Kalland, 258–76. Richmond, Eng.: Curzon Press.

Peet, Richard, and Michael Watts, eds. 1996. *Liberation Ecologies: Environment, Development, Social Movements.* London: Routledge.

Peluso, Nancy Lee. 1992. *Rich Forests, Poor People: Resource Control and Resistance in Java.* Berkeley: University of California Press.

Peristiany, J. G., ed. 1966. *Honour and Shame: The Values of Mediterranean Society.* Chicago: University of Chicago Press.

Perks, Robert, and Alistair Thomson, eds. 1998. *The Oral History Reader.* New York: Routledge.

Poffenberger, Mark. 1998. "A Report on Community Forest Management in Kota Division, Eastern Rajasthan." Unpublished manuscript, files of the author.

Poffenberger, Mark, and Betsy McGean, eds. 1996. *Village Voices, Forest Choices: Joint Forest Management in India.* Delhi: Oxford University Press.

Prakash, Gyan. 1990. *Bonded Histories: Genealogies of Labour Servitude in Colonial India.* Cambridge, Eng.: Cambridge University Press.

———. 1991. "Becoming a Bhuinya: Oral Traditions and Contested Domination in Eastern India." In *Contesting Power: Resistance and Everyday Social Relations in South Asia,* ed. D. Haynes and G. Prakash, 145–74. Berkeley: University of California Press.

———. 1999. *Another Reason: Science and the Imagination of Modern India.* Princeton: Princeton University Press.

Price, Pamela G. 1996. *Kingship and Political Practice in Colonial India.* Cambridge, Eng.: Cambridge University Press.

Price, Richard. 1990. *Alabi's World.* Baltimore: Johns Hopkins University Press.

Radcliffe-Brown, A. R. 1965. *Structure and Function in Primitive Society.* New York: The Free Press.

Raheja, Gloria Goodwin. 1988. *The Poison in the Gift: Ritual, Prestation, and the Dominant Caste in a North Indian Village.* Chicago: University of Chicago Press.

——. 1994. "Introduction: Gender Representation and the Problem of Language and Resistance in India." In *Listen to the Heron's Words* by Gloria Goodwin Raheja and Ann Grodzins Gold, 1–29. Berkeley: University of California Press.

——. 1996. "Caste, Colonialism, and the Speech of the Colonized: Entextualization and Disciplinary Control in India." *American Ethnologist* 23: 494–513.

——. 1997. "The Pradoxes of Power and Community: Women's Oral Traditions and the Uses of Ethnography." *Oral Traditions* 12 (1): 1–22.

——. n.d. " 'Hear the Tale of the Famine Year': Colonial Ethnography and the Politics of Famine Relief in Nineteenth-Century India." Unpublished manuscript, files of the author.

Raheja, Gloria Goodwin, and Ann Grodzins Gold. 1994. *Listen to the Heron's Words.* Berkeley: University of California Press.

Rajasthan State Archives. 1980. *A List of the English Records of the Ajmer Commissioner (1818–1899).* Bikaner: Rajasthan State Archives.

Rajasthan State Gazetteer. 1995. *History and Culture,* vol. 2. Jaipur: Directorate, District Gazetteers.

Rajendran, S. 1995. "Plant Prospects." *Down to Earth,* December 31, 20.

Ramusack, Barbara N. 1978. *The Princes of India in the Twilight of Empire: Dissolution of a Patron-Client System, 1914–1939.* Columbus, Ohio: Ohio State University Press.

Ranciere, Jacques. 1994. *The Names of History: On the Poetics of Knowledge,* trans. Hassan Melehy. Minneapolis: University of Minnesota Press.

Rangarajan, L. N. 1992. "The Kautilyan State and Society." In *The Arthashastra,* ed. L. N. Rangarajan, pp. 42–98. New York: Penguin Books.

Rangarajan, Mahesh. 1996. *Fencing the Forest: Conservation and Ecological Change in India's Central Provinces 1860–1914.* Delhi: Oxford University Press.

Ray, Rajat K. 1978. "Mewar: The Breakdown of the Princely Order." In *People, Princes, and Paramount Power: Society and Politics in the Indian Princely States,* ed. Robin Jeffrey, 205–39. Delhi: Oxford University Press.

Reichel-Dolmatoff, Gerardo. 1996. *The Forest Within: The World-View of the Tukano Amazonian Indians.* Tulsa: Council Oak Books.

Richards, John F. 1993. *Power, Administration, and Finance in Mughal India.* Aldershot, Eng.: Variorum.

Richards, John F., Edward S. Haynes, and James R. Hagen. 1985. "Changes in the Land and Human Productivity in Northern India, 1870–1970." *Agricultural History* 59 (4): 523–48.

Rival, Laura, ed. 1998. *The Social Life of Trees: Anthropological Perspectives on Tree Symbolism.* New York: Berg.

Robbins, Paul. 1996. "Negotiating Ecology: Institutional and Environmental Change in Rajasthan, India." Ph.D. diss., Clark University.

——. 1998. "Paper Forests: Imagining and Deploying Exogenous Ecologies in Arid India."

Geoforum 29: 69–86.

———. 2000. "The Rotten Institution: Corruption in Natural Resource Management." *Political Geography* 19: 423–43.

Roberts, John W. 1989. *From Trickster to Badman: The Black Folk Hero in Slavery and Freedom.* Philadelphia: University of Pennsylvania Press.

Rockefeller, Steven C., and John C. Elder, eds. 1992. *Spirit and Nature: Why the Environment Is a Religious Issue.* Boston: Beacon Press.

Rose, Deborah Bird. 1992. *Dingo Makes Us Human: Life and Land in an Aboriginal Australian Culture.* Cambridge, Eng.: Cambridge University Press.

Roseberry, W. 1989. *Anthropologies and Histories: Essays in Culture, History, and Political Economy.* New Brunswick: Rutgers University Press.

Roseman, Marina. 1991. *Healing Sounds from the Malaysian Rainforest: Temiar Music and Medicine.* Berkeley: University of California Press.

Rosin, R. Thomas. 1987. *Land Reform and Agrarian Change.* Jaipur: Rawat Publications.

Ross, Andrew. 1991. *Strange Weather: Culture, Science, and Technology in the Age of Limits.* London: Verso.

Rubin, Barnett R. 1983. *Feudal Revolt and State-Building: The 1938 Sikar Agitation in Jaipur.* New Delhi: South Asian Publishers.

Rudolph, Lloyd I., and Susanne H. Rudolph. 1967. *The Modernity of Tradition: Political Development in India.* Chicago: University of Chicago Press.

———. 1984. *Essays on Rajputana: Reflections on History, Culture, and Administration.* New Delhi: Concept Publishing Company.

Rushdie, Salman. 1991. *Imaginary Homelands.* London: Granta Books.

———. 1997. "The Firebird's Nest." *The New Yorker* June 23, 122–27.

Sagar, Vidya, and Kanta Ahuja. 1987. *Rural Transformation in a Developing Economy.* Jaipur: Kumar and Company.

Sahlins, Marshall. 1985. *Islands of History.* Chicago: University of Chicago Press.

———. 1999. "Two or Three Things that I Know about Culture." *Journal of the Royal Anthropological Institute* (New Series) 5: 399–421.

Sahlins, Peter. 1994. *Forest Rites: The War of the Demoiselles in Nineteenth-Century France.* London: Harvard University Press.

Saint, Kishore. 1989. "Aravalli Abhiyan—Save Aravalli Campaign." In *Deforestation, Drought, and Desertification: Perceptions on a Growing Ecological Crisis,* 110–15. New Delhi: INTACH.

Samaddar, Ranabir. 1996. "Territory and People: The Disciplining of Historical Memory." In *Texts of Power: Emerging Disciplines in Colonial Bengal,* ed. Partha Chatterjee, 167–99. Calcutta: Samya.

Santapau, H. 1966. *Common Trees.* New Delhi: National Book Trust.

SAPROF Team for the Overseas Economic Cooperation Fund, Japan. 1991. "Final Report on Afforestation Project in Aravalli-Hills State of Rajasthan, India, March 1991." Unpublished document, files of the author.

Sarda, Har Bilas. 1911. *Ajmer: Historical and Descriptive.* Ajmer: Scottish Mission Industries Company.

Sarkar, Sumit. 1997. *Writing Social History.* Delhi: Oxford University Press.

Schama, Simon. 1995. *Landscape and Memory.* New York: Vintage Books.

Scheper-Hughes, Nancy. 1992. *Death without Weeping: The Violence of Everyday Life in Brazil.* Berkeley: University of California Press.

Schneider, David M. 1976. "Notes Toward a Theory of Culture." In *Meaning in Anthropology,* eds. Keith H. Basso and Henry A. Selby, p. 197–220. Albuquerque: University of New Mexico Press.

Schomer, Karine, Joan L. Erdman, Deryck O. Lodrick, and Lloyd I. Rudolph, eds. 1994. *The Idea of Rajasthan: Explorations in Regional Identity,* 2 vols. Columbia, Mo.: South Asia Publications.

Schulte, R. 1994. *The Village in Court: Arson, Infanticide, and Poaching in the Court Records of Upper Bavaria, 1848–1910,* trans. Barrie Selman. Cambridge, Eng.: Cambridge University Press.

Scott, James C. 1985. *Weapons of the Weak: Everyday Forms of Peasant Resistance.* New Haven: Yale University Press.

———. 1990. *Domination and the Arts of Resistance: Hidden Transcripts.* New Haven: Yale University Press.

Sen, Geeti, ed. 1992. *Indigenous Vision.* New Delhi: Sage Publications.

Sen, Sudipta. 1998. *Empire of Free Trade: The East India Company and the Making of the Colonial Marketplace.* Philadelphia: University of Pennsylvania Press.

Seremetakis, C. Nadia. 1996. "The Memory of the Senses; Part I: Marks of the Transitory." In *The Senses Still: Perception and Memory as Material Culture in Modernity,* ed. C. Nadia Seremetakis, 1–18. Chicago: University of Chicago Press.

Seshadri, B. 1986. *India's Wildlife and Wildlife Reserves.* New Delhi: Sterling Publishers.

Sharma, Brij Kishore. 1990. *Peasant Movements in Rajasthan (1920–1949).* Jaipur: Pointer Publishers.

Sharma, K. L. 1998. *Caste, Feudalism, and Peasantry: The Social Formation of Shekhawati.* New Delhi: Manohar.

Sharma, O. P. 1994. *Universal Literacy: A Distant Dream (Based on the Census Data).* New Delhi: Kar Kripa Publishers.

Sharma, O. P., and Robert D. Retherford. 1993. *Literacy Trends in the 1980s in India.* Faridabad: Government of India Press.

Sharma, Shiva, and B. Tiagi. 1979. *Flora of North-East Rajasthan.* New Delhi: Kalyani Publishers.

Shastri, M. M. Haraprasad, trans. 1982. *The Art of Hunting in Ancient India of Raja Rudradeva of Kumaon.* Delhi: Eastern Book Linkers.

Shetty, B. V., and V. Singh, eds. 1987. *Flora of Rajasthan,* Calcutta: Botanical Survey of India.

Shiva, Vandana. 1988. *Staying Alive: Women, Ecology, and Development.* London: Zed Books.

———. 1991. *Ecology and the Politics of Survival: Conflicts over Natural Resources in India.* New Delhi: Sage Publications.

Simmons, I. G. 1993. *Interpreting Nature: Cultural Constructions of the Environment.* New York: Routledge.

Singh, Dool. 1964. *Land Reforms in Rajasthan: A Study of Evasion, Implementation, and*

Socio-Economic Effects of Land Reforms. Alwar, Rajasthan: Sharma Bros Electromatic Press.

Singh, Hira. 1998. *Colonial Hegemony and Popular Resistance: Princes, Peasants, and Paramount Power.* New Delhi: Sage Publications.

Singh, Kesri. 1977. "Pig-Sticking, a Vanishing Sport of Rajasthan." In *The Natural Resources of Rajasthan,* ed. M. L. Roonwal, 497–98. Jodhpur: University of Jodhpur.

Singh, Munshi Hardyal. 1990 [1894]. *The Castes of Marwar (Census Report of 1891).* Jodhpur: Books Treasure.

Sinha, Nandini. 1993a. "A Study of State and Cult: The Guhilas, Pasupatas, and Ekalingaji in Mewar, Seventh to Fifteenth Centuries A.D." *Studies in History* 9: 161–82.

——. 1993b. "State and the Tribe: A Study of the Bhils in the Historic Setting of Southern Rajasthan." *Social Science Probings* (March-December): 55–67.

Sinha, Subir, Shubhra Gururani, and Brian Greenberg. 1997. "The 'New Traditionalist' Discourse of Indian Environmentalism." *Journal of Peasant Studies* 24: 65–99.

Sivaramakrishnan, K. 1995. "Colonialism and Forestry in India: Imagining the Past in Present Politics." *Comparative Studies in Society and History* 37 (1): 3–40.

——. 1997. "Wild Landscapes and the Politics of Memory in Southwest Bengal." Paper presented at the Annual Meeting of the American Anthropological Association, Washington, D.C.

——. 1999. *Modern Forests: Statemaking and Environmental Change in Colonial Eastern India.* New Delhi: Oxford University Press.

Skaria, Ajay. 1998. "Timber Conservancy, Desiccationism, and Scientific Forestry: The Dangs, 1840s–1920s." In *Nature and the Orient,* ed. Richard H. Grove et al., 596–635. Delhi: Oxford University Press.

——. 1999. *Hybrid Histories: Forests, Frontiers, and Wildness in Western India.* Delhi: Oxford University Press.

Slyomovics, Susan. 1998. *The Object of Memory: Arab and Jew Narrate the Palestinian Village.* Philadelphia: University of Pennsylvania Press.

Smith, John D. 1991. *The Epic of Pābūjī.* Cambridge, Eng.: Cambridge University Press.

Sontheimer, Gunther-Dietz. 1997. *King of Hunters, Warriors, and Shepherds: Essays on Khaṇḍobā.* New Delhi: Manohar.

Soper, Kate. 1995. *What Is Nature? Culture, Politics, and the Non-Human.* Oxford: Blackwell.

Spiegelman, Art. 1986. *Maus: A Survivor's Tale.* New York: Pantheon Books.

Spivak, Gayatri Chakravorty. 1995 [1985]. "Can the Subaltern Speak?" In *The Postcolonial Studies Reader,* ed. Bill Ashcroft, Gareth Griffiths, and Helen Tiffin, 24–28. New York: Routledge.

——. 1999. *A Critique of Postcolonial Reason.* Cambridge, Mass.: Harvard University Press.

Spooner, B., and H. S. Mann. Editors. 1982. *Desertification and Development: Dryland Ecology in Social Perspective.* London: Academic Press.

Srivastava, Vinay Kumar. 1997. *Religious Renunciation of a Pastoral People.* Delhi: Oxford University Press.

Stebbing, E. P. 1922–26. *The Forests of India,* vols. 1–3. London: The Bodley Head Limited.

Stern, Robert W. 1988. *The Cat and the Lion: Jaipur State in the British Raj.* Leiden: E. J.

Brill.

Stevens, Stanley F. 1993. *Claiming the High Ground: Sherpas, Subsistence, and Environmental Change in the Highest Himalaya.* Berkeley: University of California Press.

Stoller, Paul. 1997. *Sensuous Scholarship.* Philadelphia: University of Pennsylvania Press.

Strathern, Marilyn. 1980. "No Nature, No Culture: The Hagen Case." In *Nature, Culture, and Gender,* ed. Carol MacCormack and Marilyn Strathern, 174–222. Cambridge, Eng.: Cambridge University Press.

Sturken, Marita. 1997. *Tangled Memories: The Vietnam War, the AIDS Epidemic, and the Politics of Remembering.* Berkeley: University of California Press.

Sukumar, R. 1994. "Wildlife-Human Conflict in India: An Ecological and Social Perspective." In *Social Ecology,* ed. Ramachandra Guha, 303–17. Delhi: Oxford University Press.

Sullivan, Lawrence E. 1995. "Memory Distortion and Anamnesis: A View from the Human Sciences." In *Memory Distortion: How Minds, Brains, and Societies Reconstruct the Past,* ed. Daniel L. Schacter, 386–400. Cambridge, Mass.: Harvard University Press.

Sundar, Nandini. 1997. *Subalterns and Sovereigns: An Anthropological History of Bastar 1854–1996.* Delhi: Oxford University Press.

Sundardas, Shyam. 1965. *Hindi Śabd Sāgar.* Banaras: Nagari Mudran.

Sutton, David E. 1998. *Memories Cast in Stone: The Relevance of the Past in Everyday Life.* Oxford: Berg.

Tambs-Lyche, Harald. 1997. *Power, Profit, and Poetry: Traditional Society in Kathiawar, Western India.* New Delhi: Manohar.

Tedlock, Dennis. 1983. *The Spoken Word and the Work of Interpretation.* Philadelphia: University of Pennsylvania Press.

Tedlock, Dennis, and Bruce Mannheim, eds. 1995. *The Dialogic Emergence of Culture.* Urbana: University of Illinois Press.

Thompson, E. P. 1975. *Whigs and Hunters: The Origin of the Black Act.* New York: Pantheon Books.

Thompson, Paul. 1988. *The Voice of the Past: Oral History.* New York: Oxford University Press.

Thorner, Daniel. 1956. "Feudalism in India." In *Feudalism in History,* ed. R. Coulborn, 133–50. Princeton: Princeton University Press.

Tod, James. 1978 [1914]. *Annals and Antiquities of Rajasthan.* New Delhi: M. N. Publishers.

Tonkin, Elizabeth. 1992. *Narrating Our Pasts: The Social Construction of Oral History.* Cambridge, Eng.: Cambridge University Press.

Trouillot, Michel-Rolph. 1995. *Silencing the Past: Power and the Production of History.* Boston: Beacon Press.

Tsing, Anna Lowenhaupt. 1993. *In the Realm of the Diamond Queen.* Princeton: Princeton University Press.

Tucker, Mary Evelyn, and John A. Grim, eds. 1993. *Worldviews and Ecology.* Cranbury, N.J.: Associated University Presses.

Turner, Victor. 1967. *The Forest of Symbols: Aspects of Ndembu Ritual.* Ithaca: Cornell University Press.

——. 1977 [1972]. "Symbols in African Ritual." In *Symbolic Anthropology,* ed. Janet L. Dolgin, David S. Kemnitzer, and David M. Schneider, 183–94. New York: Columbia University Press.

Ujwal, Kailash Dan. n.d. *Bhagwati Shri Karniji Maharaj* [The Great Goddess Shri Karniji]. Jodhpur: Jodhpur University Press.

Unnithan-Kumar, Maya. 1997. *Identity, Gender, and Poverty: New Perspectives on Caste and Tribe in Rajasthan.* Providence: Berghahn Books.

Van Hollen, Cecilia. 1999. "Invoking *Vali:* Painful Technologies of Birth in South India." Paper presented at the Annual Meeting of the Association for Asian Studies, Boston.

Vansina, Jan. 1985. *Oral Tradition as History.* Madison: University of Wisconsin Press.

Vasavi, A. R. 1999. *Harbingers of Rain: Land and Life in South India.* Delhi: Oxford University Press.

Vidal, Denis. 1997. *Violence and Truth: A Rajasthani Kingdom Confronts Colonial Authority.* Delhi: Oxford University Press.

Vidal-Naquet, Pierre. 1996. *The Jews: History, Memory, and the Present.* New York: Columbia University Press.

Visweswaran, Kamala. 1994. *Fictions of Feminist Ethnography.* Minneapolis: University of Minnesota Press.

Vyas, Ram Kishore. 1976. "Twenty-Point Economic Programme and Implementation of Land Reforms in Rajasthan." In *Agrarian Reform and Rural Development,* ed. Hari Mohan Mathur, 5–26. Jaipur: The HCM State Institute of Public Administration.

Wadley, Susan S. 1994. *Struggling with Destiny in Karimpur, 1925–1984.* Berkeley: University of California Press.

Waghorne, Joanne Punzo. 1994. *The Raja's Magic Clothes: Re-Visioning Kingship and Divinity in England's India.* University Park: Pennsylvania State University Press.

Wallot, Jean-Pierre, and Normand Fortier. 1988. "Archival Science and Oral Sources." In *The Oral History Reader,* ed. Robert Perks and Alistair Thomson, 365–78. New York: Routledge.

Weaver, Mary Anne. 1999. "Gandhi's Daughters." *The New Yorker,* January 10, 50–61.

Weisgrau, Maxine K. 1997. *Interpreting Development: Local Histories, Local Strategies.* Lanham, Md.: University Press of America.

Wilce, James M. 1998. *Eloquence in Trouble: The Poetics and Politics of Complaint in Rural Bangladesh.* New York: Oxford University Press.

Williams, Raymond. 1976. *Keywords.* Oxford: Oxford University Press.

———. 1980. *Problems in Materialism and Culture.* London: Verso.

Wiser, William Henricks. 1988 [1936]. *The Hindu Jajmani System.* New Delhi: Munshiram Manoharlal.

Wolf, Eric R. 1982. *Europe and the People Without History.* Berkeley: University of California Press.

Wolpert, Stanley. 1989. *A New History of India,* 3rd ed. New York: Oxford University Press.

Worster, Donald. 1990. "Transformations of the Earth: Toward an Agroecological Perspective in History." *Journal of American History* 76: 1987–1106.

———. 1993. *The Wealth of Nature: Environmental History and the Ecological Imagination.* New York: Oxford University Press.

Yang, Anand A. 1989. *The Limited Raj: Agrarian Relations in Colonial India, Saran District,*

1793–1920. Berkeley: University of California Press.

———. 1998. *Bazaar India: Markets, Society, and the Colonial State in Gangetic Bihar.* Berkeley: University of California Press.

Yugandhar, B. N., and P. S. Datta, eds. 1995. *Rajasthan—Feudalism and Change.* New Delhi: Sage Publications.

Yule, Colonel Henry and A. C. Burnell. 1990 (1886). *Hobson-Jobson.* Calcutta: Rupa and Company.

Zelliot, Eleanor. 1992. *From Untouchable to Dalit: Essays on the Ambedkar Movement.* Delhi: Manohar.

Zimmermann, F. 1987. *The Jungle and the Aroma of Meats: An Ecological Theme in Hindu Medicine.* Berkeley: University of California Press.

Zonabend, Francoise. 1984. *The Enduring Memory: Time and History in a French Village.* Manchester: Manchester University Press.

INDEX

Index ❦ 399

Ann Grodzins Gold is Professor of Religion and Anthropology at Syracuse University. She is coauthor of *Listen to the Heron's Words: Reimagining Gender and Kinship in North India* and author of *Fruitful Journeys: The Ways of Rajasthani Pilgrims* and *A Carnival of Parting: The Tales of King Bharthari and King Gopi Chand.*

Bhoju Ram Gujar is Headmaster of the Government Middle School in Maganpura Village, Bhilwara District, Rajasthan, India. He has been a visiting scholar at Syracuse University, received grants from the Spencer Foundation and the Cornell University Branch of ASHA, and published articles based on ethnographic fieldwork in Rajasthan. He lives in Ghatiyali, in the former kingdom of Sawar.

Library of Congress Cataloging-in-Publication Data
Gold, Ann Grodzins.
In the time of trees and sorrows : nature, power, and memory
in Rajasthan / Ann Grodzins Gold and Bhoju Ram Gujar.
p. cm. Includes bibliographical references and index.
ISBN 0-8223-2808-9 (cloth : alk. paper)
ISBN 0-8223-2820-8 (pbk. : alk. paper)
1. Rajasthan (India)–Rural conditions. 2. Kings
and rulers—India—Rajasthan. 3. Rajasthan (India)—
Social conditions. 4. Rajasthan (India)—Economic
conditions. I. Gujar, Bhoju Ram.   II. Title.
HN690.R3 G65 2002   306'.0954'4—dc21   2001047512